UNCOVERING WORLD MYTHOLOGY: THE ULTIMATE COLLECTION (5 BOOKS IN 1):

The Perfect Beginners Guide On Greek Mythology, Norse Mythology, Celtic Mythology, Egyptian Mythology and Japanese Mythology

LUCAS RUSSO

CONTENTS

UNCOVERING GREEK MYTHOLOGY

UNCOVERING NORSE MYTHOLOGY

UNCOVERING CELTIC MYTHOLOGY

UNCOVERING EGYPTIAN MYTHOLOGY

UNCOVERING JAPANESE MYTHOLOGY

UNCOVERING GREEK MYTHOLOGY

A Beginner's Guide into the World of Greek Gods and Goddesses

LUCAS RUSSO

Introduction

For all the remarkable and awe-inspiring traits that make us humans who we are, the single most impressive is our ability to explain the world around us through story and pass that information down through subsequent, surviving generations. The tall tale, the caught fish which grows as large as the arms can spread, and even the fable all contribute to an ever-increasing wealth of knowledge that connects us through time and space as a disjointed but unified people. It is through common elements of story that we build a culture, religion, and society, and none of the above had a greater impact on the Western world than the Ancient Greeks.

Additionally, nothing has had a more significant impact upon the telling and codifying of stories than the written word, of which the Greeks claim the oldest surviving language in the Western world. The Sumerian language in ancient Mesopotamia, to be clear, lays claim to the title of "oldest" written alphabetic language, but it fell into disuse sometime after the third millennium BCE. Through the arrangement of their alphabet into syllables and words, the Ancient Greeks forged a series of explanations about the world that are still alive and breathing today. They are still full of wonder and power, allowing us as readers a glimpse into the minds, hearts, and fears of an entire people separated from us by time but not by emotion or intelligence.

The Ancient Greeks and their mythology occupy an undeniably foundational part of Western literature. Its figures and events have been alluded to and personified increasingly by each generation of writers who engage with it. The Trojan Horse, for instance, has wheeled its way from the wilderness of the Iliad into the stern, stone fortress of modern English euphemism, where it has settled into usage typically far less dramatic. We must conclude, then, that the primary reason for the survival of these texts is due to their written dissemination, and as such, we must use this fact to establish "when" we are talking about Ancient Greece and its myths.

We come to an interesting point: Specifically we must establish the factual context in dealing with works of fiction. "Ancient Greece" can be taken as a nebulous, primarily geographic area that spans from the island of Crete, south of the "fingers" of the Greek mainland and as far east as the shores of Turkey. These borders persisted up until and even into the Roman conquest of Greece and, based on archaeological evidence, most likely further back, all the way to 7000 BCE. Between those two points, leaders exchanged lands and titles, people exchanged goods and cultures, and armies exchanged bodies and blood, all of which became increasingly difficult to map without any method of documentation. As such, for the purposes of this book, we will safely pin our version of "Ancient Greece" somewhere between the two furthest historical points: between the eighth and seventh centuries BCE, or around the first-known emergence of the writings of Homer, the great Greek poet.

Why start with Homer? Why not trace the mythology back to its roots, attempt to unearth its essences and origins, its "truth"? These are fair questions, and certainly interesting approaches to the topic, but they do not belong to the realm of the strictly historical; these questions are more at home in the realm of the archaeological. We are not concerned here with the reasons that the myths came to be, simply that they have already arrived packaged and ready for our enjoyment and admiration. In essence, our approach is not one of the botanist, concerned with how each part of the plant comprises and sustains the plant, but rather the gardener, who, with the same level of care, keeps the plants alive for the sake of the flower.

Therefore, we choose Homer as our starting point because his work marks the first instances in Ancient Greek history where the ethereal, cultic realms of Greek mythology and its writings intermingle with the realm of human affairs. We are treated at this time to the codification of demigod myths, a testament by the Greeks to both the power of the human being and the attention Mount Olympus could pay its creations. Homer's work balanced the power between mankind and those once-wrathful, omnipotent beings above and beneath the earth. By giving human reasoning and emotions to the Greek pantheon, the deities became more understood, less feared, and thus, more respected. No longer were the myths and religion of the Ancient Greeks separated much as they once envisioned the heavens split from the earth, but at the horizon of Homer's centuries, they had merged, never again to be divided in writing.

What did our Ancient Greece look like, then? We know its borders, but as with any civilization anywhere in space or time, it is always more sophisticated and complex than marking off land on a map, particularly in the case of Ancient Greece. By Homer's time, our Greece had divided itself into many small, self-governing settlements, which emerged primarily due to the geography of the region. Comprising mountains and valleys on the mainland and chains of islands in the south, mass transportation and communication was incredibly difficult. Each community was essentially cut off from its counterparts by either peak or sea, and as such, by necessity, had to rely on self-sufficiency for survival.

There were, however, several "dominant" city-states in Greek affairs: Athens, Sparta, Thebes, and Corinth, all of whom, due to their population and geographic advantages, held a loose control over smaller states and through series of intricate alliances and treaties could call upon them in defense or times of conflict. We know Athens for its cultural and political importance as the cradle of democratic thought. Sparta for its military dominance and austerity, from which we gain the words "sparse" and "spartan," and which paved the way for the expansion of Greece's borders and, in turn, its population. With this population explosion and overcrowding of established city-states in the seventh century, new colonies were established all over the newly conquered territory of the Greek Mediterranean. Colonists founded these cities in the names of deities of the city-states from which they came, praying and sacrificing for prosperity and protection; it is a small proof that one of the binding agents of Ancient Greece was a universal religion.

By Homer's time, that religion was a complex web of intertwined meanings, interpretations, and representations; deities were no longer representative of single events or concepts, but rather shared the burden of their fellow divines. A colony of a city-state devoted to Demeter, as a hypothetical example, might share the same deity as her city-state, although the needs of the settlements might have differed significantly, thus resulting in Demeter's responsibility for the harvest as well as legal precedence. By the time the Parthenon was completed in the mid-fifth century BCE, the pantheon of Greek deities had come more and more to resemble the individual columns of Athena's palace. While each had their individual role, they served together, supporting a roof to protect their patrons from the unknown.

This is where this book comes in. There are countless sources on Greek mythology, in fact, one could devote an entire book to how these myths have changed hands and readings throughout the centuries, and I am almost positive that has been done. What this book looks to do is untangle the strings that comprise that web of divine columns and see them stand on their own. In the simplest terms, the aim is to present these deities, demigods, and creatures as they were understood and appreciated through the stories woven about them and their realms. Its intent is not to overcomplicate the myths through citation and counter-citation, but to elucidate and compress through the simplicity of organization and articulation of commonly held understandings. Ideally, the reader will walk away with questions of their own and investigate further reading about the mythologies and their impact on the Western world.

As such, this book is to serve as a foundation of knowledge as to the myths and figures of Ancient Greece and has no intention of exhausting all sources and questions. It is an introduction into the world of Greek myth. In the end, it is to serve as an appreciation of the storytelling's history, of dispelling the fear of the unknown through human and divine conflict, cooperation, and compromise. It is to help illuminate the depth and breadth of the universal comedies and tragedies that, across space and time, resonate with us because we have lived them ourselves in a sense. These are stories we must approach without searching for an objective, scientific, or even religious "truth" and instead give way to the truths they communicate human to human. Though polytheism has long since fallen out of Western religious thought and practice, I believe we must, when engaging these myths, hold some reverence for these once omnipotent and ubiquitous creations; they were sparked by the human mind, which in itself is the most powerful creative force ever known.

CHAPTER 1

Remember the Titans

When delving into the world of Greek mythology, just as any religion and its texts, it is imperative to start at the beginning of the world. Who created it? How did it come into being? Why does it look like it does now? Was it always like this? These questions are particularly important in Greek mythology, as their answers serve as a basis for the emotional responses and reasons for all major Greek deities as they move through their history. One concept we must come to terms with when evaluating these stories is that omnipotence never equals contentedness or confidence. Indeed, the Greek pantheon operates in a similar fashion to the aristocratic court of Louis XIV; that is, its players move covertly, gracefully, manipulatively, and above all: jealously. We, as readers, or maybe mere mortals, cannot escape the thought that plagues us when we look at these stories: are the gods simply bored of eternal life? Perhaps yes, but as we will see when evaluating the beginnings of the Olympian pantheon, the only thing more difficult than obtaining control of the cosmos is maintaining it.

Chaos, Uranus, & Gaia

The Greek cosmos began with Gaia, the "Mother Earth," a concept which we still carry to this day, and Uranus. Before these two, Greek philosophers speculate, there was Chaos, translated as chasm or abyss, which was neither deity nor demon, though possessed qualities of both. One thinker, Pherecydes of Syros, asserted that Chaos most resembled water in that it is "something formless that can be differentiated." It has been articulated as the unified space of heaven and earth before their splitting apart, yielding our two divine entities. Interestingly, the Ancient Greeks deferred the debate regarding the world pre-creation to the realm of philosophy, not religion, and dubbed this field "cosmogony."

Some sources, like Hesiod's Theogony and Apollodorus' Bibliotheca, point to an immaculate conception of Uranus by Gaia; others, from Spartan poets to ancient Rome's Cicero in his De Natura Deorum, point to Aether as Uranus' father, who was the god of the "upper air," or the air which was breathed by the gods. Though parentage may be disputed, the important concept to take away is that both these deities exist for the ancient Greeks in a time and space before form, and are responsible, through experimentation and offspring, for bringing about shape to the otherwise shapeless world. It is not until subsequent generations of deities that we see the emergence of divinity resembling mankind, one Titan going so far as to create humanity with his own hands.

Despite not giving these original deities a specific, recognizable form, it is nonetheless important to note that the Ancient Greeks still bestowed them with personality; these divines were governed by, as we will see, something eerily close to human emotion. The early gods and their children lend us a terrific insight into Ancient Greek logic: ubiquitous as divine energy and nature was, it was always under the flawed thumb of human dominance. Though there were many mysteries surrounding the ancient world, the Greeks nevertheless positioned themselves in the very middle of it and were convinced their modes of thinking were as close to divine as any could get.

Uranus, by all accounts and despite his contested origin, is universally agreed upon, as Apollodorus writes, "the first who ruled the world." Here we see for the first time the Greeks giving preference to the sky, given Uranus' realm of the heavenly air. It could be that the sky is given this weight because of its intangibility. It could also be that the Ancient Greeks structured their physical surroundings in a simple hierarchy; naturally, the sky exists above the earth and sea, and the earth and sea above the underworld. This is a theme that will articulate itself and become more apparent throughout our whole study of Greek mythology: the domains, and thus deities, of sky and sea, perpetually dominate the realm of land due, in part, to their immense unknowable and therefore frightening qualities.

Regardless of whence he came, Uranus with Gaia produced twelve children, the Titans, who further divided up the cosmos into their realms, ranging from the expansive and concrete, such as the oceans, to the unfathomable and intricate, like time. The two had additional children who walked the earth and carried the early, grotesque marks of the human form: these were the five Cyclopes, hulking one-eyed creatures, and the three "Hecatoncheires," or the "Hundred-Handed Ones." These, as one may guess, were behemoths, unsurpassed in "size and strength" covered with one hundred hands and fifty heads. The names of these creatures the reader can search out easily enough; they are not important enough to our exploration of mythologies to delve into. Of the sets of children, those who demand our most pressing and scrutinous attention will be the twelve Titans, although it is important to set the stage for their rise via the Cyclopes and their Hundred-Handed brothers.

The human-like offspring of the two original deities were despised by Uranus, who, setting the thematic stage for many myths to come, tied together and thrust the five Cyclopes and all three "Hundred-Handed Ones" into Tartarus, the emptiness beneath the earth, a place "as distant from the earth as the earth from the sky," according to our old friend Apollodorus. Greek cosmogony points to Tartarus as below Chaos in the ancient layer cake of the world, while Chaos is below the earth. This left the twelve Titans as the sole eventual heirs of the earth and cosmos, although, as we will see, nothing could possibly be that easy, even for the divines.

Cronus & Rhea

Though there were twelve Titans, thirteen by some counts, those that concern us are Cronus, the youngest Titan and ruler of time, and Rhea, his older sister and eventual wife, the "mother of the Gods." From these two sprang the most recognizable and immortal of the ancient Greek religion; the Olympian gods and goddesses, those who live on today as the noble subjects of literature and art.

Cronus, much like his mother Gaia, has survived in concept through the ages. He is pictured in various ways and interpreted in a variety of ways; from the benevolent Father Time, sometimes at certain festive times of the year referred to as Santa Claus, to the scythe-wielding, hooded specter of death we call the Grim Reaper, Cronus is, in some sense, the only remaining true master of his ancient domain.

That he was the youngest of all twelve Titans is important to note as well. The cosmos would have been divided up according to spaces and divine objects; the oceans, the moon, and the sun all had their respective Titanic rulers, but until Cronus came to be, all was static. As the youngest of the Titans, he represents action, youthful energy, and constant change and shuffling. He is a symbol, according to many Greek and modern sources, of the bridging of gaps, of moving simultaneously toward and away objects and goals; small wonder, then, that as the mythology of the Greeks unfolds, his appearance and aims shift considerably, as do his worship purposes.

Rhea, on the other hand, holds a place much less concrete in these stories. Aside from her role as mother of the Olympians, she has been excluded from Mount Olympus herself; the Ancient Greeks did not regard her as an Olympian in her own right for some reason. She has been cited in ancient debates regarding the origin of the Olympians as perhaps a river, and in later texts, she is determined to be the "Great Mother," upon whom depend, according to Apollodorus, "the winds, the ocean, [and] the whole earth beneath the snowy seat of Olympus." It is not too far a leap, then, to imagine Rhea occupying the ever-changing world within time, the manifest changes we witness with time's passing; every Father Time requires his Mother Nature.

But how is Rhea different from Gaia? It's a fair question to ask. Both are female representations of the planet or surrounding world; surely it is tenuous to separate them along merely hereditary lines? True, both goddesses are similar in their domains, and this may lend confusion to their roles, but one important distinction must be made: it is in the manifestations of change in the physical world that differentiates Rhea from Gaia. The latter remains the divine representation of the static, solid earth, devoid of change.

One interesting difference emerges between the parents of the Olympian deities: their forms of worship and appreciation. One can undoubtedly state that the Greek pantheon was patriarchal; the most powerful of all the divines was male, as were nearly every single demigod. However, when it came to worshipping the older, primordial divines, we find staggering evidence that Rhea enjoyed a level of cultic activity that her male counterpart did not. Across the ancient Mediterranean world, there exist ruins of temples presumably devoted to Rhea, whereas monuments and devotions to Cronus are limited to a single feast day. Perhaps this was due to the individual roles they each played through the history of Greek mythology; Cronus, as we will see, certainly lives up to his robed, skeletal persona. One should consider, though, the notion of tangibility in the appreciation and worship of Rhea.

The ancient Greek world, as we have established, was full of the unknown. What was beyond, let alone beneath the ocean, was left to the terrible toys of the mind's imagination. The same was true for the air; it was an infinite, unfathomable space. It is important to note that both domains were male-dominated in terms of mythology; not only was the earth and its personification female, but it was also the realm of the seen, the felt, and the heard, where the Greeks lived and breathed, fought and died.

What we see with the introduction of the first generation of divines is the emergence of a single theme: change. Before Cronus, Rhea, and the other pairs, the world was merely still and immobile, two distinct traits that are far removed from the human experience. Thus, we are again confronted with the notion that the Greeks infused human elements into their religion and did not let the religious elements and practices govern or justify their human counterparts.

The Dawn of the Golden Age

Despite the myriad of disagreements among mythological sources regarding the early Greek deities, one thing is certain: at some point, Cronus usurped his father Uranus' throne in the heavens through violence. This first act of destruction opened the door for all divine conspiracies to follow.

As we know, Uranus had cast several sets of his children into the depths of the earth: The Cyclopes and the Hecatoncheires, which incurred the wrath and spite of Gaia, and by some accounts, physically injured her as well. According to Hesiod's Theogony, Uranus would descend upon the earth every night, covering the world with darkness to mate with Gaia. We are told that he banished his children to Tartarus because he found them hideous and wished them never to see the light of day. Having birthed the Titans, Gaia, furious of course with Uranus for his maltreatment of his firstborn children, recruited, according to Hesiod, the "wily, youngest, and most terrible of her children," to exact revenge upon the ruthless Uranus.

Cronus, in this affair, was not entirely innocent himself; in many sources, he is cited as being either cruel, hateful toward his father, or oftentimes both. Though Gaia had initially summoned all her sons to avenge the banishment of her children, only Cronus answered the call due to his unyielding envy of Uranus' power. Equipping him with a sickle, or in some retellings, a scythe, she had fashioned from flint, she instructed the young Cronus to hide in ambush and await the nightly descent of his father. Armed with his weapon, and night having fallen, Cronus seized his opportunity and castrated his father, throwing his genitals into the sea.

The castration of Uranus yielded two interesting results. The first was that the blood from Uranus' wound, upon hitting the soil, gave rise to the race of giants, another creature like the Cyclopes and Hecatoncheires who had the physical characteristics of human beings, although the giants were notably much closer in appearance. Uranus' blood also birthed the three Furies. We can understand this in several ways. One, perhaps overly gloomy, interpretation is that violence begets humanity; those acts of great physical harm render us closer to our true selves than any pleasurable experience. Another way to look at this result is to read that change is inevitable, and if one remains complacent and overly content, time will render a person impotent, so to speak.

The second happening due to Uranus' misfortune was the emergence of the first Olympian. After Cronus had dispatched the parts into the ocean, they took to the water, creating an immense white foam. From that foam blossomed the goddess Aphrodite, who came to represent beauty, love, passion, and procreation. In separating the divine from himself, so to speak, the Greek mythos is moving ever closer toward humanity. On the one hand, we are left with the sexless body of Uranus whose blood yields the hardened, rock-like multitudes of giants; on the other, the severed sensitive pieces swallowed up by the sensuous sea conjuring up a single presence of undying passion.

The dispatching of Uranus brought forth what Ancient Greek scholars, poets, and mythographers refer to as a "Golden Age." Cronus ruled over the entirety of the cosmos unopposed, immorality was unknown, and as such, there was no need for legal custom; those of the time were carefree, and food was in vast abundance. The Golden Age makes its appearance first in the works of Hesiod, who we have referenced before, and seems to transcend the realm of the religious or mythological, and dip slightly into the pseudo-historical. Of course, we cannot be looking into these stories as holding any historical weight, but it is intriguing to note that there was some held belief that a version of mankind existed in Cronus' Golden Age. Conceptually, perhaps the closest thing we can equate to this mythological belief is the garden of Eden, where, according to the Bible, humans were, although they behaved with the instincts of animals.

Iapetus & Clymene

It is important to note, when dealing with mythological genealogies, those important but peripheral couples whose reference early on will save excessive confusion and explanation later when discussing the myths of their children. With such fanfare arrive the Titans Iapetus and Clymene, who, as related as Cronus and Rhea, brought into being the second generation of Titans, most notably Atlas and Prometheus.

It is said that Iapetus, brother of Cronus, is responsible for the growth and multiplication of mankind, that his sons, the next Titans, bore the burden of the most wicked of humanity's traits. Indeed, this seems to be the case; we can point to the downfall of both Prometheus and Atlas as human folly, and less divine interference or wrath. Iapetus has survived, according to some scholars, all the way to the time of the Bible, where parallels have been drawn between himself and Japeth, the son of the Old Testament's Noah. We can see the similarities for ourselves in looking at both personalities; Iapetus, like Japeth, is viewed in both religious contexts as the "progenitor of mankind."

While Iapetus was a Titan of the first generation, his wife Clymene was an Oceanid, a nymph of the sea, a daughter of the Titans Oceanus and Tethys. The Oceanids were charged with the care of the young and, surprisingly, were not strictly associated with the water. Several of the Oceanids appear as rocks, trees, and even entire continents throughout Greek myth. Though they were often held in high regard, they were never elevated to the plane of deification themselves.

It seems fitting, then, that the sons of a Titan, a hulking immortal, and a decidedly undivine nymph should produce children as powerful as they were flawed. Atlas, we see pictured incessantly as the man carrying the earth upon his shoulders; a punishment passed down for his all too human transgression, which we will address in more detail in the following chapters. Alongside Prometheus, his brother, the two form what will be marked as the first evidence of physical punishment in the Greek myths, and as such, lends itself nicely to a semblance of a moral compass.

Hyperion & Theia

Hyperion and Theia, our third set of prominent Titans, owe their importance, much like Iapetus and Clymene, to their offspring. Hyperion tends to wallow in relative obscurity compared to his brothers and sisters, and indeed, extraordinarily little is known or recorded about him as far as stories are concerned. What we do know, through several ancient sources, is that he was watchful and observant, diligent in his attention, and as such, became the first entity to fully comprehend the change of seasons and the movement of time. He was revered as a god of light, watchfulness, and time, albeit in a different capacity than Cronus, who was a master of time itself. We see further movement toward the intersection of divine and human with the properties given Hyperion; to observe, comprehend, and analyze are all three very distinct human traits.

Theia's place in the pantheon seems just as opaque, unfortunately, as many of her fellow primordial goddesses and Titans. By some accounts, she occupies a similar standing as the mother of the earth, as she is addressed by Pindar in one of his many odes as "Theia of many names." She is the supposed reason mankind is fascinated with gold; because it shines and gleams by her blessing, she is regarded as a goddess of "shimmer," not of wealth or prosperity. She seems to be a perfect match for Hyperion, as one of the greatest qualities that light bestows upon anything is its glow.

Between them, they bore three children: Helion, Selene, and Eos, the sun, moon, and dawn, respectively. According to myth, across the entire cosmos, none were more admired for their beauty and chastity than these three, which, given their cosmological locations, makes sense. The sun and moon, being isolated not only from each other but from the earth as well, do strike within us even today a sense of wonder and awe.

By one account, Helios and Selene were not born as immortal sun and moon but rather became so through, as is so common in the ancient Greek mythologies, acts of jealous violence. Theia was said to have garnered the title of "Great Mother" because of her standing as the eldest female of all twelve Titans and subsequently raised her siblings as a mother might. Eventually, however, her desire for her own children and thus heirs to the cosmic throne emerged, and she took Hyperion for a husband and had her three children. Naturally, this sparked jealousy in the remaining Titans, who conspired against their brother by executing him and kidnapping Helios and drowning him in the river Eridanus. When Selene discovered what had happened to her brother, she threw herself off a roof, while Theia, in a daze, wandered the banks of the Eridanus in search of her son's body. While she was wandering, she beheld a vision of her son. He told her not to mourn the deaths of either of her children, for, in the future, vengeance would be swift and terrible for the offending Titans, and her children would be transformed into the immortal Sun and Moon. While we cannot say for certain that her children are, in fact, those two celestial bodies, we do know that the first half of Helios' prophecy is devastatingly accurate.

CHAPTER 2

Dawn of the Olympians

Tracing the Greek mythologies back to their creation myths is an entangled and convoluted process. The difficulty arises in that none of the early, primordial gods had specific forms, or rather were representative of all things. In looking at source materials, the early Greek scholars, poets, and philosophers, it seems the only unsatisfactory reward for our scrutiny appears to be a shrug of those ancient, rhetorical shoulders. Those accounts which survive seem to differ; those mythological agreements those documents point to are, for the most part, nonexistent and thus exceedingly difficult to verify. Nothing seems for certain in the creation of the universe despite how confidently the mythology was taken for fact by these thinkers; the universe before the Olympians was vague and difficult to pinpoint in a series of events. As the ancient world became divided up among deities, elements within the physical world became codified and easier to explain and develop through story. In this chapter, we will see the division of the natural world further, and the movement away from the primordial deities into the realm of the familiar Olympian pantheon that is still celebrated today.

Cronus & Rhea

We begin, yet again, with our set of indispensable Titans: Cronus and Rhea. In prior myths, we saw that Cronus conspired with his mother against Uranus, his father, castrating him and removing him from power, ushering in what mythographers and poets deemed the "Golden Age." How Cronus achieved this was by imprisoning his brothers and sisters as well as the Cyclopes and "Hundred-Handed Ones," thus achieving sole possession of the realms of the universe.

In these times of peace and monarchical rule, Cronus and Rhea, much like their father and mother before them, birthed and raised several sons and daughters. Their offspring would become the core deities of the ancient Greek pantheon: Zeus, Demeter, Hera, Hestia, Poseidon, and Hades. These gods would eventually divide the world up further than their ancestors along more concrete lines, opening the door for more myth and morals, though we are getting ahead of ourselves.

To return to the Golden Age: though Cronus and Rhea controlled the known universe in times of unrivaled peace, it was prophesied by Gaia that Cronus should be overthrown by his children, much in the same way that he had overthrown his own father. Prophesy plays an immense part in Greek mythology and practice; from the earliest myths, there is a foretelling of even deities' destinies. Thus, the Greeks took the words of the oracles very seriously all over the ancient Mediterranean.

Cronus, in his wily and terrible way, was determined to deny his fate. In a cannibalistic spectacle before the unknown, he resorts to devouring his children upon their births, consuming them, and holding them within his body. What we see are a decided shift in Cronus' values and representations: in the early primordial days, he is a liberator and progenitor of his family of divines, and by the end of his Golden Age, he has come to represent stagnation, the slowing of time, and ultimate death. Here he lives up to his image as the Grim Reaper; still bearing his scythe, he is the timeless march toward the end, consuming the years and multitudes of youth.

Just as conspiratorial as her mother, Rhea could not bear witness to the destruction of her children by their father and smuggled her youngest child to the island of Crete, to the south of mainland Greece, far away from Cronus by ancient measurements. Having seen Cronus devour her first five children, she refused to allow the same fate to befall Zeus. Cleverly, she knew she would be unable to hide the birth of Zeus from Cronus, so she wrapped a stone in swaddling clothes and gave it to Cronus to consume as he had his other children. This stone became known as the Omphalos, the center, or "navel" of the world, whose mythological and literary symbolism is still conjured today. She entrusted the care of her youngest child, in some accounts, to a goat named Amalthea and a troop of armored dancers whose shouts and claps kept Cronus from discovering the young Zeus' cries. Other accounts state that Zeus was entrusted in the care of Adamanthea, a nymph who suspended Zeus by a rope between the realms of sky, earth, and sea to hide him from the all-seeing eyes of Cronus.

No matter how or under whom, Zeus grew to be a powerful, divine being, and after reaching maturity received a poison from Metis, who was one of the many sea nymph daughters of Oceanus and a representation of magical cunning. He forced it upon his father, who vomited up all the youth he had consumed, although in reverse order: first, the stone fell from his mouth, followed by his children from youngest to oldest, Poseidon to Demeter, Hestia, Hades, and Hera in between. Cronus, of course, being divine and cruel, would neither die nor abdicate, and the assault on his throne erupted into a full-scale, apocalyptic war known as the Titanomachy, which we will explore in the next section.

Looking at the first part of this myth, we are treated to the emergence of new themes and some themes we have visited before. The first, and most prevailing, is the oppression of youth, and youth's eventual and inevitable revenge. Uranus imprisoned several sets of children beneath the earth; Cronus imprisoned all his children except one within his body. Both had revenge exacted upon them by their youngest sons with the help of their mothers, which leads us to a second theme. Again, we see that although the Greek pantheon is primarily a patriarchy, divine female wisdom and input are essential to these stories. This notion carried over into practical religious worship for the Greeks, as oracles and soothsayers throughout the ancient Mediterranean were decidedly young women.

A new theme that emerges in Zeus' rise is that of the divine gift; throughout Greek mythology going forward, gifts from above are imperative to the success of heroes, particularly demigods. It is through these gifts, stemming from Metis' simple poison all the way to Perseus' winged horse, that the righteous triumph over the wretched, despite any divine-ordained odds. Through the concept of divine gift-giving, the Greeks bring themselves in their stories ever closer to their divines and bring those deities closer to the realm of the human. It also serves as a theme to justify the exploits of demigods as such, as we will see; if a human being receives an object from Mount Olympus, how could he not bear some closer resemblance to Zeus than a man who has received nothing?

Finally, what comes from this story are specific places. In the primordial eons of Uranus, there were no "locations" as we imagine or know them; the world was as nebulous as night itself, events flashing quickly within it and without context. We see that with the rise of the Olympians, the Greeks are bestowing a sense of their constructed world upon their myths; while the river which drowned young Helios was fictional, the island where Zeus was reared is rooted in the realm of fact, even if his story is symbolic.

The Titanomachy

The battle between the gods, the Titanomachy, lasted, according to Hesiod, ten years, and pitted Cronus and his old regime against his sons and daughters, known as the Olympians. After having forced his father to disgorge his siblings, Zeus set to work liberating the Cyclopes and the Hundred-Handed Ones from Tartarus so that they may help him to overthrow Cronus. Cronus called upon his Titan brothers and sisters, once so reluctant to engage in conflict, and the battle lines for the war of the fate of the cosmos had been drawn.

It is important to note that while allegiances in this war fell along generational lines, the Titans Themis and Prometheus broke rank and sided with the Olympians. Themis, for her part, was the primordial representation of order, fairness, and natural law. Prometheus, we know, is a Titan bearing human traits and flaws, and is one of the four children of Iapetus. Again, the combination of these two further bridges a gap between the human and the divine for the Ancient Greeks. We can read this choice by the two Titans as dogmatic: that it is part of the natural order of the world for human beings to side with the new natural order, or that it behooves them not to resist cosmic change.

In freeing the Cyclopes, Zeus rendered a set of allies who would ultimately bestow upon him his greatest symbol and source of his power. From their forges, the Cyclopes crafted for Zeus his everlasting symbols: the thunderbolt and lightning, weapons that would help turn the tide of the war against the Titans. Interestingly, both thunder and lightning had previously been hidden from the world by Gaia, the primordial mother. His Hundred-Handed uncles, though bound to the earth by grotesque corporeal form, hurled giant rocks and boulders toward the heavens to dislodge Cronus and his siblings.

With thunder and lightning in hand and allies on earth, Zeus unseated Cronus and the other Titans, imprisoning them deep within Tartarus in a fitting, poetically just punishment. To distribute justice further, he dictated that his Hundred-Handed uncles should guard the Titans' prison for eternity. One of Cronus' primary leaders, Atlas, brother of Prometheus, was met with special punishment. For eternity, he would be responsible for holding the world in place upon his shoulders, and we always see his image rendered so.

Dividing the Earth

Order had been restored to the cosmos after ten years of constant struggle, and the remaining task was to divide the spoils of war between the victors. All the Olympians agreed: Zeus would take control of the skies as supreme ruler, while his brothers Poseidon and Hades would claim as their territory the sea and the underworld, respectively. The earth, at which we will take a closer look, was to remain neutral ground, free to all and beyond divine interference unless deemed necessary by the Olympians.

The earth has been divided after the ten-year struggle, we can see, into three parts, and all of them are controlled by male entities. What of the Olympian sisters? In carving up the known world, they appear to be utterly neglected and shut out of sharing any potential power. While this is true in a certain sense, in other ways, the female Olympians garner more precious and potent power than all three of their male siblings combined.

The original three Olympian sisters, Hera, Hestia, and Demeter, were given realms not as concrete or even nearly as quantifiable, but rather were entrusted with entire worlds that ensured growth, happiness, and prosperity among the newly established cosmos. While the earth was to remain an essentially neutral arena to be merely observed by the divines, the nuanced domains of the three Olympian sisters almost guaranteed a direct control over its destiny. Their worlds were the intangible necessaries of mortal life: the bounty of harvest, the wooing of hearts, and the propagation of mortal species. What jumps out to the modern reader regarding the Olympian division of the world is that the aforementioned "female" domains seem to relate directly to human survival, that while there may not be direct divine "interference" upon the earth, there is a gentleness guiding it. Without these crucial pieces, the earth remains stagnant, just the same as if not worse off than the times before Cronus' Golden Age.

The Seat of the Gods

The Olympians are named for their home in the clouds, the legendary Mount Olympus. The seat of the gods is striking because it holds a tangible geographic location; it is in the eastern central part of mainland Greece. It is technically not a single mountain, but a chain of peaks, and owes its geological distinction due to its peaks' smooth, almost circular appearance, and relatively flat tops. These mountains can be, and in fact are, climbed and conquered, and countless photos and postcards bearing its image are strewn all over the modern world. There is certainly nothing mythological about the course of nature that formed this impressive range, though the ancient Mediterranean would have seen it differently.

From the Ancient Greek perspective, we can presume that the world was bordered on four sides: to the south, the inhospitable deserts of Egypt, to the west, the unfathomable ocean and the ends of the earth, to the east, the savage unknown of Persia, and to the north, the awesome heights of Mount Olympus. The Greeks presumed that between these four borders sat their country and beyond them, the world's end. The remarkable similarity between three of these four borders is that they are flat; there are no mountains atop the ocean, the closest thing resembling a peak in Egypt would be the man-made pyramids, and Ancient Persia was perched upon a plateau, which, while elevated, is essentially a plain.

As such, we are left with Greece's northern border, the fabled chain of mountains that separates it from its northern contemporaries, the Macedonians. We have already seen that the Ancient Greek world's smaller states owed their independence and self-sufficiency due to their relative geographical isolation. Is it so difficult to imagine that such ideas regarding geographic borders could expand to include an entire culture with a shared religion? Who better to protect the Greeks from the threat of their northern neighbors than the divines themselves? What could be more simultaneously intimidating for an enemy and comforting for a Greek than knowing that Zeus and his brothers and sisters were directly observing the movements of the country and simultaneously preventing any intrusion upon Greek soil?

While we do have the physical "northern border" of Mount Olympus, it seems that throughout mythology and Ancient Greek history, Mount Olympus occupies a largely symbolic space as well. In keeping with the Ancient Greek self-sufficient and geographically isolated thinking, it seems that by many accounts, "Mount Olympus" was a point of reference to every early city-state. Thessaly, for instance, had its Olympus, and Olympus existed as far outward as Cyprus. The islands of Ionia and Lesbos each claimed a Mount Olympus as well. It seems that, on the one hand, to these early states, Mount Olympus was merely the highest visible point of their surroundings. On the other hand, a culture devoted to physical representations and housings of deities as spaces of worship and protection could have seen their peaks as a sort of temple. While each city-state had its patron deity and a temple devoted to it, it is understandable that the population of a place would enjoy the security of the watchful eye of all twelve Olympians. This "together but separate" concept surfaces and resurfaces throughout the stories atop Mount Olympus as well: oftentimes, the domain of a deity, though clearly marked off and isolated, will share some conceptual heavy lifting with another divine.

The Stage is Set

We now have, in what I hope was presented concisely, accurately, and without confusion, all the necessary background information to truly begin looking at the major figures in Greek mythology. Before proceeding, however, I do believe it is important to note a few simple, philosophical evaluations regarding these stories.

Of course, we know that none of these myths or figures hold any religious sway in the current century, but they are certainly valuable literary symbols. Its believers are long gone, and all that truly remains are wind-pocked columns and edifices of once-proud temples. In analyzing these ancient stories, the reader often makes the mistake of seeking a moral conclusion, or a compass needle pointing them toward "good" and away from "evil." The Ancient Greek pantheon and its practitioners did not operate in such a capacity; these stories and figures were explanatory and taken for granted as fact; the moral compass and the roots of the universe were left to the realm of philosophy.

Mythology, then, if we can imagine it, existed in a place where science now stands; it was a method of understanding the physical world and humanity's place within it. It is a misstep to try to obtain a glimpse into the ethics of Ancient Greece through these stories; they do not hold the same textual or structural elements as later texts we equate to the religious. "But," you might be correct in asking, "haven't you already dissected several of these early creation myths to draw some governing principle from them?" I cannot deny this fact; flipping back even three pages will reveal it. Though I have and will continue to conduct a rudimentary analysis of many of these major myths going forward, I do not believe they fall into the world of moralizing. There are plenty of surviving Greek philosophical texts regarding morality, and even one of the great Greek writers, Aesop, has devoted his Fables to fundamental moral principles. However, we notice that the subject of Aesop's work is not the divine Olympians hovering over the plane of earth, but rather the animals that inhabit it, illustrating that in the eyes of the Ancient Greeks, the moral compass was a purely mortal concern.

The gods, as such, act as closely to their original oath as possible; they truly let the earth and its inhabitants govern themselves and establish a moral code befitting of their times. While they do not necessarily interfere, there are, as we will see, countless instances where they meddle, take on the form of beasts and manipulate people among other trickeries, and even turn individuals into a variety of things. It is not until we get to the epic poems of demigods that we see true intervention; however, the instances in which we see it are usually fraught with hesitation by the powers that be.

So, to conclude, in order to begin, we know the creation story of the Ancient Greek world, the basic realms inhabited by the male and female Olympians, how they are related, and that these stories are intended at their heart to explain the natural world. We see, in simple terms, how the Greeks perceived that world and how their surroundings helped give rise to the notion of security within the temple structure. We know that the further the divines divided their world, the closer they came to humanizing themselves, and as such, the closer humans came to becoming divine. We will see that gap grow even smaller with the emergence of demigods in later chapters. We have hopefully established a relatively coherent timeline of events for the creation of the cosmos and the rise of the Olympians despite differing and diverse sources scattered throughout time. We should have a basic working framework to operate within when it comes to these myths and figures of Ancient Greece, and all that remains is to dive headfirst into the stories themselves.

CHAPTER 3

The Big Three

Now that we have a sketch of the roots of the broader mythological workings of the Ancient Greeks, we will change our approach going forward from a narrative perspective to a more encyclopedic one. We will be looking at deities individually and in clusters less through their interconnection through story but rather according to their importance and prevalence in the mythologies, though, of course, some overlap is bound to occur. I hope to avoid retracing previously established information as much as possible; although most myths in the Greek tradition hold more than one primary deity as characters, I will try to devote each tale to the deity who most occupies its foreground. We will start with the most visible and "legendary" deities and work our way through the pantheon to hopefully render a basic understanding of how the Greek divines operated.

Our first three we have chosen because of their ubiquity; in nearly every single myth available for the reader in the modern day, at least one of these three deities make themselves known to figures in the story as well as to the reader. These are the three major Olympians: Zeus, who we have covered briefly in the establishment of the Greek world, Hera, his wife and sister, and Poseidon, the lord of the depths of the sea. From these three come nearly all the gods and demigods to follow; they are responsible for the propagation of the Olympians and mortal Greek heroes.

Zeus

The immortal Zeus, having banished his Titan predecessors to the depths of Tartarus, presided over the Ancient Greek world as its supreme ruler from his seat on Mount Olympus. With his iconic thunderbolt, he was lord of the skies and king of all Olympians. He was, for the Greeks, a manifestation of the sky, lightning, law, and order and bears considerable resemblance to other European chief deities: the Norse Thor and Roman Jupiter, most notably. There are many more associations made with Zeus throughout religious iconography and tradition, and to go into each in detail would distract from our main ideas, but should the reader be curious, there are a multitude of texts devoted to just such a subject.

As we know, he was the youngest of all Olympians, or by some arguments the oldest, as his siblings had spent their lives in Cronus' stomach. He ultimately married his sister Hera; by some accounts, however, the two deities had begun their relationship in secret. Between the two, the pantheon ballooned in number from the small six who had snatched control of the world to a staggering 18 deities, not counting those countless demigods whom Zeus also fathered. Among his offspring, we count Ares, Hephaestus, Artemis, Apollo, and Athena, to name only a handful. His virility granted him the title of "All-Father," and was celebrated across the ancient Mediterranean as the sole representation of Greek strength, power, and religious thought. As his realm was the endless, expansive sky, any event or seemingly random occurrence that could not be attributed to a specific deity automatically fell into the hands of Zeus. In this way, his image and realm grew even more far-reaching.

Just as every region of the Greek world had their own Mount Olympus, temples to Zeus were no less common. Given his stature as king of all deities, nearly every Greek city center had a temple devoted to him, some, of course, larger than others. Fittingly enough, the center of Zeus worship, and Olympian worship in general, lay in a city called Olympia, which boasted the site of the fabled Olympic Games. The city hosted these games every four years in the name of the king of the gods, complete with animal sacrifices and feasting. One story claims that the sacrificial altar of Zeus in Olympia was carved from ash instead of stone due to the thousands of animals that had been sacrificed there.

Myths

One thing we can read about Zeus' personality through his myths is his obsession with youth and beauty, going so far as to destroy the lives of those mortals he finds attractive.

We see that many of his myths are centered on the possession of the young and ideal by manipulation, force, or coercion. For example, in the myth of Europa, Zeus had become so infatuated with the eponymous Phoenician king's daughter, who was the ideal representation of mortal beauty, that he disguised himself as a virginal white bull among her herds. According to Hesiod, the bull breathed a "saffron crocus" from his mouth. Europa grew enchanted by the bull, ultimately climbing upon its back. The bull, Zeus in disguise, took off running into the ocean, whisking Europa away to the island of Crete. Zeus then reveals himself and "seduces" Europa, to put it mildly, beneath an evergreen tree. The result of their Cretan retreat was the birth of Minos, a powerful king who would lend his name to that great beast of legend: The Minotaur.

Another instance where Zeus' obsession with youth and beauty emerges is in the myth of Ganymede. Ganymede was a Trojan and, by Homer's account, another devastatingly beautiful human being. "The loveliest born," Homer dictates in his Iliad, "of the race of mortals," and of course, Zeus took notice of the young man and became infatuated. Just as with Europa, Zeus finds the youth among herds of animals and transforms himself into an animal again, albeit this time a proud, giant eagle. He abducts the boy and carries him into the sky, where he is to become the immortal cupbearer for all the gods upon Mount Olympus. Ganymede is transformed into the constellation Aquarius and is visually manifest as a cloud: that which brings water and is closest to the sky.

Our humanlike Titan, Prometheus, plays an important role in the mythology of Zeus. On one occasion, humanity offered Zeus a sacrifice of animal bones wrapped in fat instead of meat swaddled in cloth. Furious with the deception, the lord of the sky decided to withhold fire from mankind, thus thwarting its development. Through trickery and cunning, sympathetic Prometheus smuggled fire in a stalk of fennel from Olympus and bestowed it upon humanity. Of course, all-knowing Zeus discovered this treachery as well, and to punish Prometheus, he chained him to a rock where every day an eagle descended upon his body to devour his liver, which would regenerate overnight, and upon which the eagle would descend the next day again. Why Zeus chose the liver to be devoured is intriguing;

according to many, the Ancient Greeks presumed the liver to be the location of all human emotion. Perhaps Prometheus is to be punished for becoming too close to mankind.

We are also given parity between Zeus and other Indo-European religious texts when it comes to the flood myth; it seems every major deity at some point must decide to wipe the slate of the earth clean. In Zeus' case, as with many other supreme beings, he had grown tired of humanity's decadence and summoned his brother Poseidon to aid in the destruction of the species via inundation. He granted mercy to one couple: Deucalion, who is the son of the perpetually half-eaten Titan Prometheus, and his wife, Pyrrha. As these stories go, the two construct an ark and eventually find solid ground at the foot of Mount Parnassus, north of Corinth near Delphi. Offering sacrifices to Zeus, the two throw "the bones of the earth," or rocks, over their shoulders, which Zeus then transforms into humans.

Hera

Hera, the eldest sister and wife of Zeus, is arguably the most ancient figure in Greek mythology; by many accounts, her presence and image in Ancient Greece predate Zeus. She is the goddess of marriage, childbirth, women, and family, and most notably surrounds herself with graceful, noble animals. The lion and peacock, to name two, are symbols often associated with Hera in Ancient Greek lore.

Images of Hera can be found all through ancient temple ruins up through contemporary literature. She, along with Zeus, was a near-ubiquitous presence in the worship centers of Greek cities; more than a representative figure, she was rendered by her marriage to Zeus as the queen of the gods. Indeed, traces of Hera's value to Ancient Greek worship can be seen through some of the oldest and largest ruins strewn about the Mediterranean; of all the temples still standing, Hera's are the most impressive. Though she had a large presence in her husband's patron city, Olympia, Hera's primary temple was located on the island of Samos, far to the east of mainland Greece, the ruins of which still stand to this day.

Herodotus described it as "the largest temple we know of," and one can imagine that to be the case merely by looking at what remains. While the temple rose far from the bulk of Greece, it remained an important part of Greek religious culture as the mythological place of Hera's birth.

Myths

We see that the most common trait associated with Hera through her myths is jealousy. It is easy to dismiss her reactions against Zeus, his mortal lovers, and illegitimate children on these grounds alone, but we must keep in mind that Hera above all, as a deity symbolizing marriage and family, is a representation of stability. When such structure as the family and marriage becomes threatened, or as in poor Hera's many cases, violated, the natural reaction is revenge, particularly for the divine-minded, as we have seen in previous generations.

One interesting disparity we see between the king and queen of Olympus comes in the form of transformation, no pun intended. While Zeus has the impulse and ability to transform himself into any creature he wishes, Hera's abilities are inverse; her strengths lie in transforming others into what she wishes. One reason for this could be that as a goddess, Hera's form must necessarily be perfect or ideal; she cannot become anything less than befits her. We see this manifest many times in Greek mythology: Hera turns her wrath outward, cursing and destroying the lives of those who interfere with her marriage. Take, for instance, the myth of the nymph Echo. In one of his many marital transgressions, Zeus insists on covering his tracks by recruiting Echo to occupy Hera by talking incessantly. The conversation sours, of course, when Hera learns of its true purpose and subsequently curses Echo; for all eternity, the nymph will be doomed to lend her voice only to mimicking the voices and words of others.

We see Hera protecting her house and crown once more in the myth of Io, another of Zeus' mortal lovers. To protect Io from the wrath of his wife, Zeus had her transformed into a cow, though Hera, wise and clever as she was, begged Zeus to give her the cow as a present.

What strikes the reader is that throughout these myths involving Hera, though Zeus seems to run rampant and with unchecked authority throughout the mortal world, he can never deny his queen. As such, he forfeits the cow, Io, to his wife, who locks her up with golden chains and sets the hundred-eyed Argus to guard her around the clock. Argus, with all his eyes, only closed fifty at any given time, and thus was an excellent watchman. The story holds that Zeus, overcome with a desire to see Io, recruits Hermes to distract, or by some accounts, kill Argus and set Io free. In one account, Hermes does so by lulling all one hundred eyes to sleep with pan pipes, in other accounts, by blinding and killing the hundred-eyed watchman, but nonetheless freeing the white heifer Io. Hera, in response, sent a gadfly to the earth to perpetually sting Io for all eternity, never allowing her to rest, and so, Io wanders the earth forever.

What is striking is that for all the vengeance Hera takes upon her husband's consorts, for all the jealousy she feels, she never once exacts her revenge upon her husband. Perhaps this is because it would violate one of her tenets: that her intent is always to tend toward stability and security within the family circle; undermining or overthrowing the king of the gods, we can easily imagine, would certainly go well against that.

Poseidon

The third major Olympian we have already briefly mentioned in one of Zeus' stories: Poseidon, the lord of the depths of the ocean, master of horses and storms. In his representations, we see him most often proudly striding forward, his telltale trident held aloft. From this trident's forks, springs would erupt from the earth, and rivers would carve their way through the land. His other symbols include a horse, a dolphin, and a fish.

In addition to his mastery of the watery world, he also garners the title "Earth Shaker" in several Greek stories, and as such, has additionally been known as the harbinger of earthquakes. Perhaps he owes this honor to his association with horses, as herds of the creatures have been known to shake the earth as they move. The Ancient Greeks also presumed that the phenomenon of the earthquake was the result of water eroding the rocks of the earth, which also contributes to Poseidon's title. In his role as king of the sea, Poseidon is also responsible for the well-being of sailors and seafarers, though, as we will see in some of his stories, he can be anything but benevolent.

Given that much of Ancient Greece's territories were chains of islands and its people unrivaled sailors, it is no small surprise that Poseidon featured prominently as the principal deity in more cities than Zeus. While he had a prominent presence in Olympia, as with his brother and sister, Poseidon boasted magnificent temples in Corinth, Magna Graecia in southern Italy, and even vied for dominance with Athena for the city of her namesake, Athens.

Poseidon fathered many children with many lovers, not all of them human. From him, we get the winged horse Pegasus, the Cyclopes Polyphemus, the hero and king Theseus, and Orion the hunter, to name only a prodigious few. We see again the prominence Poseidon held in Greek culture; as he was so prolific in reproduction, it could be argued the Greeks understood the value of water as a direct correlation between life and death. Of all the Olympians, Poseidon, possibly due to the proximity of his domain, is the most often tempted to violate the divine agreement regarding the earth's self-governance. In many of his stories, we see his desire to take revenge on the mortal world for trespasses committed against him or his children.

Myths

One of the most iconic myths surrounding Poseidon lies in Homer's Odyssey. In the legendary Trojan War, Poseidon had chosen the side of the ultimately victorious Greeks against the Trojans. On Odysseus' seafaring journey back home, he crosses paths with Polyphemus, who we know is Poseidon's son, and ultimately blinds him, which invokes the unbridled rage of the sea god. Poseidon begs his brother and sister to allow him to punish the transgression of the mortal Odysseus, a request which is denied. Poseidon, Zeus, and Hera agree to a compromise, however. Poseidon may delay Odysseus' journey home, punish those around him, but must not harm Odysseus himself. As a result, we are given the Odyssey, a magnificent work of man's struggle against himself and the world, a story positively worth reading, and within which Poseidon's behaviors and actions are expounded upon in astounding detail.

As hinted earlier, Poseidon was in direct competition with Athena for the city of her namesake, wherein priests and priestesses of both cults maintained an extremely healthy presence. The myth states that on a mutually agreed upon feast date, to decide the patron deity of the city, both cultic processions would set up altars to their respective deities. Seeing this, Poseidon and Athena agreed to each give a gift to the city and let the people decide which divine should hold court in the principal temple. Athena bestowed upon the people of Athens an olive tree, a gift that provided wood, food, shade, and beauty to the Athenians. Poseidon, for his part, struck the ground with his trident and caused a spring to rush forth from the earth; the water, however, was ocean water, salty and briny and entirely unfit for a use other than sailing. Naturally, the Athenians chose Athena's practical and graceful gift, and a furious, rejected Poseidon, his pride wounded, struck the earth once more with such force and rage that he flooded the entire Attic plain to punish the Athenians. The flood reached all the way to the halls of the Erechtheion, an all-marble temple atop the Athenian acropolis devoted to both Athena and Poseidon, which still stands to this day. From the north porch of the temple, the only place in Athens not to be affected by the mythical flood, one can see in the distance where Poseidon allegedly struck his trident: rocky pools known as the "salt sea."

We see that Poseidon is just as vengeful, violent, and jealous as his two siblings, although, as evidenced by his stories, his wrath manifests in a unique way. Both his brother and sister, the king and queen of the Olympians, tend to exercise their power by transforming and dominating individuals, altering physical forms of themselves and others to attain their desired result, coercing them through trickery and deceit. Poseidon, on the other hand, has no such ability; he, as the "Earth Shaker," prefers to unleash his retribution through sheer, natural force. He has no qualm with laying waste to entire peoples for the transgressions of one person. He, unlike any other Olympian, manipulates with unrelenting savagery the weather and natural world, which, coupled with his notoriously short fuse and protective, paternal instinct, make him arguably the single most feared and revered deity in the entire Ancient Greek pantheon.

CHAPTER 4

Girl Power

We move now from our most prominent three deities to three somewhat less visible, but no less powerful goddesses: Athena, who we mentioned briefly in our quarrel with Poseidon, the goddess of wisdom, Artemis, the chaste, untamable huntress, and Aphrodite, the most sensual and passionate of all the divines. We are placing these three in the same chapter not based on any generational or genealogical lines but because they occupy distinctly feminine places in Ancient Greek culture, and as we will see, oftentimes, these places are infinitely more powerful and influential than the male-dominated, location-based domains.

We can argue that the trifecta of female deities hold much more power because their domains are primarily internal: they are the heart and mind, which yield the cosmic magic of emotion and language, which dominates the world of mortals and permeates the realm of the divines. We will see that for all their infallibility and rage, their jealousy and omnipotence, even the fiercest and mightiest Olympians must succumb at some point to the eternally dominant intangibles of love and logic.

Athena

By this point, we have become briefly introduced to Athena; we know her patron city, and we know how it came into her possession. She was the goddess of wisdom, warfare and its strategy, and handicraft, three things that her namesake of Athens excelled at in the ancient world. She is often depicted in a traditional Greek warrior's helmet and holding a spear, and is one of, if not the only, Greek goddess who is depicted exclusively fully clothed. From her gift to the Athenians, we can gather that one of her symbols is the olive and its tree, symbols of Greek prosperity, and she also claims the owl as her bird, the snake as her animal, and a pendant depicting the head of a Gorgon, called the *Gorgoneion*.

Of all the Greek pantheon, no deity is so quick to aid a righteous mortal than Athena. Throughout her stories, she incessantly appears in various disguises to support a hero or thwart a malevolent divine hand. She, according to myth, aided nearly every single prominent Greek hero: Jason, Heracles, Perseus, and Bellerophon, among others. She is the guiding light for mortal man through the darkness of the unknown, and thus it is no surprise that her image in the Western world of art has become synonymous with democratic principles and the idea of freedom. According to Plato, Athena's name can be broken down to mean "divine intelligence," which, given her myths of guiding heroes toward their goals and belaying ill-intended plans of the gods, gives her an air that floats toward the concept of "fate;" she operates in spite of and above the divine level of her siblings.

Myths

Athena, by all accounts, is said to have been birthed by unique circumstances. She was the child of Zeus and Metis, one of Zeus's early wives. According to a prophecy, as are so common in the ancient world, it was said that Metis would birth two children more powerful than Zeus himself: a son and a daughter, who, of course, would ultimately overthrow Zeus. Following in his own father's footsteps, Zeus turned his pregnant wife into a fly and swallowed her before she could give birth to the children. Within Zeus's stomach, to protect her first child, she began forging Athena's iconic Grecian helmet and her ever-present robe, understanding that in time her child would be born. The constant hammering of the helmet's construction gave Zeus an immense headache, and he demanded Hephaestus, or by some accounts, Prometheus, obtain a double-headed ax and split his head in two. From the wound, Athena sprang forth, fully grown and donning her helmet. Because she emerged from the head of Zeus, she is given her domain of divine intelligence and is often regarded as Zeus' favorite child.

What is interesting is that she uses this divine intelligence not to control the realm of the divines, but rather, as we have mentioned, aid in the accomplishing of mortal tasks. Countless images of Athena have been collected portraying her alongside Heracles, and several poetic sources show her lending a hand to the nearly defeated hero. She is given reign over the hearts and minds of humanity in a way unique from all other divines; undoubtedly, being the favorite child of the king of the gods comes with certain privileges, and perhaps more than one blind eye. What we see manifest in her "divine intelligence" is lending her power to those who prefer cunning and strategy over those who rush headlong into any combat.

For example, we see in Homer's Odyssey, one instance in which Athena favors those mortals gifted with wit. Odysseus, who is a master of cunning and a highly intelligent and practical combatant, becomes a protégé of and thus protected by Athena. She reveals herself to him on many occasions and speaks on his behalf atop Mount Olympus, pleading to her father to let Odysseus return home after his ten years at sea. She speaks to his friends and relatives, bringing discoveries and news of Odysseus' whereabouts and condition to their attention. Odysseus, meanwhile, has fallen into countless traps and captures, all through his human folly, though with his intelligence and practical thinking, emerges relatively unscathed, though the same cannot be said of his compatriots. We are treated to an Ancient Greek version of "creating one's own luck;" it is due to the similar, intellectually creative natures of Odysseus and Athena that bring them together.

Though Athena appears to meddle benevolently in the affairs of mankind, being a divine and a direct offspring of Zeus, she is not without her wrathful side. There are many myths featuring a side of wise Athena that is just as jealous and vengeful as her father. One of the more interesting stories to emerge is the tale of the Gorgon Medusa. Medusa was a priestess in one of Athena's many temples and was, according to myth, exceptionally beautiful. Poseidon, with his insatiable appetite, lusted after the priestess, disregarding the vow of chastity she had taken, and seduced her on the floor of Athena's temple. Once she had learned of this desecration, Athena turned the beautiful Medusa into the snake-haired monster we imagine today, with a gaze that would turn any mortal into stone.

Artemis

Our second powerful female deity comes in the form of the elusive and cunning Artemis. The goddess of the hunt, Artemis, is often shown brandishing a bow and quiver, which are symbols of her efficacy in the wilds. Alongside her, most commonly, are deer, her sacred animal, and like her counterpart Athena, she too claims a tree as a divine symbol: the cypress. She is the divine huntress, the goddess of the wilderness, protector of young women, and guardian of the moon; indeed, above all other deities in the Greek pantheon, not a single one is more ethereal, and not a single one is more graceful. In the true fashion of the divine huntress, myths and stories of her exploits are difficult to track down; not many texts regarding her history survive.

Another child of Zeus, she was a twin of Apollo, as the stories go. By some accounts, she is older and even assisted in the birth of Apollo, and by others, the two were born simultaneously. Her mother was Leto, a daughter of the two Titans Phoebe and Coeus. Despite the lack of surviving written work about Artemis, there is a myriad of physical representations that have passed through the centuries; this shows that perhaps while not as important in the codification of religious or cultic mythologies, she could have played an immense part in the daily life and worship of the Greeks. Her domain is adjacent and runs parallel to many of her sisters, as she helps to ensure the survivability of mankind through the prosperity of their hunts and protection of their women. What is interesting about Artemis' personality is that she seems not only to insist upon her chastity for all eternity but also seems to remain a young girl forever, like an Ancient Greek Peter Pan.

As she was one of the most-worshipped deities in the ancient Mediterranean, it stands to reason that her temples would befit that title. Her patron city was Ephesus, in modern day Turkey, wherein a temple was constructed in her name that became one of the Seven

Wonders of the Ancient World. Unfortunately, due to centuries of conquest and human negligence, only ruins remain at the site of the once-towering temple. However, its presence reinforces Artemis' divine importance as a goddess in practical, everyday life, as though her existence is a harbor in the storms and divine wrath of the unknown.

Myths

We are told and can most likely deduce, given our experience with the hyperbolic pantheon, that Artemis is a young woman of staggering beauty. She is so beautiful that she catches not only the eye of Zeus and several other male divines but also the eye of Hera. Hera, however, is extremely jealous of Artemis' beauty and the attention lavished upon her by her male counterparts, and as is her way, cursed her to remain in the form of a young girl. In Homer's *Iliad*, we are treated to a glimpse of Artemis after her transformation, as she is represented as a crying child upon the lap of Zeus, and in a poem by Callimachus, the weeping child Artemis is granted ten wishes by her father, which effectively establish her domain. Among her ten wishes, she asks for: any city, which we know to be Ephesus, to remain chaste forever, a bow and arrow forged by the Cyclopes, a choir of nymphs comprised Oceanus' daughters, and a knee-length tunic so that she may not be impeded while hunting. She also asked for the ability to relieve the pains of childbirth, as she had witnessed them firsthand with the birth of her brother Apollo.

Another myth surrounding the elusive Artemis involves the protection of her chastity, a recurring theme throughout the surviving stories about her. In this instance, during a hunt, Artemis stops to rest and bathe in a stream. Through the woods comes Actaeon, an extremely skillful hunter in his own right, nearly as quiet and observant as Artemis herself. He chances upon the goddess bathing, which means he has seen her in the nude and is caught in the act by Artemis herself. To punish him for watching her, she turns the hunter into a stag, who is then viciously and mercilessly hunted down by his own pack of hunting dogs who cannot distinguish the animal from their master.

Though Artemis was pursued by many male suitors, only one man ever won her heart: the great, giant hunter named Orion, one of the many sons of Poseidon. Myth states that Artemis and Orion were hunting partners, and he charmed her through his skill with a bow. He boasted that he could successfully hunt any creature upon the earth and threatened in his time with Artemis to kill them all. Gaia, the earth mother, having heard this, became determined to create a creature whose skin could not only withstand the arrows of Orion's bow but also equal the hunter's lethal talent with a dagger. Thus, the scorpion was born. According to one version of the myth, Artemis' brother Apollo conspired with Gaia to create the scorpion to destroy Orion, as he disapproved of his sister's cavorting with a male and was overprotective of her maidenhood. By some accounts, during the ensuing combat between the two hunters and the scorpion, Artemis mistakenly shot and killed Orion with her own divine bow and arrow; in her grief, she immortalized Orion as the constellation we see today.

Aphrodite

Born of the waves and erogenous zones of the first Father Time, Aphrodite is by far the most seductive and irresistible goddess in the entire pantheon. Hers is the realm of love, passion, the erotic, and physical beauty. No other deity in any other pantheon comes close to Aphrodite's charm and sensual persuasiveness; even certain foods have come to carry her namesake for their purported qualities. "Aphrodisiacs" are said to accelerate sexual appetite and desire, which fall almost too perfectly in the basket of our goddess of love.

Her symbols have survived the centuries, maintaining their erotic and passionate connotations: the pearl, the scallop shell, the rose, and mirror, all have attributes that orbit the world of carnal passion and sensual delight. Her animals were the dove and tortoise, and some sources indicate her affinity for the dolphin as well. We know she emerged from a union between the sea and Uranus' severed genitals; the mythological location of that union is, according to the poet Sappho, the bay of Paphos on the island of Cyprus. Others place her birth off the island of Crete, along a major sea trade route for the Greeks.

Wherever her birthplace, we know that by all accounts, she was born a fully grown adult with no childhood, skilled in the ways of passion, and a highly desirable woman. Among her many epithets, one of the most telling of her domain is Aphrodite, the "Genital-Lover." Given her domain of the purely sexual, one can easily imagine that she is often portrayed in the nude, or when she is clothed, the fabric seems to be mere drapery, concealing little of her assuredly feminine figure. She and her niece Athena are the only two Olympians to have been born immaculately: Athena from the head of Zeus, and Aphrodite from the sea.

Aphrodite, for all her appeal, was widely worshipped across the ancient Mediterranean, from Athens to her birthplace Cyprus, and even as far south as Alexandria in Egypt. She had major temples and sites of worship all throughout Greece, and every year in Athens, a celebration would be held in her honor: the Aphrodisia. During this festival, priests would sacrifice a dove to Aphrodite in gratitude for her role in uniting Greece. She has been the inspiration and basis for countless works of art, ranging from paintings to sculptures and character archetypes in novels, plays, and stories, and continues in many regards to represent a certain form of ideal sensuality.

Myths

One theme that emerges from Aphrodite's mythological history is that her beauty and amorous nature tend to get other people in trouble. It also ignites repeatedly the all too quick tempers of the fickle Olympians, particularly her sisters and nieces, who, in turn, insist on punishing the unsuspecting mortal population. Unlike her siblings, though, Aphrodite never seems to care about the consequences of her actions; she is the manifestation of moments of passion, not the guilt or regret that follows.

Take, for example, her feud with Hera and Athena, two major players in the Greek religious world. All three claimed ownership of a golden apple cast to the earth by Eris, the goddess of discord, which held the inscription "to the fairest." Naturally, all three goddesses thought themselves the fairest, and took their case before Zeus. Unable, or perhaps unwilling, to decide himself, Zeus handed the decision to a mortal prince: Paris of Troy. As all divine beauty is unparalleled to mortal eyes, Paris could not decide, and the three resorted to bribery. Athena promised Paris fame and glory in battle, Hera offered him control of the continents Asia and Europe, but Aphrodite, with her unique power over the hearts and parts of man, confided in Paris that if he should choose her, he would be able to marry the most beautiful woman in the world. Naturally, given his mortal weaknesses, Paris chose Aphrodite and was gifted his prize: Helen, wife of King Menelaus of Sparta. Paris' decision enraged Hera and Athena, who broke from Mount Olympus and instigated the legendary Trojan War on the side of the Spartans. Aphrodite, fitting her personality of momentary passion, was content with her apple and title, and never rushed into battle herself, though she did find her way into several heroes' bedrooms.

Aphrodite, to a degree far surpassing her Olympian counterparts, favors mortals whom she finds physically attractive, while giving no real preference for the divines. While it is true that she is technically married, this is not by her choice, as we will see later when we dive into the stories of Hephaestus. She seems obsessed with manipulating the hearts of men, particularly those who devote their worship entirely to her. In that way, she can certainly be the most selfish of the Olympians, even though her actions, for the most part, seem flippant and impulsive. One prominent instance of this is in the myth of Pygmalion. Pygmalion was a brilliant sculptor who could carve the most magnificent figures from marble. He was convinced that all women were immoral and essentially evil, so he refused to marry or keep the company of any female. However, he was a devout worshipper of Aphrodite, even going so far as to carve her likeness out of stone. During the artistic process, Pygmalion fell in love with the statue and longed to marry it. Aphrodite, impressed by his devotion to her, granted life to the statue and thus Pygmalion's wishes.

To Conclude

We see that these goddesses are equally terrifying and beautiful in their power. They occupy the spaces of mortal minds, bodies, and hearts, although not in the purely physical way. Each of their strengths comes from indirectly controlling and guiding those internal impulses that lead us away from the purely animal and toward the distinctly human. The powers of wit, the hunt, and procreation are three of the most essential elements of survival in the ancient world for mankind. Entrusting those necessary pieces to three of the most widely-worshipped deities in the pantheon illustrates in a small way the importance of the female presence in Ancient Greece, and with what quiet respect it was regarded.

CHAPTER 5

Let's Hear It for the Boys

A truth of the universe is that everything must ultimately come into balance; the Greek pantheon is no exception. For the subtle powers in the realm of the psyche bestowed upon the earth by the three major female deities, there must be brothers who reign from Mount Olympus with heavier, more blatant hands. This brings us to our next triad of male deities in the subsequent generation of Olympians: Apollo the miracle worker, the raging and violent Ares, and the swift Hermes.

This trio is grouped as such as they bear genealogical resemblance to the previous three goddesses; Apollo, we know, is Artemis' sister, Ares, a lover of Aphrodite, and Hermes, a favorite son of Zeus. We will see that their realms are more concrete than their female counterparts, although they seem to share conceptual lifting; it could be said that they and their sisters are two sides of the same coin. We will see that all three are, without a doubt, sons of their father Zeus, as in some capacity, they all carry a specific trait of his character.

Apollo

The younger twin of Artemis, Apollo, shares many of her qualities. His weapon is the bow and arrow, just as is Artemis', though he claims the swan as his bird, and the python as his animal. While his sister is the protector of young women, Apollo is charged with the protection of young men, and, as such, he is the principal figure of the ancient Greek nation. A distinction should be made: it could be said that Zeus is the principal representative of the Greeks, but he is specifically chief of the gods, religiously speaking. That is, he is the surviving religious artifact that the Greeks gave to the Western world; when it comes to national and international affairs, it is Apollo who is the representation of Ancient Greece's cities and people. He is seen as a deity of healing and, specifically, medicine; his python,

44

along with his son, Asclepius, intertwine around that eponymous symbol of Western medicine, the Rod of Asclepius.

In addition to his role as a healer, Apollo was music and art made manifest; he is often depicted in the company of the Muses, strumming his lyre. Initially, in the Greek tradition, he was a deity rurally inclined; he looked over shepherds and their flocks, presumably in his role as protector of the young. Later, as Greek civilization grew to become more urban and less nomadic, he was the ever-watchful patron over the blossoming democracy and the founding of new Greek cities. Given his importance and rise to prominence along with Greek civilization, he is deemed by several sources as an amalgam of all gods; in essence, he is the perfect eternal youth, brimming with potential.

Though he had temples devoted to his many faces throughout the ancient Mediterranean, his most important place of worship was at Delphi, the fabled site of the legendary oracle. This site housed that eponymous oracle, who, in fact, was a worshipper of Apollo and was traditionally a young woman. Unlike other deities and their followers, Apollo's worshippers touted the strongest connection with the oracular and clairvoyant; should any person of note wish to discover their fate, they would ultimately head for Delphi in hopes of obtaining the blessing of the keeper of Greek civilization.

Myths

Leto, one of Zeus' many wives, gave birth to her children on the floating land of Delos, as Zeus had forbidden her to give birth on earth. First, she gave birth to Artemis, who acted as a midwife for the delivery of her brother, Apollo. When Apollo emerged, he held a golden sword, and the story says that everything on Delos then turned into gold. Swans were said to have circled the island. He was fed ambrosia and clothed in fine, white cloth held in place with golden bands. After having eaten the nectar of the gods, the child Apollo tore the bands from his body, announcing that he alone would be the interpreter of Zeus' will to mankind. Allegedly, it was the god's birth that anchored Delos to the earth and rendered it an important place of Apollo worship throughout Ancient Grecian history.

Apollo, according to myth, was responsible for slaying Python, the enormous snake, the midwife of the giant Typhon, and supplicant of Hera. As per Hera's orders, Python attempts to assassinate the pregnant Leto to prevent the birth of Artemis and Apollo. Python, while successful in harassing and assaulting Leto, failed to kill her. After his birth, the child Apollo vowed revenge, and picking up his bow and arrow, hunted Python down and killed it in the very cave at Delphi that would bear his temple and oracle.

While Apollo was known chiefly as a healer and protector, he could also be known to dispense suffering and death. Several accounts show him as a plague-bringer, particularly during times of hardship. During the Trojan War, for example, when, on the side of Troy in defense of that city, he sent a terrible plague upon the invading Greek camp. During that conflict, he was responsible for the destruction of many Greek heroes, Achilles included.

The laurel wreath as a symbol of triumph stemmed from Apollo as well. Myth states that Apollo, having been struck with Cupid's fabled arrow, fell in love with Daphne, a forest nymph. As a chaste devotee of the woods, Daphne scorned Apollo's advances, who, in turn, took to pursuing her through the forest to try and change her mind. Daphne, whose cries for help Gaia heard, was transformed into a laurel tree. In some stories, Gaia hides Daphne deep within the forest and replaces her with the laurel tree, but the fact remains: Apollo loved the tree and donned its leaves and branches as a symbol of his victory. Even today, we see the connotation of Ancient Greek culture and the laurel leaf; it seems that when the iconography of Ancient Greece emerges, one of the first images to appear is the laurel wreath.

Ares

Just like his sister Athena, Ares is a manifestation of warfare. Unlike his sister, who centers herself on the tactics, planning, and leadership of war, he is the image of and delights in the horrors of combat; his is the realm of brutality, carnage, and indiscriminate slaughter. While Athena is pictured with her iconic helmet and robes, Ares is often depicted entirely nude, sporting a similar helmet, and wielding a shield. Among his symbols, he counts his shield, spear, chariot, and flaming torch; his animal companions consist of the boar, the dog, and that most vile of all avian beings: the vulture.

Though a decidedly warlike people, the Ancient Greeks surprisingly held little regard for Ares as a powerful, prominent deity. There appears to be a differentiation in Greek thinking between the necessity of war and the senseless destruction it causes; in no means do they elevate that carnage above its status as a "necessary evil." Ares' influence in the world of man as well as atop Mount Olympus is significantly diminished when compared to his sister's; Zeus himself tells his son in one story that he, in Zeus' eyes, is the most despised of all gods. In Sparta, however, Ares was elevated beyond his role as the harbinger of pain, death, and destruction and became associated with the ideal soldier, though this image is widely regarded as different than the majority of Greece.

Ares had few temples devoted to him in the ancient world, unlike his Roman counterpart Mars, who was a pivotal deity in that culture's pantheon. It could even be argued that due to his maligned place among the Olympians, that Ares was not Greek at all; indeed, myths point to Thrace as his birthplace, in modern day Turkey, which housed a people the Greeks thought entirely barbaric. We know, however, that as an outlier, Sparta housed a temple devoted to Ares, as well as an enormous statue of the deity in chains outside the city, according to Pausanias.

Upon his chariot, Ares rides into the maelstrom of battle with two of his sons by Aphrodite: Deimos and Phobos, "dread" and "fear," respectively. Decimating the ranks of both sides in battle, Ares chooses no favorites but insists upon rewarding courageous acts and valor in combat. His is a role as indifferent toward the fate of the Greeks as the Greeks are to him; he cares for nothing other than the clash of swords and the falling of bodies around him.

Myths

One of the most widely depicted myths involving Ares is his legendary fight with Heracles. It has been emblazoned on countless numbers of ancient pottery and repeatedly rendered in pigment by classical painters. The story goes that one of Ares' sons, Cygnus, a powerful Thessalian king, would detain travelers and pilgrims on their way to the Oracle at Delphi. In his cruelty, he would treat the travelers to food and drink, and then kill them without compunction. Naturally, this aroused the fury of Apollo, who dispatched Heracles to take revenge on Cygnus. In Apollodorus' Bibliotheca, he writes that the two met in single combat, and with Athena's intervention, Heracles thrust his spear through Cygnus' neck, killing him. Ares, furious not only with his son's murder but with his sister's intervention on behalf of Heracles, rushes to earth to confront Heracles. The two belligerents meet in battle, and again with Athena's aid, Heracles manages to inflict a wound on Ares' thigh. A thunderbolt from Zeus ends the fight, and Ares' two sons, Deimos and Phobos, carry the god of war away from battle and back to Mount Olympus to heal. Other stories recount similar events, though instead of Cygnus' murder by Heracles, he is simply turned into a swan, Apollo's bird, as penance, and became the eponymous constellation we see today.

Another popular myth involving the god of war comes in the form of his conflict with the Aloadae: Otus and Ephialtes, two giants and sons of Poseidon. According to myth, the two giants were responsible for bestowing civilization upon mankind; they grew, according to the writer Hyginus, "nine fingers every month," and were "surpassed in beauty only by Orion." Literally translated, the pair's names are "insatiate" or "insatiable," and "nightmare." They plotted to overthrow the gods atop Mount Olympus by constructing mountains to rival Olympus and claiming Hera and Artemis as their wives. In their war with the Olympians, they managed to capture hotheaded Ares and hold him captive with chains in a bronze jar for thirteen months; the whole time, Ares was screaming and raging for his freedom. However, Eriboea, the mother of the two giants, made the mistake of relating to Hermes her sons' conquest, who, with Artemis' help, freed the captured god of war. Artemis then tricked the giants into impaling each other with their spears by turning into a deer and jumping between them.

What we see time and time again in the myths of Ares is his rashness and headstrong mentality often lands himself in danger or at the mercy of those he strives to fight against. He is often outwitted and outclassed, relying solely on his ability to unleash havoc with brute force upon the earth; it is no surprise then, that for all the fear and terror he strikes into the hearts of the Ancient Greeks, he is easily dispatched and diluted through the workings of other, more "diplomatic" deities.

Hermes

The third wily son of Zeus is Hermes, the young herald, and messenger of Mount Olympus. Renowned for his cleverness and fleetness of foot, he was the ever-alert guardian and protector of the roads, merchants, and traders of the ancient Mediterranean. He also was known as a trickster, and thus became a patron deity of thieves. From him, we have the image of the winged sandals, and among his other symbols are the airy lyre, the crowing rooster, and his winged helmet, known as a Petasos. His tree is the palm, and in his representations, a goat or lamb is usually found somewhere nearby.

His iconography is one of the most interesting of all the Olympians; in early images such as gravestones and stone fragments, he is depicted as a fully grown and bearded adult, his hair curling proudly around his ears and forehead. Later, in Hellenic Greece and even into Roman times, he is shown most often as a child, closer to the Hermes we recognize; he tends to be nude save for his winged sandals, cape, and helmet, clutching his staff of two intertwined serpents.

In addition to his position as guardian of transportation and commerce, Hermes also played the part of divine guide; it was he who helped recently deceased souls into the afterlife. He has also been recognized as the mediator between the visible and invisible worlds. That is, in his role as divine messenger, it is his duty to make the will of Zeus manifest in the material world, while it is his brother Apollo who interprets it. Pieces of evidence of Hermes' places of worship are scant in the ancient world, although there is some reason to believe that he was primarily worshipped extremely devoutly in rural areas of Greece, primarily as a guardian of flocks, shepherds, and farmers. Only three ruins of his temples remain today; all three of these ruins are within the northeastern portion Arcadia, the southern, three-fingered "hand" of mainland Greece. The lack of temples in Hermes' honor might be because his spaces of worship were the roads of Ancient Greece itself; markers bearing Hermes' image have been discovered all along supposed Grecian highways.

While a notorious trickster and confounder of mortals and divines alike, Hermes, according to Pausanias, was dubbed by Zeus to remain entirely amoral. Zeus, according to Homer's hymn to Hermes, decrees that Hermes alone "should be the appointed messenger to Hades, who, though he takes no gift, shall give him no mean prize." Interestingly, his presence in Greek households was supposed to ensure good luck, as Hermes was a "gift giver" and one who bestowed blessings. There is even evidence that in his early cultic years, he was a deity of prosperity and fertility, which we can imagine, for one as agile and swift as Hermes, is not so great a leap. As Ancient Greece became more connected beyond the family circle, who better to look after its prosperity and connections than the deity responsible for creating them?

Myths

We are treated to Hermes' tricks nearly from the moment of his birth. One myth surrounding him states that when he was merely hours old, he snuck from his crib and made off with several of Apollo's divine cattle, hiding them away in a cave in Pylos, along the southwestern coast of Greece. To disguise his footsteps, he first donned his now famous sandals, thus making his feet unidentifiable. Thinking he had gotten away with his theft, he slaughtered several of the oxen in gratitude, performing what the Ancient Greeks agreed was the first animal sacrifice. He then took muscle fiber from one of the sacrificed animals and strung it across a tortoise shell, thus creating the lyre. Apollo, noticing several of his prize cattle missing, tracked them down to Hermes' cave, where Hermes denied ever having seen them. Apollo appealed to his father, Zeus, who, having seen everything, demanded the oxen be returned to Apollo. However, upon hearing the strum of the lyre, Apollo grew infatuated with its music and offered a suitable trade for all parties: the remainder of his herd for Hermes' newly invented instrument. Apollodorus writes to conclude the myth that Zeus was so amused by his young son's gumption that he immediately made him an immortal Olympian.

In addition to helping Zeus free his lover Io and liberating Ares from his bronze jar, Hermes was no stranger to aiding mortals in times of overwhelming crisis. It is shown across many surviving stories and works of ancient art how the messenger god bestowed upon Perseus the necessary equipment to dispatch Medusa. Loaning Perseus his winged sandals, cape, and golden sword, Hermes instructed the hero Perseus in their use: the winged sandals so as to not be heard by the monster, the cape so as to not be seen, and the sword for severing Medusa's head.

In Homer's Odyssey, Hermes appears before a wandering Odysseus with words of warning, in effect, comically chastising him. He tells Odysseus it is dangerous to wander, as the magic-wielding temptress Circe lives on the island, who will undoubtedly try to bewitch the hero with a strong, enchanted drink. Hermes offers Odysseus an herb, telling him to eat it, as it will dispel any harmful effects Circe could place upon him. Odysseus does as the messenger commands, and sure enough, the magic of Circe fails in turning the hero into a pig, saving him from the fate of many of his shipmates.

We can see Hermes draws some distinct comparisons between himself and Athena, our wisest, most measured Olympian. Both deities see the value in assisting humans with their advancement; indeed, it could be argued that it is part of their job descriptions. Athena, due to her wisdom, was often equated with education and, specifically, human growth through technology; the advent of farm equipment, for example, is a gift from the goddess. Hermes occupies a similar space, although his methods of aiding human development come from trade, commerce, and intercommunication between peoples; his gifts to mankind include the alphabet, currency, and the wheel.

To Conclude

Between the three looming male figures and the previously exalted female deities, we can decipher striking similarities; beyond the familial relationships, many of these six gods share the roles of their siblings. As we have stated, these pairs of deities are essentially two sides of the same coin, adhering to more or less "traditional" behavior patterns; the male counterparts tend toward the side of the boastful, rash, and aggressive in their interactions with the world. This does not necessarily mean they occupy an "evil" side of Greek religious thought; as has been stated previously, it is impossible to brand any of these stories or figures with a moral tag. They are figurative representations of ill-understood concepts, offering, despite the terror they inspire or gifts they bestow, a working model for the people of Ancient Greece.

CHAPTER 6

Last But Not Least

While we seem to have the most prominent of the Greek pantheon covered, surely there must be parts of the world, both divine and mortal, left undefined. We have seen that many of the roles of the most famous deities intersect and overlap, but between them all, they certainly must have let some parts of the world slip through their widely-cast net. What of the crops that sprout from the furrows of Athena's plow? What of the revelry reaped from a good harvest? What of the home behind the grain that holds the revelry? And what of the steel that crafts the plow, and those who craft the steel? Are not all these just as, if not more important to humanity than wisdom, war, or water?

These questions bring us to our final four Olympians: Hephaestus, Demeter, Dionysus, and Hestia. While they dwell mostly in the shadow of their boisterous and interloping brothers and sisters, the four are an essential part of Ancient Greek life and culture. They, above all, represent the peace and security that civilization and family can provide. While their brothers and sisters are the pillars of Greek religion, hoisting the divine shelter above the Greek people's heads, our remaining deities can be seen as the four corners of the temple foundation upon which those pillars stand, holding them unshakably firm and tall through the centuries.

Hephaestus

The lord of craftsmanship, its tools and metal itself, Hephaestus' work is renowned across Greece and throughout the pantheon. He claims the anvil, tongs, and hammer as his tool, and from beneath Mount Olympus, he alone is responsible for controlling the fires of the earth. Due to his exemplary, almost miraculous metalwork, he is the patron of sculptors and artists alike and the ever-watchful friend of the carpenter. He is known to look after the work of blacksmiths, going so far as to infuse his own metalwork into that of chosen mortal workers.

To the Ancient Greeks, Hephaestus occupied an important, if oftentimes uncelebrated, role as the master of industry and artisan craftsmanship. His presence could be noticed, fittingly, in the urban city centers of the Ancient Greek world; these were, of course, the primary locations of workshops and armories. According to Homer's Iliad, the island of Lemnos was Hephaestus' home when he struck out from Olympus. Today, evidence of cultic activity can be seen strewn about the north Aegean island's ruins, and in particular, through the distinct, exceptional quality of the ancient tools unearthed there.

A son of Hera, he was cast from the top of Mount Olympus and his seat with the divines for a deformed or misshapen foot. He is the only deity in the Greek pantheon to have a noted physical deviation; all the other divines are repeatedly lavished with the praise of perfection and represented as ideal forms. As he could not be physically perfect himself, he devoted his divine talents to crafting physically perfect objects: swords, armor, even Hermes' winged sandals. Among his companions and assistants, he counted the Cyclopes, the very three who forged Zeus' thunderbolt, as well as automatons composed of metal.

Hephaestus' iconography, just like his deformity, is unique to the Greek pantheon as well. As he possessed unrivaled skill in metal and stone, it was written of Hephaestus that he could bring life to any inanimate object; we see one instance of this in his workshop automatons. What this meant for his iconography was that it became imbued with the god's presence; the images rendered of Hephaestus in stone or metal, on a tombstone or edifice, were not mere representations of the god, but a literal manifestation of the god himself. Given the awe-inspiring artistic and architectural works produced by the Ancient Greeks and their influence on the Western world, it is easy to see how, even back then, the Greeks found the beauty of craftsmanship divine.

Myths

Hephaestus, the master craftsman that he is, was recruited by Zeus to construct all the thrones in the Palace of Olympus. This, of course, was after his casting off the mountain by his mother, Hera. Hephaestus did as he was told, building the immaculate seats for his eleven relatives. Upon sitting on her throne, Hera found that it began to levitate, and suspended her between the realms of heaven and earth. When she demanded that her son and throne's builder help her down on matriarchal grounds, Hephaestus replied famously, "I have no mother." To make amends, Hera offered her son any hand in marriage he could desire; Hephaestus chose Aphrodite, the goddess of love.

Some of the most interesting myths surrounding Hephaestus are tied to his marriage. His wife is Aphrodite, the picture of beauty and desire. It seems incongruous that a sulking, lame blacksmith and the queen of sexuality would match, and in a certain sense, one would not be wrong for thinking so. Aphrodite's infidelity is widely touted throughout Greek mythology; her numerous affairs are each of a mythological caliber, even for a deity. One affair in particular catches our eye, just as it caught Hephaestus': her transgression with Ares, the god of war.

We know that Ares, for all his terror and bluster, is irrational, short-sighted, and frankly, none too intelligent. During the Trojan War, he took up a secret relationship with Aphrodite, and due to his carelessness, was caught in the act by Helios as he was driving his chariot of the sun across the sky. Naturally, as the bringer of light, Helios informed Hephaestus of his wife's infidelity to which the blacksmith responded in silence, crafting and drafting plans for revenge. He set to work in his workshop, crafting by some accounts a net, by some accounts chains, but by all accounts bronze and fine as threads of silk, and strong enough to ensnare even the mightiest of gods. He set his trap upon his bed, and sure enough, caught the two lovers. Hephaestus then called down from Olympus all the gods to bear witness and humiliate the two paramours. Seeing the state of the two entangled gods, Poseidon pleads to Hephaestus to release them, vowing that all penalties shall be paid by

Ares, and if he should fail, Poseidon himself will take up the shackles of Hephaestus. Satisfied, the divine craftsman releases the two, whereupon a disgraced Ares returns to his distant homeland of Thrace, and Aphrodite to the sea from whence she came, bathing herself to restore her virginity. The punishment alluded to by Poseidon was never paid by Ares directly, though we are told that his children would bear ill-fated destinies.

Given his stature as an artisan, it is no surprise that Zeus entrusts his forging and crafting to no other than Hephaestus. It was the divine sculptor himself who was charged with bringing to form the most beautiful mortal woman known to the world. Tired of the advances of his female counterparts upon the men of the mortal plane, and as a price demanded of mankind for illicitly acquiring fire, Zeus commanded that Hephaestus bring to life Pandora, which he did from clay and water. Zeus instructed Hephaestus to render, according to Hesiod, her "face like the immortal goddesses, [with] the bewitching features of a young girl." She was to be so fully beautiful, charming, and intelligent that she would be "a sorrow to men who eat bread." In addition to giving form to Pandora, Hephaestus also crafted Pandora's infamous *pithos*, a jar often mistranslated as a "box," from which, opening in her curiosity, she released all evil into the world.

Demeter

For putting food on the table, the Greeks have Demeter to thank. She is the mother of the harvest, a culmination of Gaia and Athena, the giver of growth and grain. In addition to her role as the proverbial founder of the feast, she also holds in her hands the cycle of life and death; she dictates the natural order of things. Genealogically speaking, she is among the newer Olympians, though one can trace her existence in her form as the mother of agriculture further back than almost any Olympian deity.

Demeter's symbols include wheat, the torch, the cornucopia, and bread. Curiously, she does not claim an animal as her living symbol, nor is she often associated with many male lovers. As the manifestation of the bounty of the earth, she is represented alongside or within various flowers and greenery, most specifically the poppy, which thrives in fields of grain throughout the Mediterranean. If not rendered alone, she is often pictured alongside her daughter Persephone, whose absence from the earth via her marriage to Hades brought about the advent of winter.

Demeter boasted one of the largest and most famous cults of the ancient world. Her patron city was Eleusis, along mainland Greece's southeastern coast. Every year, pilgrims would flock to Eleusis to take part in the Eleusinian Mysteries, a festival devoted to the harvest goddess and her daughter Persephone. The festival was ancient even by Grecian standards; elements of it can be traced to the Mycenaean period several hundred years before Homer's epics, and it survived to be adapted by Romans in their worship of Ceres. The Mysteries centered on the myth of Persephone's disappearance into the underworld and her journey back to earth and was divided into ritual parts as such: her descent, the search for her, and her ascent.

The goddess of the harvest also enjoyed the splendor of a universal, localized festival throughout Greece, known as the Thesmophoria. This ritual took place in late October, and according to various sources, restricted its attendance to adult women. This festival was intended to promote fertility and reproduction for women, which may explain its yearly occurrence around the time when the harvest would take place.

Myths

Given the allegorical prominence of Demeter's festivals, it stands to reason that the most important myth surrounding the Grain Mother has to do with Persephone's disappearance into the depths of the underworld. The story is rendered most vividly and coherently by Homer, in his hymn to Demeter. Homer writes that one day in Zeus' fields, Demeter's daughter Persephone and several nymphs of Oceanus were singing and gathering flowers in a Grecian Garden of Eden, which by Gaia were "made to grow at the will of Zeus, and to please Hades, to be a snare for the blossom-like [Persephone]." Hades, seizing his opportunity, mounted his chariot and kidnapped Persephone from her garden, dragging her to the underworld. Persephone cried for help, though all her shouting went unheard by Zeus and his Olympian companions atop the mountain except for her attentive mother.

Having heard her daughter's cries for help, Demeter threw off her cloak and descended Mount Olympus with all haste. She ran over land and sea, searching everywhere for her Persephone. She asked every man and animal she came across what had become of her daughter, though none would answer truthfully, if at all. Homer writes that this pattern of searching continued for nine days. Just before the dawn of the tenth day, Demeter encountered on her travels a torch-wielding Hera, who consequently had been searching for the missing Demeter. The harvest goddess revealed to Hera why she had fled Mount Olympus, that her daughter had vanished amid cries for help, and that it was her motherly duty to rescue her. Remaining silent, Hera took Demeter by the hand, and by the light of her torch, she escorted her to the foot of Helios' chariot.

Helios' responsibility, as we know, is riding the chariot of the sun across the sky every day. He is also the eternal watchman of both realms: the mortal and the divine. As no man or beast would reveal truthfully Persephone's whereabouts, it was left to the forthright Helios to alleviate Demeter's grieving. He informed her that he had seen Persephone whisked away by Hades' chariot to the underworld, where, Hades claimed, he would make a wife of Persephone. As is in his objective nature, however, Helios makes the argument that as far as a husband goes, Persephone could do a lot worse; Hades, after all, is a god of an entire domain himself, and close brother to the king of all gods.

The reasoning and perceived apathy of the sun's charioteer did little to raise Demeter's spirits. She cursed the sun, the underworld, and Zeus himself, imposing upon herself an exile and resigning herself to grieving. According to Homer, she took the form of an old woman in the city of Eleusis, which we know would become the site of her annual Mysteries. Taken in by the king of Eleusis' daughters, she became a confidant and midwife to the queen and was charged with raising the newborn boy Demophoon. According to the hymn, she fed the child neither milk nor solid food but anointed him with ambrosia, much in the same manner of Apollo. Unbeknownst to the mortal court, she would bathe the child nightly by fire to cleanse him and move him toward the path of immortality. Upon discovering this, the queen and her court snatched the young Demophoon from Demeter's care; this infuriated her. Dropping her disguise, she cursed the island with perpetual civil war. The harvest goddess then took her leave, vowing to build upon the highest hill a temple in her honor, where her rituals will be studied and performed each year to appease her wrath. Thus, the reason for the location of the Eleusinian Mysteries.

Alone in her Eleusinian temple, without daughter or newfound son, Demeter set once again to mourning. She plucked from the earth its fruits and grains, dried it to a husk, and left its cattle destitute. Her famine deprived the people of food and the deities atop Mount Olympus of their customary sacrifices. Her exploits upon the earth had, by this time, reached the ears and wounded the pride of Zeus, who had grown tired of Demeter's meddling in the mortal world. He dispatched Iris, a minor winged goddess, down to the Eleusinian temple to demand on Zeus' behalf Demeter's return to Olympus. Of course, Demeter denied the pleas of a perceived lesser deity. However, this did not dissuade the Olympians, who, annoyed that the population of the earth was no longer sacrificing in their honor, went one by one to Demeter's temple to demand her return. To each visitor, Demeter provided the same answer: she would neither return the bounty of the earth nor Olympus until her daughter had been returned to her.

Man was left without food to eat or sacrifice. As king of Olympus, it was Zeus' duty to find a suitable compromise between Hades and Demeter. To satisfy all parties, he proposed that while Persephone should remain Hades' wife, he could not possess her in the underworld alone, and she would be allowed to split her time between Hades' realm and alongside her mother. For one-third of the year, while Persephone was enclosed in the underworld, Demeter bestowed starvation and drought upon the earth, yielding the season of winter. When that season passed, Persephone brought with her in a sudden surge all the growth that had been repressed, aided in celebration by her mother. This we know as the season of spring, where the bounty of the earth once again comes to life.

Dionysus

In keeping with the theme of celebration, we are met by the lord revelry himself: Dionysus, the patron deity of festivals, wine, general carousing, and the theatre. Naturally, from these, we can infer that he also holds some sway over the "ritual madness" of intoxication; he is essentially the king of the drunks. He is often depicted completely nude, and unlike his Olympian brothers, not necessarily in the most chiseled shape. His form borders on the feminine; he is portrayed usually with soft features and hair that tumbles down his back and shoulders, though typically not unkempt. It could be argued that Dionysus is truly the most benevolent of all Olympians; certainly, he is the most difficult to anger.

Dionysus seems, compared to his Olympian counterparts, a proverbial "black sheep." He cares nothing for the struggles of man, is not so vain that he covets a mortal or divine position, and seems content to spend his days in repose with a glass of wine or twelve. The Ancient Greeks explain this stark deviation from the Olympian norm by asserting that Dionysus is, in fact, a foreigner, a Thracian by divine birth who essentially weaseled and charmed his way into the immortal halls of Mount Olympus.

As the god of celebration, Dionysus boasts an enormous domain; it touches nearly all facets of Greek society. He is present at weddings, funerals, harvests, and sacrifices, not to mention all religious rites and rituals. When oracles fall into their soothsaying trances, Dionysus, it is said, is pulling the strings.

As vintner of the gods and giver of fruit to mankind, Dionysus' symbols include the grape and its vines, the goat, the chalice, and a staff of fennel wound tight with ivy known as a Thrysis. Just like Demeter, Dionysus had an immense, ancient cult following across Greece that existed even before Homer. There is some speculation that, due to their similar realms, the Eleusinian Mysteries were devoted both to Demeter and Dionysus; this is supported by evidence of a large Dionysian following on the island of Eleusis.

Dionysus also claimed in addition to the Mysteries, the festivals of Dionysia and Anthesteria. The former was divided into two parts: the rural Dionysia, and the city, or "greater" Dionysia. Both shared the same purpose: to celebrate the grape harvest throughout Attica, in gratitude for the gift of fruit Dionysus bestowed upon the Greeks. Plays and poetry recitations were held in honor of the god of revelry to celebrate, and naturally, the wine flowed freely. The Anthesteria, on the other hand, was a three-day festival that mirrored some concepts of modern-day Halloween. Though it was celebrated at the vernal as opposed to the autumnal equinox, it marked the days when the wine from the previous year was fit to drink, and thus induce the "ritual madness" which the Greeks believed thinned the barrier between the living and the dead.

Myths

Unlike his stationary Olympian siblings and counterparts, Dionysus was renowned as a chronic, compulsive wanderer, carrying with him the grapevine and the knowledge of how to cultivate it. It is said that Semele, Dionysus' mother, threw him into a fit of madness, which sparked his wanderlust; the myth states that throughout his travels, he left behind him swaths of vegetation and the knowledge of how to cultivate the grape. Some versions of the myth state that Dionysus' obsession with the grape stemmed from a love affair he had with a young man named Ampelos, who died falling from an elm tree following Dionysus' request that he guard the god's sacred vines. In his mourning, Dionysus turned his lover into the fruit that the vines produced and sowed it throughout the world in his sadness.

In his interactions with humanity, Dionysus tends toward the ambivalent, even the flippant, as opposed to his brothers and sisters, whose main motivation remains vengeance of selfishness. One of the most famous stories in the Western canon involves Dionysus, who causes a mighty king great sorrow and regret for choosing his words carelessly. The king Dionysus plays this cruel trick on is King Midas, whom Dionysus stumbles across while sowing his grapes and pressing his wine. Dionysus, impressed with Midas' generous hospitality, reveals himself as an Olympian god and allows the king one wish, to which we know exactly how the king replied. Unable to eat, drink, or hold his children, Midas despaired at his golden touch and begged the god of revelry to recant his wish. Dionysus agrees in good spirits and takes Midas down to a river, where he washes himself clean and turns the river golden.

Dionysus, being no stranger to madness, once descended blindly into the underworld to bring back his wife and mother from the realm of the dead. He did not know the way to the underworld, and in his travels, asked an old man named Hypolipnus for help. The old man, lovestruck by the handsome Dionysus, promised to show him the entrance to the underworld if the god, in return, promised to remain with his guide forever. Eager to rescue his family, the young Dionysus consented to the old man's demands. When he returned from the underworld, however, Dionysus discovered that the old man had died. On his return with his wife and mother to Mount Olympus, it is said that Dionysus picked up Hephaestus along the way, helping the deformed craftsman back into the immortal Olympian fold. The myth has been interpreted as a triumph of revelry and celebration of mortal life over the grimness of death, an ancient rendition of the old phrase, "Love conquers all."

Hestia

Arguably the most important peripheral deity in all Greek religion is Hestia, goddess of the home, the hearth, the family, and the state. Greek legend states that upon the christening of any new building or completion of any new house, the first sacrifice to be offered was to Hestia, to ensure the prosperity, security, and longevity of the structure and its inhabitants. Given the condition of the many remains of Greek buildings throughout the centuries, it could be argued that Hestia has done a fair job holding up her end of the divine bargain.

The ubiquitous Hestia has but one true symbol: the hearth and the fire within it. Hers is a simple, safe world devoid of ravenous animals or the terrors of the sky and water. Her goal is to provide comfort and community beneath a roof and behind a door. Her domain was the culmination of all the previous divine realms; the harvest of the grain from the earth having been completed, Hestia remained responsible for turning that grain into bread through fire and ensuring there was enough to feed and warm the household. She is the most closely human of the Greek Olympians in that humanity exercises just as much control over her realm as she does. Hestia provides wealth and warmth to a home equal to the amount of work a man puts into it.

Curiously enough, as prominent as Hestia was in Ancient Greek mythology, she never possessed standalone worship sites. Other deities had their temples and monuments, we know, but Hestia's temples were considered by the Greeks to be the fireplaces of every home and public building. That she had so diffused herself into Greek culture and custom gave rise to a mode of Greek thinking that placed her outside the twelve Olympians; in fact, it was said that she forfeited her place among her brothers and sisters to Dionysus to maintain cosmic harmony.

Hestia is the oldest and youngest of all the Olympians, according to the myth of Cronus' disgorging. She was the first daughter of Cronus and Rhea. Due to her seniority among the Olympians, she is often pictured in a subdued, mature fashion, a striking deviation from many of her Olympian counterparts. Above all the Olympian goddesses, she radiates a matronly air in many of her representations; she often appears cloaked and robed, complete with a head covering, and extending an arm with a beckoning finger. When the Olympians erected their temple atop that eponymous mountain and divided the world, Zeus instructed that Hestia would be charged with keeping the fires of the hall lit and hot with the discarded portions of animal sacrifices.

Myths

Though Hestia had arguably the greatest, most immediate presence of all her Olympian counterparts, there are surprisingly few stories involving her. We see that one reason for this is that she may not have been considered an official "Olympian," or perhaps that her duties as goddess of the hearth are essentially invisible. She works to make the home, family, feast, and warmth all plentiful, and as such, it seems she has no use for intervention on the lives of men. However, we do know at least one small myth addressing how she got her position as keeper of the divine hearth.

Like her sister Artemis, Hestia wished to remain chaste for eternity. It is said that at one point, both Poseidon and Apollo once sought to make a wife of Hestia. When Zeus was ready to commit his sister to the bonds of marriage, Hestia pled to let her stay on Olympus, which she loved above all, keeping the hearth of the massive temple warm and inviting. Swayed by her devotion, Zeus allowed her to stay, giving her the position not only of the divine homemaker but bestowed upon her the gift of every fireplace past, present, and future as an altar to her service. She would be placed "in the midst of the house and receive the richest portion [of all offerings]," according to Homer's hymn.

To Conclude

We see that our remaining Olympians hold a humble yet elevated presence compared to the other deities covered thus far. Each of our four holds control of a world that exists primarily in the material, and within those material worlds, the divine rulers work to ensure a better quality of life for mankind. These four are, above all, the most benevolent and charitable to humanity, bestowing upon them the technology, tools, and wisdom that allow for advancement through the ages and mastery of the harsh, oftentimes lethal natural world.

We see that all four of these divines are connected to the earth in more intimate ways than their counterparts. As mankind sprang from the clay of the earth, it is a small wonder that those gods whose tools and spaces are similarly tied to the planet would occupy a greater prestige in daily Greek life. These four deities provide the basis for interpersonal communication and celebration, linking the chains of ancient islands together with food and festivity.

CHAPTER 7

The Love Below

It would appear at this point that we have hit a bit of a snag in rounding out our mighty Olympians; we are left with a proverbial "elephant in the room," or perhaps more fittingly, the "elephant below the room." We have omitted from our discussion thus far Hades and his domain, the underworld. There are multiple reasons for this. The most in line with Ancient Greek mythological and religious thinking is that Hades is technically not an Olympian; in claiming the underworld, he abdicated his seat among the gods in favor of full sovereignty and autonomy over the realm of the dead. The second reason, in keeping with the first, is that Hades' realm is so vast, touching so many facets of divine and mortal life throughout Greek mythology, that devoting an entirely separate chapter to its places, people, and stories seems almost necessary to begin to understand it.

Death, as in all ages, held especially peculiar importance to the Greeks. Given the terrors of the surrounding environment, the expansion of hostile forces through conquest, and that medical technology was next to nonexistent, the ancient Mediterranean people would have been surrounded by death for reasons beyond their comprehension. Naturally, based on their religious thinking, it would stand to reason that the Ancient Greeks would create an entire mythological ecosystem to attempt to answer the questions that seem to be incongruous with the behavior of their more visible and benevolent Olympian divines. To the Ancient Greeks, as to many other cultures, death was a sort of theft; a life was removed from the visible world. The questions then arose: Who stole that life? Where did they take it? It could not be the many Olympians who snuffed it from the mortal plane; while it is true that they were vengeful and oftentimes cruel, the Olympians were much more satisfied transforming humans than outright killing them. Nor could the life be taken by Mount Olympus, for only those deities could set foot there.

If lives undeniably disappeared but retreated neither to the top of Mount Olympus nor to Poseidon's depths, then, mythologically, the one remaining place they could go was the most mysterious and opaque of all: beneath the earth itself. It was a world unimaginable to the Ancient mind; from beneath the earth grew all life grew and withered, so logically there must be something there. What was that something; what did it look like? Who controlled it, and above all, did it mean to instigate violence against the living? The answers came in another, albeit shadowy, form of the divine: Hades, his black horses and strange abominable creatures, the god with least concern for mortal activity beyond claiming their souls to populate his gloomy underground kingdom which today shares his name.

Hades

Up until this point, we have mentioned the lord of the underworld as a passing character in several preceding myths; mostly, he has been a selfish, cunning character bent on abduction or theft to benefit himself. We have seen that it is essentially his fault we have winter, among other earthly misfortunes. Hades, sometimes referred to as the "Zeus of the Underworld," occupied a position certainly self-serving but surprisingly apathetic. The commonly held belief was that for all the evil Hades could inflict upon the earth, his primary desire was to maintain balance on the planet by offsetting his brother's actions.

Unsurprisingly, Hades had few sites of worship in Ancient Greece. Superstitious as they were, they avoided calling attention to the lord of the underworld as they were afraid of summoning him; taking an oath in his name may result in an untimely end for those who swore it. Bizarrely, however, all across Greece, he was nearly as revered as he was feared and loathed. We are told that he often received sacrifices and that in worship, Greeks would avert their eyes from his image and bang their heads against the ground to ensure that Hades would hear them.

It seems Hades left his estate beneath the earth only a handful of times in his mythos. Once, we know he departed to ensnare the young Persephone, but other than that, Hades seemed to remain covetous of his sovereignty and what he deemed a perfect, natural, and legal order. We are treated to many colorful descriptions of Hades' realm, particularly in Homer's works, where he describes the lord of the underworld's estate as "full of guests," which is, for all its macabre context, a pretty funny way to describe the eternal entrapment of souls. He was jealous of those who managed to escape his tyrannical legal system, who, coincidentally, always seem to be at least half-god. His love of order, justice, and balance is often his undoing; Hades is entirely his own master, but a slave to his own rules.

Myths

It seems that most of Hades' direct myths employ demigods; frankly, they seem to be stories where the half-divines outwit, outlast, or outrun the order-loving, law-abiding lord of the underworld. Heracles, Perseus, and Odysseus all took their turns confounding the rules laid out by Hades, who, with metaphorical hands tied and literal fists shaking, had no choice but to let them return to the upper world of the living.

One instance where Hades emerges a victor by his own design is in his dealings with Theseus, the mythical king of Athens. Having unrivaled power among the Greeks, Theseus, in his hubris, plotted with his best friend Pirithous, a Thessalian king, to take daughters of the gods for wives, as they could seemingly find no mortal woman that pleased them. Theseus kidnapped Helen of Troy, holding her hostage until she was of marrying age. Pirithous, foolish as he was, chose to kidnap Persephone. Having some degree of omniscience, Hades caught wind of the Thessalian king's plans and readied an immense feast. The two kings arrived and were met with hospitality to rival that found on Mount Olympus; though as they ate, Hades quietly unleashed serpents to bind the two to their chairs, where for eternity they would sit, their senses tempted by food, but their stomachs always empty.

Hades also plays an essential part in another extremely popular, surviving myth: the story of Sisyphus in his attempt to cheat death. The story goes that Sisyphus, the man with a self-proclaimed greater wit than Zeus, broke a promise to Zeus that he would not reveal the location of Aegina, an invisible nymph kept hidden by the king of the gods. Furious, Zeus ordered Hades to take Sisyphus down to his kingdom and chain him up as punishment. Having been escorted to the underworld, Sisyphus encounters Hades setting up the chains of punishment. Sisyphus asks Hades if he can show him how the chains work as a means of punishment, to which Hades obliges. Sisyphus then locks Hades up and flees back to the upper world, seemingly having bested death itself.

The problem arises when Hades is unable to fulfill his duties as the claimer of souls; if he is detained, nothing can die. The Olympians cannot receive their animal sacrifices, grain cannot be harvested, the old cannot pass on, and plague spreads, unhindered by the culling of its hosts. The earth is thrown into chaos, and Zeus takes notice. He sends a fuming Ares, no stranger to entrapment himself and furious that war has lost its fun, to free Hades from his chains, and deals with Sisyphus himself. The now famous punishment handed down to the king who cheated death was the eternal rolling of a boulder up a mountain, only to have it tumble back down to its foot.

Places of the Underworld

The underworld offers us an opportunity to glimpse the imagination of the Ancient Greek writers, unlike its exalted counterpart Olympus, of which we have scant physical descriptions. One reason for this may have been that many Greeks understood and agreed to some capacity what Olympus looked like, so rendering it upon a page or in a spoken poem would seem redundant or unnecessary. The underworld, however, was and still is a place of great mystery. Nobody has ever seen it, but given the many terrors that bring about death, one can imagine that the destination for those taken souls is anything but paradisiac. Comprising rivers dividing souls by their quality and fields wherein those souls spend eternity, the underworld's geography is rigid, severe, and abysmal.

The River Styx

The River Styx is the single most famous and recognizable locale in all the Greek underworld; behind Mount Olympus, it might be the most recognized in all Greek mythology. It is the river that supposedly separates the world of the living from the realm of the dead. It is an indispensable part of the underworld's ecosystem, as it provides the main highway of transportation into Tartarus for the newly deceased. As with many elements of the Greek mythological world, Styx is also personified as a nymph; she is a daughter of Oceanus punished by Zeus for siding with the Titans during the Titanomachy.

The Styx is one of five hellish rivers that converge upon the marshy center of the underworld; this is referred to as "the Styx," a term that today we colloquially carry to mean any backwoods, sparsely habited wilderness. We are told that the nymph and her fluvial incarnation can grant invulnerability to anyone who bathes there. In fact, it is said that as a boy, Achilles was dipped therein yet braced by his heel, later the location of his undoing by Paris' well-placed arrow during the Trojan War.

Tartarus

The deepest depths of Hades' realm, Tartarus can be described closest as a dungeon. To reach it, Hesiod says, would take nine days of descent from the plane of Hades, which in turn is nine days descent from the earth, which is nine days descent from Olympus. It is the paragon of the abyss; completely devoid of light and hope, it is the most severe punishment an eternal soul can undertake. Tartarus, in effect, is the "nothingness" of death. It is a vacuum from which there is no escape save divine intervention.

Naturally, Tartarus was deified, as is the Ancient Greek habit. He is one of the three original offspring of the cosmos; he is the middle child, stuck between his older brother Chaos and his younger sister Gaia. He is the one Greek deity whose realm remained intact after the Titanomachy; in fact, it is said that he guards the defeated Titans within his cells.

Those who inhabit Tartarus are said to be the most wretched of all beings; our cunning King Sisyphus is among them, eternally rolling his boulder. The Titans, as mentioned, take residence there, as does the king Tantalus, who, according to myth, murdered his son Pelops and served him as a meal when invited to dine with the gods upon Olympus. We can see that these are wholly unsavory characters, and Given Hades' love of justice, understand why they were fated to the chains of Tartarus.

Elysium & the Asphodel Fields

Though the punishments handed down may have been harsh and severe in many cases, for the most part, the underworld was less to be feared by the ordinary mortal. The worst of the worst were sent to Tartarus, but those who lived without severely offending the divines were sent to the Asphodel Fields.

The fields were described as flowery and peaceful, though not as we mortals would imagine. They were alive with blooms, certainly, but according to Homer, in his Odyssey, they were a dark place without joy or laughter. The impression one gets from the fields is that although one's mortal work may have ended, paradise in the afterlife remains reserved only for the divines.

On the other hand, those souls touched or deemed worthy by the gods would be escorted to Elysium, an exclusive paradise, which technically was separate from Hades' realm, but existed on the same plane. Elysium, split from its dismal underworld counterpart by the river Lethe, was a place of easy, bright, colorful life; stories state that there was always a light western breeze which kept the temperature manageable. Homer writes of Elysium that, in addition to the warmth, there is no snow, nor rain, nor drought; it is the perfect, ideal afterlife, though it seems populated almost entirely by demigods.

The River Lethe

Another one of the five rivers of the underworld, we know the mythical Lethe bordered Hades' domain and that of Elysium. It was the "river of forgetfulness," in that should one fall in or drink from it, their soul would forget everything it had known. It was a commonly held belief among those Ancient Greek cults of mystery that all souls drank copiously from the river before reincarnation. The story goes that as part of his punishment for trying to steal away Persephone, the king Pirithous was dropped into the river, thus wiping his memory completely.

The river traced its path around the interior of the underworld, looping the cave Hypnos, where wayward souls were drawn to sleep for eternity. According to some religious sources, the river has an opposite sister on the mortal plane named Mnemosyne, which provided those who drink from its waters omniscience and infallible memory.

The Rivers Cocytus & Phlegethon

Two of the remaining rivers both ringed the border of Hades, though they flowed in opposite directions: the Cocytus, the "river of wailing" or "river of lamentation," and the Phlegethon, the "river of fire." Both served to deter mortal interference and trespassing into Hades' realm, and both struck utter despair in the Ancient Greek imagination.

The Cocytus is unique among the underworld's rivers in that it varies in depth; this is because its purpose is to contain those souls who behaved traitorously or treasonously in their mortal bodies. Depending on how great the transgression, the backstabber could be submerged anywhere from their knees to above their heads; no matter how much water the victim takes on, however, they would be resigned to screaming and wailing for all eternity.

The Phlegethon is a more subtle river, despite its contents. It is a river of fire from which we draw some connotations of the Judeo-Christian ideas of "Hell" and its inferno. After winding around the border of Hades, the river plummets in a fiery cascade into the depths of Tartarus, the only of the five rivers to make that plunge. One myth surrounding the river of fire comes in relation to the nymph Styx. Supposedly, before being turned into rivers by the vengeful Zeus, Phlegethon and Styx were lovers before the Titanomachy. Having chosen the losing side in that conflict, the two were punished simultaneously. In turning into the river that bears her name, her physical being was consumed by the fires of Phlegethon, whom the retributive Hades charged with bordering his underworld. Not without his sense of justice, however, Hades, upon seeing the punishments carried out to a suitable conclusion, allowed the two rivers to be reunited in their meanderings through the underworld.

Two Flowers and a Dog

The locations of Hades' world provide a wondrously rich locale for the afterlife, and just as its cousins on the material plane, the rivers and fields are populated with all manner of symbolic plant and animal life. Some species of earthly vegetation, according to Greek myth, even originated in the underworld, and through either fruition or folly, wind up growing upon the earth.

Mint

One of the most intriguing stories of underworld flora comes in the form of the mint plant. According to the Greek myth, it is not a wholly earthly plant. Mint finds its roots in the underworld because of the all-too-common jealousy that pervades the ancient deities. The story goes that Hades, after marrying Persephone, falls in love with one of his subjects, a nymph of the river Cocytus named Minthe. Some accounts say that the nymph attempted to seduce Hades, who consequently fell under her spell. No matter how the lord of the underworld came to fawn over Mithe, Persephone would have none of it. Taking matters into her own hands, she transformed the nymph into the mint plant, scattering it across the underworld and the mortal plane, giving it so strong an odor and taste that it repulsed all animals.

Jonquil

Growing along the banks of the famous Styx and throughout the Asphodel Fields are splatters of jonquils, also known as narcissus. The white petals and yolky centers sprouting in clusters throughout the underworld are named for the young man so transformed:

Narcissus, the most vainly handsome of all Greek men. Having been turned into the flower for scorning those who loved him, he remained fragrant, striking, and poisonous, perfectly suited as a lure for the unsuspecting Persephone. As she was dragged away by Hades' chariot, Persephone, according to myth, clutched a handful of the flowers between her fists, and thus they took root all throughout the underworld.

Cerberus

One of the most fearsome and famous creatures throughout the Greek mythos, Cerberus was the fierce and loyal companion of Hades. He is pictured as a dog with multiple heads, ranging from three to one hundred, and most often sitting obediently at Hades' side when he is atop his throne. In some depictions, Cerberus is presented as a single-headed hound, albeit with hundreds of snake's heads slithering down his back. He varies in size, though it is commonly accepted that he is, at the very least, the size of a man and often much larger. Though he was Hades' best friend, he was tasked with the important job of preventing wayward souls from escaping Hades' underworld. He was like Hell's guard dog, although he was supposed to keep people in instead of out.

The most well-known myth surrounding the hound of Hades involves the hero Heracles, who, as one of his twelve labors, is sent to the underworld to capture Cerberus. The hero arrives, confronts Hades by asking politely to forfeit his possession of the multi-headed hound. Ever the legislator, Hades agrees to part with Cerberus on one condition: that Heracles defeat the giant dog in combat without the use of his weapons. Heracles subdued the creature and dragged him to the surface of the material world, where it is said that the dog vomited, and from that, the poisonous monkshood plant sprouted its first flowers on the earth.

To Conclude

There are countless other locales, symbols, and varying stories within Hades' underworld; to dive any further into their depth and breadth would almost assuredly yield an entirely new book, which is not this book's objective. I have attempted to convey efficiently those outstanding stories and elements which form the foundation for discussion about the belief systems and symbols of the Ancient Greek afterlife; I hope that while this chapter has provided a coherent map of Hades' world, it leaves many landmarks undiscovered, so that the reader may embark on that journey themselves.

CHAPTER 8

The "Half" and "Half-nots"

We have made great allusions to this idea of Ancient Greek religion gravitating toward a world more human than divine, but all that is essentially speculatory. Of course, it makes sense that early, sophisticated human beings would understand the control of the world in relatively simple terms: those universal human emotions and motivations. How could it be possible to bring the two worlds even closer together, to entirely bridge the mythological gap? The very idea of worship or religious ritual is insufficient; it only elevates deities above mankind. Oracularity, while mystical and mortal, provides less a bridge to the divine realm and more a connection to it, and indeed one that can be severed quite easily.

What if, then, for all their temptations to control the lives of men, the gods were responsible for the birth and rearing of mortal men? Where would they rank? Surely, they are not fully divine; and yet neither are they completely human. Is their purpose on earth to abet mankind, or dissuade it from more noble goals? Are they acting solely on behalf of their Olympian superiors, or might it be that given their humanity, they have a genuine altruistic side? Many questions emerge when considering those half-immortal humans, the demigods; we can find their answers sprinkled throughout their stories. They affirm not only the Ancient Greeks' belief in the strength of mankind but ours as well.

There are an exceptional number of demigods planted throughout Greek mythology. However, we must lend our focus to the most visible, whose stories have been told and rehashed throughout the ages; again, our job is to provide an introductory framework to the mythology. We will be focusing on Achilles, Heracles, and Perseus because they all share the common elements of divine birth, world-shaping tribulation, triumph over seemingly insurmountable odds, and most importantly, a multitude of surviving texts and contemporary allusions upon which to draw.

Achilles

Touted as the mightiest of all Greek warriors, the great Achilles played a pivotal role in the Trojan War, and as such, Homer's Iliad, the ancient poem centered on the legendary conflict. Son of the sea nymph Thetis and the king of the ancient nation of the Myrmidons, Peleus. There are several stories surrounding Achilles' conception, though one myth stands out due to its humor. It comes in Aeschylus' play Prometheus Bound, where Achilles' mother, the chaste Thetis, is said to have been pursued without rest by many of the Olympian divines. Hera, the wife of Zeus, one of the amorous gods, prophesied that the child Thetis bore would be infinitely stronger than his father and would usurp any claim his father had in the world. Upon hearing this, the Olympian gods immediately dropped their conquest ideas and forced Thetis to marry Peleus, a mortal king.

If we are not familiar with the stories of Achilles, we certainly are familiar with his fabled body part, the heel. It is said that Thetis, fearing the destruction of her only child at the hands of the Olympians, fled to Hades' underworld and the safety of her sister Styx, the river of invulnerability, and dunked Achilles beneath it, holding him by his heel and thus keeping it dry. As such, Achilles' heel remained the only vulnerable place on his entire body, and it is a term we carry today to mean a weakness in an otherwise seemingly strong entity.

As mentioned previously, Achilles was the central figure in the Trojan War, fighting on the side of the Greeks against Troy. We are told by Homer that Achilles arrived at Troy with fifty Myrmidon ships, each carrying fifty soldiers of his nation. After having engaged in several battles with the Trojans and their hero Hector, the Greeks under Achilles and his lifelong friend Patroclus had been pushed back to the beaches harboring their ships, whereupon Patroclus donned Achilles' armor and rallied his troops for a counterattack. It proved to be successful, forcing the Trojans all the way back behind the famous walls of their city, though Patroclus was killed in the onslaught, and Achilles' armor was stolen by Hector.

Seeing his best friend downed in battle, Achilles is whipped into a rage. He demands of Hephaestus to craft him new armor, a new shield, and a new spear, and sets out onto the field of battle, where with his godlike invulnerability and proficiency in weapons slaughters every enemy soldier he encounters in search of Hector. Homer writes that his rage is so great that if the gods had not intervened, he would have single-handedly sacked Troy. Ultimately, Achilles finds Hector and chases him around the walled city several times before Hector sees his fate is inescapable. Accepting his death, he begs Achilles to let his body be treated with the respect of a fallen warrior; Achilles does no such thing, tying Hector's corpse to the back of his chariot and dragging it around the battlefield in front of Troy. With his last breath, however, Hector prophesies the downfall of the legendary Achilles: that later in the war, Hector's brother Paris' arrow would bring about the hero's destruction.

Analysis

In this brief story of Achilles, as with many of the stories of the Greek demigods, what we see is the strength of humanity when inspired through the divine. In Achilles' case, he is brought to a godlike rage and seeks his revenge, not through any direct offense to him, as would be the case with Zeus or Poseidon, to name two, but because one of his closest friends has been unjustly slain in battle. We see that the gods themselves must intervene against the strength of one man, who is driven not only to great deeds on the battlefield but great shame in his desecration of Hector's body. This shows that although there is nobody on earth more powerful than this single, half-human warrior, he is dominated by those dark shades of humanity which haunt all mortal men.

Heracles

If Achilles is the most legendary Greek warrior, the place of greatest hero must belong to Heracles. Arguably the most famous figure in Greek mythology, Heracles' stories are blooming with rich symbolism of mortal strength and determination. He is, by all accounts, the divine protector of mankind, acting as the bridge between the mortal world and Mount

Olympus. It is upon his shoulders that the fate of humanity rests, and he is, above all, its greatest champion; we can imagine him simply as an Ancient Greek Superman. His labors and conquests have helped shape the Western literary canon. His myths have been told and retold throughout history, but always point to the belief that mankind possesses those unique qualities of tenacity and internal fortitude that put even the seemingly divine efforts well within mankind's reach.

The result of Heracles' birth was one of Zeus' many extramarital affairs. Among the many stories of Heracles' conception, we are told that Zeus seduced the mortal Alcmene by disguising himself as her husband. Hera, knowing full well the affair had taken place, and true to her character, plotted vengeance not against her husband, but against her half-human offspring. She sent into the crib of the young Heracles a pair of snakes to dispatch the hero, although to no avail. Heracles' divine strength and constitution, even as a baby, prompted no fear but an instinct of domination; he was found by his earthly mother playing with the snakes as though they were toys. Astounded by the sight, Alcmene summoned Tiresias, a soothsayer, who foretold that the child would fulfill the destiny of a god, that he would be the conqueror of countless creatures.

Heracles' story picks up again when, as a young man, he killed his music teacher Linus with a lyre, and thus was forced from the city into the role of a shepherd, where he was supposedly visited by the divines in the form of two travelers. One offered the young Heracles a life of ease and pleasantness, one without severe conflict or great reward; this was Vice. The other, Virtue, offered the hero a difficult, harsh existence, one plagued with strife and brutality, but for all his struggle, he would be thrust into the halls of glory, with a seat on Olympus as his ultimate prize. Naturally, we can gather, Heracles chose the latter and propelled himself along the track that would yield his legend.

We are told that after choosing the path of Virtue, Heracles married the king Creon's daughter Megara, and had ten children. Driven to a fit of madness by the divine saboteur Hera, he winds up killing his family, his wife included. Heracles then wandered the earth, ultimately curing his madness at the Oracle of Delphi, of whom Hera had taken control. She instructed Heracles that, to atone for his crimes, he should lend himself to the service of the king Eurystheus for ten years, one for each slain child, and fulfill any request or task the king demanded of him. Other stories state that the service was a result of a compromise between Zeus and his vengeful wife; that if Heracles should complete twelve nigh-impossible tasks, he shall have proven worthy of immortality. Either way, we are given the meat of Heracles' life: his Twelve Labors.

There are many sources readily available regarding Heracles' Twelve Labors. Thus, it would be tedious to focus on them individually; as such, we will cover them briefly, though the reader is encouraged to seek out these stories on their own. According to myth, the tasks Eurystheus bestowed upon Heracles were accomplished with Athena's help, who had taken an interest in the hero's life. He was to, in varying order, slay, capture, and steal his way to freedom. He would be pitted against the terrible Hydra, the aggressive and vigilant Amazons, and the ever-defecating three thousand cattle of Augeas. He relies on his divine strength and human intelligence to bind horses' mouths shut, scare off man-eating birds, lie in wait to capture seemingly elusive beasts, and swipe golden apples from a jealously guarded orchard. His final impossible task, we know, was conjured up by a fearful Eurystheus who had grown wary that Heracles would, in fact, complete all his labors. He was to descend into the depths of the underworld and bring back Hades' multi-headed guard dog Cerberus, which he does, successfully evading death and earning his prophesied place atop Olympus.

Analysis

While there are many more stories surrounding Heracles, the ones mentioned occupy a space in the imagination that is as permanent as his seat of immortality. The common thread that strings these myths together is Heracles' human traits. Even after being driven mad by Hera, he accepts his guilt, takes responsibility, and seeks to make amends for his transgressions. He learns to be patient, clever, and diplomatic; he comes to rely less on his divine, unmatched physical strength, and more on his mortal traits. Therefore, due to his commitment to self-improvement, Athena takes an interest in his development. What we can learn from Heracles' stories is that it behooves a person to become well-rounded and fully developed. It is not simply enough to be gifted with great talent; it is necessary to cultivate those strengths and mitigate those weaknesses which a person is given in life, because, even if someone is born half-god, nobody is perfect.

Perseus

The oldest of our demigods, mythologically speaking, is Perseus. Before the days of the famous Heracles, Perseus was widely regarded as the greatest monster slayer in history. A contemporary of Bellerophon, Perseus is the only demigod who, in his mortal life, occupied a place of royalty; he was the king of the ancient nation of Mycenae and the Perseid dynasty, of which an unborn Heracles was prophesied to inherit. Though he was of divine birth, it seems that Perseus relies less on the help of his Olympian family and more on his own native intelligence and strength; he is truly the picture of a good king, eager to raise arms only in defense of the weak and in the name of justice.

The story goes that Perseus was a son of Zeus and Danae, daughter of the king of Argos. As is common, it was prophesied that the king would be overthrown by the impossible strength of his son, and as such, he imprisoned both Perseus and his mother in a wooden casket and floated them out to sea. Thanks to a prayer from Danae, the two washed up unharmed on the shore of Seriphos, where they were taken in by the king Polydectes.

As Perseus grew, he noticed Polydectes shower his attention and affection upon his mother, which he felt was ignoble, as he deemed the king a less than virtuous man. Polydectes, true to Perseus' assumptions, planned to thwart the hero's defense of his mother by fabricating grounds to dispatch him. He held a sprawling feast, asking that all guests bring a gift; specifically, the king demanded that all guests bring a horse. Having no horse to offer, the noble Perseus promised to bring the king any other gift he could possibly want; Polydectes, deeming it impossible, requested of Perseus the head of the Gorgon.

Perseus set to planning his impossible task; no mortal had approached the Gorgon and lived, much less taken its head. In his dismay, he was visited by the goddess of wisdom and strategy, Athena; she had taken a special interest in Perseus as a dedicated man of his word and offered the hero her divine assistance. Athena knew, as she was the one who turned Medusa into a Gorgon, exactly how to defeat it. She guided Perseus to the Greae, the three much older "grey sisters" of Medusa, who, sitting in a circle atop a mountain, shared one eye for seeing and one tooth for speaking. The Greae, according to myth, knew not only the whereabouts of Medusa but the tools to destroy her as well. Though the three refused to willingly give up their sister, Perseus, with his natural smarts, took from the three their only eye as they were passing it between them, holding it for collateral and promising to return it once his quest had been completed.

Perseus ultimately found the secret orchard of which the Greae spoke and collected a knapsack which could contain the Gorgon's gaze. He was given Hermes' sandals and sword and Hades' helm of invisibility; Athena furnished him a divine shield. With Athena's aid, he found the Gorgon's cave, and with his divine tools, severed its head; according to some stories, Pegasus the winged horse flew from the Gorgon's neck.

Analysis

What we see in Perseus' encounters is the humility of the human spirit. True, he is gifted as his descendent Heracles with unrivaled strength and mettle, but Perseus differs in that his great labors are essentially selfless and for the benefit of others. He is an excellent judge of character, and although he does not see eye-to-eye with Polydectes on moral issues, he understands his place in the king's court and is grateful for the life the king has provided for him.

Perseus also embodies the noble human traits of honesty and accountability. He vows to return to the king the head of the Gorgon, and does just that, despite the ulterior motives of Polydectes. Sure, he steals the eye of the Greae, but only to vow to return it when his quest is complete, which he does. He is the picture of the upright and admirable human being; he does not seek glory to immortalize his own name, but rather to elevate those around him. These are the very traits that give him the sympathetic benefit of the gods; he is, in a way, the Greek mythical embodiment of "karma," getting from the world exactly what he puts in.

To Conclude

We can see that the demigods of Ancient Greece, and these three, in particular, possess those traits which even today we deem as most noble; they are generous, ambitious, hounded by determination, and tenacious in their pursuit of success. However, in their fallible humanity, they also claim those shadowy pieces of personality that dwell deep within us all: they are, in some instances, naïve, rash, and irrational; full of pride and short-sighted, they tend to rush headlong into conflict, and only afterward evaluate their judgments. They are characters whose explicit purpose is to amplify both the human and the divine; they are completely hyperbolic, and yet their presence sparks within us some sympathy, for their reasons in their struggles are not unfamiliar to us, though the situations and creatures might be.

CHAPTER 9

"It Came from the Greek!"

We have seen that there is a plethora of intriguing myths regarding the creation of the earth, those divines who watch over it, and those chosen heroic individuals who act on behalf of and to benefit mankind. In addition to those wonderful personifications, the Ancient Greeks gave us a bestiary of unparalleled imagination. For all the huffing and puffing and pushing and pulling that the Olympians cause upon the earth, it is the creatures of Greek mythology that truly inspire the awe or fear of the worshipper.

The creatures of Greek mythology are some of the most iconic and inspired in any system of beliefs. What strikes the reader about these creatures is that while they apparently occupy a world of the imagined, there is always some relative plausibility to their existence. One can place them in the uncanny valley of believability; we know nowadays that they do not exist, but to the Ancient Greek mind, with all the tumult and unknowns the material world hid from the eye, who could say whether or not a creature with several different animal heads could exist?

In this chapter, we will be taking a closer look at several of the most prevalent beasts in Greek mythology: the centaur and its variants, Pegasus, Chimera, and the Hydra. All of these creatures hold a concrete place in the Greek mythos; each were so much a part of Greek religious thinking that they had developed their own narratives alongside their divine and semi-human counterparts.

Centaur & Demihumans

The centaur, it could be argued, is the most sophisticated of all Greek creatures; indeed, it is the closest to mankind, and even provides guidance and wisdom to the two-legged race, according to some stories. The centaur is a cross between a horse and a man; its lower body is equine, while from the waist up, it is decidedly human, thus endowing it with the powers of speech and reason. While they do possess the noble human traits of communication, many Grecian myths portray them as primarily brutish and animalistic; in some sense, they can be interpreted as the opposite manifestation of the demigod. Some scholars have taken their split form to represent early humanity's split between their instinctual, purely animal past and the cerebral, more analytical present and future. Still, others more historically oriented claim that the centaur is a misfired memory: that the creatures were in a sense "real," but were simply nomadic horsemen misremembered.

Chiron

The most well-known of all centaurs is Chiron, the mentor of Achilles and guardian of Prometheus. Apollo's foster son, Chiron, was held in great esteem among his half equine brothers because he was deemed the wisest and most measured of them all. As his brothers lived according to their animal instincts, debasing themselves with carnal pleasures and intoxication, Chiron devoted his time to artistic and intellectual development. He was renowned for his mastery and skill in healing, medicine, and the hunting arts, so much so that he is attributed throughout the pantheon as the inventor of botany and herbal remedies.

Even his appearance differed from that of his brothers. Chiron possessed more human elements than the average centaur; in depictions of the mythical beasts, one can always tell which Chiron is by his human front legs. In effect, he was an entire human with half a horse attached to his back, while other centaurs claimed all four hooves. We can read that Chiron possesses these distinctly human features because he is, through his actions and behavior, more human than animal, though he acts as the connecting bridge between man and nature, as is evident through his teaching.

Minotaur

A creature that belongs to the same category as the centaur is the Minotaur, the great bullish beast of King Minos. It has the inverted physical qualities of the centaur: its body remains fully human, while its head takes the form of a bull's. It also has the bull's tail. The Minotaur is said to be the reason why the great inventor Daedalus created the labyrinth, the halls of which the Minotaur supposedly wandered as its prison.

The story of the Minotaur begins when King Minos, in competition with his brothers for Poseidon's favor and control of the kingdom, set to sacrifice a bull in the name of the sea god. Upon retrieving the animal, however, Minos noted how beautiful it was and kept it for himself, sacrificing a lesser animal to Poseidon. Catching wind of this, Poseidon, furious as always, swore vengeance on the king and made Minos' wife Pasiphae fall in love with the beautiful animal. Pasiphae then recruited Daedalus to construct a hollow cow made of wood so that she could mate with the bull. Thus, the Minotaur was born. Under protest of his wife, who loved the child, Minos could not bring himself to kill the bullheaded child. He had Daedalus construct the legendary labyrinth, where the Minotaur stayed until Theseus descended it and killed the beast.

Satyr

The third half-animal varies from its counterparts in many ways. The satyr, unlike its centaur and minotaur cousins, is fully divine. It is a forest spirit, often pictured with the ears and tail of a horse, and short, stubby hoofed and hairy legs like that of a donkey. They are depicted as walking upright, often dancing or in possession of an instrument: typically, a lyre or a pan flute. In some instances, they are lent the traits of a goat such as horns, as well as the occasional hyperbolic erection.

More closely related, mythologically speaking, to the nymph than the centaur, the satyrs are the forest spirits of the Ancient Greek world; they are symbols of youth, joy, new growth, and harnessed animal passion. They are known as devout followers of Dionysus and are imagined throughout plays and myths as possessing an insatiable sexual appetite, a taste for wine, and above all, a desire to play tricks and pranks on mortal men and women. All these traits are distilled down to their essence in the manifestation of one iconic satyr alone: Pan.

Pan

Pan is the very picture of a satyr in that he is the god of the field, the cave, springtime, improvisatory music, and sexuality. He is a mentor and teacher, though not with his mischievous side. It is from his stories that we are given the myth of the pan flute, and in fact, his name lends itself to our word panic.

We are told, due to his satyr's appetite, that Pan once attempted to seduce the nymph Syrinx, a devout follower of Artemis, and thus devoted to chastity. The story goes that Pan chased the nymph through the forest, and Syrinx, unwilling to yield but unable to keep running, transformed into a reed nestled within a marsh. When Pan came across the marsh and reeds, a breeze blew through them that made a sound that enchanted Pan's ears. Not knowing which reed his desirous Syrinx had turned into, he plucked several of varying lengths, tied them together, and blew through the ends of all, creating the pan flute.

In addition to his musical inspiration, Pan also claims total victory on behalf of the Olympians during the Titanomachy. As the war was raging, Pan claims in one of his stories, he was taking a nap in a field beneath a tree, as he can often be found. The action of the combat, or perhaps a stray thunderbolt, apparently disturbed his sleep so suddenly that he woke with a start and let loose his divine voice. Pan shouted, so loud, he claims, that he startled the Titans; they fell off Mount Olympus all the way into Tartarus. As we can see, this is where panic arose into the common vocabulary.

Pegasus

A famous symbol in the world over, Pegasus the winged horse occupies a pivotal part in Greek myths; he is seen at the side of a multitude of ancient heroes, aiding them in their seemingly impossible tasks. He is regarded as a symbol of man's triumph over nature as well as a manifestation of purity of heart and motive. He is commonly believed to be completely white, with wings that are usually pictured as larger than the horse itself sprouting from its foremost shoulders. When his powerful hooves strike the ground to launch himself skyward, some myths say, springs rush forth from the earth.

It is said that Pegasus is either one of the many offspring of Poseidon, or, as we have illustrated earlier, born immaculately from the blood of the Gorgon's neck. One myth that reconciles the two stories is that Pegasus emerged from the Gorgon's blood as it trickled into the sea, so that, in a similar fashion to the birth of Aphrodite, the horse sprang forth without a true "father," though Poseidon had a hand in his creation.

Regardless of his birth and parentage, we know for certain that the winged horse's guardian was the goddess Athena; who better to stable mankind's greatest ally than the divine most inclined to lend humanity a hand? Whoever Pegasus is charged with assisting on any given day, we can be sure that the myths provide our hero with a path through Athena. Some stories state that after Pegasus sprang into being, he made a beeline straight for the birthplace of thunder and lightning, by the side of Zeus within the clouds. There, in Zeus' pastures, the goddess Athena is said to have tamed him under the king of the gods' instruction, and thus became the sole master of the winged horse.

Bellerophon, one of the great pre-Heraclean heroes, for example, was united with Pegasus when he was charged with the task of dispatching the Chimera. The story goes that, unable to ascend the mountain wherein the Chimera lived on his own, he was instructed by the soothsayer Polyeidos to spend the night in the Athena's temple, which he did. The goddess came to him in his dream and bestowed upon him a golden bridle, and when Bellerophon awoke, he found that it had materialized. He came across the elusive winged horse at a spring, and ultimately tamed him using Athena's gift. Pegasus helped Bellerophon destroy the Chimera with immense ease, although the manner of his victory gave the hero an inflated sense of self-worth, and he began to think himself equal to the gods. To thwart his hubris, Zeus struck Pegasus with a gadfly while Bellerophon was riding him, and the winged horse threw the hero from his back, where he crashed to the earth, breaking his body.

Pegasus played his part in Perseus' rescue of Andromeda as well; he is an integral part of that most famous of Greek myths, which has been told and retold on page and screen many times. Part of that story involves the hero tracking the winged horse to where Athena had tamed it, and, seeing Perseus in need of a steed and deeming his character worthy, offers up Pegasus to the hero.

In addition to his role as helper to heroes, Pegasus was a necessary sidekick to the king of the gods himself. We know from several stories that Pegasus' role was to carry Zeus' thunderbolts and other weapons into battle. He also shared the same responsibilities as Zeus' fabled giant eagles as a divine peacekeeper and an agent of mortal surveillance.

Chimera

The Ancient Greeks seem to associate the sinister or ungodly with deformations, amalgam and unbalance. This is made evidently apparent in their imaginings of the Chimera, a terrifying three-headed beast that lived in a cave atop an enormous mountain. Some stories claim it is the explanation behind the volcano, others that its purpose was to guard some unearthly treasure. Whatever its reason for being, it is arguably one of the most horrible and vicious creatures conjured up by the Greek imagination.

One of the reasons the Chimera strikes such fear into the Ancient Greek mind is that it makes its home on the mortal plane; Cerberus, the sea serpent, and Hydra, while all equally sinister, cannot be encountered by mankind during their earthly travels. The beast boasts the fire-breathing head of a lion, from its flank the head of a goat, and its tail the head of a snake. It is a porridge of creatures who share one thing in common: for one reason or another, they are to be feared by man.

Chimera, unlike many of its mythological family, was widely accepted and depicted as a female creature. It is written that Chimera was mother to the Egyptian Sphinx and Nemean lion, that massive beast slain by Heracles as his first labor. We are told that Chimera's homeland was Lycia, in modern day Turkey, where several geothermal features have been long referred to as "the eternal fires of Chimera."

Where most creature mythology depends on oral and written tradition, the stories of Chimera are interesting in that they are predominately told through artistic expression; while Homer and later sources make mention of physical descriptions of the Chimera, source materials regarding her stories survive primarily on vases, jewelry, and other shards of pottery. This could be because, as an essentially "foreign" creature, the conception of Chimera was brought into Greece, wherein it flourished and disseminated throughout Greek culture, though was never entirely codified into the mythology. The myths tend to support this, in that Chimera is a foreign, unknown, and seemingly insurmountable and yet wholly mortal foe, who is vanquished by the "homegrown" Bellerophon with the aid of the decidedly Greek pantheon.

Hydra

The giant many-headed reptile known as the Lernaean Hydra was the victim of Heracles' second labor, and for good reason. The snakelike monster was a terror to those of Ancient Greece, said to possess not only intelligence but, by some accounts, the ability to regenerate entire portions of its body.

The creature was said to be the most poisonous and lethal of all mythical beasts; even its scent, in some stories, was lethal. It had disease-carrying blood and toxic breath and was outfitted with hundreds of razor-sharp, venomous teeth. Though the number of its heads varied according to different sources, some placed them at three, others fifty, it is agreed that the creature was gargantuan in size and would regrow two heads for every head it lost.

Hydra's mythological home was the lake of Lerna, somewhere on the eastern portion of the Peloponnesian peninsula. The lake is significant as a location of myth as it was considered one of the many entrances to the underworld, and as such, is one of the gatekeepers to

Hades' realm. According to myth, the many-headed Hydra is the only creature under Hades' domain who lives primarily outside of the underworld itself.

The Hydra met its end, as we know, when Heracles vanquished it as one of his Twelve Labors. As the creature's scent alone could have killed him, he covered his mouth and face with a sheepskin so he would not breathe the noxious gasses emitted by the creature. Then, having snuck up on Hydra, Heracles severed its heads and deemed the labor complete. Hydra, on the other hand, was not quite vanquished, growing twice as many heads as Heracles removed. Seeing his predicament, and quickly becoming overwhelmed, Heracles called upon his nephew Iolaus to help him. With his nephew's aid, Heracles brandished a sword of fire and cauterized each wound he inflicted upon the Hydra's various necks, thus thwarting its potential growth. Having slain the creature, Heracles then dipped his arrows in the Hydra's bile, thus poisoning them. The resulting wounds would be unable to heal.

To Conclude

The bestiary of Ancient Greek mythology is brimming with truly inspired creatures. Even those neglected in this brief account hold a mystique that sparks the imagination and provokes eternal questions about the ancient Mediterranean. Logically, these creatures could not exist in a literal sense; what, then, were they? Were they misremembered human beings? Or, like the fabled caught fish that keeps growing larger, some encounter with a literal creature that became inflated to mythical proportions over time? Whatever the case may be, the bestiary at its most exquisite provides modern day human beings an intriguing and coveted glimpse into the more earthly fears and perceived perils of the average Ancient Greek.

Conclusion

Though the pantheism of Greece and its worshippers have all but vanished from the earth, we are fortunate to have been handed down through the centuries those cultural artifacts that tie us intimately to our past and connect us to the future. It is the imagination and longing to understand and interpret the world that the Ancient Greek pantheon bestowed upon us, the people of today.

In this nowhere near exhaustive work, we have begun a simple evaluation of those features most prominent in Greek mythology; hopefully, with some degree of success, those stories have been brought back to life, and their importance underscored. We have seen the creation of the world, the construction of humans, creatures, and the end of life itself condensed into a small space, but this by no means should betray or undervalue the complexities and nuances of the Greek pantheon or the Ancient Greek way of life. Indeed, any given element of the themes and stories discussed in this work are worthy of countless books and studies; in part, it is this very inexhaustible intricacy of Ancient Greek culture that has allowed it to survive through the ages despite shifting spiritual trends. With a crumbling marble hand outstretched, it reaches even now for speculation, holds tightly human history, and points toward art.

Through those tumultuous ages of human history, mankind has always seemed to turn its gaze backward to these classic, immortal subjects and stories. It seems that mankind looks back, less for the nostalgia of the polytheistic culture, but to help guide it forward through whatever seemingly insurmountable obstacle that faces it. From the stories of Ancient Greece, we draw hope, inspiration, and confidence that humanity is a noble species. In a sense, the myths of the Greek pantheon operate as the Athena to our Odysseus; we trust we have the knowledge and experience to see ourselves through hardship, but we certainly will not turn down a little outside help.

We have seen in our brief study several themes as omnipresent as the Olympians themselves: that youth is to be valued as much for its energy and beauty as age is for its wisdom and experience, that pride, of all folly, is most rewarded with pain, and that although the world may be a hostile, destitute, and inhospitable place, family and community can greatly ease that burden.

We have become acquainted with the physical symbols of the Ancient Greek divines: their trees, animals, weapons, and clothing, and how and where their images were codified throughout Greece so that even today, they are immediately recognizable. We can identify Hermes, Hades, and Hestia at first glance, and can even explain to a certain extent why they are pictured the way they are.

We have constructed a bridge between the worlds of the divines and their supplicants, showing that for all the fear and respect the Ancient Greeks placed upon their deities, they had the utmost faith in the power of mankind to craft his own destiny and bear his own moral responsibilities. We see that although the Olympian gods are by no means accountable for their wrath and destruction, the sources of these outrages are undoubtedly human emotion.

Although the Greek pantheon has a reputation for the fantastic, the otherworldly, and the truly impossible, when we take a closer look at it, we see that though the conclusions about the world and its mechanisms tend to be farfetched, the reasons and logic behind those conclusions is, by ancient standards, quite sound. Creatures were not simply brought out of the imagination from fear, but with the intent of a measured explanation of a phenomenon or event. Natural disasters and even precise locations are usually explained as the result of a god or goddess' particular action or as a consequence thereof, not because their omniscience "willed it" into being.

Beyond any religious fervor or ideology, truth or falsehood, the Ancient Greek mythologies have handed down through the centuries the timelessness of narrative and storytelling. While we no longer look to explain the world through the inner machinations of naked, angry, invisible overseers, we are somehow still drawn to those ancient themes, symbols, and names that resonate within our imaginations. We carry the forms and structures of these ancient narratives into our modern-day storytelling; even the myths themselves have been reshaped and retooled to fit our contemporary sensibilities. Where the sciences of today are accustomed to explaining the world in the strictest, most technically accurate terms, they still acknowledge the importance of the Greek mythos through its nomenclature.

It is through the Greek myths, their characters and places that allow us to see deeper into ourselves as a species, and thus understand the world in a more holistic way. In that sense, the mythology of the Ancient Greeks is alive and well; it still serves its primary purpose of elaborating and expanding the world around, beyond and behind us, albeit in a far less dogmatic fashion. We see that, despite the near constant fluctuation in views, customs, nations, and languages across time and space, there is one thing from which we are never very far removed: the belief that above all, it is the power of the human imagination which can shape the world.

A Short Message from The Author:

As a small author, reviews are what help me out the most! It would mean so much if you could please leave a review of the book.

If you enjoyed reading this book and it left an impact in you, please scan this QR code below with your camera to leave a review!

It won't take more than a few seconds and will help me out tremendously.

Thank you, I can't wait to read what you thought of my book!

References

Aeschylus, & Griffith, M. (1983). *Prometheus bound*. Cambridge, UK: Cambridge University Press.

Apollodorus, & Frazer, J. G. (2002). *Apollodorus: The library: With an English translation*. Cambridge, MA: Harvard University Press.

Apollodorus, & Frazer, J. G. (n.d.). Apollodorus, Library Sir James George Frazer, Ed. Retrieved August 20, 2020, from http://www.perseus.tufts.edu/hopper/text?doc=urn%3Acts%3AgreekLit%3Atlg0548.tlg001.perseus-eng1%3A1.2.1

Apollodorus, Higino, C. J., Smith, R. S., & Trzaskoma, S. (2007). *Apollodorus' Library and Hyginus' Fabulae: Two handbooks of Greek mythology*. Indianapolis, IN: Hackett Publishing Company.

Bulfinch, T. (1913). *Bulfinch's Mythology: The Age of Fable the Age of Chivalry Legends of Charlemagne*. New York, NY 1913: Thomas A. Crowell Company. Retrieved from http://www.gutenberg.org/files/56644/56644-h/56644-h.htm

Burkert, W. (1985). *Greek religion: Archaic and classical*. Oxford, UK: Blackwell.

Callimachus, Mair, A. W., Mair, G. R., Lycophron, & Aratus. (1921). *Callimachus and Lycophron*. London, UK: Heinemann. Retrieved 2020, from https://archive.org/details/callimachuslycop00calluoft

Callimachus. (n.d.). CALLIMACHUS, HYMNS 1 - 3. Retrieved August 20, 2020, from https://www.theoi.com/Text/CallimachusHymns1.html

Clayton, P. A., & Price, M. (2015). *The seven wonders of the ancient world*. London, UK: Routledge.

Diodorus, & Thayer, B. (n.d.). (Book III, continued). Retrieved August 20, 2020, from http://penelope.uchicago.edu/Thayer/E/Roman/Texts/Diodorus_Siculus/3D*.html

Frazer, J. G. (1994). *Studies in Greek scenery, legend and history: Selected from his Commentary on Pausanias' "Description of Greece".* London: RoutledgeCurzon. Retrieved from http://www.gutenberg.org/files/56002/56002-h/56002-h.htm

Grant, M., & Hyginus. (2019). Hyginus, Fabulae. Retrieved August 20, 2020, from https://topostext.org/work/206

Hadas, M. (1950). *A History of Greek Literature.* New York, NY: Columbia University Press.

Herodotus, Flower, M. A., & Marincola, J. (2002). *Herodotus: Histories.* Cambridge, UK: Cambridge University Press.

Hesiod, & Lattimore, R. (1991). *Hesiod: The Works and days, Theogony, the Shield of Herakles.* Ann Arbor, MI: University of Michigan Press.

Homer, Fagles, R., & Knox, B. M. (2001). *The Iliad.* New York, NY, NY: Penguin Books.

Hurwit, J. M. (2001). *The Athenian Acropolis: History, mythology, and archaeology from the Neolithic era to the present.* Cambridge, UK: Cambridge University Press.

Morford, M. P., Lenardon, R. J., & Sham, M. (2011). *Classical mythology.* Oxford, UK: Oxford Univ.- Press.

Sealey, R. (2003). *A history of the Greek city states: Ca. 700-338 B.C.* Berkeley: Univ. of California Press. Retrieved from https://books.google.com/books?id=kAvbhZrv4gUC&hl=en

Simon, E. (1983). *Festivals of Attica: An archaeological commentary.* Madison, WI: University of Wisconsin Press.

Smith, W. (n.d.). A Dictionary of Greek and Roman Biography and Mythology. Retrieved August 20, 2020, from http://www.perseus.tufts.edu/hopper/text?doc=Perseus%3Atext%3A1999.04.0104%3Aalphabetic+letter

UNCOVERING NORSE MYTHOLOGY

A Guide into Norse Gods and Goddesses, Viking Warriors and
Magical Creatures

LUCAS RUSSO

Heil

I've come to the conclusion that mythology is really a form of archaeological psychology. Mythology gives you a sense of what a people believes, what they fear.

~ George Lucas

Oh, how we love to read mythology. At least, if Hollywood's adaptations of many of the Greek and Norse gods, heroes, and myths are any indication, we certainly do. We love to read about Thor, Freya, and Odin and all their amazing adventures. There is something in the ancient runic writing and oral tales that speaks to our deepest roots when we read or listen to Norse mythology.

In studying Norse mythology, I have found out about myths, the Norse gods and their personality traits, the apocalypse and creation stories, and fabulous creatures too. It is fascinating how an ancient culture has the power to influence popular culture today. From toys to movies, the ancient Norse gods and goddesses have risen once more. However, I find the Norse ways, stories, and myths truly inspiring (apart from being entertaining), don't you?

As renowned movie maker George Lucas said, mythology is an excavation of our psychology. What we read in myth and history tells us so much more about ourselves as humans than the mere wording in the ancient 13th century texts. It tells us about our own trials and tribulations too. We all want the courage of the handsome hammer wielding Thor or the wisdom of Odin, the one-eyed raven god. Even being in the presence of the massive runestones in Northern Europe or at the sites of the Viking ship graves in Norway has the power to move a deep part of our psyche.

From the Norse runic writing that dates back as far as 200-300 AD, making it some of the oldest runic writing sources on earth, we have managed to learn a great deal about the Norse culture and times. The Norse made sense of their world with the telling of great stories to inspire, delight, and educate their people. Just as we tuck our children into bed at night, I can just imagine a Norse dad also telling his child a bedtime story featuring the adventures of Thor or the deceptions of Loki.

Wanting to learn more about this fascinating culture and its accompanying traditions, I began extensive research, collecting stories, myths, and a vast glossary of uniquely beautiful old Norse words. As rugged and unforgiving as the Northern landscapes are, I found these stories to perfectly match an ancient people shaped by time, tragedy, and triumph.

How to Use This Book

This book is written not only to share Norse mythology with a curious mind. Instead, I have tried to create a comprehensive view of Norse mythology across the ages and how it survives even today. How you use this book is up to you as the reader. You can choose to skip to a chapter you are particularly interested in, such as the myths of the gods. However, I strongly recommend reading it cover to cover. You will find the experience so much more enriching. This is a complete overview of the gods, their characters, their inter-relatedness and how they affected the people their belief was founded on. Also, considering their effect on our modern society today will give you a much more nuanced view of the Norse gods, giants, creatures, themes, fates, and their stories.

So, if you're like me, you enjoy a sneak peek. You may already be familiar with some of the Norse myths or gods or stories, but here's what you can expect in the chapters that follow:

- **Once Upon a Time**

Find out who the Vikings were, what beliefs they held, and why their myths still survive till today. Discover the skalds or poets and explore the themes that we find in Norse myths, and consider how these themes can speak to our own lives today.

- **Norse Culture and Myth**

Find out more about the ways in which the oral traditions of the Vikings were recorded, their unique writing system, and how this affected their beliefs.

- **Where It All Began**

The best place to begin is in the beginning, and like Christianity and every other major religion on earth, Norse mythology has its own creation story, starting with a void. Here you can explore the Nine Realms, learn about the major gods, giants, creatures, and other forces that affected Norse mythology. Learn how the genealogy of the gods worked for and against them as alliances were crafted and enmities formed.

- **The Royal Family**

Norse mythology revolves around a few central figures, specifically the royal house of Asgard, and these gods deserve special mention. The characteristics and quirks of the gods are expanded on with tales specific to each god, where lessons are learned and history is made.

- **Asgardians**

The Asgardians included many powerful gods such as Tyr and Heimdall and influential gods like Idun. In an expansion on their abilities, skills, and challenges, you can get a real feel for these gods and how they will feature in the final days of Ragnarok.

- **The Vanir**

Having learned about the Aesir, it is important to also discover their arch enemies, the Vanir. By learning about Njord, Freya, and Freyr, you will learn how magic came to the Norse gods, and how making friends of your enemies can be rewarding in the end.

- **Deadly Offspring**

My love of myth often centered not only on the good guys, but it also thrived on the bad guys, and Norse myth has some of the best baddies around! We all love Loki's trickery from the Avengers movies, but I found the myths to be even better. I provide you with a detailed overview of Loki and his strange and dangerous children. It is in their own tragic and slightly demented tales that the seeds of fate are planted, leading up to the end of days and the twilight of the gods.

- **The End Times**

Final battles are always the most dramatic of events, and Ragnarok is the epitome of final conflicts. Discover the signs that hail the end of time, grip the edge of your tablet as you read about your hero's fate, and see the whole plot come together.

- **The Norse Gods Today**

When I wrote this book I was trying to find an ending, only to realize—it doesn't end. Norse mythology has no end. Not even in the sense of Ragnarok. Instead, it is resurrected and reborn with each generation in new and unusual ways.

- **Glossary**

And finally, I wanted to share the exciting and amazing words of Old Norse, what they mean, and some of the ways in which they were used in a glorious glossary that will gift you the skald tongue of Bragi. The glossary has a treasure trove of terms from Old Norse, along with their phonetic pronunciation (so you can sound like the Vikings did), with the emphasis bolded for easy use.

Why Read This Book?

In these digital pages, you will learn all about the major gods and goddesses of the ancient Nordic lore. I will share how the Nordic people believed the world was created and how they thought it might end. The Nordic people had a strange but advanced sense of how the world interacted, which they explained with their belief in the Nine Realms, connected by the World Tree called Yggdrasill. While the Nine Realms were each unique and separate, they all connected through this central trunk of the World Tree. I have always found this a beautiful metaphor for how we humans may be from different races and cultures, but that we all follow the same trunk from creation too.

The Norse myths were so strong and potent that they have been preserved even to today and still serve to entertain and educate many European cultures. The influences of these mythical stories still echo in the world today, and not just on the big screen or in comic books. Many of the same Viking greetings of old are still used today, and in 2018, a couple tied the knot in "the first Viking wedding in a thousand years" (Rach, 2018) with a ceremony presided over by a gothi (priest) and featuring longboats, hog roasting, blood offerings, and traditional throat singing.

From Norse myths, we learn about concepts like honor, valor, family, destiny, and time. We discover what sacrifice means, how tricksters can infiltrate our lives, and how we can master our time and our power to change our world. But the greatest power of these myths is the ability to make me want to read. I wanted above all to share that love with readers all over the world, who loved reading myths just like I do.

I grew up loving to read, but as life got busier, I read less and less, much to my great loss. Now, in my 30s, as a single guy interested in ancient histories and traditions like stoicism and the warrior's way, I have become passionate about self-development and mythology. Self-development and mythology may seem like a strange combination; it isn't. What you experience in yourself can be stimulated by myths and stories. Through myths we can discover new insights. This is, after all, where the hero's journey began. Renowned psychologist Joseph Campbell (1904, 11) so eloquently put it, "They're stories about the wisdom of life."

By reading Norse myths and the mythology of other ancient cultures, we learn things our modern world has not prepared us for. We lose a little part of what it means to be human in an age driven by technology, not magic; by equipment, not heroes. Reading mythology can help us dream again, reach into the very deepest parts of our psyche and discover our own inner hero again.

Reading these stories, I rediscovered the joy of storytelling and myth and the thrill of going on fantastical journeys with a childlike innocence. Like the Greek myths, these Norse myths have also shaped my concept of what it means to be a man in today's world. I would like to share those stories and influences with you here.

So, *Heil*—be healthy and happy—and *Til Árs ok Friðar*—a year of peace—as you travel along the World Tree with me.

CHAPTER 1

Once Upon a Time

All good stories start with this phrase: once upon a time, or as in George Lucas' case, "a long time ago." The Viking era is, for practical purposes, documented as being from 793 AD lasting to 1066 AD, making it a relatively short-lived period in history. Yet, Vikings were documented through implication, if not specificity, in manuscripts earlier than 793 AD. We can also be fairly certain that their days extended beyond 1066 AD. It is simply that this period was their hey-day. The Norse traditions, which began with the Vikings, have expanded far beyond this time, persisting even today.

Reading the tales, myths, and traditions of the Vikings, the Norse gods they believed in, and thinking about how these influence us in our modern (but equally dangerous) world, makes for an enjoyable pastime.

Image 1: Image by WikiImages on Pixabay. Scandinavia, which includes Sweden, Norway, and Iceland, is the ancestral home of the Vikings.

Who Were the Vikings?

The Viking kings originated from Scandinavia, which is where they launched their fierce and much dreaded raids from. They raided up and down the British coastline, and also parts of Europe, even discovering North America more than 500 years before Christopher Columbus's trans-Atlantic voyage.

Vikings ruled the seas. They were the first major sea-faring nation, and definitely one of the first to use their longboats to attack and raid other nations. Their longboats were so important to their culture that they would bury a Viking's boat with him. Today, Norway has several historically preserved longboats in their museums. And in 2018, a Viking ship graveyard was discovered where whole ships had been buried on land during the Viking era.

But back to ancient Viking times. The Vikings were so influential to European history that I was astounded to learn their conquest of nations meant not ruin, but civilization. Peoples conquered by the Vikings developed laws and learned to write in runic script, and the Vikings brought concepts about trade and commerce that had previously not existed. The Viking conquest of Eastern Europe led to the Rus empire, which became known as Russia today (McCoy, n.d.-a).

As you might imagine, a people so advanced and well-traveled as the Vikings would have a rich history, filled with stories and beliefs that lasted well past their own empire. Much of this history and storytelling happened in an oral tradition, but fortunately, the Vikings were also given to recording their histories, events, and stories on runestones, and many of these were later recorded into Latin once the Vikings' descendants were conquered by the Roman empire. Thanks to these scripts, we have a strong recorded history for the Viking or Norse kingdoms and their traditions.

While the Vikings were known as seafarers, they were also farmers, and most of their homesteads in Scandinavia were constructed to farm, produce food, and give shelter in times of famine and disease. When the prime days of Viking raids ended with the creation of sea forts to protect the British Isles, the Vikings turned to trade routes. Many of the Viking warriors went from raiders to caravan guards, traveling as far east and south as Baghdad.

With travel and trade, the Vikings were known to keep slaves or serfs (servants) as property. Their society consisted of three tiers:

Nobles

Firstly, the noble lords (earls) owned large sections of land that were worked by their subjects. These lords were responsible for caring for their subjects, keeping them safe, ruling in the cases of disputes, and enforcing the law. They, in turn, paid taxes to the kings who ruled the lands. The earls or chieftains gained power through military victories such as raids and dominating their neighbors.

Free Men

The second tier of Viking society was the free men. These were smaller landowners who lived independently, fending for themselves, and being responsible for their own well-being.

Slaves/Serfs

The last tier comprised slaves or serfs who had to work submissively for the landowners who owned them or owned their service. The members of this tier had little power or entitlement, but they were still reasonably well-treated, and they were given a place at the hearth to stay and enjoy safety and protection.

What Is Norse Mythology?

Norse mythology is a collection of the stories, beliefs, customs, and the history of the Germanic-speaking peoples of Northern Europe. Essentially, it is an amalgamation of the myths and stories of the pre-Christian Germanic people and their cultures from Denmark,

Finland, Iceland, Sweden, and Norway. Once Christianity took hold, the Norse beliefs began to wane.

However, today, we can still see influences of Norse mythology in our world. Even the days of the week stem from Norse mythology with Tuesday being Tyr's day, Thursday being Thor's day, and Friday being known as Freya's day.

How Did the Myths Survive?

What we know about the Norse or Viking mythology is mostly extrapolated from two ancient texts compiled in the Middle Ages in Iceland. These texts are known as *the Poetic Edda* or *Elder Edda.* They contained Norse history and myth captured in poetic form. While nobody knows exactly who the author or creator of these manuscripts were, it is known that they captured the history and beliefs of the Norse culture from 800 AD to 1270 AD. The claim is that the chieftain Snorri Sturluson wrote these collections of poems and battle songs around 1222 AD.

The most famous of these poems is "Völuspá" (meaning Sibyl's prophecy), which was a lengthy poem covering the shaping of the world and the prophesied ending or Armageddon that would come with Ragnarok or the final battle.

Much of Norse mythology is contained in the "Völuspá." It is where we learn about the polytheistic religious views of the Norse. The ancient Vikings and Norse cultures believed in as many as 66 deities. Some of these were mightily renowned, from Odin to Freya and Heimdall to Thor and Loki. But some deities were lesser known and only featured occasionally in the great saga of Norse mythology.

There are also other less well-known texts that contain Icelandic poetry, which refer to mythic events or figures such as Odin or the Valkyrie. Even family histories were interspersed with mythological subjects. What we see as fiction today was considered fact and religion to the ancient Norsemen. Heroes and legends were recorded as faithfully as births and deaths. For the ancient Norsemen, it was as if Odin himself (and many other gods and goddesses) walked among them daily.

The first actual historical account that was recorded was begun in the 1200s and was compiled by a Danish scholar known as Saxo Grammaticus. In this account, he recorded the history of the Danish people as well as their pagan gods and the ancient heroes they believed in. In turn, Grammaticus was recorded along with some mention of his work in the Roman and medieval historians' works. And so, history began to record the world of the Vikings and their rich tapestry of myths, gods, tales, songs, battles, and otherworldly kingdoms, all arranged along the World Tree.

The Skalds—Poets and Bards

History was recorded in poetic form. Prose writing style didn't feature as strongly as later Latin history records were wont to do. This might have been since singing was a powerful part of Scandinavian and Norse culture. Since it is easier and more entertaining to sing poems around the hearth, the role of the bard or *skalds* took on new prominence in Norse society. The skalds were permanently at the different courts and long halls of the lords, earls, chieftains, and kings of the Norse lands. Most of these were Icelandic by the 11th century, which is why so much of Norse recorded history and myth is Icelandic in origin today.

Since these myths were orally presented through singing and performances, there was quite a lot of variation in the recounting of the tales and legends. Each skald was likely to create their own flavor of myth dependent on what their lord liked to hear. However, with the discovery of the *Poetic Edda* in the later 11th century, there emerged a more standard version of the myths and histories of the earlier Norse accounts.

Writing started to dominate, and many myths were recorded into Latin by skalds. History and myth began to spread more widely, influencing more cultures and peoples throughout Europe. Who could resist the poetic presentations of the adventures of Thor or the mighty justice of Odin or the beauty of the fickle Freya? This was more than the entertainment of the day—it was their education system too.

Major Themes and Myths

Through songs and recitations, the Norse people learned their history, culture, and myths. The stories usually had definite themes that were used to teach values to the people. Common themes emerged based on the living experience of the Norse people:

Bravery Despite Harshness

This is an overarching theme in Norse mythology. No matter the odds you faced, you were expected to be brave and steadfast in an emulation of the warrior code. While this may seem depressing, it was aimed at motivating the people by telling them that everyone has a harsh fate, even the gods. In the barren northern wastelands with its cold and unforgiving landscape where hunger and conflict was often a daily existential experience, the consolation that even the gods suffered helped people face up to their challenges. This theme encompassed the acceptance of your fate with courage and bravery. Honor was to be found at the end of a harsh journey or trying existence. Complaining about life wasn't something the Norse did.

Everything Ends

Norse mythology has different and powerful gods and goddesses, but they are also very human and they also die. While they are sometimes reborn, they are not truly immortal and also have to face the end of the world. This concept helped prepare the common man, woman, and child for the reality of death. In the harsh environment of the northern lands, death was a daily reality, and only by living bravely could you be assured of being remembered.

Even Gods Don't Always Win

Greek and Roman mythology created a picture of immovable and completely aloof gods who were drunk on their own power, believing they would live forever. In stark contrast, the Norse gods and goddesses were almost human in their characteristics. They knew they didn't have everything under their ultimate control and they accepted that things would go wrong. Sons betrayed fathers, and brothers slew brothers, and other real-life themes were often experienced by the Norse gods. This made the Norse people experience their gods as more than human but still relatable. Like humans, the Norse gods knew they would one day die.

Creation

Image 2: Image by Yuriy Chemerys on Unsplash. When considering the rugged and unforgiving landscapes of the Scandinavian countries, it becomes quite a haunting experience to listen to their creation myths read or sung aloud.

The creation myth was a powerful story that helped Norse people come to terms with their lives, accept their environment, and continue striving to reach their potential. The story begins with a place that was empty and deep; it had existed before anything else did. This endless abyss was known as Ginnungagap where there was endless silence and darkness.

Lying between the homeland of elemental fire and the homeland of elemental ice (between Niflheim and Muspelheim), this endless abyss is where the cosmos was spawned and where it will one day collapse and end.

In the creation myth, frost and flames met in Ginnungagap, where the fire melted the ice. The resulting drops became the frost giant Ymir, and the thawing ice became a cow, nourishing him. This cow licked salt blocks, freeing the first man, Buri.

Buri had married Bestla, the daughter of a frost giant, and they had three sons, Odin, Vili, and Vé. According to mythic legend, the three sons killed the frost giant Ymir, making the world from his corpse.

The frosty and mountainous landscape of Scandinavia indeed makes one think of the body of a frosty giant slain in some terrible battle, and it is then no surprise that such a strange story would be their creation myth.

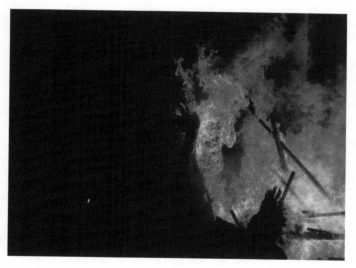

Image 3: Image by ella peebles on Unsplash. The end of days myth is like most such myths apocalyptic in nature, and the world ends in a mighty battle between fire and ice.

End of the World ... Ragnarok

The end of the world in Norse mythology is a series of terrible events as foretold by the poem "Völuspá." In the poem, the frost and fire giants unite against the gods and man in a final battle that destroys everything, sinking the world under a great sea. After many years, the earth will resurface, and the surviving gods will join together. The world will be repopulated by the last two human survivors.

This is a typical doomsday prediction, with the world ending in fire and ice. Yet, it is fascinating that it is humans who will repopulate the earth, not the gods who will magically save it. Instead, the message is to embrace your fate, even if that fate is to die. Even the gods die.

~~~~~//~~~~~

The Norse beliefs may not have purely religious value today, but aside from their entertainment factor, they offer unique insights into our own humanity. They allow us to consider our own belief in creation, end of days prophecies, and concepts such as personal honor, valor, and bravery. It's time to see where it all began ...

CHAPTER 2

Norse Culture and Myth

The Norse culture and myth is still very much alive and present in the Scandinavian countries of the world. While you can go on tours of the sacred sites in Norway, Sweden, and even Denmark, you can also learn about these cultural traditions today through an amazing network of sites online and through social media. But let's look a little further back at how the information we do have about the Norse gods and their lives have come to us.

Recording Norse Histories

Much of the early Norse histories, beliefs, traditions, and cultural expressions have not been recorded accurately. Resources from that time are somewhat limited. The ancient Norse were given to an oral tradition. This meant they remembered their history instead of recording it. Only later as the Vikings progressed to creating a complex system of runes to record their history did the concept of "writing" enter Nordic culture.

These runes were mostly created and read by the Norse priests, shamans, and bards or skalds. The common folk didn't know how to read runes, which imbued the runes with a mystical power. They were said to be signs of power, and these runes were often carved into wood, stone, and bone as charms of protection that were worn by warriors and common folk alike. Today still, the use of runic pendants as jewelry is popular among those who favor the ancient traditions. Runes also feature prominently in full body tattoos that are quite popular among the more traditional Norse descendants.

The *Poetic Edda* and the *Prose Edda* are two volumes created by the Icelandic scribe Snorri Sturluson, who recorded the poems and stories from the Viking era during the 13th century. While he faithfully recorded what he read and translated from the runestones found all across Northern Europe, Snorri was of Christian origins, making some of his records somewhat biased against traditional Norse concepts and beliefs.

One primary source for information that Snorri used was from the medieval manuscript known as the Codex Regius. The *Poetic Edda* contained a number of poems that were copied from the rune stones and the Codex Regius, including "Völuspá," "Lokasenna" and "Hlöðskviða."

Reading the Runes

The ancient runes, not to be confused with the ancient ruins, offer both knowledge and visual appeal and presence. Visiting any of the standing stone sites and seeing the runes first-hand can have a profound effect on you.

Runes are symbols that represent a type of alphabet that are arranged to create words or concepts. To make matters a little more complicated, there were also many different runic alphabets, which meant different interpretations when these were later translated into the Latin alphabet.

The power of runes is that they make visible the sound of simple units called phonemes. Each rune, like the alphabet, is a visual representation of a sound. This concept was like magic to the early Norse, who had never seen people produce sounds from symbols before. The conceptualization of rune creation as magic is also represented in myth through the act of making fate depicted as weaving or rune carving.

While each rune represented a sound such as "A," they each also had a name that represented something else. So, the rune for the sound "F" was called Fehu, which meant "cattle." The rune for the sound or phoneme "Th" was called Thurisaz, which meant "giant." Apart from meaning "giant," it also implied "suffering and danger."

Reading the runes was, therefore, more of an art than a science as the runic meanings are constructed from sight and sound. There is certainly a magical quality to the runes, and no magical tale is complete without runes or some other magical inscription.

The presence of runes is found in many of the Norse myths. Odin learns to read the runes carved on the trunk of Yggdrasil, while Bragi, the famed skald is said to have runes etched on his tongue, which might be where the expression "to have a silver tongue" comes from.

Runes provide an intriguing glance back into the past, but it is a time that is made up of history and magical that we see.

Norse Beliefs

The Norse had a wide range of beliefs, and many of these still have some relevance today. However, I wanted to look specifically at the cornerstone beliefs of ancient Norse culture. Here are a few pivotal views that these antique warriors and their families held to:

- **Fate**

For the Norse, fate (old Norse word: Urðr) set the path before your feet to walk in life. While you may try to step off that path, or hide in a hole, you would still end up at the same end. The belief was that all living things, including the gods, were tied to their fates. Whether you accepted it or fought against it, your fate was your fate.

The only beings who were outside of fate were the Norns, who created fate. Practitioners of the Norse magic known as seidr could sometimes get glimpses into the future, seeing what fate had in store. What is markedly different between Norse and Christian views on fate was that the Norse saw fate as being completely a-moral and there was no good or evil, right or wrong. There was simply your place in time.

Talking to the Norns or trying to influence your fate was quite like talking to a tree as they had no interest in any attempts to sway fate. Since fate was so out of the hands of the humans, gods, or giants, it lends a certain tragic feeling to the Norse myths.

While the Viking view on fate may seem defeatist, it is far from that. Your fate is not something you simply passively accept. Instead, it is about riding into battle with courage, even if the outcome is known. In modern day life, this could be seen as accepting the potentially bad hand of cards you are dealt and still striving to achieve greatness before the end.

- **Magic of the Seidr**

Viking or Norse magic was known as seidr. It was a form of shamanism that, while it accepted fate, believed it could make some minor changes. So, if a warrior's fate was to die in battle, then a seidr shaman could help that warrior to first vanquish their enemy and then die in battle. The aim of a seidr practitioner was usually to bring about prophecy, send a blessing, or invoke a curse. The Norns used seidr magic to create fate, so the two forces were intertwined. Both Odin and Freya were accomplished practitioners of the seidr. Traditionally, seidr magic was a woman's activity, and all three Norns were female. Yet, Odin was proficient at it too, and it's suggested in some ancient texts that Odin was temporarily kicked out of Asgard for practicing a woman's art, namely magic. The act of weaving, which is involved in practicing seidr magic, is a woman's art. Weaving makes this form of magic practice extremely ill-suited to men.

In Norse culture, the term "völva" is used to define a woman who is a practitioner of seidr magic, and this woman is both revered and shunned. The völva lived outside of society, yet she also participated in it.

Norse beliefs held that all living things had spirit, which extended to plants and animals too. Hence, these could be influenced by magic. This gave the practitioners of magic the ability to control things like animals, plants, and even the weather. Due to the magical nature of the forces at work in Norse times, dreams were taken very seriously. So, when Baldur had a nightmare about his own death, it was taken very seriously by his mother, Frigg, who was herself a seidr practitioner.

- **Their Sense of Self**

In modern day psychology, we have learned the theory that our sense of self is made up of three parts: the ego, the id, and the superego. Most commonly, we see ourselves as having a body, a mind, and a spirit. The Vikings had a slightly different view on their sense of self, which supports their shamanistic practices and cosmological beliefs.

For the ancient Norse, the self was made of many different parts, and some of these could work on their own, or they could even detach from the rest and leave the body for a while before returning. While there is no definitive answer as to just how many and what kind of parts constitute the self in Norse beliefs, these are some of the more commonly acknowledged ideas:

The Hamr

(meaning: skin)

It is something you look like, your appearance. Since hamr can change, this is the core word or concept at Norse shapeshifting. When changing your appearance, the term skipta hömum (meaning: changing hamr) is used.

The Hugr

(meaning: thought or thinking)

The Norse believed your thinking can help you connect to other people without your conscious thought leaving your body. This might be related to some form of astral projection or speaking to someone over great distances with the power of your mind.

The Fylgja

(meaning: an attendant spirit)

When the Norse had animals who helped them, they could use these animals as a kind of second sight or familiar gift. Ravens, cats, and all manner of animals could be seen as being someone's fylgja. Odin had two ravens, Hugin and Munin, that he could interact with and gain information about the outside world. These animals or attending spirits are seen as part of the person's self.

The Hamingja

(meaning: luck or talent)

The Norse believed the luck or talent of an ancestor could be separated from their self upon death, and it was this part that was reincarnated in a relative. Even without death, a person's hamingja could be temporarily lent to someone. That person would gain the talent and insight of the person whose haminja they have acquired temporarily.

This concept tied into their beliefs, and warriors might implore a god such as Thor to lend them his hamingja for a battle. When imbued with Thor's power, the warrior was said to have the god's strength and skill. Those who claimed Thor as their family god might have more of a sense of warrior-spirit in them than the Norse who claimed a softer god or goddess like Frigg.

▪ Their Belief in the Afterlife

The Norse didn't really have a well-defined sense of the afterlife. Some sources claim that the spirit goes on to a spirit hall such as Valhalla or even Hel's hall upon death. In the world of the dead, the spirits did the same things they did in real life too. They dueled, drank and ate, and they practiced their magic more. It's not quite clear how a soul was picked to go to Valhalla or Helheim, but the choosing seemed to have something to do with whether the dead were warriors or lived plain lives.

The warriors went to Valhalla if they died honorably in battle. Those who died without a sword in their hands were probably sent to Helheim. This might also be why Viking warriors were burned with their sword in their hands when they died. However, historians quickly point out that we only have this distinction between Valhalla and Helheim due to the early Christian scholar Snorri Sturluson who recorded most of the Viking myths and runes in the *Poetic Edda*.

There was also a belief among early Vikings that the dead can be reborn into a relative. Thus, when Thor died, he could have been reborn into one of his sons. This is quite likely as there are some accounts of Viking myth that indicates the fallen gods would be reborn again.

Lastly, there is also no concept of punishment or reward for life in death with the Vikings. They didn't believe you went to Helheim as punishment or to Valhalla as reward. Instead, it was simply another place to exist in. The idea of heaven and hell were very Christian and didn't feature in Viking myth until much later in the Norse history when Christianity had begun pollinating Nose culture with biblical beliefs.

- **Why Choose These Gods**

As I stood on the blackened volcanic soils of Iceland, I looked at the great burial mounds and the museums that abound throughout the countryside, and I found myself wondering what had made the Norsemen of antiquity come up with the gods they did. Why Odin, Thor, Freya, and Baldur? Why does any culture come up with the gods that are so particular to their beliefs?

While Christianity believes that God made man in His image, the Norse mythological system might be the other way around. The Norse peoples had to find a way to explain their amazing countryside, make sense of warring tribes, and bring some sense of belonging and order to their physical existences. So, by creating and believing in gods like Odin, Thor, and Heimdall, the Vikings were making gods that they could turn to in times of need, gods who would represent the land, and gods who inspired acceptance of a harsh lifestyle. After all, if the gods could accept their own fate to die in battle, then surely the humans could accept their own fate to survive or perish in harsh winters, to win or lose in battle, and show courage in the face of adversity.

Traditional Viking Daily Living

How would the gods have impacted the lives of the ancient Vikings? Let's look a little closer at a traditional Viking's days with the gods:

Sven is a typical Viking. He lives on a small landholding with his family, and their household god is Freyr, since they are blessed with many children and live closer to the land. Life is tough, and in summer, they eke out a living from a rocky patch of land that is fertile but hard to farm due to the limitations of the agricultural tools of the time. His oldest son, Erik, who is 10 years old, fishes in the local fjord for trout, eel, and other fish to add to their diet as they can't slaughter the livestock regularly. While Sven had seven cows, which was quite a nice herd for a lowly farmer, he had lost five to the raiders from nearby villages. They had also sold two of his children into slavery when they raided and stole the children.

Their small home is a roundhouse made of turf since they can't afford timber, and trees are scarce in this part of Norway. There's a central fire pit, and the fire is kept going throughout the day and night to warm up their home. This is also where their cooking takes place. At night, they sleep in a circle around the fire, their feet pointing towards the coals.

It is not an easy lifestyle, but Sven doesn't grumble. Even the gods face their challenges, and he will face his too. He knows his fate is to die in battle, for aside from farming in summer, he also participates in Viking raids in late summer before returning home before the deepest snows of winter. He joins a local warband, and they raid the shores of the nearby British Isles. The objective is to gather gold, precious gems, textiles, and other valuables that can add to his wealth and be sold to buy essentials for his family.

Going on raids presents opportunities to gain wealth, esteem, and honor as he can distinguish himself on the battlefield and please the gods. After the battles, they honor the dead, taking them home for burial near the small town. Sven is happy with the warband he is in as their leader is a good man who follows the ways of Odin.

He is wise, first scouting out an area they want to raid, and he will always look for ways to win that will not cost his men their lives. They aren't afraid to die. What warrior wouldn't want to be blessed by the Valkyrie and taken to Odin's hall in Valhalla? But they all have families, and if they fall in battle, who will protect their families from other raiders?

The eve before battle, Sven prays to his gods. He asks Thor for courage and power. Odin, he asks for wisdom and strategy. Freya, he asks for protection as she can use the seidr magic to cast a spell of protection over him. Sven also asks for luck and blessings from his ancestors, whom he honors daily.

Battle upon battle, the warband fights, wins, and gains glory. Sven is soon quite rich for a farmer, and he can purchase another three cows to enlarge his herd. This also means more work though, and he hires two young men to help him in running his farm. He also buys a slave at the market to help plough up the more difficult fields for planting.

To ensure a good crop, Sven pays a local priest of Freyr to come and bless his land. While they are ploughing the land, the priest walks over the newly turned soil, sprinkling apple cider or mead over the ground. He also asks for the last ear of corn from the previous harvest, which he threshes with a sharp knife and scatters to the four corners of the wind. The priest now announces that the land is blessed by Freyr himself and a good crop will grow. This ritual also shows the delicate relationship the Norsemen had with the land spirits.

At night, Sven tells his children the stories of the gods, always including a little lesson for them. He tells them of Odin's sacrifice by hanging on the Tree of Life, and here he teaches them to always be resolute in their wishes. Odin hung for nine days; how many humans could have said or done the same? These tales are meant to teach and inspire the children.

When it's bedtime, Sven and his wife, Hilga, tuck the children in. While they fold in the woven blankets, they mutter a traditional blessing over the head of each child. The boys, Sven mentions to his house god, Freyr. But the girls, he mentions to Freya.

At the start of the next winter, Sven is blessed with another child, but he is still off raiding. During the birth, the local women gather and sing songs to Frigg and Freya, asking for healing and health for the child and mother. Sven is not yet back from the raids, and the family prays for his safe return. They pray to Njord for fair weather as they wait for Sven and the other warriors to return. Finally, nine days after the birth, Sven marches over the nearby hill. Luckily, he was just in time as he only had nine days to get home, for on the ninth day, he had to hold his child on his knee and name the babe.

Sven names his new boy, Thorian. Choosing a name that is based on the god of lightning is due to an omen that Sven experienced. He had been walking home when he saw a lightning streak flash over the sky above a rune stone. When he returned from a fierce battle to learn his child had been born, he saw it as a gift from Thor. While away raiding, Sven had been sorely pressed during a battle, and he had prayed to Thor to help him defend his comrades and win victory. Victory had been granted, and Sven now believed that Freyr may have been off on an adventure and didn't hear his pleas, so Thor had answered instead.

Winter is long, and back at home, there is little to do outside as most of the land is covered thickly by snow and ice. The livestock sleep inside with the family who will care for them in separate little camps inside the home. The family survives off the grain they harvested in summer, the fish they caught and salted, and what meat they could cure and store. While waiting for the winter months to blow over, the family talks about their ancestors, recount tales of the gods, and they may even have performed mini plays about the gods. This is also a time for the women to weave cloth and repair clothing. The men might mend nets, carve runes on stone and wood, and if they were skillful enough, they might make weapons or tools with some minor metal work. These weapons would probably be consecrated by using a blessing or calling on the approval of the family god.

During the following summer, Sven makes offerings of mead and fresh meat to the land spirits or wights, ensuring they are content with the new field he is ploughing. If he does not do this, he may anger them, causing crops to fail or disease to strike.

Near the end of that summer, his son, Thorian, falls seriously ill. They call on a traveling völva to come and help them. This requires deep magic and beyond their normal rituals that the family performs. At the völva's instruction, Sven buys a boar from the market, which he slaughters in a ritual sacrifice in the meadow beyond his house to appease a restless spirit that has poisoned his son. The völva works ancient land magic known as seidr, and she calls on the healing powers of the land. Reading the child's fate, she knows the boy is not meant to die before he reaches manhood.

She tells Sven and his family to pray to Eir, who is considered a goddess of healing (though she was thought to have been Frigg's handmaiden). His prayer might have been something like this:

Hail Eir, goddess of healing who sits on the hill. *Heil*, healer, physician, and keeper of ill children. We implore you, Eir, shelter this needy child. Heal this sick child. Bring a remedy with your soft voice, and shower blessings with your gentle eyes. May you bring health and vitality to this child. Make him hale and whole again. Eir, we call to you, we call to you.

The boy may or may not recover; either way, the gods are thanked for his life (or death) and honored. To the Vikings, death was not a bad thing, though they would then mourn that the boy died of illness and not in battle with a sword in his hand.

Sven thanks the gods and goddesses daily for looking after his farm, and much of what he does is to build a reputation and ensure his stature as a warrior, which will earn him a seat in the halls of Valhalla.

The Telling of Tales

Before we get into the tales and characters of Norse mythology, I wondered why and how these stories might have been told, and Neil Gaiman's interview with Shadow Writer might hold the answer to these questions. Brown (2012) relates how Gaiman believes the writer of the *Poetic Edda* Snorri Sturluson might have sat around a fire with his friends sharing a tale such as "The Meeting of the Utgard-Loki Giant."

Thor, Loki, and Thor's servant (a human boy named Thjalfi) were traveling to Jotunheim. They were always looking for adventure and trouble in equal measure. Reaching a deep forest, the three were ready to make camp for the night but saw a set of caves instead. The caves were interlinked with a large central chamber and smaller side chambers, almost like a house. They decided to spend the night there.

During the night, there was suddenly a massive earthquake, and the very walls of the cave seemed to buckle and shake. Terrified, the gods and the human boy held onto their belongings and each other as they waited for the inevitable end. But morning came, and they walked out of the caves unscathed.

(Snorri might have spoken dramatically or shaken the dining room table if the story was being told at dinner.)

The next morning, as the companions stepped into the bright sunlight, they saw a giant that was far bigger than anything they had ever seen before. Even the mighty Thor was cowed, and he politely asked after the giant's name.

"Oh, but I know who you are! You are the mighty Thor … although you are a lot smaller than I imagined!" the giant said, laughing as he reached behind them and picked up the caves. "What were you doing in my glove?"

(Snorri might roar with laughter here, and there would be chuckles all around the beer hall of the Icelandic castle in the 13th century as he told this part.)

Thor and the giant soon struck up a conversation, and Thor explained that he, Loki, and the serving boy were looking for adventures in the realm of Jotunheim. They wanted some trolls to kill or … uhm, large creatures to slay.

(Snorri would be sure to look embarrassed as he pretended to be Thor telling the giant how they were looking for giants to kill.)

Well, the unnamed giant seemed kindly enough. Most giants would simply jump in and try to slay the heroes, but this giant decided to travel to a nearby castle where there were adventures to find.

At the castle, a giant king welcomed them, telling them how they could stay if they could each best a giant at something using their best talents. Thor instantly claimed to be the biggest drinker, while Loki said he could eat faster than anyone, and the servant said he could run like the wind. Their giant opponents approached, and Thor drank from the mead horn of the giant king, hardly able to drain the mead away from the brim. Meanwhile, the king drained his horn with one gulp. Loki began eating at the end of one trestle table with an assortment of meats laid out. Another giant began in the middle. They would see who could eat fastest.

After a few minutes, Loki was completely full, but looking up, he was surprised and awed to see the giant had eaten more than three quarters of the meat, bones, sinew, and even the table, clearly winning.

Thjalfi was next to race against a giant, who within the first few strides far out distanced the human boy, leaving him winded and in the dust. Thus, the three companions lost, and they felt quite miserable. After all, the gods weren't used to losing!

(Snorri might pause here to allow the mostly Christian audience to have a laugh at the expense of the pagan gods.)

The giant king of the castle suddenly turned into the unnamed giant from the forest, and he explained the following:

Loki's opponent had actually been fire, which could consume everything faster than any man could. The boy Thjalfi had run his race against thought, and there was nothing faster than thought. Thor had been competing against eternity. While you could conquer small amounts of it, you would never beat eternity.

In telling tales such as this one, there may have been a moral implication or some form of entertainment to be had. The Norse gods weren't all serious and high minded. Likewise, the early Vikings had a broad sense of humor too, and they were likely to tell mythological tales as entertainment and learning material.

I am reminded again, as a child of the eighties, that the Vikings didn't have modern day entertainment like the internet or TVs. They would gather around fires, listening to the bards or skalds weave stories that transported their minds to Asgard and Jotunheim where they were momentarily relieved of their often harsh realities. This is why the myths of the Norse gods have persisted to today. They meet some human need to challenge ourselves, learn from dramas and challenges, and become more, earning our place in Asgard too.

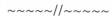

What is also unique about the bond between the Vikings and their gods is that they could serve different gods at the same time, and they could also willfully disobey their gods. There was no punishment for disobeying a god, and unlike the Greek gods, there was hardly ever any punishment for not obeying your god(s). The Vikings saw their gods as divine beings but also human beings whom they could empathize with, relate to, and learn from.

CHAPTER 3

Where It All Began

All cultures and religions have their own creation stories, detailing the way in which they believe it all began. Their version of the beginning is often a powerful indication of how that culture's members see their role in the order of things. The Norse are no different. Let's take a look at how the Norse believed the world to have begun, what creatures they saw as being created at that time, and how their belief in the nine worlds tied everything together.

Image 4: Image by Jeremy Bishop on Unsplash. The Viking or Norse belief in a world tree that connects the nine worlds is at the center of their religious beliefs about creation.

The Creation Myth

According to Norse mythology, in the beginning there was also a great void. Much like the Christian Genesis story, Norsemen believed there was nothing except the void that existed between the elemental fires of Muspelheim and the elemental frost of Niflheim. One might think of these as the first two worlds on the World Tree. Like fruit, connected to a tree, these realms existed independently but were joined by the World Tree.

In the vast emptiness of Ginnungagap (meaning: the great emptiness), the fires of Muspelheim and the frost of Niflheim met, and in this meeting, there was an exchange. Fire melted ice, and from these drops of the first waters, Ymir or the first of the frost giants was formed. These giants would form a godlike race known as the Jötnar.

Image 5: Image by Logga Wiggler from Pixabay. The giants or Jötnar had terrible powers, and their elemental natures hinted at a time of chaos.

Fortunately, the frost giant Ymir slept, as giants usually do in these creation stories. But while he slept, more giants were born from his legs and the sweat produced in his armpits.

The fires of Muspelheim and the frost of Niflheim continued their exchange and a cow known as Audhumla came forth to nourish Ymir with her milk. She was, in turn, sustained by licking the salty crystals of the ice. Licking away at these ice crystals, she soon wore them away, and Buri was revealed. He was the first of the Aesir gods to be created.

Buri was blessed with a son named Bor who wedded the giant Bolthorn's daughter Bestla. From this union came three giant half-god and half-giant sons. These sons were Odin, who later became the ruler of the gods, and his brothers Vili and Vé.

Seeing that Ymir and his ever-increasing family of frost giants were evil and cruel, Odin and his brothers planned to kill him. When they succeeded, they dragged his body to the center of the great void and created the world (one of the Nine Realms) from his corpse. Specifically, his blood became the sea and lakes, his flesh the earth, his hair grew into trees, and his bones shaped the mountains. The sky was made from his massive skull, and this was upheld for all eternity by four dwarves who represented the cardinal points.

As Ymir's flesh rotted, it filled with maggots, which the gods gifted with human insight and they gave to them the appearance of men. However, these were not men but dwarves, and they dwelled in the earth or hid in the rocks. The first four dwarves were Nordi, Vestri, Sundri, and Austri (north, west, south, and east), and they upheld the skull of Ymir. These dwarves also created magical weapons for the Aesir, including Thor's hammer Mjöllnir.

Ymir's brains became the clouds. With Ymir's death, a massive deluge of blood was released that washed most of the frost giants away, with only a few remaining.

The three godly brothers observed all that had happened, and sensing that the remaining Jötnar, two giants Bergelmir and his wife (and their offspring), would always threaten the new world, they made a protective wall (from Ymir's eyebrows) to safeguard this new land, which they called Midgard.

The word Midgard is loosely translated as "middle yard" or "middle earth," a term that has so been ingrained in mythology that it even appears in the story of *The Lord of The Rings* many centuries later. The reasoning behind the Norse use of Midgard is that since this new realm was halfway down the World Tree's trunk, it was suitable to call it thus. It also located earth as the center of the World Tree cosmos.

Finally, the three gods decided to create the first man and the first woman, Ask and Embla. Suitably, they made them from two tree trunks. Ask was made from an ash tree trunk and Embla from an elm trunk, although some legends indicate they were born from the Ymir's sweat, like the giants.

Other elements of the Norse creation myth are equally fascinating:

The Sun and the Moon

One man on Midgard was so arrogant and self-obsessed by the birth of his two beautiful children that he named them Mani and Sol (moon and sun), which angered the gods.

As punishment, the gods placed Sol (the girl) into a chariot (the sun) that rushes through the heavens. The chariot is drawn by two magical horses, Árvakr (early awake) and Alsviðr (very quick). The earth was shielded from the sun's fire by a shield strapped to the bottom of this stellar chariot.

The beautiful son, Mani, was forced to rush across the heavens in a chariot drawn by one horse Aldsvider, with two wolves called Sköll (treachery) and Hati (hate) chasing him. The wolves would bite him (giving the moon it's carved shape), but each month he would heal again.

Asgard

When Midgard had been formed, the three gods decided to create a world of their own, Asgard. They built this world high over Midgard, and the two worlds (and later the other worlds too) became joined by a rainbow bridge known as the Bifröst. Within Asgard, there are many realms, each belonging to different gods or goddesses.

The golden hall, Valhalla, is ruled by Odin and receives the souls of warriors slain honorably on the battlefield.

Himinbjörg is the realm ruled by Heimdallr who guards the entrance to the Bifröst. While there are other realms within Asgard; however, these two are important as they contribute specifically to the creation and Armageddon beliefs of Norse mythology.

When picturing what Asgard looked like, it is interesting to remember that it was the Viking idea of "heaven." Thus, it would have been a place of great beauty. There would have been great mountains, glittering oceans, magnificent sunsets, tall forests, and of course, the different halls of the gods, which were each more majestic than the rest.

The Nine Realms

Among the Germanic tribes, the numbers nine and three are quite auspicious. Throughout their mythology, we encounter these numbers. With the nine worlds along the World Tree, we find but the first instance of the number nine. These nine worlds or realms are Niflheim, Muspelheim, Asgard, Midgard, Vanaheim, Alfheim, Jotunheim, Svartalfheim, and lastly, Helheim.

Niflheim and Muspelheim had been made out of the great void, but the other realms were all made from Ymir's body. A closer look at each of the Nine Realms provides an interesting look at the mythological views of the Norse people.

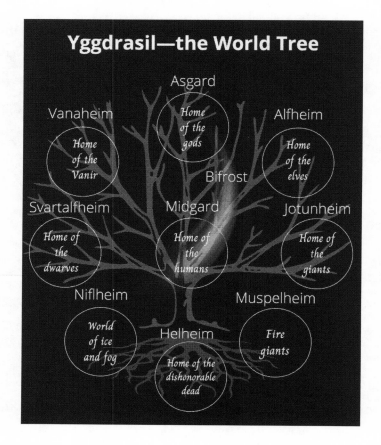

Image 6: Russo self-designed image. Diagrammatic representation of the World Tree with the Nine Realms and the conditions or inhabitants of each shown.

- **Niflheim**

Meaning: World of Fog

One of the oldest realms or worlds of the World Tree, Niflheim is a cold and dark region. It contains the oldest spring, Hvergelmir, which is protected by a fearsome dragon called Nidhug. From this fountain comes the 11 rivers that feed energy to the rest of the universe. All the living energies or people will eventually return to this fountain. Not much is known about the landscape of Niflheim, but it is assumed to be a frozen world since the ice giants or ice energy came from there.

- **Muspelheim**

Meaning: The World of Múspell

Ancestral home of the fire giants and polar opposite to Niflheim in the north. This is a place of fire, lava, ash, sparks, and soot. The sparks from Muspelheim are rumored to have been the first stars. Home to the fire giants and demons, its landscape is loosely equivalent to the Christian idea of hell.

The ruler of Muspelheim is a savage giant known as Sutr or Múspell. His destiny is to attack Asgard during the end of days of Ragnarok. True to myth, this ending of the world through the actions and attacks of Sutr will be in the form of fire. It is through his doing that Asgard will burn.

- **Asgard**

Meaning: Enclosure of the Aesir

The fortified home of the gods and goddesses, located in the middle of the World Tree, high above Midgard. This is the epitome of order and justice, while the home of the frost giants is the antithesis of this, being made up of chaos and injustice. The human world, Midgard, tried to emulate the world of the gods, basing their laws on the divine ones.

Valhalla is located in Asgard, and this is where fallen warriors go, making Asgard the concept of heaven to the Norsemen and women. It is a golden hall that is under the authority of Odin, the Allfather.

During Ragnarok, Asgard is destroyed in fire, and many of the gods perish along with it. However, after the destruction of the old world, a new Asgard is said to arise, and this is one that is wealthier and more magnificent than before. In Christian terms, this is the new Jerusalem concept of heaven being recreated for all humans.

- **Midgard**

Meaning: Middle enclosure

This is the world or earth created from Ymir's body, and it is the concept of civilization. It is also where the humans live. For the ancient Norse or Vikings, their world was made up of land surrounded by dangerous seas with "monsters" such as storms, sharks, and whales that destroyed their ships and threatened their communities. To represent this, they created the mythology that Midgard was surrounded by hostile seas with giants and other creatures (Jotunheim) that threatened the humans of Midgard. These hostile lands that surrounded the earth were represented by Jotunheim, the home of the frost giants and the symbol of chaos.

Image 7: Image by Jonas Friese on Unsplash. The fearsome creatures that small wooden vessels had to face in the world's oceans may have inspired the mythic creatures that threatened Midgard.

The main creature that threatened Midgard was Jormungand, a terrifying serpent that lived in the seas of chaos around Midgard. During the end time or Ragnarok, the world Midgard sinks beneath the ocean of blood. It drowns in the massive waves that the great serpent makes as it writhes in the waters surrounding Midgard.

- **Jotunheim**

Meaning: World of the Giants

The feared frost giants live here, and these are the sworn enemies of the gods and of men. Mostly, this land is rough and barren with occasionally dense and impenetrable forests and abandoned frozen regions on the ocean shores. In terms of earth's geography, this might have been the Greenland and the North Pole, which was frightening to the Norse sailors to behold.

According to myth, the giants have no society of their own, and in the chaos, they live off what they can find such as fish, deer, and birds from the ocean and forests. The giants have their own version of Asgard called the stronghold of Utgard. This is carved from blocks of snow and ice. The giants hunger for the days of Ragnarok, and they wish to storm forth and swamp civilization, spreading their chaos to the rest of the World Tree.

- **Vanaheim**

Meaning: Homeland of the Vanir

This world is home to the Vanir gods who are more nature spirits than the newer Asgard gods. These gods have powers over fertility, health, and other forms of sorcery. The only Vanir who are mentioned in Norse mythology are Njord, Freya, and Freyr. These gods are like the Greek muses, and through their magic, they can see the future and mold it, but never change it. They predict that Ragnarok will see the destruction of Asgard and the other worlds.

- **Alfheim**

Meaning: Homeland of the Elves

Situated next to Asgard, this is the world of light bringers or angels. This world is ruled by the god Freyr, and these elves or angels have power over nature and fertility and are known to inspire the poets or bards. Given the warrior mentality of the early Norsemen, Alfheim doesn't feature strongly in the myths, although many records from that time may be lost due to the oral traditions not always having been recorded on parchment with the later influence of Latin scholars.

- **Svartalfheim/Nidavellir**

Meaning: The Dark Fields or Home of the Black Elves

When the maggots that formed in Ymir's body were turned into dwarves, this is where they moved to. The dwarves, who were also referred to as the black elves, lived here among the rocks and in caves. This would probably have been an extensive system of subterranean caves and caverns where the dwarves had mines, forges, and workshops. The dwarves were master craftsmen, and they were rumored to have forged many of the Asgardian gods' weapons such as Thor's hammer and Odin's spear. They also created the fabled chain that finally bound Fenrir in a last attempt to stave off Ragnarok.

- **Helheim**

Meaning: Hel's home

Loosely, this is hell since it is where the dishonorable dead are sent. Though, this world is not anything like the Christian idea of hell. This world is ruled by Loki's daughter, Hel. Those who die without honor are sent to this place to spend eternity. This army of miscreants will become Hel's weapon against the other gods during Ragnarok.

The Major Gods

The gods that feature in Norse mythology include groups of deities and individual gods or goddesses too. Each is a unique character with their own personality and characteristics, which makes Norse mythology truly interesting.

The name Aesir is the collective noun for the gods who lived in Asgard. Also, the Aesir mythical gods of war and sky included Odin, Thor, Tyr, Loki, Baldur, and other gods too. Initially, the Aesir gods and the Vanir gods made war upon each other, fighting for dominance, but eventually, they reached a peaceful accord, living in relative peace on the World Tree.

In a move toward a more amicable relationship between the Aesir and Vanir, prisoners were exchanged between the two sides to keep the peace. This may have explained the similar practice among the Norse tribes where conflict was ended with the exchange of prisoners to keep a peaceful relationship going.

Living in Vanaheim, the Vanir were believed to have power over the earth, prosperity, and fertility. The gods Njord and his children Freyr and Freyja were known to be of the Vanir. They were sent to the Aesir gods as an exchange to preserve peace. Due to the prisoner exchanges, the two sides later united and would fight together against the giants during Ragnarok.

The Aesir sent Hönir and Mimir as exchange for Njord, Freyr, and Freyja. However, legend has it that when the Vanir noticed how Hönir looked to Mimir for guidance, they beheaded Mimir out of vengeance. Odin didn't declare war in return for the affront, choosing instead to preserve Mimir's head with a magic ritual and placed it over the fountain of wisdom below Yggdrasil.

What has been pointed out is that the exchange of prisoners brought great things to Asgard, with Freyja possibly marrying Odin and becoming his wife (Skjalden, 2020). Though there is some ambiguity in this regard as this implies she was Frigg as well as being Freya. In Norse Mythology, there is often some interchange between similar gods. Perhaps this is due to different tribes telling the same story but with subtle changes. Freya also taught Odin magic, since she was believed to have been a sorceress and the goddess of love.

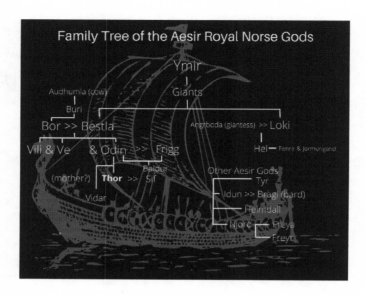

Image 8: Russo self-designed image. The gods of Asgard were mostly descended from the royal lineage of Odin's family; however, some were descended from giants like Loki.

- **Ymir**

Ymir (also called Aurgelmir) was technically not a god. It was the ancestor of the giants, and it had terrible powers. Therefore, we can consider it a deity too.

Ymir was the first creature to be created in the Norse mythology. It formed in Ginnungagap. From its death at the hands of Odin and his brothers, Ymir's body became the world. In a sense, we can consider Ymir to be the creation act or raw energy that the world was shaped out of.

- **Odin**

Eldest son of Bor and Bestla, Odin is known as the "Allfather" or the "father of battle." The character of Odin is complex and filled with dualities. While he is fearsome and unforgiving, he is also wise and all-knowing. He was the god of poetry and war, wisdom and death. He, in turn, fathered Thor and Baldur, among some other lesser known gods.

Odin was the patron of kings and bandits alike, again showing his duality of nature. While he favored stern governance, he had little time for laws. His very name meant "master of all." And while Odin could be the life of the party with his friends, he was a terrifying sight to behold on the battlefield. His characteristics were often ascribed to fearsome Nordic warriors or berserkers who lost all sense during battle and fought without any awareness of injuries.

Being born of a mother who was a giant, Odin was different from the other gods. He was also known to be both Asgardian and Vanirian. With Odin, nothing was simple or straightforward. He was many things. We'll dive into more detail on the enigmatic and multi-layered Odin in Chapter 3.

- **Vili and Vé**

Odin's two brothers represent the other sides of the creation diad, "Inspiration, Conscious Intention, and the Sacred" (McCoy, n.d.-d). The two brothers killed the giant Ymir with Odin, and they created the world from the giant's body. There are also other myths involving these two brothers, and they were prominent figures in early Germanic mythological beliefs.

One other mention of them in the *Poetic Edda* is when Odin was banned from Asgard for practicing forms of magic that were considered "unmanly." The two brothers allegedly slept with Odin's wife Frigg while he was away, which, if true, might question the parentage of at least one of Odin's children.

- **Frigg**

Frigg or sometimes Frigga was Odin's wife and mother of Baldur. In literature, Frigg is sometimes used interchangeably with Friya, and at other times, they are two distinct goddesses. Frigg is shown as using Norse magic, which is known as seidr.

She had many magical skills that were depicted in her ability to weave, her shapeshifting into the form of a falcon (which she kept feathers for), and her ability to know the future.

In mythology, Freya had a husband, who is essentially Odin. This implied the two goddesses shared Odin as husband.

- ■ **Thor**

The oldest son of Odin, Thor's name means "thunder." Most of the Germanic tribes worshiped Thor before their conversion to Christianity. With his representation as a noble, honorable, and physically superior god of war, he was well liked and respected by the Norse tribes. Thor was the tireless defender of Asgard from the chaos of the giants. His most famous possession was the hammer, Mjöllnir, which represented lightning.

Yet, Thor also owned several other weapons and treasures that were spectacular. He had a pair of steel gloves that were specially made so he could handle the magnificent Mjöllnir, which could fly through the air with tremendous speed. These gloves, called Járngreipr (meaning: iron grippers), allowed Thor to catch the hammer as it returned to him when he threw it.

While Thor was powerful and physically superior to any of the other gods, he also had a magical belt called Megingjörd (meaning: belt of power) that doubled his incredible strength. To say that facing Thor was an intimidating prospect was certainly an understatement.

Thor's nemesis is the great serpent, Jormungand, which he fights against during Ragnarok. Here, Thor and the serpent slay each other though legend has it that Thor revives himself again after the battle.

The claim is that Thor's mother was a giant, and since Odin was half-giant, that meant Thor supposedly was a "three-quarter giant." Thor had a particular relationship with the humans of Midgard who often appealed to him for aid. Nordic tribes asked Thor to bless their land and marriages as well as guide them in battle.

Thor is said to be married to a little-known goddess called Sif, whose golden hair was representative of grain or harvests.

- **Baldur**

Odin's son from his wife Frigg, Baldur loosely means "bold." However, he was more than just bold. He was said to be so cheerful that he gave off light. Baldur was the god of light and purity. In most of the literature, Baldur is portrayed as being mild and pleasant, but there is evidence that Baldur was as fierce a warrior as his half-brother Thor. Most of the myth surrounding Baldur concerns his death and the visions he had, as well as a magical journey to try and rescue him from death.

- **Vidar**

Known only as a distant son of Odin, Vidar's claim to mythological fame is that he survived Ragnarok and was the god who slew the great wolf Fenrir once it had killed and devoured Odin. He is involved in Norse religious practices, and at least two places in Norway are named after him: Virsu (meaning: temple of Vidar) and Viskjøl (meaning: rocky outcropping of Vidar). Due to his role as the Slayer of Fenrir in retaliation for the wolf's slaying of Odin, he is known as the god of vengeance.

- **Tyr**

Known primarily as the god of justice and law, Tyr is remembered today still in the naming of Tuesday (Tyr's day). He was one of the most dominant Norse gods in the early Viking era. In the *Poetic Edda*, the Valkyrie Sigrdrifa tells the human hero Sigurd to ask for Tyr's blessings before battle (McCoy, n.d.-c).

- **Bragi**

Some Norse myth and later translations of documents from the later Viking era held Bragi to be a Norse god when he was reported to have been a human bard or poet. He was so popular in life that he was believed to have been made a god in death by Odin to entertain and regal the fallen warriors who traveled to Odin's hall (Valhalla) upon their deaths. Later, he was believed to be the god of poetry, which is unlikely as Odin drank the mead of poetry and was known as the god of poetry too.

- **Idun**

Wife to Bragi, Idun was the keeper of the fruits of immortality. Her fruits were said to sustain the immortal gods, and she is mostly known to appear in the story of the kidnapping of Idun, where she was said to have been kidnapped by Loki.

- **Sif**

Wife to Thor, there is little mention of her in the *Poetic Edda,* other than the incident when Loki, the trickster, cut off her hair, which resulted in Loki having to approach the dwarves to make her a head of golden hair and Thor's hammer too.

Sif was said to be a goddess of fertility or the harvest, and this makes sense in ancient Norse beliefs where Thor was the lightning god, who fertilizes the earth, creating a perfect union of this marriage.

- **Hermod**

Another distant son of Odin, this god is mostly known as the god who rode Sleipnir to the underworld to plead for Baldur's release. Other passing references to Hermod have him welcoming fallen warriors to Odin's hall and receiving armor as a blessing from the Allfather. Like many of the other Asgardian gods, he was also known to have occasional interactions with the humans of Midgard.

- **Loki**

Known as the trickster, Loki features prominently in Norse mythology. He is often an ambiguous figure in mythical tales, and his actions rarely serve in the best interest of the gods. When Loki is involved, he will always do what is right for him.

His father was the giant Farbauti (meaning: cruel striker) and his mother was the giantess Laufey. Loki had a daughter, Hel, by the giantess Angrboda (meaning: anguish boden), who had an assortment of vile creatures at her bidding to inflict all manner of painful injuries upon the other gods. One of these, the wolf Fenrir, even killed Odin during Ragnarok.

- **Hel**

Daughter to Loki, Hel ruled the underworld (also called Hel). While little is known of Hel, the poet Snorri referred to her as being half black and half white, and he wrote that she had a fierce and terrifying expression on her face. She was said to be the sister of the great wolf, Fenrir, and the serpent, Jormungand.

- **Heimdall**

One of the better known Aesir gods, Heimdall is known to be the guardian of Asgard and specifically the Bifröst. He was characterized as being a fearsome warrior with exceptional powers of hearing and sight, and he could see enemies approach from miles away and hear the grass grow. He sat at the entrance to the Bifröst with the great horn Gjallarhorn, which he blew upon when enemies of Asgard drew near. The greatest of these events that caused him to blow the horn in warning is the start of Ragnarok.

While Heimdall is the loyal and ordered god of Asgard, Loki is the trickster who will betray him. During Ragnarok, the two will slay each other. Heimdall's birth is somewhat mystical and makes for an exciting tale, which I'll share in Chapter 4.

- **Njord**

One of the most powerful Vanir gods was Njord, who was sent to Asgard during the Asgard-Vanir war as a prisoner along with his two children, Freyr and Freya. Njord was the god of the sea and prosperity.

- **Freyr**

Son of Njord, Freyr was also sent to Asgard to secure peace between the Asgardians and the Vanir after their war. He is venerated as the god of fertility, and he was often invoked at marriages and harvest festivals. Traditionally, he is shown with his totemic animal, a huge boar, and a massive erect phallus. He was also reputed to have been sexually involved with many goddesses and even giantesses, including his own sister, Freya. The Vanir seemed to have had little problem with incestuous deeds among their gods.

Being associated with festivity and prosperity, Freyr was well liked among the early Germanic tribes. He is also said to have been instrumental in the origins of many tribes and royal lines.

- **Freya**

Daughter of Njord, she is later also said to have been married to Odin. She is renowned to be the goddess of fate and destiny. Freya was sent as prisoner to Asgard with her father Njord and brother Freyr. She is, therefore, considered both a Vanir and Aesir goddess.

- **Sigyn**

The wife of Loki, this Asgardian goddess features in several tales about Loki. Not to be confused with the giantess Loki sired Hel, Jormungand, and Fenrir with, Sigyn is the mother of Loki's two Asgardian children, Vali and Narfi.

The Giants

There are many giants mentioned throughout Norse mythology, and several of these possessed powers akin to those of the gods. Their influence on the gods and presence in the tales of Norse mythology make them an unmissable component to the worlds of Yggdrasil. Here are a few of the prominent giants who feature in mythology:

- **Skadi**

While many of the giants were portrayed as being violent and aggressive towards man and gods, Skadi was associated with winter. She was known as a more benevolent giantess. While she had been married to Njord, a god of the Vanir, her union didn't last as she preferred icy weather, while he preferred beach landscapes and mild weather.

- **Surt**

This fiery giant is quite important as he is the commander of the army of giants that descends on Asgard during Ragnarok. The fiery sword of Surt could also have been the volcanic eruptions that characterized Iceland during that historic era.

- **Aegir and Ran**

These two giants were known to live under the ocean, and they were attributed with generous spirits and divine culinary skills. They often socialized with the Asgardians, and they participated in cooking for the gods and making mead for Odin's feasts.

While there were many other giants also mentioned in the *Poetic Edda*, these are better known and had more unique characteristics that are worth noting.

Other Creatures

The worlds of Yggdrasil were also populated by a mix of strange creatures other than the gods, giants, and men. The world of Svartalfheim was populated by the dwarves (or black elves), while the world of Alfheim was home to the elves. These creatures also featured in a supporting capacity in most of the mythological tales of the Norse gods. In addition to these two races, there were also other beings that feature in mythology that are ambiguous in their origin but are worth mentioning nonetheless.

- **The Elves**

The Vanir seemed to have a particular bond with the elves who were described as being light and made of light. Freyr, a Vanir god, was noted as being the lord of the elven homeworld Alfheim. With the Vanir gods being associated with harvest, nature, and fertility, it is no stretch to assume the elves shared these characteristics.

Humans and elves had a strange relationship according to myth, with the elves both causing and healing diseases among the humans, and instances of interbreeding were strongly hinted at. The Norse peoples were known to venerate the elves for centuries after their conversion to Christianity and the lapsing of the worship of the Norse gods.

- **The Dwarves**

According to Norse myth, the dwarves were formed from worms that burrowed from Ymir's flesh after his death. They were black in color and were renowned as miners, craftsmen, and also magicians. Dwarves also had to live underground as sunlight supposedly turned them to stone.

- **Mimir**

The shadowy being who guards the well of wisdom (the Well of Urd), Mimir is a wise and steadfast counselor who guides the gods. He was savagely beheaded during the Asgard-Vanir war, but Odin kept his head, using magic to preserve life and wisdom in the appendage. There are instances when Mimir's head counseled Odin during great tribulations.

- **Kvasir**

While not a creature as such, Kvasir was a magical human who was made from mead brewed at the end of the Asgard-Vanir war. All the gods had chewed berries and spat these into a vat to be fermented. This mead turned into the human Kvasir, who possessed wisdom to know the answer to all questions.

Kvasir deserves mention since his death produces a mead that could turn anyone who drank it into a poet or scholar. This is also an interesting tale involving Odin on another of his quests to gain wisdom. But I'll share this interesting tale in the next chapter.

- **Völva**

The Völva was a long dead seeress or witch who dwelled in Helheim. Using seidr magic, the Völva could perceive the future, and she could tell what would happen. Baldur's death was predicted by the Völva, leaving Odin in much grief. Following Völva's prediction, Frigg set out to find a way to save her son's life.

- ## The Norns

These magical beings were responsible for fate. While they were hardly imposing women, these female beings determined what would happen to every living being in the cosmos. There were three Norns: Urd (meaning: past), Verdandi (meaning: what is being shaped right now), and Skuld (meaning: what will be).

The Norns had several fate-making rituals or tasks they used to decide what would happen in the present, the past, and the future. Likely, each of the Norns were predisposed to the time-aspect corresponding with their names. To decide fate, they would use wooden lots, create a magically woven cloth (as destiny unravels), or carve rune symbols into wood, such as with the carving of the runes into the trunk of Yggdrasil when Odin learned to read the runes. The Norns were simply fate creators, and they did so in a completely impartial way. The ancient Norse didn't worship them, and while they didn't fear them, they respected their powers.

- ## Valkyrie

These female spirits (meaning: choosers of the fallen) were Odin's helpers to choose fallen heroes from the battlefield. Once a hero had been chosen by a Valkyrie, they would bear him on their wings to Odin's hall, Valhalla. While some texts promoted the Valkyrie as being noble spirits, others suggest the Valkyrie chose the slain *before* the battle, thereby *causing* death.

In the "Darraðarljóð," a poem from Njal's Saga, the Valkyrie are portrayed as grotesque spirits who weave a dark magic using a weaving loom, intestines, skulls, and terrifying enjoyment as they plot which warriors would live and which would die.

- ## Hugin and Munin

The two ravens are often seen with Odin, and they assist him with gathering information about what is happening in the cosmos, and they assist his spirit helpers by carrying his orders and returning with updates on how things were with the realms of Yggdrasil.

Their names were so interlinked in meaning, they are commonly just known as "thought and memory." In Norse traditions, they were seen as a blessing whenever a blood sacrifice was made to Odin, as seeing ravens circle the freshly slaughtered animal offering was a sign that Odin had accepted the offering. Like Odin, the ravens are intelligent and they are also fierce fighters, showing Odin's dualistic character through these familiar animals.

Hugin is most often referred to, and Norsemen would use a kind of literary device almost like personification by referring to warriors as the ones who redden Hugin's beak or drown the field in Hugin's blood.

- **Einherjar**

The best soldiers and warriors who fell in battle were chosen by the Valkyrie and taken to Odin's fabled golden hall known as Valhalla. There they were trained daily to become part of his Einherjar, which is a host of warriors who would fight with Odin during Ragnarok. These warriors enjoyed an exemplary life as Vikings, fighting by day, feasting by night, and come the morning, all their wounds would be completely healed. The feasts came from magical sources too, with the meat being from the Saehrimnir, a boar who was slaughtered for the warriors, but was then reborn the next day, only to be slaughtered again. The mead was from the goat Heidrun, and every night, the warriors could drink all the mead they could milk from its udder. In the morning, the goat's udder would be filled with mead again.

~~~~~//~~~~~

The gods and goddesses of Norse mythology are often interconnected in strange familial relationships, making for conflict-rich events. Represented in myths and tales, we can learn more about their character and powers through the stories they feature in. Each tale is an opportunity not only for learning about Norse beliefs but also for reflecting on our own in the modern world we live in. The Aesir royal family were certainly involved in an assortment of strange, terrifying, and even humorous tales.

CHAPTER 4

The Royal Family

Image 9: Victor B on Unsplash. The Viking myths and tales were often depictions of massive battles, conflicts, war, and victories or losses. As a warrior culture, courage was proven in sacrifice. Odin's sacrifices rank chief among these.

Odin

Odin has much the appearance as the modern representation of Gandalf the Gray from *the Lord of the Rings* movies, and he appears as an old man with a long white beard and one missing eye. He is shown in ancient illustrations as wearing a cloak and a hood with his spear Gungnir in his hand. Sometimes, he travels with his wolves Geri and Freki as well as his two ravens.

Odin's triple horn, which was made from three interlocking mead horns also appears in Norse mythology. The mead horn had great importance in Norse traditions where it was used to toast during feasts.

Being all-seeing, Odin traveled the land, but his two ravens Hugin and Munin (meaning: thought and memory) would soar through the skies of Midgard and report all they saw in the realm of men to Odin.

Unlike modern depictions of Odin as being a benevolent ruler, he was historically noted as being a warmonger, inciting violence and conflict among tribes (McCoy, n.d.-b). Other war gods like Thor were seen as being much more noble of character. Odin's totemic representation is usually as a bear or wolf. All of the warriors who swore affiliation to these enjoyed Odin's patronage. He favored strong-willed people, but mostly warriors and kings or outlaws. Average people were of little interest to Odin.

Odin was always questing for more knowledge or magic, and he would take extreme measures to attain this, even going as far as to sacrifice an eye to gain knowledge from the fountain of wisdom. In another legend, Odin performed a self-sacrifice by hanging on the World Tree or Yggdrasil for nine days and nights to gain magical insight into the writing system of the Norse, the Germanic runes, or alphabet.

Known to undertake shamanic journeys, Odin practiced advanced magic and was known to enter a deep sleep state known as Odinsleep where he gained magical insight.

Image 10: Russo self-designed image. Odin, the Allfather, is a prominent figure in many tales and myths from Norse mythology. He was both wise and fearsome.

Odin's Quest for Wisdom

Odin was so obsessed with wisdom that he was willing to make any sacrifice to gain it. When he learned of the Well of Urd at the roots of Yggdrasil (as per the "Völuspá"), he journeyed down to the twisted roots, hoping to gain knowledge and wisdom from the well. The waters of the well contained wisdom, and those who drank from the well would be imbued with wisdom and great knowledge.

However, the Well of Urd was guarded by a shadowy figure known as Mimir, which prevented all from drinking from the well. Odin stopped and asked the guardian for a drink of water from the well as he was so thirsty from his journey. Mimir refused, saying that those who wished to drink from the well would have to sacrifice an eye first. Having seen how passionately Odin wanted the waters of the well, Mimir had decided that Odin could drink of the waters and sate his thirst for knowledge if he made a great enough sacrifice to earn the valuable reward of wisdom. Hence, Odin had to choose between sacrificing his own eye for the right to drink the waters of wisdom. Odin bravely plucked out his own eye to seal the deal. Mimir, honoring their deal, dipped his horn or cup into the well and offered Odin a drink.

While Odin left the well with only one eye, he had gained much wisdom. It is unclear what wisdom Odin gained in exchange for his eye, but it is believed that many of his following quests and visions were based on his hard-earned insights. This story of self-sacrifice may have been a parable that reflected on the concept that losing some of your earthly vision (represented by an eye) in exchange for wisdom (personal insight) is a wise deal.

Odin and the Mead of Poetry

Kvasir, who was created out of the mead brewed after the Asgard-Vanir war, was slain by two dwarves. He had been traveling the land, dispensing wisdom to all, and the dwarves, greedy to possess his power, slew him, making mead from the man's blood.

This mead gave all who drank it the ability to act with wisdom. Of course, this was a gift the gods desired, especially Odin, who was constantly questing for greater wisdom. It was said that drinking this mead could give you wisdom and make you either a poet or a scholar.

The gods soon tracked Kvasir's path, and finding the dwarves who had seen him last, they wanted to know what had happened, to which the dwarves lied, saying Kvasir had choked on his own wisdom.

These two dwarves had developed a taste for killing immortal and magical beings, and they set out to kill the giant Gilling by drowning him in the ocean. When his wife cried and lamented too loudly, the dwarves also killed her. However, this earned them the wrath of Gilling's son, Suttung, who took the two dwarves to a shallow reef as the tide was changing, threatening to drown them. As it goes with these tales, the giant was swayed from his vengeance by the offer of treasure. In this case, the treasure was the mead made from Kvasir's blood.

Letting them go in exchange for every last drop of the special mead, Suttung hid the mead in a mountain fortress where his daughter guarded it.

Enter Odin.

Hearing of the mead being hidden away, Odin decided he had to find out where. So, he set off in disguise (which was Odin's way), traveling to Suttung's brother's farm. There Odin deceived the nine farm hands, who worked for Baugi (Suttung's brother). He tricked them into killing each other, leaving Baugi without labor for the season.

Odin (in disguise as a lowly farm hand) offered to work for Baugi, bringing in the harvest by doing the work of nine men. In exchange, Odin asked for a sip of Suttung's magical mead. Baugi said it wasn't really up to him as Suttung was jealously guarding his mead, but he agreed to help Odin find it.

Bringing in a harvest when you have the skills of magic and godly strength is hardly an issue, and Odin easily brought in the harvest, claiming his reward from Baugi, who took him to see Suttung. However, Suttung refused to give a mere farm hand even one sip of his mead. So, Odin pleaded with Baugi to take him as close to the mead as he could, which Baugi did.

Standing next to a rock face that joined onto the chamber where Suttung's daughter guarded the mead, Odin took out an auger (a drill called Rati) and instructed Baugi to drill a hole into the chamber. Baugi tried to deceive Odin by only drilling halfway, but when Odin blew into the hole and the dust blew back into his face, he knew the hole wasn't complete, so he asked Baugi to drill further. Finally, satisfied that he could blow the dust into the chamber beyond, Odin quickly changed into a snake and sped through the hole.

Realizing who the farm hand was, Baugi tried to stab the snake with the auger, but Odin made it into the chamber where he seduced the giantess into giving him the mead. In exchange for sleeping with her for three nights, Odin drank all three casks that contained the mead, draining them to the dredges.

Odin then changed into an eagle, and with the mead in his stomach, he flew back to Asgard. The giant Suttung also changed into an eagle and flew after Odin, but in typical Norse style, Odin reached Asgard in the nick of time.

Taking wooden vats, Odin then regurgitated the mead into them, and this mead was shared among the gods Odin felt were worthy of it. In a comical twist, a few drops of the mead fell from Odin-eagle's beak, trickling down to Midgard, which accounts for all the bad poets and ill-informed scholars on earth. Those who had real talent in poetry and prose were gifted by Odin himself and not those last few drops.

Odin's Learning of the Runes

On another quest, Odin learned that the trunk of Yggdrasil, which grows from the well of Urd, had been carved with runes by three maidens known as the Norns. What the Norns carved in the tree affected all nine of the realms of Yggdrasil. Anyone who could read these runes were then able to see all nine the realms of Yggdrasil. These realms were normally invisible to the eye.

The runes were more than just an alphabet. Rather, they held great cosmological value and were closely connected to the power of control over the forces of life and magic. Being able to read the runes imbued the reader with great power and insights that far exceeded their contemporaries. Odin's search for the knowledge to read the runes was about his quest to control magic.

Again, to acquire this powerful gift, Odin was required to make a sacrifice, which enabled him to "earn" the knowledge to read the runes. As an act of self-sacrifice, Odin hung upon the tree of Yggdrasil by impaling himself on his spear, Gungnir. For nine days and nine nights Odin hung from the tree, dying a little each day. He stared into the waters of the well, refusing help from any other gods as he bore the terrible pain in stoic silence.

On the ninth night, Odin's mind opened and he learned the knowledge and wisdom to read the runes. This gave him great wisdom, and he could cure the sick, nullify the weapons of his attackers, and make women love him. Perhaps this is also where he gained the knowledge of what was fated to happen during Ragnarok. There is little chronological order to Odin's mythical journeys and quests, so we don't know if he gained this knowledge before building his golden hall and creating Valhalla so he might create his army of brave warriors who had fallen in battle. Was Odin preparing for the great and final conflict?

Image 11: Husein Bahr on Unsplash. Wife to Odin, Frigg was a great practitioner of magic.

Frigg

Odin's search for knowledge and wisdom culminated in his quests to understand magic. He often indulged in magical rites to gain wisdom despite this not being seemly for a man in Norse tradition. Odin's marriage to Frigg, which means beloved, may also not have been one of romance, but rather of convenience and valuable exchange. Frigg (or Freya according to some conflicting interpretations of the *Poetic Edda*) taught her magic to Odin.

Frigg was the queen of all goddesses and had power over love, fertility, the sky, motherhood, marriage, and other domestic aspects of the female psyche. As she was a fertility goddess, she was associated with the full moon.

The gods were often involved in the affairs of the men of the North (Norsemen). One instance is recorded of the Vandals and the Winnilers (two warring Germanic tribes) fighting each other and Frigg and Odin each choosing an opposing side. Wanting the conflict to stop spilling into their home, Odin swore to support whichever side he saw first thing in the morning. He knew he would see the Vandals first as his bedroom window faced that way.

Frigg was a talented strategist, and she cleverly told the women of the Winnilers tribe to place their long hats under their chins so they might look like long beards. Then, while Odin slept, she turned their bed, so Odin would wake while facing towards the side of the Winniler tribe. When Odin awoke, he was confused by the long beards he was seeing. Odin knew Frigg had fooled him. Yet, he still kept his word and sided with the Winniler tribe, granting them victory (Geller, 2016).

Frigg and the Gift of Future Vision

Frigg and Freya, who was Njord's daughter, were both highly skilled in magic. On one occasion, Loki was crashing a party at Odin's hall. Being the god of trickery, Loki proceeded to taunt the gods, especially Frigg, whom he provoked by saying that he had been the one to decide that her son Baldur would never be released from Helheim again. Frigg was unable to respond to this, but Freya responded by warning Loki that teasing Frigg was not wise as Frigg had the gift of foresight and knew the fates of all men and gods. Thankfully for Loki, Frigga was prevented from speaking these fates aloud.

In the "Lokasenna," or Loki's Truth Game (North, 2010), a poem from the *Poetic Edda*, Loki confronts Frigg publicly. He accuses her of taking both Odin's brothers as lovers while Odin was away on one of his quests, and this is why Freya warned him to mind his manners or face a grim truth of the future.

While Frigg is mentioned frequently, she doesn't participate in any major quests or myths where she features dominantly. Her main claim to notoriety is being Odin's wife and mother to Baldur.

Image 12: Image by ANIRUDH on Unsplash. Today, one of the most widely recognized symbols and weapons of antiquity and myth is the hammer of Thor (Mjöllnir).

Thor

Unlike the Hollywood depiction of Thor as being a blonde giant with a square jaw, the Norse depiction of the god of thunder shows him to be a large red haired and bearded giant. His size was impressively large, and in most images, he more than dwarfs those around him.

Thor was a son of Odin, but his mother was not Frigg. Instead, it is reported that Thor's mother was a giantess, Jord, indicating the brutish physical power that Thor would have possessed. There are many myths and stories that are recounted in the *Poetic Edda* in which Thor features.

While Thor married a goddess named Sif, and he had three children, but only two with her, namely Thrud and Magni. His other son was Moi; his mother might have been a giantess but the information about this isn't conclusive. Thor represented the three pillars of manhood: procreation, protection, and providing. While Thor wasn't known for anything other than his ability to produce violence, he did protect those who needed him, and the gods and mortals were quick to summon him. He was a favorite god to call upon before battle, during marriage celebrations, and if you were facing an angry giant, like the gods did during the building of Asgard's wall (but more on that in Chapter 5).

Thor's magical hammer, Mjöllnir, features prominently in his tales. It brought lightning when he struck the ground, and he could pulverize both gods, giants, and creatures with it. The hammer was supposed to be passed down to one of Thor's sons in true Nordic tradition, though this did not happen due to the events of Ragnarok.

With his characteristics of being quick to act, being rash, having nobility of spirit, and protecting others, Thor was the archetypal warrior that Norsemen tried to aspire to.

The Feast and Killing of Hrungnir

This fable perfectly portrays Thor's commitment to family. Odin had been riding his magnificent stallion Sleipnir through the countryside. Meeting the giant Hrungnir (also on a horse) along the way, a race ensued. With eight legs, Sleipnir easily won the race back to

Asgard. The giant and Odin were quite civil to each other, and Odin invited Hrungnir to stay for a feast that night.

During the feast, Hrungnir gorged himself and drank barrels of mead, soon becoming quite drunk. He looked around, noticing the many beautiful goddesses that were present at the feast, and in a boastful tone, he said, "I will destroy Asgard, but not before I have claimed each of the goddesses here as my concubines!" Roaring with laughter, the giant continued to leer at the goddesses, including Sif, Thor's Aesir wife.

As honor dictated, Thor quickly challenged the giant to a fight, and the drunken giant instantly sobered a bit when he beheld the sheer size of Thor. Quickly, he agreed to the fight but only if they could meet in Jotunheim where his weapons were. This was quite a journey, and Hrungnir sent word ahead to the other giants that they might devise a clever plan to slay the god.

They constructed a clay figure that was 30 miles high and 10 miles in breadth. And it was this juggernaut figure whom they hoped would slay Thor. However, the clay golem offered no real challenge to Thor and his mighty hammer. When it saw Thor, the clay giant ran.

When Thor threw his hammer, Hrungnir hurled a whetstone with his slingshot at Thor. Mjöllnir passed through the clay figure, shattering it, and it passed on to crush the giant's head. The whetstone lodged in Thor's head, and rumor had it that the whetstone was lodged in Thor's skull until Ragnarok.

The Making of Thor's Hammer

Loki, being a great mischief-maker, had cut the golden hair from Sif's head. Thor, her husband, was enraged and he was about to smite Loki when Loki claimed that he could go to Svartalfheim, the home of the black elves or dwarves, and instruct them in how to make a new head of hair for Sif.

Ever the silver-tongued devil, Loki convinced Thor who allowed him to journey to the mines of Svartalfheim. A dwarf, Ivaldi, had his two sons make the head of golden hair for

Loki as well as two other treasures that he sent back to Asgard. These treasures were Odin's spear (Gungnir) and a marvelous ship (Skidbladnir), which could be folded up small enough to fit into your pocket.

However, Loki was far from done trickering around on Svartalfheim, and he challenged the dwarven brothers Brokkr and Sindri to make better and more advanced crafted items than the spear and the magical ship. Overcome by jealousy, the dwarves worked tirelessly, crafting their magical objects. The first was a golden boar (Gullinbursti), which gave off light with its golden bristles. And the second item was a wonderful and magical ring (Draupnir), from which eight golden rings dripped every nine nights.

Finally, the dwarf brothers made a very powerful and costly gift. It was the pinnacle of their creations, but they had to focus and pay strict attention. However, Loki, being devious, changed into a fly and bit Brokkr's eyelid, causing blood to run into his eyes, distracting the dwarf from his work. The work the dwarves made was truly spectacular. They had made a metal hammer (Mjöllnir) that was powerful and magical. It could be thrown, and it would then boomerang back to the wielder. Yet, due to Loki's interference, the hammer had one flaw: it's handle was short, making it ungainly to wield.

The dwarves traveled to Asgard to present their costly gifts and claim their fees. Thor was given the hammer and the golden hair for Sif. Odin claimed Draupnir as well as Gungnir. Freyr was awarded with Skidbladnir and Gullinbursti. For his treachery, Loki was given to the dwarves as payment, who sewed his lips shut.

Thor Goes Fishing for Jormungand

The gods were going to host a massive feast with the two ocean giants Aegir and Ran who offered to brew mead for all the gods who would attend. However, this would require a massive kettle to brew the honeyed wine in as the gods were many and had legendary appetites. The only kettle large enough to brew such a massive batch of mead was owned by the giant Hymir who was hardly friendly towards the gods.

Thor, being brave and well-versed in communicating with the giants, offered to go to Hymir to ask for the kettle. When Thor arrived at Hymir's home, the giant slaughtered three bulls to provide meat for them during Thor's visit. However, Thor had a legendary appetite, and he easily devoured two of the three bulls in one meal.

The giant angrily said they would have to go fishing for the next day's food since there wasn't enough meat left over. Thor happily agreed, and Hymir sent him to get bait for the fishing trip. He didn't consider that Thor would slaughter his prized bull with the intention of using the bull's head as bait. Enraged, Hymir wanted to take vengeance against Thor, but he also hoped the young god's strength and courage would help them in their fishing trip.

Boarding a boat, Thor began rowing. They first visited Hymir's regular fishing waters, where the giant easily caught two whales to eat. Thor then pulled up anchor and began to row, but he wasn't rowing back to land. Instead, Thor was rowing them out to deeper water, and Hymir became anxious.

The deep ocean was where the terrifying serpent Jormungand lived!

He begged Thor to turn back to land. However, Thor anchored the boat and cast his line with the bull's head as bait. After some time, a massive pull almost capsized the boat. Thor held onto the fishing rod with all of his prodigious strength, bracing so hard that the boards at the bottom of the boat buckled and began to leak. After a short struggle, the head of the grotesque sea serpent rose above the water, the cruel hook caught in its mouth.

Grinning, Thor reached for his hammer, ready to slay the beast, but Hymir panicked and cut the line to save his boat. Thor had missed out on the opportunity to slay the beast. Angry at the giant, Thor threw him into the waves, then he tossed the two whales over his broad shoulders and waded to shore. Taking both the whales and the giant's cauldron, he returned to Asgard for the feast.

Baldur

Son of Frigg and Odin, Baldur was also reportedly handsome and fiercely brave. He was associated with light and cheerfulness. He was known as the god of love, truth, and light. The only substantial myth concerning him is the story of his death and the attempts to resurrect him. Baldur married the goddess Nanna, and their child was Forseti, who later became the god of justice.

Baldur had long hair and a coarse beard. While he was masculine and handsome, Baldur was not an aggressive god, which made him well-liked by all. Depictions of him often show him as an attractive man who is armed with a spear and a shield, but these are usually not held in his hands as if for combat, but they are rather lying on the ground.

Living in a palace called Breidablik, Baldur and his wife Nanna were popular among the Midguardians. Baldur was known to possess knowledge of runes and herbs, which he used to heal the sick and injured.

Baldur's Death and Attempts at Resurrection

Baldur was considered the fairest of the gods, and such was his pleasant nature that all loved him. When he suddenly began having troubling dreams of his own death, he spoke to his mother Frigg, who was a powerful sorceress and goddess. She instantly turned to Odin, Baldur's father, and implored him to find out what these dreams meant.

Odin knew a dead seeress who dwelt in the underworld (Helheim), and dressed in a disguise as a wandered, Odin rode upon his eight-legged steed, Sleipnir, down to the depths of Helheim. Reaching the cold and desolate realm of Helheim, Odin was amazed to see a feast had been laid out, as if expecting some important guest. He began questioning the seeress, who happily told him they were awaiting the arrival of a prominent guest who was sure to die soon. She was about to tell Odin how the guest was supposed to die when she looked at Odin and wondered at the panic in his questions. Finally, she only revealed that the guest was Baldur, but she refrained from saying how the godling was going to die.

Crestfallen, Odin returned to Asgard and related all that he had learned to Frigg, who was inconsolable upon the news that her beloved son would die. In desperation, Frigg traveled to all of the realm, begging and securing promises from every living thing that they would not harm her son. Even the rocks and sand gave their consent that they would not harm Baldur. He became invincible.

Such was his new power and safety from harm that the other gods would make a sport out of throwing anything they could lie their hands on at Baldur, watching these bounce harmlessly off him. Nothing could harm Baldur, it seemed.

Of course, Loki wouldn't approve of such a sport, unless he was the maker of it, so he decided to wreak havoc. Donning a disguise, he asked Frigg if she had really gotten all things to give their consent not to harm Baldur. This was truly an amazing feat, and Frigg was happy to admit she had gotten all these consents, but then as a side note, she admitted that she had not acquired consent from the mistletoe, which was so soft and kind it wouldn't harm her son in any case.

Gleefully, Loki left and went to the first mistletoe tree, carving a spear from its trunk. Then he approached Hodr, a god who was blind, and seeming to sympathize with Hodr, who couldn't participate in the other gods' fun by throwing things at Baldur, Loki passed him the spear and suggested he throw the spear at Baldur to also join the fun. Loki helped Hodr aim and then disappeared as the blind god threw the spear.

The spear sailed through the air, cleaving into Baldur, who dropped dead. The gods were in a state of panic and fear. While they were anguished that Baldur had been slain, they were also afraid since this was reportedly one of the first signs of the impending doom of Ragnarok. Frigg was beside herself with grief, but she finally asked if there was a brave enough god there who could journey to Helheim and entreat Hel to release her son that he may be resurrected. There was nothing that Frigg and Odin wouldn't pay in ransom.

Hermod, a lesser son of Odin, stepped forward and swore to do this task. Odin quickly placed Hermod upon his own steed, Sleipnir, and sent him off to the underworld. On the journey to Helheim, Hermod traveled for nine days and nights to reach the river Gjoll, which was guarded by a giantess Modgud. She asked why he would want to enter Helheim when he was still among the living, but Hermod cleverly told her that he had come to negotiate for a relative's release from death. Satisfied, the giantess let him pass into Helheim. Reaching Hel's enclosure, Hermod didn't enter by the gate, but instead, he leapt the wall with Sleipnir and snuck closer to the area where a massive feast was happening.

There, Hermod saw Hel sitting with the cold and pale Baldur next to her. Hermod approached Hel and began to entreat her to release Baldur that he may be resurrected in the world above. However, Hel wasn't interested in letting go of her latest pet.

Finally, in an act of spite, Hel said that if all beings in creation could weep for Baldur, then she would release him. With this news, Hermod rode Sleipnir back to Asgard where he told Frigg what she had to do to secure her son's release.

Frigg easily secured the tears of all living things in creation except for one giantess, Tokk, who responded by saying that she wouldn't cry and Hel could keep what she had. This giantess was, of course, Loki in disguise. And so, Baldur remained in Helheim, never to be resurrected again.

Following the full death of Baldur, the Aesir decided to give him a magnificent funeral. In Viking tradition, they prepared his great ship, Hringhorni, stacking it with kindling as they lay Baldur's body on the craft. As they were preparing to torch the funeral pyre, the gods realized the ship had become stuck in the beach sand. They were unable to heave it into the waters, so they were forced to call on the strength of the giantess Hyrrokkin to push the craft into the ocean.

When Hyrrokkin arrived in Asgard, she rode in on the back of a wolf, and she used two poisonous snakes for reins. One can imagine what a terrifying sight she was. Even her name meant "shriveled by fire." Taking hold of the ship, she gave one terrific shove, launching the ship into the ocean.

While the ship was in the shallows, Baldur's wife, Nanna, had a heart attack and died on the spot. As was tradition, the gods placed her body with Baldur's on the ship as well as leading his horse aboard. The fire was then lit, and Thor blessed the funeral pyre with his hammer.

~~~~~//~~~~~

The royal family of Asgard was quite extensive, with Odin having many sons who are occasionally mentioned in the *Poetic Edda*. While these tales are quite strange and unusual, they do cover themes that humans deal with on a daily basis. Odin's sacrifices to gain treasures and knowledge appealed to the beliefs of the Norse that achievement is only found through self-sacrifice. Frigg's tragic efforts to protect her son indicates a very real human challenge to stave off death. Thor's myths center around being brave in the face of overwhelming odds, facing your nemesis, and acting with courage. Baldur's story is one of warning: never to take life for granted, as you never know when a spear might slay you (even one cast by a blind god). The other Asgardian gods provided other valuable tales and experiences to learn from and reflect on.

CHAPTER 5

Asgardians

Image 13: Steven Erixon on Unsplash. The stories of the Asgardians are recorded on the rune rocks scattered all across the Scandinavian lands, and in these strange writings, we can learn all about Odin, the other gods and goddesses, and the trials they went through.

Tyr

Little is known about Tyr, and like many other gods and goddesses who have faded into the past due to oral traditions not being captured in writing, we may have lost a large chunk of what was known of him. Tyr's weapons were a spear and magical gloves. While history and time has all but forgotten this noble god, we do know he was once revered as one of the prime gods of the Aesir by the Norse tribes.

Remembered still in the naming of Tuesday, Tyr was associated with justice and order. However, he was also revered as a battle god and honored for his bravery and courage in battle. Well established as one of the main war gods, Tyr held his place with Thor and Odin when it came to battles. Early Norsemen would invoke his blessings before entering battle. While Loki accused Tyr of only being able to cause conflict between people, Tyr was more concerned with justice than warmongering.

During Ragnarok, Tyr was destined to battle the hellhound Garm. While it was foretold that he would slay the beast, he would be so severely injured that he would also succumb to his injuries and ultimately die. This is an appropriate conclusion to the tale of the binding of Fenrir, which is said to be the same as the hellhound Garm. In slaying Garm/Fenrir, Tyr could finally take retribution for the loss he suffered when he bound Fenrir.

He ruled in disputes, and his actions contributed in settling conflict between the gods. In the story of the binding of Fenrir, Tyr preserves peace at great personal cost. His psychological instruction is then that it is better to sacrifice than to encourage strife.

The Binding of Fenrir

Loki, being ever the contrary god, had sired three offspring with the giantess Angrboda (meaning: she who bodes anguish). These terrible beasts had posed some trouble to the gods who were unsure of their destiny in the scheme of things. Thus, to maintain some control over them, the gods sent Hel to Helheim, and they confined Jormungand to the sea that surrounded Midgard. However, they especially feared Fenrir, the massive wolf pup. Him they didn't want to let out of their sight, and so, they decided to raise this offspring of Loki where they could keep an eye on it and bind it.

Yet, Fenrir grew more powerful with each passing day, and while the gods tried to come up with a plan on how to bind the beast, the wolf easily broke through any bindings they placed on it.

Wolves, being clever beasts, were not easily deceived, and the beast refused to have any bindings placed on it. Only by pretending they were training the beast to grow stronger could they get it to agree to being bound. And only Tyr who was the most just among them could get close enough to wrap chains and ropes around its limbs. Each time the wolf broke through a new set of chains, the gods cheered and pretended to be in awe so they could convince the wolf to let them put more powerful bindings on it in future.

Meanwhile, the gods grew desperate in their fear of the mighty beast. They sent an envoy to the dwarfs of Svartalfheim, asking the dwarves to use their incredible skill and craftsmanship to make a binding that could finally keep the wolf bound for all eternity. The dwarves came up with an unusual solution: They fashioned a chain out of the soft padding sound of a cat's steps, a woman's beard, the deepest roots of a mountain, a fish's breath, and a bird's spit. By using things that didn't exist, the dwarves made a binding that Fenrir couldn't oppose.

The magical chain was light as a feather, and the dwarves had named it Gleipnir (meaning: open), and it was the only thing in the cosmos that could bind Fenrir if it was tightly fitted.

Now, with all the preceding bindings the gods had tested on Fenrir, the beast had only allowed the bravest and most honorable of the gods, namely Tyr, to come close enough to bind it. However, Fenrir had grown mistrustful of the bindings the gods wanted to tie and chain it down with. So, it demanded that the god who placed the new binding on it needed to place their arm in his great jaws as surety of their pure intentions. None of the gods were willing to risk this except for Tyr who placed his arm in the wolf's jaws while binding it with Gleipnir.

When Fenrir realized this chain was stronger than him and he couldn't break it, he snapped his jaws close, amputating Tyr's arm. So, Tyr secured the deal at the cost of his limb. With Fenrir bound, the gods moved him to a place that was far away and completely isolated. They set a sword between his jaws, forcing the wolf to keep his mouth open so he might never chew through the chains.

Legend has it that the drool that dribbled from the wolf's open mouth became a river known as Ván (meaning: expectation). Fenrir was forced to wait in this miserable state until he was freed during Ragnarok.

Bragi—The Bard God

It's unclear if Bragi was a god named after a real bard, Bragi Boddason, or if the Norsemen were so in awe of Bragi's skills that they believed he was elevated to godhood upon his death. Either way, Bragi was known as the bard god. He was said to entertain the brave dead in Odin's hall with his wonderful tales. Such was his skill that it was rumored he had runes carved upon his tongue.

Bragi was married to the goddess Idun, who symbolized youth and vitality, and even his name was said to have inspired the word for "poetry." His symbols were the harp, lyre, and other traditional bard's instruments. He was especially venerated on long winter nights, around traditional log fires, and in front of fireplaces where stories were told and tales were sung. Traditional throat drumming may have originated in Bragi's traditions. There are few complete stories involving Bragi as the protagonist, but he features prominently in the poem "Lokasenna."

Bragi Confronts Loki

In the "Lokasenna," Loki arrives uninvited to a feast at Odin's hall. He tries to force entry, but Bragi tells him that his kind is not welcome in this hall. However, Bragi is overruled when Odin invites Loki inside. Loki then toasted all the gods and goddesses, except for Bragi, whom he singled out as being unworthy of his toast.

Bragi responded by offering his arm band, a horse, and a fine sword to Loki as appeasement gifts, since he warns Loki not to anger the gods. When Loki tells Bragi off and remarks that Bragi is always impressed by dishonorable gifts, Bragi threatens that if they had been outside, he would have cut Loki's head from his shoulders. At this point, Idun intercedes and calms Bragi, preventing all-out conflict. However, Loki insults her as embracing her brother's slayer, hinting that Bragi may have slain Idun's own brother. Bragi doesn't feature again in this tale.

Idun—The Goddess of Rejuvenation

The goddess Idun's claim to notoriety is her magical fruits (represented as apples), which she gave to the gods, ensuring their immortality. Therefore, Idun was a vital personage to the gods of Asgard. She was married to Bragi, and she always appeared as a beautiful young maiden. The magical apples (although this is probably an error in the recorded history as the Norse didn't know apples until much later in history) were kept in a box made from ash wood. Her importance is emphasized in the story of her kidnapping.

The Kidnapping of Idun

Idun provided magical fruits to the gods. These fruits or nuts were enriched with immortality. The gods had never before had to face such a dilemma. What would they do if the gods lost their immortality?

In the tale, three gods (Odin, Loki, and Hoenir) were traveling far from Asgard into the desolate lands. Feeling really hungry, the gods slaughtered a herd of oxen they came upon. However, once they had built a fire, the meat would not roast on these flames and they couldn't cook their meal.

"This is my doing, gods of Asgard," a voice said from above them. It was a giant eagle, sitting in the tree. "With my magical powers, I have frozen your flames. If you will give me my share of the meat, then I will let you cook the rest of the oxen."

Unable to deny their hunger, they agreed with the eagle, who ate the very best sections of meat from the ox, leaving only the stringy bits for the gods to eat. The gods were enraged, but what else could they do?

Loki was unhappy with this bargain, and he decided to kill the eagle with his club as it was busy devouring the meat. However, much to Loki's surprise, the eagle spun, grabbed the club and launched into the sky with the surprised Loki still clinging on to the weapon. The eagle flew high into the air with Loki still hanging there.

Begging for the eagle to let him down, Loki's pleas fell on deaf ears, and the eagle (which was actually the giant Thjazi in disguise) flew back to his mountain nest. In this eagle's nest, the eagle struck a deal with Loki. If Loki could give Idun and her immortal fruits to the eagle/giant, then it would release him.

Loki rejoined the other gods and returned to Asgard. Once there, Loki tricked Idun to follow him as he had found fruits more magical than her very own. Idun followed Loki to a forest that surrounded Asgard where Thjazi swooped in as a giant eagle, grabbed Idun and her magic fruits, and sped off.

With immortality removed from Asgard, the other gods and goddesses began to shrivel and grow old. The gods, realizing they would grow old and die, were desperate to have Idun and her fruits returned. They were still unaware of her kidnapping or of Loki's involvement. However, they quickly put the pieces of the puzzle together and found out that she'd last been in Loki's company in the great forest.

The gods seized Loki, threatening him terribly until he spilled the beans and admitted to being a part of her kidnapping. The gods demanded that Idun be returned, but Thjazi had taken her to his home, the mountain stronghold of Thrymheim.

Freya gave her hawk feathers to Loki, allowing him to turn into a hawk that he might fly to the mountain stronghold on Jotunheim and rescue Idun and her fruit. Once Loki arrived, he was thrilled to find the fortress abandoned, except for Idun and her fruits. He quickly changed the goddess into a nut so he might easily carry her, and gripping the nut in his talons, he flew as fast as he could back to Asgard, knowing the giant would be in hot pursuit as soon as he found out his prize had been stolen away.

Loki was drawing near to Asgard when the giant eagle started to gain on him. The gods had been watching the skies in desperation as they waited for Idun's return, so they saw the great race happening overhead. They built a large bonfire near Asgard's wall. As Loki flew over with the eagle close behind, the gods lit the fire at that moment, and it exploded, roasting the eagle in the sky.

Idun was safely returned, and that is where the story ends, though we can imagine there were some serious repercussions for Loki for having betrayed Idun to the eagle in the first place.

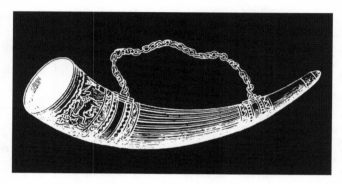

Image 14: Russo self-designed image. The great horn of Heimdall, Gjallarhorn, was said to herald the start of Ragnarok.

Heimdall

The guardian of the Bifröst, Heimdall is the defender and watchman of Asgard. His home, Himinbjörg (meaning: sky cliffs) is perched high above the Bifröst, and it gives Heimdall a bird's eye view of any approaching enemies. Heimdall has some excellent abilities, including that he sleeps less than a bird, can see for hundreds of miles with the clarity of an eagle, and he can hear grass grow and even wool growing on a sheep's back. Truly, he is equipped to be an ever-present watchman who sees all that happens in and around Asgard.

When the great horn of Heimdall, the Gjallarhorn, sounds an alarm, it will signal the start of Ragnarok and the approach of the giants coming to slay the gods in Asgard. It is fated that during this conflict, Heimdall and Loki would slay each other as the world went up in flames around them.

Heimdall is also born of Odin, and in a magical twist, he has nine mothers called the Nine Undines. Their names are representative of the power of the ocean.

First, there was Duva (meaning: hidden one) and also Kolga (meaning: cold one), who reminds one of the ocean depths. Then came Blodughadda who had red hair and was truly bloodthirsty. She was named after the red tide when the very seafoam would turn red. Fourth was Bara (meaning: foam fleck), which referred to the moment a wave hit the shore. There was also Bylgja (meaning: billow), which might refer to the wind over the sea in the ships sails or the breaching of whales when they blow. Hrǫnn (meaning: wave welling) and her twin sister Hefring (meaning: wave that rises) were also known for their blood-thirsty appetites. Unn was named for frothing waves, while the youngest of the sisters, Himinglava was the transparency of waves. These were the nine sisters who were said to have covered for each other when Odin slept with one of them, conceiving Heimdall. However, there is also a rumor that Odin had slept with all nine of these ferocious maidens (quite the feat) and one of them fell pregnant with Heimdall.

The number nine features quite strongly in Norse mythology. While Heimdall is involved in many stories, he is rarely the central figure. However, he is known as the father of all humans, not to be confused with the Allfather as Odin was known. Heimdall was said to have visited three married couples in the beginning when Midgard was made. He stayed with a poor family, then a farmer and his wife, and lastly, a wealthy lady and lord. Nine months after his visit, all three couples were blessed with a child each.

These children were respectively Thrall who was strong but ugly and became the ancestor of the serfs or slaves; next, Karl was skilled with the land, and he became the ancestor of all farmers; and, lastly was Jarl, who was the first of the noble classes.

Heimdall appears in the story of the building of the wall of Asgard, and he also features in the story of Ragnarok. We'll be looking more closely at those in the following chapters.

~~~~~//~~~~~

Chapter 3 and Chapter 4 has given us an idea of what the Asgardian gods were like, the tales they were involved in, and the adventures they enjoyed. Now it's time to look at the Vanir gods in more detail. The conflict and unity between these two god tribes are not only a major axis in Norse mythology but also representative of the conflict the warring tribes of the Viking era faced.

CHAPTER 6

The Vanir

Image 14: Russo self-designed image. The Vanir were gods of nature, wealth, abundance, fertility, and magic. They were the very opposite of the Asgardians who were brawnier, relying on their brute strength as opposed to magic.

Njord—The God of Seas and Wealth

One of the most prominent Vanir gods, Njord was sent as hostage to the Aesir after the Aesir-Vanir war in a prisoner exchange. The early Vikings believed that Njord was the god of the sea. They believed he could control the wind and the waves, and he was said to be immeasurably rich. Hence, the expression "to be as rich as Njord."

Njord's two children Freyr and Freya also accompanied him to Asgard where they were well received. While these two gods were supposedly begotten by Njord with his own sister, he later wedded a giantess named Skadi. This union was doomed though as Skadi loved the ice and snow of winter, while Njord loved the milder climates of the ocean.

Fate decreed that Njord would be one of the few Norse gods to survive Ragnarok.

The Marriage of Skadi and Njord

This tale came about as Idun was returned with her magical fruits to Asgard following her kidnapping. The gods, having suffered greatly the effects of old age while she had been gone, were reveling in the sun and warm glow of their restored youth.

Skadi was meanwhile waiting for the return of her father, Thjazi; however, she knew deep inside that her father had been murdered. Finally, after a night and a day, Skadi gathered up her spear and her hide-covered shield. She took her father's sword with special runes engraved on the blade and set off to Asgard, ready to seek vengeance.

Now, the gods were in a light spirit after regaining their immortality, so they had no wish for further bloodshed against the giantess as she neared Asgard. Heimdall sounded the alarm with his great horn, and the gods gathered to face the angry giantess. At first, they offered her money in exchange for the loss of her father, but she retorted that she had no need of more wealth as her father had been wealthy beyond comparison.

Finally, Odin asked what would satisfy her sorrow and her need for revenge. The giantess replied that she would choose a husband from among the gods (keeping her eyes on the beautiful Baldur) and she would laugh again. The giantess believed these two tasks would be beyond the Asgardians and she could then have her revenge.

So, Odin agreed upon the condition that Skadi choose a husband by only seeing his feet and legs. She agreed, and the gods blindfolded her so she could only see a small section above the ground, where the male gods lined up so she could view their legs. Believing that only Baldur could have the most shapely legs, and she chose quickly. Believing that everything was perfect on a god as handsome as Baldur, she chose the most attractive legs she could see. However, when she saw who the legs belonged to, she was shocked. The husband she had chosen was none other than Njord, the sea god!

Skadi began to complain, saying she'd been tricked, but Njord cautioned her to think carefully as her words were the start of their marriage. Njord further teased her that her choice could have been Loki, so she ought to count herself lucky. Still confident she would outwit the gods, Skadi announced she had not laughed since her father's death and she was unlikely to laugh now. So, Odin called upon Loki, having full confidence in the trickster's ability to make the giantess laugh.

Loki was somewhat bashful, which is contrary to his nature, but he had been the reason her father had kidnapped Idun and he had also been the reason Thjazi had been killed as he flew over Asgard's walls. Hoping the giantess would never learn the truth, Loki set out to make her laugh—no mean feat considering her frozen countenance.

So, taking a leather thong from his pocket, Loki told Skadi he had been to market and with his arms laden with food and parcels, he had no hand left to hold his goat's leash. In desperation, Loki had apparently tied the goat to a sensitive part of his body, making the beast follow him home.

"What 'sensitive part?'" Skadi asked, a bemused expression on her face.

"Well, lady, I had no option but to tie the beast to my … uhm … testicle," Loki said and began to demonstrate by tying the leather thong to his testicle on one end and to the goat's beard on the other. When the goat pulled back, Loki squealed in pain, and when Loki pulled back, the goat bleated in agony. It was a tug of war! Finally, in pain, Loki stumbled backward and fell in the giantess's lap, and unable to stop herself, she chuckled softly.

Thus, having secured the giantess's laughter, she and Njord were wedded. Odin, in an act of wisdom, further appeased the giantess's sorrow by producing her father's eyes, which he cast into the night sky where they became stars, looking down on her always.

Njord had planned they should live in his home by the seas of Asgard, but Skadi wanted no such thing. So, they compromised, and decided to live nine days and nights in Thrymheim, high in the mountains of Jotunheim, where there was only ice and snow and wolves howling at the moon. Njord was most unhappy, hating everything about Skadi's home.

They then traveled to his home on the shores of Asgard's seas, and stayed nine days and nights in Noatun, where the seas whispered and the gulls cried every morning and night. Skadi was most unhappy there, and realizing they could never live together, they decided to live separately. Njord remained in Noatun, and Skadi returned to Thrymheim.

Freyr—The God of Fertility and Weather, Peace, and Prosperity

Freyr, like his father Njord, was sent as hostage to Asgard following the Aesir-Vanir war. He was known as the god of fertility, prosperity, and abundance. He was, therefore, one of the most loved gods to Norse peoples as he blessed marriages with children, and he was represented with an enormous erect phallus. His totemic animal was the golden boar Gullinborsti. Freyr chose to live among the elves on Alfheim where he was lord of the elves. Even his name Freyr meant "lord" in old Norse.

While Freyr was a skilled and experienced fighter, he was popular with the farmer and serf class of Norsemen because he could secure crops and children for his followers. This meant they could feed themselves and have families, which, in an odd way, made Freyr the protector of the simple man (and woman) too. Most Aesir gods were venerated for their war-like abilities, but Freyr was worshipped for his ability to bring peace and prosperity, revealing the duality of Norse culture.

Freyr was known for his magical sword, which could fight on its own, and he also had the golden boar the dwarves had made. In addition to this, he also had a superior horse called Blodughofi, which means "blood hoof." But most spectacular among his treasures was surely the magical ship Skidbladnir, which was the fastest vessel on the oceans, and it could fold into his pocket. It was also rumored to be unsinkable and always steered true.

According to legend, Freyr traveled by sea with this magical ship, which was made by the dwarves from thin slivers of wood. On land, when Freyr wasn't astride his magnificent warhorse, he traveled in a chariot drawn by wild boars. As Freyr was the god of love, lust, and fertility, his appeal to both goddesses and giantesses was well noted.

Freyr and Gerdr

In Odin's hall, there was a special seat called Hliðskjálf, which allowed anyone who sat upon it a view into all nine worlds. Freyr had the opportunity to sit on this seat, and gazing throughout the realms, he saw a woman, a giantess, who was so fair as to steal his heart.

Freyr was so overcome with grief at the thought of never having this woman, he fell into a deep depression, wasting away. Concerned, his father, Njord, sent his servant Skirnir to check on Freyr and find out what ailed him. Freyr confessed his longing for the giantess Gerdr, and that if he could not have her, life was not worth living.

Skirnir said he would go woo the giantess for Freyr, but Freyr had to give "the sword of Freyr," his magical sword that could fight on its own, to Skirnir to take with. Freyr agreed without any second thoughts, and the servant set off to woo the giantess.

This had seemed a small price to Freyr in exchange for Gerdr's consent to marry him, but the cost would be more than he could imagine, as this exchange meant he would have to face the giant Surt without his magical sword during Ragnarok. Ultimately, it would lead to his death.

Freya—The Goddess of Fate and Destiny

Sister to Freyr and daughter to Njord, Frey was the goddess of virility, blessings, and love. She was a milder version of the other gods, and her talent was more in the realms of magic than that of physical combat. While she was said to be gentle and mostly achieved her goals with bargaining and by using sex as a tactic, she was also known to be the most fearsome killer on the battlefield, claiming more than half the dead during conflict.

Despite her darker side in conflict, Freya's name meant "lady."

Having mastered the art of the seidr, Freya could change the future and influence the past. It is said that she taught this skill, which was primarily a woman's magic, to Odin.

With Freya and Frigg sometimes being the same goddess and being able to predict the future, she gave the fated prediction regarding Ragnarok and the death of the gods when the giants attacked. She also predicted the falling of Asgard and the burning of Odin's hall.

Friday is likely named after her, and the lustful nature of this goddess is captured in the revelry that usually accompanies Fridays when people celebrate the end of the work week.

While Odin welcomed half of the slain dead to his hall of Valhalla, Freya ruled the other half in her palace at Sessrúmnir (meaning: seat room), which was located in the Fólkvangr (meaning: field of the host).

Freya married an obscure god named Odr, which is thought to have been Odin. This has caused some confusion about whether Freya and Frigg were actually the same goddess. With Odr, she had two children, Gersemi and Hnoss. Some narratives portrayed Freya as a goddess of loose morals who was willing to turn tricks for any fancy trinket that she desired. If Freya and Frigg were indeed the same goddess, then it explains why Odin was so obsessed with Freya.

Odin's obsessions are manifested in the story of Freya and the golden torc. It once again shows Loki's ever-present annoyance and manipulations that interfered with the affairs of the gods.

Freya didn't have any special weapons, but she did possess many magical objects that she used to reach her own goals. She owned a cloak with falcon feathers, which she used to fly with or transform into a falcon. It is from here that she plucked a few feathers to transform Loki into a falcon so that he may rescue Idun from the giant when she had been kidnapped. She also had a torc, Brísingamen (meaning: gleaming torc), which she was quite obsessed with. She allegedly purchased this torc from the four dwarves who gave it to her upon her agreeing to have sex with each of them. Freya also had a golden chariot drawn by two blue cats.

Freya and the Golden Torc

Freya loved all things beautiful. When she saw the golden necklace being made by four dwarves in a darkened cave, she instantly wanted it. The dwarves were born opportunists, and they demanded that Freya sleep with each of them in turn. Loki, always lurking in the shadows, happened to pass near the cave, and he witnessed Freya copulating with the dwarves in exchange for the necklace.

Aiming to sow discord among the Aesir gods, Loki revealed this to Odin, who was furious. He instructed Loki to retrieve the necklace that Freya loved so much and bring it to him.

Loki turned into a flea and managed to get into the goddess's sealed tower that night. Freya lay sleeping on her bed, the golden necklace clasped around her neck. Such was the position of her head that Loki was unable to retrieve the necklace. So, he bit her on the cheek, making her turn over in her sleep. Now Loki could slip the necklace off, and taking it, he quickly scurried off to the waiting Odin.

When Freya awoke, she was distraught to discover her beloved necklace was gone. Believing there to be a thief on Asgard, Freya went to Odin to complain. However, Odin coldly revealed that he had the necklace and also knew how she had come by it. Freya begged forgiveness. However, Odin said he would only give back her necklace if she performed a certain task for him. She had to cause two kings (who each ruled over 20 kings) to go to war with each other. This was to be an endless war though, and Freya did this to regain her treasure. These kings fought for years, and they only knew peace when Olaf Tryggvason, the Christian King of Norway, gained power.

Tales such as this one did not do much to build the goddess's reputation, and while it may have been a smear campaign by early Christians, it did discredit Freya by portraying her as a whore.

Freya and the Building of the Wall of Asgard

Freya had been greatly desired by the giants, and when a giant approached Asgard, offering to rebuild their wall within a short time and to impenetrable strength in exchange for marriage to Freya, it seemed like a good deal to the other gods. They agreed upon the condition that the giant, whose name is never mentioned, complete the wall within one year.

Within a matter of months, the gods noticed that the giant did indeed seem capable of building the wall in a year, since his stallion, Svadilfari, was strong and powerful and managed to do most of the work for the giant by moving stones on its broad back. The gods were fearing they might have to sacrifice Freya in exchange for the wall if the giant could uphold his end of the deal.

However, sly Loki came up with a plan. He transformed himself into a beautiful mare and so tempted the stallion that he was no longer capable of working with the giant, and the work fell behind schedule. The giant, realizing he had been tricked and wouldn't be able to finish the wall on time, became enraged and he grew aggressive. In fear, the gods called on Thor to come save them from the ferocious giant. Thor arrived, and without a second thought, he drew his mighty hammer and smote the giant, killing him instantly.

So, Asgard gained an impressive wall and Freya was safe from having to wed the giant. In a strange twist, Loki who had been entertaining the giant's stallion had been impregnated and foaled, giving birth to a colt named Sleipnir, which he gifted to Odin. This magnificent horse had eight legs and was the fastest and most powerful horse ever known.

In another twisted story, Freya was again almost pawned off as a bride to a giant when Thor's hammer disappeared.

The Disappearance of Thor's Hammer and Freya's Wedding

Thor awoke one morning to find that Mjöllnir, his powerful hammer, was missing! He was so upset that his hair stood on end and his beard bristled. As one can imagine, he must have been quite a terrifying image. When he finally did calm down somewhat, Thor went to the other gods, asking their help to find Mjöllnir.

The other gods were all upset as well. With Thor's powerful hammer missing, Asgard was vulnerable to attack! They all set out to find Mjöllnir as quickly as possible, and even Loki borrowed Freya's falcon cloak to go find the hammer.

With these swift wings to assist him, Loki flew to Jotunheim. He soon discovered that the giant Thrym (meaning: noisy) had indeed taken Thor's hammer. Thrym had hidden the hammer more than eight miles below the earth, and he was only willing to return it on one condition: that Freya marries him.

Now, the gods were not at all interested in this union, and serious debate raged in Asgard as the gods tried to come up with a solution. While they wouldn't willingly lose Freya to a giant in marriage, they also couldn't afford to lose Thor's hammer, which was their primary weapon for Ragnarok.

Heimdall was known for his wisdom and insight, and he came up with a solution. The gods would send Thor disguised as Freya to "marry" the giant, and once the giant produced Mjöllnir, Thor could then grab his hammer and strike at the giant. As you can imagine, Thor was less than pleased with this plan as it meant he would have to dress like a woman! He feared that all of Asgard would jest with him for all of eternity (since the gods were immortal, they would literally never forget), and he believed he couldn't live with the shame.

However, Loki cleverly pointed out that without Mjöllnir, Asgard would be overrun by giants when Ragnarok came, which would mean even more shame for Thor. Grudgingly, Thor agreed to the plan and allowed the gods to dress him up in a suitable wedding dress with a thick veil to hide his masculinity. Loki agreed to also dress in disguise as "Freya's" maid-servant, thus hiding their real intent. Thus, Loki and the disguised Thor traveled to Jotunheim for the wedding.

Thor was well-known for his incredible appetite, and at the wedding feast, he almost gave up the clever plot when he ate a huge spread of food, including one ox, eight salmon, all the pastries and tarts that the women were supposed to eat, and drank enough mead to drown a sailor.

Thrym began to suspect that something was amiss with his new bride, and he remarked heavily, "Never in all my many long years have I seen a woman eat and drink as you, Lady Freya."

Knowing that Thor couldn't disguise his heavy timbered voice, Loki quickly interceded, and he replied in a high-pitched voice, "The lady Freya has been starving herself for days with want for seeing you, my Lord!"

Now, Thrym accepted this response as he was already quite full with mead too, and he suddenly couldn't resist the urge to kiss his bride, so he pulled back Thor's upper veil, but when he saw Thor's burning eyes, he was stunned.

Blushing at the dark look in his bride's eyes, Thrym remarked that he had never before seen such a look of passion in a maiden's eyes, to which Loki again replied in his feminine tone of voice, "The Lady Freya has been so excited at the thought of her wedding night that she hasn't been able to sleep for days, Lord Thrym."

Then followed the ceremony, and as was tradition, Mjöllnir was brought forth to sanctify the union between Thrym and "Freya." But as soon as the hammer was placed in Thor's lap, he grabbed it and smote the giant and the rest of the wedding guests in a bloody rage. Happy to have his beloved hammer back in his control, Thor traveled back to Asgard where he jauntily changed back into his own clothes.

Image 15: Enrique Meseguer from Pixabay. War was a common occurrence of the gods. They regularly engaged in battles, waged conflicts, and went off to slay creatures. This may have been a mimicry of the tribes of Scandinavia that often raided, looted, and made war on neighboring tribes. The war of the Aesir-Vanir was one such conflict between the gods.

The Aesir-Vanir War

While the focus of Norse Mythology seems to always be on the end days of Ragnarok, we should not neglect the tale of the Aesir-Vanir War, when the Aesir and the Vanir battled without cease. While the two godly races were later unified, this was a time of great bloodshed and sorrow. However, only through the prisoner exchange did the Asgardian gods, like Odin and even some of the other gods, gain their magical powers.

The Aesir hailed from Asgard, and they were renowned for their physical prowess in battle, while the Vanir were from Vanaheim, and they were known for their magical ways. Freya, who was a sorceress without par, wandered the worlds of Yggdrasil, and using a disguise, she traveled while dispensing her magical skills. The Asgardians knew her only as Heiðr (meaning: bright). It is unclear if things would have turned out differently if the Asgardians had known that Heiðr was secretly Freya, but they became obsessed with her skills.

Chasing after desires and ideals that were against their own laws and warrior codes, the Aesir soon realized they were changing as a people due to their new obsession with magic. So, they decided to blame Freya, and they tried to murder her. Three times they tried to burn her as a witch, but each time she simply protected herself with her magic and walked from the ashes like a phoenix is reborn from its own funeral pyre.

The violent acts of the Aesir against Freya, who was an important figure to the Vanir, soon stirred up feelings of hatred between the two races as they grew to despise each other. It wasn't long before their hostilities blew into open war.

Both sides fought using their respective means. The Aesir fought with terrifying weapons such as Thor's hammer, Odin's spear, and Heimdall's sword. The Vanir used their magic in terrible ways. Both sides suffered terrible losses, and the war raged on for years.

Finally, both sides grew weary of fighting and quarreling, and a truce was called. As was the tradition, the two sides agreed to pay restitution to each other, and the truce was sealed with an exchange of hostages.

As has already been mentioned, the Vanir sent Njord and his two children, Freya and Freyr, to live among the Asgardians, while the Aesir sent Mimir and Hoenir to live on Vanir. One could imagine Freya may not have been happy with living in Asgard after she had been burned three times before by the Asgardians. Likewise, the unfortunate slaying of Mimir caused the Asgardians to feel a surge in hostilities, although the peace held between the two races of gods.

The tale ends with the gods gathering and making the magic mead by all chewing berries and spitting it in a barrel. From this mead, Kvasir, the wisest human, was born.

~~~~~//~~~~~

The Vanir were opposing forces to the Aesir, yet they could set their conflicts aside, even forgiving terrible atrocities committed on both sides, eventually fighting side by side in Ragnarok. While there was great nobility of spirit among the gods, they could be cruel and fickle at other times as we will see in the tale of Loki's binding.

CHAPTER 7

Deadly Offspring

Image 16: Russo self-designed image. Loki, being the offspring of two giants, had his own troublesome children that he added to the world of the Norse gods. These would be intricately involved in the final conflict of Ragnarok.

Loki—The Trickster God

The trickster was one of the four main Norse deities, and together with Odin, Freya, and Thor, Loki was the best known and most involved in Norse mythology. Loki was the absolute chameleon, shapeshifting, re-aligning, betraying, and defending the worlds and gods of Yggdrasil. There was incredible duality to Loki's persona, and where he might help

Thor one day, he would betray Sif the next. With Loki, what you saw was never what you got. When you try to class Loki as being a good or an evil god, you will fall short as he is neither. Loki is simply an agent of chaos, and he casually upturned the views of others.

His father was the giant Farbauti, and his mother was the giantess Laufey (though there is some uncertainty of her ancestry).

Even the meaning of Loki's name is ambiguous, and it could mean either "fire" or "knot" or even "spider" based on interpretation and usage. Unlike the other gods who had their own accoutrements, Loki only had his wits and shapeshifting powers. Loki had assumed various forms from fish and fleas to birds, and even the old giantess who refused to weep for Baldur. His symbolic animal was a snake.

Loki married the goddess Sigyn, which again was strange, as he is not a half Asgardian like some of the other gods and goddesses. His parentage was fully giant, which makes it strange that he resided in Asgard and was considered an Aesir god. Loki was even able to give birth to another offspring of his own: the eight-legged stallion Sleipnir that he gifted to Odin. There is certainly no more interesting deity than Loki in Norse mythology.

While Thor was powerful, Odin was wise, and Freya possessed magical skills, Loki had intrigues that made him very much a shadowy figure who recklessly influenced the fates of the Aesir, Vanir, and creatures of the Nine Realms alike. It is because of Loki that the end of the world, Ragnarok, takes place.

We may at times feel sorry for Loki, yet his often deceptive and misleading actions are what lands him his fate and the ultimate decision to see Asgard burn.

Loki's Imprisonment

One of the most unpleasant tales is Loki's part in Baldur's death and what happened after. Loki had orchestrated Baldur's death, tricking the blind Hodr into casting a spear made of mistletoe, which was the only living thing that had not given its promise to never harm Baldur. To make matters worse, when Hel agreed to let Baldur be resurrected upon condition that all living things shed tears for him, Loki transformed into the shape of an old giantess, Thökk, and he refused to weep for Baldur. His dismissive attitude towards Baldur is shown in his words: "Let Hel keep what she has then!"

When the gods learned of Loki's involvement, they were beyond enraged, and Odin, having loved his son Baldur dearly, was the most angered. Odin conceived a child, Vali, with the giantess Rindr. Váli grew to manhood in a day and slew Hodr. For Loki, Odin had something far worse in mind.

Loki had realized his taunts and interference in the gods' affairs had made him fall from favor, and following Baldur's death and the gods' inability to resurrect Baldur, Loki fled. Building a house atop a tall mountain, Loki watched day and night for approaching gods who came to claim vengeance for his slaying of Baldur. It is said that he changed into a salmon during the day and hid in a waterfall where nobody could see him. But there was no way to avoid the all-seeing eyes of Odin.

Image 17: Russo self-designed image. Odin sat in his chair Hliðskjálf from where he could see all of Yggdrasil's Nine Realms, and he soon spotted Loki's hiding place.

On one fateful night, Loki was sitting by his fire, mending the net he used to catch fish for food. He saw the gods approaching, and casting his net into the fire, he ran to the river where he transformed into the salmon once more to hide away.

Arriving at Loki's house, the gods saw the net smoldering on the fire, and they quickly decided that Loki must have changed into what he had been catching. They walked to the river, made nets of their own, and surrounded the rocky pool where Loki hid. Casting their nets in, Loki barely managed to wiggle past their attempts to catch him, but they drew closer and closer, and Loki became desperate to escape.

In one final desperate move, Loki jumped from the water in his fish form and tried to leap into the river leading to the ocean, but mighty Thor had never been slow. In one sweeping gesture, he grabbed the salmon by its tail and held on tightly. The Norse believed this was why salmon have a strangely thin tail fin even today.

What followed was a particularly brutal punishment, which one can only surmise must have angered Loki so that he fought on the side of the giants in Ragnarok, which soon followed.

The gods forced Loki to transform back into his normal form and then they dragged him back to a cave high in the mountain. Here, they brought his two sons with Sigyn to him. The boys, Vali and Narfi, were still young, but the gods transformed Vali into a wolf, who promptly slayed his brother and began eating him while Loki watched. The wolf spilled his brother's entrails all over the cave floor, which then hardened into chains of steel. Taking these, the gods bound Loki to the cave wall.

With Loki bound, the gods then took a venomous snake, which they tied above Loki's head. The snake dripped venom, which burned Loki. To save Loki some pain and suffering, his dutiful wife Sigyn brought a bowl to catch the venom in so it might not drip on his face. The bowl would fill up though, and Sigyn had to go empty it beyond the cave, leaving the drops of venom to drip from the snake onto Loki's face until she returned with the bowl once more.

Each time the venom dripped on Loki's face, it burned him like acid, and Loki writhed in agony. Such was his torment that Loki would convulse with a tremendous force, causing earthquakes to form in Midgard. One can only suspect that Loki must have languished in this agony for years even while he remained chained by his son's entrails. There could not be a grizzlier fate. Eventually Loki would break free, and he would fight against the gods during Ragnarok.

Hel—The Ruler of Helheim and the Realm of the Dead

Hel was the daughter of Loki and the giantess Angrboda, and her name hints at her dark persona as the meaning of Hel is "hidden." She is described as having a face that is half healthy and fleshy colored, and then rotten and skeletal on the other side.

Like the underworld or Helheim (hidden realm) that she governs, Hel is not a friendly person. She is 100% giant, which leaves no doubt where her allegiances lie during Ragnarok. With a giant wolf and a monstrous sea serpent as siblings, this makes for a rather strange and fiendish family.

As we would imagine the ruler of the underworld to be, Hel is not a charitable or kind person. She is rather obsessed with her own goals and her dark purposes of gathering up a host of the dead to fight in the final days of Ragnarok.

Helheim is populated by all people who died of sickness or disease or old age. Only warriors who die in battle can progress up Yggdrasil to reach Valhalla. The rest go down to Helheim. The journey to Helheim is not one that is pleasant or easy. To reach the hall of Hel, one has to travel for nine days and nights through a desolate landscape where the path is known to cut feet to shreds.

Then you need to cross the dangerous river Gjoll with a glass bridge suspended by strings of hair. Falling into the river is best avoided as there are knives floating in the tumultuous waters. The bridge is also guarded by a terrifying giantess, Modgud, whose name doesn't inspire friendly chatter. Her name "furious battle" clearly announces what will happen to those who dare enter without permission or purpose.

The palace in Helheim is surrounded by a tall wall, which has a single gate to allow the dead to enter. Hel rules in the halls of her kingdom as queen of the dead. True to form, all the objects in her hall have misfortunate names. The large table is called hunger, while the knives and forks are called starvation. Her bedroom is equally depressing, and her bed is known as sick-bed while the surrounding curtains are called misfortune.

Image 18: Kristijan Arsov on Unsplash. Warriors who died of old age went to Helheim, while those who died with their sword in their hand went to Valhalla. Needless to say, this fueled the bloodthirsty temperament of the early Viking raiders.

When Hel went collecting the dead on earth (Midgard), she used a rake to choose who she would take to Helheim, but when there was an outbreak of pestilence, she used a broom, simply sweeping the dead into her kingdom.

While the Christian concept of hell is not pleasant, involving torture by terrifying demons, the Norse idea of Helheim wasn't all that bad. When Baldur arrived in Helheim, he was welcomed with a feast of freshly cooked foods, and even Hel herself sat him next to her in her hall.

Hel's Role in Baldur's Remaining Unresurrected

While the story about Baldur's death is more about Loki, we do see some aspect of Hel's character in it too. When Hermod rode into Helheim to ask for Baldur's resurrection, Hel showed little concern for the worlds beyond her own realm. She seemed to have utter disregard for what Baldur's death meant for the end of days. The deal she offered, that every living being in the cosmos must weep for Baldur, was hardly a fair one, especially since her own father was a being in that cosmos, and Loki had been the one who orchestrated Baldur's death.

Image 19: Image by Deedster from Pixabay. The concept of death as an extension of life, being resurrected, and traveling to the underworld is not unique to any one culture, and whether you believed in Hel or Helheim, this was a place to avoid.

Fenrir

The giant wolf who would slay Odin at Ragnarok, Fenrir (meaning: dweller in the marshes) was a son of Loki. His sister was Hel, and his other sibling (whose gender isn't really revealed) is Jormungand, the sea serpent. Fenrir is always shown as a slavering wolf who is about to tear up some god (usually Odin).

When the wolf was born, they realized the pup was a terrible force, but they couldn't bring themselves to kill him. So, to try and maintain some control over the beast, the gods took him from his mother, and they raised him themselves. The idea was to stop the wolf from becoming too wild and doing serious damage in the Nine Realms.

However, they were ill prepared for how swiftly the wolf grew. They were soon terrified of him. The only god who was unafraid was Tyr, who could approach the wolf and feed him. Soon, the gods noted the strength and agility that Fenrir possessed, and they realized they would have to chain him up if they wanted to maintain control over him.

So, they had ropes and strong chains made, and while they stood there, pretending the bindings were to make Fenrir stronger, they had Tyr fit these restrictive devices to the wolf. However, twice they tried and twice they failed as the wolf easily broke free from the bindings. The wolf was becoming suspicious as he couldn't understand why the gods would want to tie him down. To fool him, the gods cheered and applauded him for being so strong, saying they only wanted to test him and see just how strong he could be.

Consulting with the dwarves of Svartalfheim, the gods begged the smiths to make a stronger chain or rope, anything they could bind the beast with. The dwarves designed a magical chain that was made from the sound of a cat's footsteps, a woman's beard, a mountain's roots, a bird's spit, and a fish's breath … all of which were things that didn't technically exist. The reasoning was that since the chain would then not exist within the normal laws of the universe, there would be nothing for Fenrir to fight against, and he would be bound.

When the gods brought the thin little chain to Fenrir, once again saying they wanted to test his strength, the wolf didn't believe them and he became aggressive. The wolf refused to be tied with this little chain, unless one of the gods were to vouch for their honor by putting his arm inside the wolf's mouth. Of course, none of the gods wanted to accept this deal as it would mean the loss of a limb when the wolf discovered he had been tricked.

Brave Tyr, god of truth and justice, stepped forward, laying his arm in the wolf's jaws. As the chain was secured, Fenrir discovered he couldn't break free and in fear and rage, his jaws snapped shut, severing Tyr's arm and swallowing it whole.

Fenrir was sent off to a desolate place where he was chained and bound with a sword to keep his jaws open so he couldn't chew through the chains. There he waited until Ragnarok.

Jormungand

The beast was known as the Midgard serpent, and it was the offspring of the dalliance between Loki and the giantess Angrboda. Jormungand was the beast whose body encircled all of Midgard, which was only protected by the wall the gods had created from Ymir's eyebrows. Thor is the nemesis of the serpent, and it is his archenemy.

While we know of the story where Thor almost slew the serpent when he and the giant Hymir went fishing, their enmity continued, but they would only face off against each other during Ragnarok.

~~~~~//~~~~~

The gods, the magical creatures, and the strange stories of the Norse all culminate in the end times when Heimdall's horn would blow, signaling the start of Ragnarok. And the horn is finally blowing ...

CHAPTER 8

The End Times

Brothers will fight and kill each other,

sisters' children will defile kinship.

It is harsh in the world, whoredom rife

—an axe age, a sword age—shields are riven—

a wind age, a wolf age—before the world goes headlong.

No man will have mercy on another

the Völva, Ursula Dronke translation

Prophecy is rarely pleasant, but there is a certain peace that comes from knowing your end before it begins. This is what accepting your fate is about, and it is a concept central to Viking life and Norse mythology.

The end time prophecy of Ragnarok is the Norse version of the Christian Apocalypse. It is how the world will end in fire. With the prophecies of the witches and seers (such as the Völva), the gods were forewarned of their fate, and while they prepared to meet each other on the battlefield of the end times, they also accepted they would likely not survive the war.

As with all end time stories, there were signs to look for, starting with the death of Beldur. From that point on, a series of cataclysmic events were happening that seemed to defeat all attempts to stop the inevitable. However, like the Vikings, the Norse gods were motivated by proving valor on the battlefield, and for them, death wasn't permanent or even punishment, so they prepared for their fate with remarkable fortitude.

The story of Ragnarok is oddly appealing to people of all cultures as it has themes that we can all relate to: brothers turning against brothers, fighting against impossible odds, courage, honorable death, and rebirth.

Image 20: Russo self-designed image. The final showdown between Thor and Jormungand was just one of the many battles that happened during the final conflict.

Ragnarok

The series of apocalyptic events that led up to Ragnarok were all in line with the predictions of a nameless fortune teller. For the Vikings, it meant the actual ending of their world, as they believed the gods walked among them. For the Aesir, it meant acceptance of fate and the fortitude to struggle on.

Ragnarok means "fate of the gods," or it is also read as the "twilight of the gods." By extension, what happened to the gods also happened to the Vikings, so they also saw Ragnarok as the "end of mankind."

When Ragnarok would be was up to the Norns to decide. As with their runic magic, the Norns would most likely have written the unfolding on the trunk of Yggdrasil, which may have been why Odin was so obsessed with acquiring wisdom and knowledge. It could also be why he was willing to hang from the World Tree for nine days and nights by his own spear so he may gain insight to see Ragnarok coming.

Here is the sequence of events:

The Great Winter, the Fimbulvetr

It was prophesied that there would come a great winter. This winter, the Fimbulvetr, would be unlike any winter ever seen before. It would last three times as long as a normal winter, and the seasons would stop changing. Thus, the realms would be covered in snow and ice for many, many months. This would cause starvation and hunger on Midgard, leaving the Norsemen to face famine.

With life-saving resources placed under strain, the world would turn to chaos as people struggle to survive, brother turning against brother in the battle for food, warmth, and medicines. Moral codes will perish before the bodies do. It shall be an age of swords and of axes. Kin will turn against kin and all that will matter is survival.

Desperation and Warnings

Fjalar, the red rooster, would crow in the forest of Gálgviðr in Jotunheim, warning the giants that the end had come. A golden rooster Gullinkambi would crow in Valhalla, warning the gods that Ragnarok had arrived, while a soot-red cock would crow in Hel's halls in Helheim, waking the dead to go to war. These would be forewarnings that would follow soon after the slaying of Baldur.

In Helheim, the great hellhound Garmr, upon hearing the rooster crowing, would begin to growl without end, eventually breaking free from his chains in a cave called Gnipahellir. It is somewhat ambiguous in the *Poetic Edda* whether the hellhound is Garmr or Fenrir, which had been chained up by the gods.

When the two mythical wolves, Sköll and Hati (meaning: one who mocks and one who hates), catch their prey, the sun and the moon would disappear from the sky. The stars would cease shining in the dark sky, and the land would know a second darkness. Heimdall would blow deeply into the Gjallarhorn, warning the gods of impending doom, and Yggdrasil would shudder with terror, shaking its leaves. As a result, mountains would crumble, and entire forests of trees would be uprooted, crashing on the icy land.

Wolves and Monsters

In the distant cave where Fenrir had been chained, the earthquakes would tear loose the unbreakable chain, freeing the great wolf. He would run forth across the land with his upper jaw scraping the clouds and the lower jaw digging up the earth, and he would swallow everything that came in his path.

The sea serpent Jormungand would spew forth poison, polluting the skies, the seas, and the land. There would be massive flooding due to the serpent's endless churning in the deep waters.

The Ship Naglfar

Jormungand would writhe in the seas, sending up such waves and tsunamis that the great ship Naglfar (meaning: nail ship) would be loosened from the place where it had been docked. This dreaded ship, which is made from the toenails and fingernails of the dead is destined to carry a terrible crew and cargo: giants, monsters, and a captain with hate in his heart—Loki.

Chaos and destruction would follow this army of giants wherever they go, and they would sail straight for Asgard with one intention in their minds: to slay the gods and burn the kingdom of the Aesir.

During the initial stages of the battle, the sky would be torn open and the fire giants would emerge from Muspelheim. These giants are said to be led by Surt who wields a burning sword. The giants would begin their march across the Bifröst as Heimdall continues to sound the alarm on Gjallarhorn.

Heimdall's Trumpet and the Battle

Despite knowing the outcome of the battle, the gods would still remain resolute and gear up for combat. The battle is almost scripted, but still the gods, giants, and the dead would play their parts to the full. Odin consults with the head of Mimir, but it seems there is no wise counsel on this day, and the gods would march out onto the field of battle.

Heimdall's horn would now play a specific melody, which can reach all the way to Valhalla. This sound would raise the dead, bringing them to life. In a final act of courage, Odin leads his einherjar, the fallen warriors he had kept and trained in Valhalla over the eons.

The gods meet their enemies on the plain called Vigrid (meaning: plain where battle surges), and there will be no mercy shown. While Odin and his magnificent warriors fight with the ferocity no previous army has ever shown, the dreaded Fenrir would swallow them whole, ending the illustrious life of Odin one-eye, the Allfather. Odin's son Vidar, blinded by a rage that may have been the berserker rage or battle fury, would rush into the fight, slashing at the beast.

As legend tells, Vidar will be wearing a special shoe made from all the scraps of leather ever discarded by every shoemaker ever to live, and he would use this thick and padded shoe to hold the jaws of Fenrir open as he stabs down into the beast's throat. Finishing off the giant wolf, he would stab the beast through the heart with his spear, thus avenging his father's death.

Garmr, Hel's hellhound, is destined to be slain by Tyr, though Tyr will perish in the fight. And Heimdall and Loki are to square off for a final combat that would see them slay each other. Thus, the watchman would finally slay the trickster.

Freyr will face the giant Surt, but since he had given up his magical sword that could fight on its own, Freyr will be sorely pushed in the combat, and in the end, he and Surt will also slay each other. Lastly, Thor and Jormungand will face each other in a final battle, and while Thor will slay the serpent with his lightning-wielding hammer, Mjöllnir, the serpent will have sprayed forth such poison as to cover Thor with the toxic fluid. Legend has it that Thor will walk nine steps after the serpent stops twitching before falling dead himself.

And so, the gods are destined to have fallen, with a few exceptions, all perishing in the great battle of Ragnarok. The destruction would still not be complete, though.

The Aftermath

Following the battle, the World Tree and all nine the realms would sink into the great seas, leaving nothing but a void, same as it had been at the beginning. One may think of this as a massive reset on the scale of the cosmos.

While some believe that this will be the ultimate end of all things, others hold that a new and verdant world will rise from the oceans again. Some of the gods would have survived the battle of Ragnarok, specifically Vidar, Vali, Modi, and Magni (Thor's sons). Other gods would be resurrected, with Hodr and Baldur also rising from the underworld.

One man and a woman, Lif and Lífþrasir (meaning: life and striving after life) would have survived Ragnarok too. They are destined to be the father and mother of the new human race in this new world. A new sun (daughter to the old one) would rise in the sky, and finally, everything would be ruled by one new and almighty ruler, whose identity is not specified.

There are two main and conflicting interpretations of the Ragnarok myth. One version seems to indicate there is no rebirth and with Ragnarok everything ends, nobody survives (McCoy, n.d.-e). In another, there is rebirth and new life, which may have been more inspired by the early Christians arriving in the Scandinavian countries. Certainly, there is quite a bit of similarity between Ragnarok's interpretations and the Christian concepts of Armageddon and also from the life of Christ.

For starters, there are a few similar symbols being used, and it makes for an interesting comparison:

Christ is nailed to a stake, and a spear is used to ultimately kill Him. Odin was hung on the World Tree, and he had impaled himself on his own spear. Three roosters announce the coming of Ragnarok, while in the Bible, the rooster crows three times to remind Peter of his betrayal.

The first time the earth ended in the Old Testament with a great flood. Ragnarok also involved serious flooding. During Ragnarok the mountains were uprooted, and in the book of Revelations, the mountains also crumble and fall into the sea.

What can we as modern day people learn from the myths and glorious stories of the Vikings? Is there some value that is contained in these beliefs that echo down the ages to enrich our lives, even in the age of technological and microscopical monsters? Indeed, there is one value I think is really valuable: to embrace fate and never lose hope.

The Norse gods knew they were destined to die. Yet, they lived each day as if they would have many more but still valued it for being precious. And on the final day, when the roosters crowed and Heimdall's great horn sang its song, they dressed in their best battle armor and they strode onto the field with courage, honor, and a spirit aimed at noble deeds. There is no use in cowering in a hole. Our fates were already written eons ago, and it's up to us to live it with the valor of the gods.

Whether your battlefield is at work, in your school, out in your town or city, or in your own home, you have the choice to cower or tower. By Thor's hammer, I hope you choose the right option.

CHAPTER 9

The Norse Gods Today

Thank you for going on the journey through the Norse gods, their wars, victories, and beliefs with this book. But our journey is not quite over. Perhaps it will never be over? There is some debate on whether Ragnarok has already happened or whether it is still destined to happen. Are the gods real or simply figments of the imagination of a "primitive" culture? If the gods are real, are they still around today? What did the implications of Norse mythology look like for the early Vikings, and what does it look like today? This chapter will answer the last lingering questions you may have, so join me on the rainbow bridge one last time.

Are the Norse Gods Still Smiling Down on Midgard Today?

When wondering if the Norse religious practices (or any pagan beliefs for that matter) are still hale and whole in Northern Europe, I came across the religion Ásatrú, which is a type of neo-Viking faith (which combines Norse and Celtic traditions). It is a revival of many of the same beliefs that these Norse ancestors had during the Viking era.

Ásatrú means "Aesir faith." In 1972, it was recognized as a religion in Iceland with the authority to marry couples or officiate burials. So, perhaps the old Norse gods are still smiling down on Midgard if their faithful are still here? But how does one believe in ancient stories when you've had a modern upbringing? How can you see Odin in the ravens that fly over the forests if you "know" they are just birds and not Hugin and Munin?

The answer is that Ásatrú is there to support its followers through the trials of life by focusing on the natural world (which the gods were so deeply intertwined in) and by being mindful of the characteristics the gods embodied. So, those who follow Ásatrú cultivate honor, bravery, courage, and acceptance, and they develop a deeper understanding and respect for the myths that shaped the Norse countries so fiercely.

The Ásatrú followers celebrate festive days or holidays that are closely tied to the ancient Aesir and Vanir gods. Sacrifices are made at four public dates of the year, celebrating the solstices and equinoxes:

- Freya is honored at winter solstice with Jólablót (Yule-blót), which means to make a sacrifice or offering to Freya at this time. Appropriate offerings would include food (such as goat's meat), mead, and sacred objects such as pendants.

- Freyr is honored with the spring equinox, Sigurblót (Victory-blót). Here, spring foods such as lamb and green veggies as well mead is offered to the god of fertility.

- Humans (and their ancestors) are honored by Þingblót (Þing/assembly-blót) on the summer solstice. This is also the harvest festival, and the fertility gods are also thanked and sacrifices are made to them.

- On the first day of winter, Veturnáttablót (wintery nights-blot), the faithful turn to Odin, the wise Allfather, whom they honor with gifts and sacrifices of sacred charms, mead, and offerings of food.

There are other forms of Norse religions that are also thriving in Northern Europe and across the world, including Odinism, Heathenry, and Germanic neo-Paganism. Followers of these ways scrutinize the ancient texts such as the *Poetic Edda* to formulate their beliefs. The gods of Asgard have definitely not died yet. These polytheistic religions have assigned slightly different roles to the main Norse gods, indicating how belief can change religion and the other way around too. For these Pagans:

Odin: The ruler of Valhalla, god of poetry and riches

Thor: Sky ruler who watches over all, and he's the god of community

Freyr: Still the god of fertility

Freyja (Freya): Now the goddess of love and beauty. She is now married to Thor.

These new forms of Norse Paganism are more flexible than mainstream religions, which makes them very appealing to the growing number of people (worldwide) who are beginning to integrate Paganism into their lives. Some Pagans combine aspects of Christianity with Paganism, living a smoothly blended religious life. If it works for them, who's to say it is wrong? I discovered that while any journey into Norse mythology may seem like a history project, it is a lively and vital process, and care needs to be taken as this "history" is still very much alive for a great number of people who live in the very places where the Norse beliefs began.

The Sacred Sites

There are a number of sacred sites scattered throughout Northern Europe that are particularly motivated by Norse beliefs and myths.

Helgafell, Iceland

In Iceland, we find the breathtaking view from Helgafell (meaning: holy mountain), which is traditionally believed to provide a view into Valhalla. In the ancient times, those nearing their end would climb to the top of this rocky outcropping and look across at Valhalla. This vantage point located on the Snæfellsnes peninsula, is said to be a place of great magic where, if you follow three ancient rules, you could make a wish and have it come true. The rules were to not look back as you climbed, the walk must be made in utter silence, and the nature of their wish can never be made known to anyone else.

Lofoten Islands, Northern Norway

This is the ideal place to view the Northern Lights from. There were many beliefs surrounding the rainbow-colored lights in the sky, and some of the ancient Norsemen believed the colors were reflected from the Valkyrie's armor, while others held that it was the colors of the Bifröst, the rainbow bridge between Midgard and Asgard. Whichever belief you hold to, it is still a magnificent view to behold and well worth the trip.

Gamla Uppsala

Located just outside the city of Uppsala in Sweden, this archeological site is sure to help you dig deep to your own Viking roots. The three giant mounds at Gamla Uppsala are said to be the funeral mounds of the three Norse gods, Odin, Thor, and Freyr. These impressively large mounds of earth definitely offer fuel for the imagination, and when I had the opportunity to visit this site, I could just imagine the three mighty gods lying there after the battle of Ragnarok.

The Rök Runestone

You can find this awe-inspiring stone in Östergötland, Sweden. While it was out in the open air and rugged landscape during the Viking days, the stone with its impressive display of runes is now housed inside a museum and is kept under roof to preserve the rune carvings. There are 760 characters of runes carved on the stone, telling riddles in poem form, which contribute to our knowledge of the Viking age. Standing before the large stone, one is struck by the sheer effort that was taken to carve the runes into the pitted surface. The Norse certainly lived a very different life from what we enjoy today, yet some of their beliefs still echo throughout our societies even now.

Norse Mythology and Popular Culture

When you hear a sentence with Norse mythology and popular culture in it, you would be forgiven for instantly thinking of the latest edition of Marvell's Thor or the Avengers. After all, we have been almost indoctrinated by the blonde hero with his large arms saving the day on the blue screen. However, Norse mythology has had an impact on popular culture long before Hollywood or the first comics caught wind of the Aesir gods.

The Norse gods have appeared in poetry, art, and song since before the more recent interpretations. Here are a few interesting takes to consider for a complete view of modern day Norse Paganism and popular culture:

Books

- *The Ballad of the White Horse (1911) by G. K. Chesterton*

This book, written at the turn of the century, highlighted the Norse gods as being false gods, pushing the reader towards Christianity, but it is an interesting take on the gods from a Christian perspective. It also makes one a little more sensitive to Snorri Sturluson's *Poetic* or *Prose Edda*, which might be equally biased.

- The Incomplete Enchanter (1941) by L. Sprague de Camp

Only a mere three decades after the first example, we are already finding a much more "interested" version of literature involving the Norse gods. Given the rich detail and bold characters of the gods, they are the stuff of dreams and imagination, driving a primal sense in humans.

- *The Hobbit (1937) and The Lord of the Rings (1954) by R.R. Tolkien*

These iconic books were admittedly inspired by the Norse gods and the realms of Yggdrasil. Gandalf is surely an interpretive version of Odin, with the elves and dwarves clearly seeming Norse in nature.

- *Life, the Universe and Everything (1982) by Douglas Adams*

Combining science fiction with myth, fantastical worlds, beliefs, and adventures unfold involving Odin and Thor.

Poetry

- *William Morris' poems such as Sigurd the Volsung*
- *Seamus Heaney (1999) wrote a great translation of the ancient Norse-inspired poem Beowulf.*

Music and Song

- *German composer Richard Wagner created the four operas that make up Der Ring des Nibelungen based on Norse characters.*

- *An assortment of Viking inspired metal bands such as Manowar, Unleashed, and Kampfar.*

Movies

- Vikings by the History Channel

- Thor and the Avengers (and a slew of other Marvel productions)

- Erik the Viking (which provides a humorous take on the Norse mythologies)

- The 13th Warrior

Other

There are many other media that we find Norse mythology making a serious mark on, from comics and manga to role-player games like "God of War." Norse mythology is not dead at all, and perhaps this is where the resurrection that came after Ragnarok has really happened? Either way, Norse mythology is certainly interesting, enriching, and entertaining.

Modern Day Impact of Norse Mythology on Scandinavia and the Viking Countries

- **The Countries**

For the people living in the countries where the ancient Vikings once did battle and built their long homes, Norse mythology will always be alive and all around them. It's seen and remembered in the names of places, the shape of the land, and a rich cultural undertone that is present in the different peoples of Northern Europe and the British Isles.

The traditions of the Vikings and Norse mythology deeply influenced the cultures and pastimes of these different lands. Viking culture is one of diversity, and the people of these countries have developed a different way of seeing the land, valuing sacred sites, and also creating a unique way of thinking.

- **Way of Living**

Many of the people living in the countries where Viking culture survives still practice similar habits, sports, and activities that the ancient Vikings would do.

- **Combining Norse Mythology and Christianity**

As mentioned, neo-Norse or neo-Paganism has evolved to include Norse beliefs and Celtic beliefs and also some Christian beliefs. There are also many similarities between Christianity and some of the tales of Norse mythology, which make for an interesting cross-reference discussion. The two religions aren't mutually exclusive, and in embracing differences and historical richness, thousands of Norse followers are able to successfully live their lives as both Christians and Pagans.

- **Tourism**

A final impact of Norse mythology is the massive market in tourism this has created in the countries where the Vikings lived such as Sweden, Denmark, Norway, Iceland, and the assortment of islands in the Baltic sea. Thousands of visitors stream to these areas to see the rune stones, enter the remains of longhouses, take modern day reconstructed tours, and visit Viking villages. Museums faithfully house texts, artifacts, and treasures of the ancient Norse times.

~~~~~//~~~~~

With the increased interest over the last 100 years, Norse mythology is again alive and thriving. The gods walk among the mortals once more as Midgard continues to thrive with its toes in the rich history of the Vikings.

CHAPTER 10

Glossary

No book on Norse mythology would be complete without a glossary, and this one is a bonus with the phonetic pronunciation of these Old Norse words included so you can grr and oooo with the ancient Vikings and really get a feel for the beautiful language that is still spoken in a modern form today in parts of Northern Europe. Enjoy!

~~~~~//~~~~~

Aesir: /**ey**-seer, **ey**-zeer/ collective noun for the gods of Asgard

Alfheim: /**alf**-heym/ home of the elves

Allsherjargoði: /**als**-her-jar-koi-thee/ a high priest

Angrboda: /**ahng**-ger-boh-duh/ she who bodes anguish, the giantess that Loki had three children with, namely Jormungand, Hel, and Fenrir

Ásatrú: /a-sa-tru, **ow**-sa-tru/ new religion in Iceland that combines Norse and Celtic beliefs

Asgard: /**ahs**-gahrd, **as**-gahrd/ home of the gods and goddesses

Ask: /ask, ahsk/ the first man made by the gods

Bifröst: /**be**-vrast/ the rainbow bridge that connects the Nine Realms within the World Tree

Blodughofi: /**blew**-ew-gla-fee/ meaning blood hoof, it was the magical horse that Freyr rode

Blót: /bloth/ sacrifice

Brísingamen: /**bree**-sing-ah-men, bree-seen-**gah**-men/ Freya's gleaming torc

Darraðarljóð: /**dar**-ra-tharl-yoth/ Ancient rune poem found on the Rök runestone in Östergötland, Sweden, containing the tale of 12 Valkyrie plotting the deaths of warriors

Draupnir: /**draop**-neer, **drao**-pnihr/ Odin's magical ring that made eight new rings every nine nights

Dwarves: created from the maggots that lived in Ymir's corpse

Eir: /er/ handmaiden to Frigg, she was venerated as a goddess of healing

Embla: /**em**-blah, **em**-bla/ the first woman made by the gods

Fehu: /**fey**-who/ name for the phoneme "F," meaning: cattle

Fenrir: /**fen**-reer, **fehn**-reer/ marsh-dweller, the huge wolf that would swallow Odin whole

Fimbulvetr: /**fim**-bul-vin-ter/ the great winter that would come at the start of Ragnarok

Fólkvangr: /**folk**-vang-uhr/ field of the host or place of the dead

Freya (word only): /**frey**-uh/ meaning: lady

Freya: /**frey**-uh/ Freya, goddess of fertility

Freyr (word only): /freyr/ means lord

Freyr: /freyr/ Freyr, the god of fertility

Fylgja: /**filg**-ya/ the attendant spirit, the part of your psyche that is associated with your animal familiars such as Odin and his ravens

Germanic runes: the carvings on rocks that symbolizes the ideas or concepts of Norse writing

Ginnungagap: /**gin**-oong-gah-**gahp**/ the bottomless abyss that existed prior to the creation of the cosmos and into which the cosmos will collapse once again

Gjallarhorn: /**yahl**-lahr-hawrn/ the great horn of Heimdallr, which will signal the start of Ragnarok

Gothi: /**gho**-thi/ traditional Norse priest

Gullinborsti: /**goo**-lin-burst-ee/ the golden boar made by the dwarves

Gullinkambi: /**goo**-lin-kam-bee/ the golden rooster that will announce to the hall of Valhalla the start of Ragnarok

Gungnir: /**goong**-near/ Odin's spear

Hamingja:/**hahm**-ing-ya/ the talent you possess that is unique, such as Thor's battle strength

Hamr: /**ham**-er/ skin or shapeshifting potential of the self

Hati: /**hat**-ee/ a magical wolf who chases the moon and the sun

Heiðr: /**high**-thur/ meaning: bright, this was the disguise Freya assumed when she traveled the Nine Realms before the Aesir-Vanir war

Heil: /hayl/ be healthy and happy (traditional greeting)

Heil Og Sael: /**hayl**-og-sa-el/ be healthy and happy, a traditional Viking farewell

Hel: /hel/ meaning: to be hidden

Helgafell: /**hel**-gha-fell/ small mountain in the Snæfellsnes Peninsula of Iceland, meaning: holy mountain

Helheim: /**hel**-haym/ the realm that is hidden, the underworld

Himinbjörg: /**he**-min-bjohrg/ meaning: sky cliffs, it's the realm ruled by Heimdallr, who guards the Bifröst

Hliðskjálf: the seat of Odin from where he could see into all Nine Realms

Hringhorni: /**hlith**-sky-ahlf/ ship with a circle at the stern

Hugr: /**hoo**-guhr/ thought or thinking, the mind

Hvergelmir: /**hvel**-guh-mihr/ the oldest fountain in Niflheim, meaning: bubbling and boiling spring

Járngreipr: /**yarn**-greypr/ meaning: iron grippers, the iron gloves that Thor wore allowed him to grip his hammer

Jormungand/Jörmungandr: /**yawr**-moon-gahnd, **yawr**-moon-gahn-dhr/ meaning: huge monster, also the serpent in the seas around Midgard

Jotunheim: /**yawr**-turn-haym/ home of the giants

Jötnar: /**jot**-nar/ frost giants

Lif: /leaf/ meaning: life, last remaining man after Ragnarok

Lifþrasir: /**leaf**-thrass-ear/ meaning: striving after life, the last woman remaining after Ragnarok

Lokasenna: /**lok**-kah-sen-nah/ a poem from the *Poetic Edda* that features Loki's taunting of the gods. Also known as Loki's Truth

Loki: /**low**-key, **lock**-ee/ meaning: fire, knot, or spider as a quite apt translation of the trickster god's name

Megingjörd: /**mee**-ying-jorth/ the belt Thor wore, meaning: belt of power

Mimir: /**mee**-mere/ shadowy being who watches over the Well of Urd and counsels Odin

Mjöllnir: /**mee**-ol-neer/ Thor's hammer, made by the dwarves

Múspell: /**moo**-spell/ the giant who rules Muspelheim and will attack Niflheim during Ragnarok

Muspelheim: /**moo**-spell-haym/ the homeland of elemental fire, the world of Múspell

Naglfar: /**nah**-ghl-far/ a ship made of toenails and fingernails of the dead, which carries the giant army to Asgard

Nidhug: /**need**-hawg/ fierce dragon that protects the spring in Niflheim

Niflheim: /**niff**-el-haym/ the homeland of elemental ice, world of fog

Noatun: /**no**-ah-toon/ castle by the sea where Njord dwelled

Norns: /norns/ magical female beings who rule the fates of men

Norse: Germanic peoples, their beliefs, myths, culture, traditions, etc.

Northern Lights: an atmospheric phenomenon in the northernmost parts of Europe where the sky is colored with rainbow light due to light refraction from ice crystals, said to be the Valkyrie's armor or the Bifröst bridge

Poetic Edda: a collection of poems, which records most of the known knowledge about the Norse gods and their mythical adventures and journeys, by the Icelandic poet Snorri Sturluson

Ragnarok: /**rag**-na-rock/ the end of the world, the twilight of the gods, and the fate of the gods

Rök: /rock/ meaning: a skittle shaped stone or smoke

Seidr: /**say**-der/ Norse magic

Sessrúmnir: /**ses**-room-neer/ Freya's seat hall

Skadi: /**skath**-ee, **shah**-dee/ daughter of Thjazi, who had kidnapped Idun, and she later married Njord

Skalds: /skalds/ highly revered bards and poets

Skidbladnir: /**skid**-bood-nere/ magical ship that the dwarves made which could fold up to fit in your pocket

Skipta hömum: /skipta-haw-moon/ to change one's skin or transform into a different shape

Sköll: /sk-**oll**/ one who mocks, a wolf that chases the moon and the sun

Skuld: /skoold/ meaning: something that will become, the last of the Norns

Sleipnir: /**slayp**-near/ Odin's magical horse that had eight legs and was born from Loki's tryst with a magical stallion

Surt: /soort/ the fire giant who would fight against Freyr, dying by his hand and also killing Freyr

Svadilfari: /**svadil**-far-i/ the stallion who worked with the giant to build Asgard's wall and had a colt with Loki

Svartalfheim: /**swart**-ahlf-haym, **svart**-ahlf-haym/ home of the dwarves

Thialfi: /**thee**-ahlf-ee/ the human boy who journeyed with Thor and Loki

Thjazi: /**thee**-a-tsee/ giant who kidnapped Idun

Thökk: /thawk/ the old giantess who refused to weep tears for Baldur (Loki in disguise), meaning: thanks

Thrym: /threem/ meaning: noisy, the giant who stole Thor's hammer

Thrymheim: /**thraym**-haym/ home of Skadi and Thjazi

Thurisaz: /**thoo**-ri-sats/ name of the phoneme "th," which means being formed right now, the second Norn

Vigrid: /**wee**-grid/ plain where the final battle of Ragnarok will happen, meaning: giant

Til Árs ok Friðar: /til-aars-ok-fri-thar/ a good year and peace (traditional new year's wish)

Urd: /oord/ meaning: the past, the first of the Norns

Urðr: /oor-thr/ fate or destiny (also called wyrd)

Valhalla: /**varl**-hah-lah/ the hall for the brave dead, ruled by Odin

Valkyrie: /**val**-ki-ree, **varl**-koo-ree/ meaning: those who choose the new spirits, the female spirits who chose the fallen to bear to Odin's hall

Vanaheim: /**vana**-haym/ home of the Vanir

Vanir: /**varn**-eer/ the gods of Vanaheim, enemies of Asgard until the unification

Verdandi: /**ver**-dan-dee, **wer**-dan-dee/ meaning: that which is happening

Viking Age: spanned from around 793 to 1066

Völuspá: /**waw**-**lu**-spa/ first and best-known poem of the *Edda*

Völva: /**waw**-wa/ poem from the *Poetic Edda* that refers to the end of the gods, a practicing seidr sorceress or witch

Yggdrasil:/**eeg**-drass-ill/ the World Tree that all realms exist within

Ymir: /**ee**-mir or **y**-mir/ the first of the giants, source of all other giants

Heil Og Sæl!

Viking history and myth presents a rich opportunity to look into the past and learn for the future. It is so wildly popular that the myths, gods, monsters, beliefs, and culture now appear in movies, miniseries, games, online role-playing games (RPG), and the religious beliefs in the Norse gods are still very much alive and well today. There are even online shrines and worship sites, and there are also many conferences that strive to keep the ancient Norse culture alive and vital to many new generations of "Midgardians."

Yet, culture is never static, and those who participate in it and keep it alive also serve to change it. Much of modern day Norse mythology and beliefs have been somewhat changed by the impact of technology, new ideas, and cross pollination of other cultures and religious beliefs. This is not a new concept though, as the same happened in ancient times when one culture met a new culture. In fact, the ancient Norse traditions have definitely been changed by the influence of the beliefs of Christianity that entered Northern Europe.

As such, I keep a mental pot of salt with me when I read about the Vikings, their myths, their beliefs, and their traditions. I have to pinch myself and remember that what I read may not have been captured 100% accurately from how it happened in ancient Norse times. But I hope this book has given you an authentic taste of true Norse mythology, the mystery, history, and culture of the Vikings. More than that, I also hope you can see how that mythology is all around us today in the books we read, the movies we watch, the music we listen to, and the poems we live by.

From the skalds to the Valkyrie, from the runes to the Nine Realms, and from the gods to the giants, there is always something exciting and thought-provoking to be learned from Norse mythology. We may not be able to imagine quite what a traditional Viking's life was like, but with these stories and the wonderfully rich characters of the gods and mythical figures, we can gain some small glimpse into the past.

How I would love to climb into a time machine, travel back to those cold and frosty days, see the Scandinavian coast, and experience Viking culture first hand! For now, I content myself with books, stories, new translations, and exciting archeological finds.

So, I hope you have enjoyed these stories, my insights into the Viking culture and Norse mythology, and the trip down my own Bifröst to learn about the Vikings and their gods. Here, I leave you at the end of this book, though there will be many more adventures, discoveries, and great insights to come and these will help you understand your own beliefs even better.

Heil og sæl! Be healthy and happy!

If you have enjoyed reading this book as much as I enjoyed writing it, then I would ask for a favorable review on Amazon that other wanderers may find their way to Yggdrasil too and drain a horn of mead in the golden hall of Valhalla, where the brave shall live forever.

References

Apel, T. (n.d.). *Freyr.* Mythopedia. https://mythopedia.com/norse-mythology/gods/freyr/

Brown, N. M. (2012). *Seven Norse Myths We Wouldn't Have Without Snorri: Part V.* Norse Mythology. https://www.tor.com/2012/12/10/seven-norse-myths-we-wouldnt-have-without-snorri-part-v/

Campbell, J. (1904). *The power of myth, with Bill Moyers, p. 11.* Anchor Books.

Dronke, U. (Trans.) (1997). *The Poetic Edda: Volume II: Mythological Poems.* Oxford University

Elderberg, J. (2015). *Viking mythology: what a man can learn from Odin.* Art of Manliness. https://www.artofmanliness.com/articles/viking-mythology-odin/

Geller, P. (2016). *Frigg.* Mythology.net. https://mythology.net/norse/norse-gods/frigg/

McCoy, D. (n.d.-a). *Who were the historical Vikings?* Norse Mythology. https://norse-mythology.org/who-were-the-historical-vikings/

McCoy, D. (n.d.-b). *Odin.* Norse Mythology. https://norse-mythology.org/gods-and-creatures/the-aesir-gods-and-goddesses/odin/

McCoy, D. (n.d.-c). *Tyr.* Norse Mythology. https://norse-mythology.org/gods-and-creatures/the-aesir-gods-and-goddesses/tyr/

McCoy, D. (n.d.-d). *Vili and Ve.* Norse Mythology. https://norse-mythology.org/vili-ve/

McCoy, D. (n.d.-e). *Ragnarok.* Norse Mythology. https://norse-mythology.org/tales/ragnarok/

North, R. (2010). *The longman anthology of old English, old Icelandic, and Anglo-Norman literatures* (R. North, Trans.). Routledge. (Original Work, 13th Century).

Rach, J. (2018). *Couple exchange vows in a Viking wedding on the shores of a Norwegian lake inspired by a 10th-century ceremony – complete with longboats, a pagan priest and blood offerings.* Mail Online. https://www.dailymail.co.uk/femail/article-6129259/Couple-tie-knot-Viking-wedding-nearly-1-000-years.html

Skjalden. (2020). *Vanir.* Nordic Culture. https://skjalden.com/vanir/

The Skalds Circle. (n.d.). *The marriage of Njord and Skadi (Norse mythology).* The skalds circle. https://theskaldscircle.com/norse-mythology/the-marriage-of-njord-and-skadi-norse-mythology/

List of Illustrations

Image 1: WikiImages from Pixabay. https://pixabay.com/photos/europe-map-1923-country-breakdown-63026/

Image 2: Yuriy Chemerys on Unsplash. https://unsplash.com/photos/pmCGouQQgFY

Image 3: ella peebles on Unsplash. https://unsplash.com/photos/kUkqoqwY61s

Image 4: Jeremy Bishop on Unsplash. https://unsplash.com/photos/EwKXn5CapA4

Image 5: LoggaWiggler from Pixabay. https://pixabay.com/photos/ervin-ahmad-lóránth-sculpture-giant-522837/

Image 6: Russo self-designed image.

Image 7: Jonas Friese on Unsplash. https://unsplash.com/photos/pS_S00R9_6I

Image 8: Russo self-designed image.

Image 9: Victor B on Unsplash. https://unsplash.com/photos/IYyvakvhi7I

Image 11: Husein Bahr on Unsplash. https://unsplash.com/photos/93afVrqOOyo

Image 12: ANIRUDH on Unsplash. https://unsplash.com/photos/8pgK7WMSnXs

Image 13: Steven Erixon on Unsplash. https://unsplash.com/photos/1xZzYbasToM

Image 14: Russo self-designed image.

Image 15: Enrique Meseguer from Pixabay. https://pixabay.com/illustrations/woman-female-warrior-hooded-2856014/

Image 16: Russo self-designed image.

Image 17: Russo self-designed image.

Image 18: Kristijan Arsov on Unsplash. https://unsplash.com/photos/tcw3nwoAgvs

Image 19: Image by Deedster from Pixabay.https://pixabay.com/photos/skull-decoration-halloween-spooky-1626803/

Image 20: Russo self-designed image.

UNCOVERING CELTIC MYTHOLOGY

A Beginner's Guide to The World of Celtic Myths, Celtic Folklore, Warriors, Celtic Gods, and Creatures

LUCAS RUSSO

Introduction

During my study of the Greco-Roman antiquity period, I stumbled upon Julius Caesar's encounters with the Celtic people of Gaul. Over the course of the 9-year Gallic wars, Caesar documented all that he could about the culture and beliefs of these people. While doing so, he began to draw connections between the German and Celtic gods to those that were followed in Rome. These wars were decisive to the Romans in securing victory over the many Gallic tribes. Despite the victories and colonization of these areas, the Celtic culture continued to thrive in the current countries of the United Kingdom and Ireland.

Suffice to say, the use of syncretism, or the overlap of beliefs and practices across nations, piqued my interest in the Celtic peoples and the origins of their surviving culture. The modern-day British Isles stand as a representation of the mix of cultures that swept across Europe throughout the Iron Age through the Middle Ages. Polytheistic and monotheistic societies and religions were combined and reinterpreted, resulting in unique and blended cultures.

To this day, the Celts are famed for their deeply intricate art styles, unique burial practices, and the ever-popular description of red-headed braves throughout popular media. The Celtic culture stands among other cultural and historical giants, such as the Romans, the Greeks, and the Germanic peoples. Ireland, Scotland, Wales, and Great Britain continue to hold onto the remains of this great ancient history. Historic castles and forts mark the skyline of the isles, as do oral traditions and histories of folktales, mythical creatures, and heroic figures, all told in their mother languages or the closest modern variants.

Ancient Celtic culture continues to bear influence over modern cultures and media. Many of the legends, beasts, and heroes find themselves repeatedly retold or reimagined. Of course, this isn't exclusive to Celtic traditions; we see the same with Norse, Greek, Roman, and many other polytheistic cultures. What keeps us returning to these ancient roots?

Mythological Significance

Mythology has always played a major role in cultures around the world, through every era in history. While we know in modern days how volcanoes work and how weather systems impact a variety of crops and natural cycles, in ancient times mythology provided comfort and significance in these unknown patterns. Being able to give hardship and success meaning helped to shape cultures and traditions. Mythology gave the human race a way to process life and death, explain natural phenomena, as well as give meaning to tragedies, such as the spread of illness through the tribes, famine, and any emotional or mental distress. In turning to mythology, we make sense of the deepest of tragedies, and find joy in the most overwhelming of emotions. When you look into the pantheons of polytheistic mythology, we see that the deities of worship were never made to be perfect idyllic beings, but were truly made as humans are: flawed, but capable of overcoming the greatest adversity.

When we study ancient mythology, we get a clearer view of what our ancestors lived through and the ideals they held in high regard. Throughout the ages, deities rose and fell in popularity, depending on the requirements of the culture. When faced with adversity and war, it only made sense that gods of war would come into higher worship. When it came time to bless the sown seeds, gods of fertility received offerings throughout the tribes. When it comes to seeing what it was that the ancient peoples found value in, we need look no further than the myths that were cherished and passed down through the generations.

Mythology in the Present Day

Living in a world where science meets fiction, where the phenomena that once perplexed our ancestors are easily explained by a barometer and careful observation, it can be easy to wonder why we still turn to ancient mythology. After all, when we see the lightning streak across the sky, we know better than to think that Thor is *actually* racing across our sky in his chariot, right? We understand the way lightning is created within our clouds, and released as vibrant energy. So what purpose does mythology hold in our modern world?

In many ways, these myths still hold the same significance to us as they did to our ancestors. When the Celts went to war, they turned to the Mórrígan, calling for her to stand with them and guide them as the fiercest goddess on the battlefield. Today, when we know that we are about to battle, whether it's our own internal demons or fighting with external issues and pressure, we rely on the tales of the Mórrígan so that we can draw from her strength. We turn to these stories to learn from them and aim to better ourselves as we pursue our goals in the image of these gods.

Even today, we have modern-day myths and legends. If you look into the near past, we have the stories of Paul Bunyan and his ox. In the present, we can see these stories at work within our media. One thing that carries forward is the human desire to tell stories. Instead of telling stories of Brigid, we tell stories of Batman and Deadpool, seeing ourselves in their greatness and downfalls. We retell the stories of great battles in history the same way ancient civilizations did. Instead of them being oral traditions, we instead have movies, like *Valkyrie* and *We Were Soldiers*: dramatizations based on true events, retold for both education and inspiration, as well as entertainment. We look at the greatest beings of our lifetimes and tell their stories, creating modern legends out of the great men and women who led movements and fought to make our culture better.

In looking at the great tales of ancient Celtic mythology, we can understand the culture, and the way these civilizations lived their lives. In the telling of these mythological giants and powers, we see more than just the values of these people. We see what they aspired to be, what they view to be true success and greatness, and what they understand of the world. We can see the state of their economies through what we know was being left as offerings, what they feared based on the creatures that were created, and their overall worldview. In today's world, these tales, deities, and creatures continue to inspire us to create and teach.

As you dive into these pages, you'll find a rich Celtic history as it has been preserved through the ages. The history and culture of the original Pagan peoples, predating even the Norse by almost 1,500 years, has continued to live on and flourish, providing wisdom that is deeply cherished by it's followers and practitioners even to this day. The history of the Celtic people lets us learn about the nature of ourselves and the world around us, and exactly why the stories, the landmarks, and the culture have been able to stay around despite the constant shifting, development, and evolution of the modern world. These fabulous myths and histories show no signs of their presence leaving the public awareness, and for good reason. There is a mountain of knowledge found within Celtic culture and history; all you need to do is begin the climb to reap the spoils of these marvelous ancient peoples.

CHAPTER 1

History and Origin of the Celts

The exact point of origin for the Celts is next to impossible to pinpoint. The Celtic people were not a singular group of people, but tribes that were spread across the massive land mass that is Europe. Similar to the Native Americans of North America, we find collectives that were spread over the land, sharing very similar beliefs among tribes, and passing their knowledge and stories down not through written or recorded history, but through oral traditions that were memorized by the people. The tribes differed slightly in practice, but for the most part maintained the core of their ways. Just like the practice of the Navajo differs from the Cherokee, the Welsh Celts and the Irish Celts had variances within their practice, while still maintaining the faith of the land.

Finding recorded history of the ancient Celts is no easy feat. Even after they encountered the Greeks and then the Romans, we find issues within the texts written about the ancients. After all, historical texts were often preserved by rewriting, leaving a huge margin for human error. These texts would end up being mistranslated, or errors would be made that left room to question their meaning by the translators who would follow centuries later. Human error wasn't the only negative impact on the written history of the ancient Celts. Given that the history was being recorded by people other than the Celts themselves, the influence of those who were recording is also present in the writing. The interpretations of the people recording sometimes meant that they would record the wrong information, only to be corrected later. Or they might even rewrite the information so that it more favorably reflected on the ones doing the writing, who were often the invaders or conquerors. The influence of Christianization also impacted the stories and mythologies, which will be more evident later as we discuss the stories in depth.

Oral Traditions

These tribes maintained their oral traditions until encountering the Greeks, who began documenting all that they could about these ancient peoples, referring to them at the time as the *Keltoi*. Soon after, the Romans made contact with the Celts, continuing the records. Prior to making contact with the Greeks and Romans as they continued their progression over the land, spreading their territories and colonizing those they encountered, the Druids were in charge of managing the oral history of the Celtic people, among their other duties. The Druids would spend decades memorizing the histories and stories of their people. Massive stories, thousands of words long, were memorized in rhythmic poetry and verse to be passed along to the next generation of learned men.

It was considered profane and blasphemous by the Druids to record the histories and stories into writing. This was for two main reasons. The first reason was that it would potentially weaken the memory of those who were meant to keep and maintain these stories if they were written. These people would spend years making sure they remembered every beat and rhythm to the poems, verses, songs, and stories to which they were dedicating their lives. The second reason was an issue of access; if the bards and Druids were expected to spend decades committing every beat and syllable to memory, having the stories written would invalidate that work and make the history accessible to absolutely everyone and anyone. The exclusivity of the information maintained the importance to the work being done by the keepers of the stories.

Bards, Filid, and Druids

In a time where oral traditions were so crucial, the keepers of the stories were crucial to Celtic society. These people were viewed as mystical, powerful, and well respected. They formed their own trinity as the keepers of knowledge: bards, Druids, and filid.

Bards

The bards were considered the lowest tier of the trinity, serving as both entertainment and teachers to the masses. They would entertain through songs and satire, sometimes thought to have power granted to them through their music. Some were thought to have the power to start or calm storms, to manipulate animals and life around them, induce sleep, and more. They served as disciples to the Druids, and were permitted to perform to honor the deities who were worshipped and entertained with plays, songs, and more when ceremonies were being performed by the Druids and filid. The primary focus of the bards was to tell the great stories and myths to the people.

Filid

The filid are a mysterious class, similar to bards in that they were poets in ancient Ireland and Scotland, but little is known about them. There is some discussion that suggests that they may have been a completely separate class from the bards and Druids, but in many circles, the accepted ideology is that they served beneath and with the Druids. If a Druid were conducting a ceremony, the filid would be there to assist as the Druid required. While there is much that isn't known about the filid class, we do know that their primary focus was on the material world, rather than the mythological or spiritual. The filid spent just as much time in the memorization of the stories and histories as the Druids did, but their dominating focus was on laws, genealogies, and the history of the people and land.

Druids

The Druids were widely revered over Celtic lands, even by kings and lawmakers. They would officiate over ceremonies and rituals, they were known to have the final say in lawful judgements and rulings, and even spoke before the king in the opening of ceremonies. This is impressive, given the importance of the king as the connection to the divine; when a ceremony was begun, absolutely nobody was to speak before the king, but the king would not speak until the Druid spoke to open the ceremony.

Druids were truly the upper class in ancient Celtic society. They were not only the spiritual leaders of the society, but often served as mediator and judge. They were the scholars who kept the knowledge of all things spiritual and moral. If a decision could not be made, or an agreement could not be reached, it was brought before a Druid to be resolved. Whatever choice the Druid made was considered to be the most wise and moral, and could not be questioned or overturned, even by the king himself.

Religion

Despite the many invasions of the Gaels and the Celts, nobody had ever successfully conquered them. This allowed for their religion and practices to continue to flourish in areas such as Ireland. In many areas, instead of Christianity completely taking over the way it had in other areas, some Celtic tribes chose to incorporate the Christian ways into the Celtic religion. This resulted in some odd takes on the history and mythology. For example, when reading the Book of Invasions, which makes up much of the mythological cycles of Celtic myth, we find that Christian stories of Noah and the great flood and the book of Genesis find themselves incorporated into the work. Many of the stories and legends that we have now are influenced by Christianity, so each story of the mythology should be taken with a grain of salt, as many of them were altered or lost over time.

Festivals

Like many other Pagan traditions, the Celtic people celebrated eight festivals each year. Half of these festivals were related to the change of the seasons, called *fire festivals* because of the bonfires lit to celebrate them, while the other half marked the halfway points between the seasons via the two solstices and equinoxes. Celtic traditions were heavily based around livestock and agriculture.

Fire Festivals

Fire festivals marked the changing of the seasons. Ancient Celts recognized the year being divided into two main parts: *Beltane*, the time of light, and *Samhain*, the time of darkness. The two quarterly festivals marked the halfway points between the two.

- *Imbolc* (February 1): Imbolc marks the arrival of spring. It is celebrated as a time of fertility, with the seed of the rising sun being sown. The ancient traditions celebrated the goddess Brigid on this day, as she was a symbol of health, protection, and fertility to them, all things they would hope to see in the coming season.

- *Beltane* (May 1): Beltane celebrates the success of the coming sun, and the days growing longer with the summer. The youth would celebrate the day by jumping through fires for good luck, and celebrate the fertility of the year as harvests grew. Fire was important for celebrating the day, representing the burning sun that had finally returned to the people.

- *Lughnasadh* (August 1): Lughnasadh marks the beginning of the harvest season. The day was celebrated through sport and craft. It was also a time of love; many people would be joined in engagement and handfasting ceremonies, where lovers would be united in marriage or prepare for a year and a day engaged. Observers feasted and celebrated, some making it a day of travel and spiritual pilgrimage.

- *Samhain* (October 31 to November 1): Samhain welcomes the dark days of the year, where the light fades and the weather becomes brisk and harsh. The end of the harvest is honored, and on this day, the ancient Celts would light two bonfires, herding their cattle between the fires as a way to bless them before slaughtering the animals, later casting their bones into the fires. It was said that the veil between the mortal and faery realms was thin on this day, so that even the dead could walk the earth with mortals.

Solstices and Equinoxes

Solstices and equinoxes were significant to the ancient Celts, marking the longest of the night and day, as well as the 2 days of the year where the dark and light would come into balance. Where the solstices marked the longest day and the longest night, the equinoxes were said to be a magical time, when magic would come to the people to grant blessings.

- *Litha* (June 21): Litha, sometimes also called Midsummer, was largely celebrated with fires, rejoicing in the longest day of the year, before the days began to shorten again. Great bonfires would roar to amazing heights and great wheels would burn as they were rolled down large hills to represent the descent of the sun. The fires would help to protect mortals from the faery folk, who would join them in the festival, keeping the celebrating humans safe from faery trickery.

- *Mabon* (September 21): There is little information regarding what the ancient Celts would have called this autumn harvest festival, but in modern days, the festival is referred to as Mabon. The day of Mabon is split equally, with equal amounts of daylight and nighttime leading into longer nights as winter approaches. The festival celebrates the final harvests of the year, feasting together to celebrate the bounty the earth has provided.

- *Yule* (December 21): Yule marks the longest period of darkness for the year. Feasts were held by the people in hopes that the sun would return quickly, ending the harsh winter. While we've seen Christianization of the festival, mistletoe and evergreens were always involved. Evergreen trees were brought into the home and decorated as gifts and tributes to the gods, while mistletoe was collected for it's healthy benefits and blessings.

- *Eostre* (March 20): Eostre is another celebration that has been heavily Christianized (ie, Easter) in the modern day. However, for ancient Celts, the day was the day of equal night and day, leading into longer days, showing the winter coming to an end. Many people would plant their seeds on Eostre, hoping to reap the blessings of the day for a fertile harvest.

CHAPTER 2

Tuatha dé Danann

The Tuatha dé Danann were the mythical race of beings, translated to mean "The people of Danu/Dana." These were the supernatural race of gods and goddesses that created the mythical races of the faery and Aos Si (also called the Sidhe). The Tuatha dé Danann have been said to interact with humans and the human realm, but otherwise reside in the Otherworld.

Where the Tuatha dé Danann represent the good, the beings that care for the land they created and ruled, their enemies were the Fomorians. The Fomorians were described as representing the evils of the world, such as pain, destruction, and the harmful forces found in the natural world. On the other hand, the Tuatha dé Danann were meant to represent various aspects of life and the natural world, such as the animals or qualities that we search for in a desirable being. Many of them are associated with many things, or have other names and representations in other minor deities. When Christian monks recorded the mythology surrounding the Tuatha dé Danann, they likened them to kings and queens, or otherwise great champions. In the modern day, they are better associated with the Aos Si.

There are variations to the ending of the story of the Milesians taking Ireland. In some depictions, Amergin divided the land horizontally, giving the underground to the Tuatha dé Danann, while the Milesians would walk the surface. Other stories say that Danu gave the Tuatha a choice: they could leave to live in Tír na nÓg. or they could choose to live underground. The final depiction suggested that the Tuatha dé Danann didn't bother to fight with the Milesians at all, because they'd seen prophecies that the Milesians were meant to rule the island. They chose not to battle them, instead preparing a kingdom beneath the mounds until the Milesians finally arrived to take their rightful place on the Island.

The Otherworld

There are conflicting ideas of where someone might find the Otherworld; some say that it is underground, accessible through wells and digging under faery mounds. Others say it's a parallel invisible world to ours that appears as we travel over impossibly narrow bridges or by walking into the foggy mists.

The Otherworld is the home of the gods, as well as to the mythical creatures and figures of the Tuatha dé Danann and their descendants. It was created by the Tuatha dé Danann to give them a place to live in peace, away from the battles and conflicts of the mortal realm. The creatures and beings that live in the Otherworld are said to leave the faery mounds to play tricks on the mortals they meet, sometimes offering them help and other times leading them astray.

In modern beliefs, the Otherworld is believed to be the Land of Eternal Youth, where if a human were to venture into this land, they would have to stay. If they went back to their realm, they would find that time had passed much more quickly, and if they touched the ground in the human world, they would never be able to return to the Otherworld, the passing of time catching up with them the moment they landed on the earth (see the story of Oisin in Chapter 7).

In a similar fashion to Christian beliefs in Heaven, some Celtic practitioners believe the Otherworld to be the paradise that they venture to when they die. The Otherworld is depicted as a place full of those who are most courageous on the battlefield, where great poets and artists stay to create wondrous works. In this place of sacred gifts, a mortal being waits to return to their next life, learning what they can of healing, creation, and courage.

The Four Treasures

When the Tuatha dé Danann took the land from the Fir Bolg, they brought with them four treasures of great significance. Each treasure came from a city from their original home realm. Each has elemental ties and associations.

First Treasure

The first treasure came from the great city of Falias. It is one of the only treasures that has a location on the Earth that is known, located on the Hill of Tara in County Meath, Ireland. The stone was said to sing a joyful song when the rightful High King of Ireland stood on the stone. At the same time, it would heal the rightful king, granting him a long life. On an elemental level, the stone is associated with the Earth.

Second Treasure

The second treasure, the Great Spear, belonged to Lugh. Originating from the city of Gorias, it was unbeatable, and foretold that anyone who fought opposing the spear was doomed to fail, no matter their strength. Even entire armies fell to the power of the spear. Elementally, the spear is connected to the air. It is said that this was the spear that was used to take down Balor, the most powerful warrior of the Formorians (see Chapter 5). It was made of the finest dark bronze and fastened to the rowan shaft with 30 golden rivets.

Third Treasure

The third treasure was Nuada's torch. Despite the name 'torch' it was actually a sword, sometimes called the Sword of Light. Similar to Lugh's spear, once it was drawn in battle, victory was guaranteed. Unlike the spear that ensured the victory for everyone on the side of the person wielding it, the sword only protected and ensured the victory of the single person who carried it. Elementally, the sword was linked to fire.

Fourth Treasure

The fourth and final treasure was the Cauldron of Dagda, also known as the Undry. The cauldron could serve all who came to it, given that it was magically bottomless. No matter how many hungry people came to it, none would leave unsatisfied. It was brought to Ireland from the great city of Murias and was linked to the element of water.

CHAPTER 3

Celtic Gods and Goddesses

When looking at the Celtic gods and goddesses of Ireland, Wales, and Scotland, we see a list of hundreds of deities that were worshiped at various points. The trouble with this is that, aside from a handful of these deities, there is very little known about a large portion of them. Some are found in the mythologies, but many of the stories and patterns of worship for these deities were lost with the Druids, who maintained the oral traditions of the Celts. While there were many deities through the pantheon, the Celts also had the tendency to worship figures and warriors. Some were raised to a level of deity-like status, while never actually being a deity, such as Cuchulainn, the great warrior of Ulster. What follows is a list of the most well-known deities, those that appear most often in the legends and hold what are arguably the most important places in the Celtic Pantheon.

Aengus Og

Aengus Og was the Youthful God of Love. He was born from Daghda and the river Goddess Boann having an illicit affair. Daghda, once he realized that he may be caught, made the sun stand still for Boann's entire pregnancy, so Aengus would be born in a day and hopefully Daghda might not be caught. Because of his 'quick' conception and birth, Aengus would forever represent youth. Aengus was known for the four birds that always circled his head, representing his kisses. He could make any couple fall for each other if he gave them his blessing.

For a God who could inspire love in just about any couple, he was also greatly susceptible to falling in love himself. In his most popular story, Aengus dreamed of the most beautiful girl of all the land. When he reached for her in the dream, she vanished. When he woke, he was so grieved that he couldn't move from his bed, nor could he eat. He would see her each night in his dreams, where she would play him sweet music until he woke. Aengus was so distraught over not knowing who she was that he became deeply ill. He refused to speak of why until the physician, Fergne, came to him. Just by looking at his face, Fergne knew that Aengus was suffering from lovesickness, and resolved to send Aengus to see his mother so that he could heal.

When Boann arrived, they sent her to search the entire land for the girl who was haunting Aengus's heart. After she had searched for an entire year with no luck, they sent for Daghda. He asked why they would send for him; it's not like he knew any more than anyone else. Fergne told him that, as the King of the Sidhe, he could send the messengers of Bodb (Aengus's brother) to look for the girl of the likeness that Aengus kept seeing in his dreams. Another year passed, and finally, the messengers returned to Daghda with news: they'd found the girl. Daghda sent for Aengus to be brought by chariot to the girl, so that he could make sure it was truly her.

Aengus was brought to a lake where 150 pairs of women sat chained in pairs. They asked him if he could see the girl whom he'd seen in his dreams. He looked over the crowd, recognizing her immediately. Bodb told him that she was not his to give. Aengus returned to his home, telling the news that he found, quite literally, the girl of his dreams. He found the names of her father and grandfather, knowing there was no way that he would be given her hand in marriage. Bodb suggested to him that he go to the King and Queen of Connaught, as they would have the power to grant him the marriage. King Ailil was told of the situation and sent messengers to the father of the girl, Ethal; her father refused to grant his daughter to a son of Daghda. When the messengers reported back, King Ailil assured Aengus that he would have his wife, or he would be bringing the girl's father to him along with the heads of all his soldiers.

The warriors of Daghda descended upon Ethal, and after they'd taken the heads of 300 of his best warriors, King Ailil demanded Ethal give his daughter to Aengus; he refused, saying that he could do no such thing since she was even more powerful than he was. She would turn into a bird every year on the eve of Samhain. Daghda told him that it would be handled, and his son would certainly marry her.

When Daghda returned to Aengus, he told him to go back to the lake on the Eve of Samhain to find the girl, Caer. When the day came, he went to the lake where he found the pairs of chained birds, calling out to Caer to come to him. She asked who he was, and he declared himself. He asked for her hand in marriage, and she agreed with one condition: that she be able to return to the water each year. He agreed, promising her she could return. He swept her into his arms, changing into a swan. They lay together as they circled the lake three times, and he kept his promise to her, each year returning to the lake with her in the shape of a swan.

Brigid

On the surface, Brigid is a wife and daughter, married to Breas, and born to Daghda. She is also a triple goddess, closely related to the cycle of birth, life, and rebirth. Brigid is associated with many things, making her a goddess who can cover a large range of polarities; she is a goddess of healing, as well as water and fire. Creativity, destruction, and fertility are all involved in her worship, as well as protection. She is a balancing goddess, representing the cycles of life, death, and nature.

While there are many deities that were adapted by Christianity, Brigid is one of the most visible, turning this pagan goddess into a saint of healing. However, Pagans still recognize her on Imbolc, calling on her ability to heal and protect by leaving offerings of cloth and creating dolls in her honor. Her connection to fire supports her connection to the return of the sun during Imbolc, the point at which the sun begins to return to the land, warming it for the sowing of crops and bringing the harshness of winter to an end. She is unique in the sense that she is considered a triple goddess, yet all three iterations of her are named the same.

Daghda

Daghda's name means 'good god,' Not in the moral sense of being eternally good, but in the sense that no matter the skill Daghda chooses to learn, he is successful in it. Leading as the Chief of the Tuatha dé Danann, he is comparable to Zeus in the way that he leads all of the gods, as well as being a lover to many and a father to even more. His wife, the Mórrígan, is sometimes referred to as his 'envious wife,' given that he had a habit of having children with plenty of other women. He was a charmer, despite often being depicted as unkempt, appearing more like a laborer fresh from the work day, rather than being smooth and fit like we typically imagine a god would look. He presides as the god of many things; life, death, fertility, agriculture, Druids, magic, seasons, and so much more. He collects skills and knowledge in a similar fashion to Odin of Norse mythology, forever consuming information and developing his skills. Daghda appears regularly in the mythological cycles, and can be found predominantly in Chapter 5.

Danu

Danu was worshiped as a mother, as Daghda was worshiped as a father, even though they weren't married. It is said that Danu birthed the Tuatha dé Danann, and those not born from her are directly descended from her. Very little is known about her, aside from her dominion over the Celtic deities who worship her as a leading mother goddess to the Tuatha. She is known to be powerful, often associated with water.

There are few stories of Danu that have survived, but there are some indirect allusions to her within the stories in the cycles. In most, she is a source of nurturing, and in some, it is suggested that she is the mother of Daghda. Some compare her to the goddess Brigid, as she appears to have many associations; fertility, war, nurturing, and teaching are all related to Danu, despite the difficulty in finding many direct references to her. The Irish language root of her name, *dan*, means 'knowledge,' 'wisdom,' 'art,' 'skill' and poetry, hence very fitting for her various attributes.

Eriu, Banba, and Fodla

Eriu (also known as Eire or Erin), along with her sisters Banba and Fodla, are revered among the triple goddesses of Celtic lore, simultaneously a single and triple being. The very island of Ireland receives its name from Eriu, as she was among the first of the Tuatha dé Danann to approach the Milesians when they landed upon the shores of Ireland. The story tells that Eriu had first proposed that the Milesians worship her as their goddess, but one of the Druids had refused, insulting her. She laid a curse upon him, and days later, he died. Given that there had been prophecy that the Milesians would claim the land as rightfully theirs, Eriu made a deal with them: she would help them in battle, but only if the island was named after her. They came to an agreement, and Eriu came to represent the island. Each time a new king or the High King took the throne, he would be married to Eriu; if he cared for her, the island would be healthy and prosperous. If he neglected her, the island would fall upon destitution and poverty. Today, Ireland is known as 'Erin's Isle.'

Lugh

Lugh is a god of nobility, as well as a god and master of all crafts. He was known for possessing a great number of skills, all of which he mastered. He was sometimes referred to as Lugh of the Long Arm, referring to his spear that, when thrown, would never miss its target. It also refers to the reach of his vast range of skills. While he was a god of nobility and the binding oaths they would take, he was also a trickster, willing to do whatever was necessary to achieve his desired result.

Lugh was also a fierce warrior in battle. His ability in battle had been prophesied, given that his grandfather, Balor of the Fomorians, was said to be killed by his grandchild. Refer to Chapter 5 for the story of Lugh's conception and subsequent fulfillment of the prophecy of Balor's death. Just like Manannán Mac Lir, Lugh was vastly popular in the Celtic pantheon as a God of the Sun, a fantastic warrior, and a clever, mischievous member of the Tuatha dé Danann. For further information, see Chapters 5 and 6.

Macha

Macha was a warrior goddess, closely related to the Mórrígan. The Navan Fort received it's original namesake from her, Emain Macha, or Macha's Twins (see Chapter 6 for this story). Apart from being a part of the triple goddess of the Mórrígan, she was also related to three core concepts: the first, related to female fertility and reproduction; the second, the cultivation of fertile lands; and the third, overall sexual fertility. As these three aspects combine, we have a powerful goddess commanding the realms of fertility, and the spirit of the warrior women who worshiped her. Warrior women were classically drawn to the power of Macha, and they embraced her as not only a fearsome warrior, but the divine feminine who could embrace both sides. For more in depth information on Macha, refer to "The Curse of Macha" in Chapter 6.

Manannán Mac Lir

Manannán Mac Lir was the Lord of the Sea, and ruler of the Land of Youth. His armor was impossible to pierce, and through his pigs, he granted the gods immortality. The pig itself would regenerate as long as it was cooked over the same log and killed with the same ax. All who ate from the pig could not be killed. Manannán Mac Lir was wildly popular within the Celtic mythologies, appearing repeatedly through the texts recorded. It is said that he was killed in the battle of Magh Cuilenn, his body allegedly buried off the coast of what is now Donegal. The area is home to a host of boat wrecks, legend saying that Manannán Mac Lir rides the wives of the storm, bringing the ships to their misfortune. For more on his stories, refer to Chapters 6 and 8.

Mórrígan, Badb, and Neiman

The Mórrígan is a complex goddess. She presides over prophecy, war and death, and is simultaneously a single and triple goddess. The Mórrígan was married to Daghda. Before battle, he would come to her for a prophecy about the outcome of the battle. During the battle, the Mórrígan would fly over the battlefield, gathering the dead. She was also a shapeshifter, taking many forms, ranging from a beautiful, shapely woman to an aged and decrepit crone, as well as a variety of animals. She presides over war alongside the goddesses Macha and Neman.

The complexity of the Mórrígan lies in her role as a triple goddess. While there is some dispute in the mythology as to who her two sisters are, one commonly accepted trilogy is the Mórrígan, Badb, and Neman, or respectively War, Madness, and Violence. However, depending on who is telling the story, some claim that Macha takes the place of Neman as one of the terrifying trio of sisters. She is a fearsome keeper of the dead, but not death within itself. When soaring over the battlefield, she favored taking the form of a crow; when warriors on the battlefield would see her, sometimes mistaking her for a raven, they would either be inspired to fight for their lives or succumb to the fear of death. She can be found quite regularly in the mythologies, and some of her stories are found in Chapters 5 and 6.

Honorable Mentions

The trouble with the way the mythologies were recorded, especially after centuries of exclusively passing stories down through oral traditions of bards and Druids, is that while we do have some slight knowledge of the Celtic deities who were worshiped, it is often conflicting and vague. Translations are sometimes questionable, and worse, there are definite portions of the stories and mythologies that died with the bards and Druids who spent their lives memorizing and telling the stories of these mythical beings. Those who did write the stories down were often later invaders or missionaries with their own agendas, changing names and legends to suit political or religious purposes. There are many of the hundreds of deities of Celtic mythology that we have pieced together through shreds of stories and the deities that bore similar stories and themes in Roman and other related pantheons.

While many of these beings have very limited information and only feature in other stories, this isn't to say that they aren't worthy of mention. Below is a list of some of these deities; some of these beings are featured for a brief moment in the following mythologies. They likely would have once had a massive, dedicated following.

- **Arawn**: As the ruler of the Otherworld, the resting place of the deceased, Arawn is a representative of all that is bound by honor and tradition. Due to the realm he inhabits, he is also closely tied to death, terror, war, and hunting. One of his best known stories is the theft of his lapwing, hound, and buck by the god Amatheon, the God of Agriculture. This spurred on the Battle of the Trees, but he was defeated when Amatheon's brother brought the trees to life to wage the war.

- **Cailleach**: Cailleach is a goddess of winter, as well as a powerful witch. She is said to control the harshness and duration of the winter, much like the current tradition of groundhog's day. The Celtic people paid special attention to the weather during Imbolc; if the weather was wet and miserable, it was said that the winter would be coming to a close; Cailleach was staying in her home, she no longer needed her firewood to keep her warm. If the weather was warm, bright, and sunny, the winter would continue on for several more weeks. After all, Cailleach would need pleasant weather to walk the woods to cut the lumber needed to keep herself warm through the remainder of the winter.

- **Ceridwen**: There is some debate as to whether Ceridwen was a sorceress or a goddess. For most modern Pagans, it is agreed that she is one of the most powerful Underworld goddesses, with close association to herbal practice and astrology. Ceridwen is the keeper of the cauldron of knowledge, and rules over the realms of inspiration and rebirth. She is powerful in all things magic, ranging from shapeshifting, to poetry, to fertility and rebirth.

- **Cernunnos**: Cernunnos ruled over the dominion of the wild. He was known by many names, and was commonly known as the "Horned God" due to his habit of wearing a set of stag's antlers on his head. When the Christian people reached Ireland and began their work recording (and occasionally altering) the stories of the Celtic Pagans, Cernunnos began to be associated with the devil, and sometimes even outright called the Antichrist. His stories are limited and scattered, but we do know that he was worshiped for his relationship with nature and the wildness of the animals and ecosystems he inhabited.

- **Cian**: Cian was a member of the Tuatha dé Danann, his most prominent stories surrounding his magical cow called Glas Ghoibhneann. She never ran dry, and was his most prized possession. The Fomorian, Balor, was determined to steal the cow, and upon his success, he unknowingly began the prophecy that would lead to his death. Cian and Balor's daughter, Eithne, fell in love, conceiving the child, Lugh, who would be Balor's ultimate undoing. The story may be found in Chapter 5.

- **Cliodhna**: Cliodhna was the goddess of love and beauty, but her legends came as a double-edged sword. Not only was she the most beautiful being to walk among the Tuatha dé Danann, followed by three birds whose songs could cure any ailment, she was known as the Queen of the Banshees. She was unphased by the lives and passings of mortals, luring sailors to their death in shipwrecks as they attempted to reach her. It was Manannán Mac Lir who ultimately ended her reign of terror on mortal sailors, sweeping her away with a magic wave. To this day, every ninth wave is known as Cliodhna's Wave, the most powerful of the set.

- **Eithne**: Eithne wasn't a traditional Celtic goddess. She was the daughter of the Fomorian Balor, and brought forth the birth of Lugh, who is considered important among the pantheon. This is her most prominent story, her wooing and conception of a child with Cian. The story can be found in Chapter 5.

- **Midir**: Midir is a lower tier lord, thought to have created the lakes and rivers of Ireland. He is the son of Daghda, prominently known for taking the first wife of King Eochaid, Etain. Etain was not aware of her faery lineage, thinking herself human when she married the king. She had an affair with Midir, sending his wife into a rage, resulting in Etain being changed into a butterfly to be swallowed by a mortal, so that she could be reborn without any knowledge of her faery background. While Midir is cunning, often associated with birds, Midir has a limited background. For further information on his story, refer to Chapter 8.

- **Taranis**: The name Taranis literally translates to 'thunder,' and as such, Taranis is the God of Thunder, not dissimilar to Thor of Norse mythology. He is one of the many Celtic gods who do not have a large amount of history and information readily available, but we do know that he was largely worshiped by the Celtic people. He had an association not only to storms, but also to sacred wheels. Still, there is much information that we are left without. We know that he is often depicted wielding a bolt of lighting. Most of what we know of Taranis is due to the similarities to the Roman God Jupiter, who also wielded a thunderbolt.

CHAPTER 4

Creatures and Their Myths

Celtic mythical creatures have a variety of origins. Some come from urban legends, like the Abhartach, which has no specific origin of how it became the creature that it is. Others are cryptids, creatures that are truly believed to exist but have never been captured or provided a significant amount of scientific evidence to their existence. Moreover, the mythic creatures that are described have a multitude of origins; some come from the Pagan myths prior to Christian influence, while others were created in the melding of Celtic Pagan belief and Christianity as it spread over Ireland. No matter the origin, each plays a role in the development of the Celtic mythology, as well as the Celtic culture and beliefs.

Abhartach

Unlike most mythical creatures of Celtic mythology, Abhartach doesn't originate in the world of faery but from the human world. The Irish tell of the *neamh-marbh*, the Celtic vampire. While many believe that vampire tales originate with Vlad the Impaler, some feel that the vampire chieftain Abhartach was the source of the original mythology. Little is known about the chieftain, except for how heavily he was disliked by his clan and the clans surrounding him.

Abhartach was known as a vile and jealous man, which would become his undoing. Climbing from his castle window, Abhartach attempted to catch his wife in the throes of passion with another man. Instead, he fell to his death, his body not found until the following day. His subjects were relieved, quickly burying the body so they could be rid of him. Since he was a chieftain, it was custom to bury him standing in respect of his position.

That evening the clan was horrified to see Abhartach standing before them with a bowl. He demanded that the bowl be filled by them, slicing their wrists to give him what he asked.

Once the bowl was filled and his blood hunger was satisfied, Abhartach left. The following morning, the clan raced to a neighboring clan, telling the chieftain, Catherine, their story and begging for his help. The Chieftain agreed.

Cathran met the people after dark, waiting for Abhartach to reappear. When he arrived, Cathran flew forward, killing the neamh-marbh, and Abhartach was again buried standing in his grave.

Yet again, Abhartach reappeared with his bowl, demanding the blood of his subjects. Seeing him appear again sent Cathran into a rage, and he attacked, slaying the creature and burying him in a grave far away from his clan. The following night, Abhartach reappeared.

Cathran ran out of ideas and consulted with a local saint, Eoghan. He asked the saint how it would be possible to kill what was already dead. Eoghan spent many hours in prayer and deliberation with his God, and when he returned, he instructed Cathran to pierce Abhartach's heart with a weapon made from a yew branch and then bury the creature face down. Cathran would then have to cover the grave in ash thorns and branches and place a slab of stone over the burial site to keep the beast from reemerging. This was the only method that kept Abhartach from rising again.

Aos Si

The Aos Si, sometimes referred to as the Sidhe, were a race of faery people and supernatural creatures. Some sources suggest that they were created by the Tuatha dé Danann, while other sources suggest that they actually were the surviving Tuatha dé Danann after the Milesian battles. The term *aos si* means 'the people of the mounds' and given that the Tuatha dé Danann retreated beneath the ground after being defeated, they are the best known source of these faery people.

The Aos Si operate with their own set of rules and customs. They are given offerings to keep them happy, and as long as you do not offend or insult them, they can be fierce protectors and offer many blessings. Some of the Aos Si are considered ethereally beautiful, typically associated with the Seelie court, while others are hideous and vile, associated with the Unseelie court. No matter which court they hail from, the Aos Si tend to be mischievous creatures and ferocious guardians.

Seelie Court

The Seelie court of faery is typically viewed as the benevolent court. While they could still be dangerous when insulted, they were the faery people that would help humans, as well as being willing to seek help from mortals. They find joy in mischief, and while they tend to be kind to humans, they don't always recognize when their pranks and tricks become harmful.

Unseelie Court

The Unseelie court of faery is the domain of the dark and evil faery creatures. Typically, faery of this court are malevolent, their mischief and tricks being used to cause mortals harm or even death.

Banshee

Of the faery folk in Celtic culture, the banshee is well known all over the world. The banshee scream is the siren song of inevitable death just around the corner. According to some legends, only those of pure, or near pure, Celtic descent will hear the wail of the banshee as she warns them of their own death, but it does appear to depend on the type of banshee.

The banshee legend goes back to the 8th century, referring to women known as 'keeners.' These professional mourners accepted payments in alcohol in exchange for beautiful, sorrow-filled songs sung in honor of a loved one or beloved community member passing on. Due to their preferred payment method, many were disregarded as sinful women, doomed to become the banshee in the mist.

There appear to be several forms of the banshee, depending on which Celtic origin you reference. The banshee is almost always a woman. Sometimes she was young, with red or silver hair, wearing a white dress or perhaps a shroud. She may appear as an old, wizened woman with long grey hair and terrifying red eyes in a black or green dress. In other renditions, she appears as a headless woman, naked from the waist up, holding a bowl of blood to the victim. No matter which version you encounter, it is said that if you look directly at the banshee, she vanishes into a mist, the sound of birds' wings echoing through the night.

The banshee's appearance primarily has to do with her relationship with her family in her life, as well as the circumstances of her death. If she dies with loving relationships with her family, she appears to them as a beautiful woman, singing a sorrowful song of concern and love for the one she warns. If the relationship was hateful or abusive, she appears as a twisted, horrific being, her song sounding like a celebration for the impending death. If she were young when she'd been murdered, a banshee would show itself as a horrible, terrifying old woman with eyes the color of blood, filled with rage and hate. Her mouth never closes, always screaming a tormenting scream. The banshee who lived tormented lives come back vengefully, some even crossing the boundary from being a warning that death is nearby to becoming the cause of death itself. These are the banshee that actively seek victims, tormenting them with their horrible screaming and wailing until they either lose their sanity or kill themselves.

Caorthannach

The Caorthannach is thought by some to be the mother of the Devil himself. She was the beast that Saint Patrick chased away when he banished the snakes from Ireland. The stories tell that Saint Patrick stood atop the mountain Croagh to expel not only the snakes, but also the demons of Ireland to free the people. One managed to escape him: the Caorthannach. He chased the beast through the mountains on horseback, riding the fastest horse in Ireland.

The chase was long, and knowing that Saint Patrick would eventually need a drink of water, she continuously spit fire at him, while simultaneously poisoning every well she encountered. Saint Patrick was able to resist drinking from the poisoned wells, continuing his pursuit of the beast despite being desperate with thirst. He prayed for guidance, which led him to Hawk's Rock, where he hid, waiting for the beast. When she approached, he leapt from his hiding spot, banishing the Caorthannach with a single word. The fiery creature disappeared into the ocean and drowned, leaving behind the Hawk's Well.

Clurichaun

The clurichaun is a distant cousin to the leprechaun. Sometimes it's seen as the nighttime version of the leprechaun because of the clurichaun's excessive love of alcohol. If you were to spot one, it would likely be carrying a jug of ale in its hands, and due to their drunken state, they have a nasty temper. They also have the leprechaun's love of trickery and pranks, but their drunken demeanor can make them quite unpleasant in their games.

The clurichaun loves wine cellars and pubs, pretty much any area dedicated to alcohol. If you're on the clurichaun's good side, they are avid protectors of the home and wine cellar, the goods never spoiling. To be on the wrong side of a clurichaun means that everything from wine to food to milk will spoil without any explanation. Even moving house won't get rid of the clurichaun. They'll continue to harass until they've received adequate offerings and feel that they've been satisfied.

Dobhar-Chu

The dobhar-chu is the Irish equivalent to the Loch Ness monster. They're said to be half dog and half fish, making them quick in the water and capable on land. This creature is massive, roughly 7 feet long, with a similar shape to an alligator. They mate for life, traveling with their mate everywhere they go. If one is killed, it alerts its mate with a high-pitched death whistle, summoning its mate to avenge them from the depths of the water.

Dullahan

The Dullahan is in the Unseelie faery family, appearing to his victims as a headless man riding a black stallion. He wears long, flowing black robes, carrying his head beneath his arm. The head is described as having a broad, unsettling grin, stretching from ear to ear as its eyes constantly move, seeking out its next victim. No matter how dark it is, the eyes can see far and deep into the darkness.

While a banshee is the warning call of death, the Dullahan is death itself, stealing the souls of his victims by simply speaking their name; he only stops riding when it is time to take a soul. Even looking at the Dullahan is dangerous. If you're lucky, you'll simply be doused in a bucket of blood. If you're less fortunate, you'll be blinded in one eye by his whip.

Everything about the Dullahan is marked by death. His whip is made from a human spine, his wagon covering made from dried, worm-chewed human skin, the spokes of the wheels made from femur bones. To light the way forward, skulls lit by candles sit at the front of the wagon.

The only way to escape the Dullahan is by dropping a piece of gold in his path. No lock or gate will prevent him from getting to his victim, as they spring open in his presence. His inexplicable fear of gold is the only way to prevent him from speaking your name.

Fear Dearg

The fear dearg is another cousin of the leprechaun, but more mischievous and often taken as a sign of incoming bad luck. Fear dearg, meaning 'red man,' describes their choice in clothing, as they are typically depicted as clad in all red clothing, sometimes looking like a rat. They delight in practical jokes, but the jokes are rarely funny to humans, as they delight in replacing babies with changelings, and tend to lean towards the grotesque and unpleasant with their pranks. Some have also linked the presence of a fear dearg to an increase in nightmares.

Kelpie

Haunting Scottish shores is the kelpie. Sometimes appearing as a beautiful horse or elegant maiden, they use their beauty to seduce and attract their prey into the depths of the water, where they can kill and eat their victim. In the form of a horse, the kelpie wears a saddle and bridle, tempting a rider to get onto their back before they become stuck, and the kelpie dives deep under the water's surface.

The only escape from a kelpie is to gain control of its bridle. Being able to grasp onto the bridle gives the person command over the creature, and a captured kelpie is 10 times more powerful than any horse on land. Even the kelpie's bridle can impart its supernatural power to a regular horse.

Leprechaun

The leprechaun is the best known of Ireland's mythical creatures, sometimes being treated as a mascot for the country. Often they are associated with luck and wealth. Leprechauns are typically described as quite short, no more than 3 feet tall, and are mischievous and fun-loving little creatures. They're clever and quick moving, and will do everything they can to keep from being caught by a human. They love a good party, and are fantastic dancers and musicians.

Leprechauns are often looked at as the kinder cousins to the clurichaun. They enjoy a good drink, but unlike the clurichaun they're not so mean tempered. Some associate the small creatures to cobblers, said to help a cobbler if he is behind on his work. Despite being cobblers, they are also associated with great wealth; most of us have heard the legends of a leprechaun's pot of gold at the end of the rainbow. Their love of gold is odd, given that they don't need to spend their gold, but one path of logic suggests that they collect gold so that they can use the greed of humans against them, using the gold to cause mischief.

Merrow

The merrow is another water-based faery species and the Irish equivalent of the mermaid. While the males are hideous and mean, the females are ethereal and graceful, singing beautiful songs to summon their prey. These faery women from the Land Beneath the Waves are not known to be kind or compassionate to humans, treating mortals as mere toys and meals, mating with mortal men to satisfy themselves since their men are so horrendous to look at.

The merrow can assume a human form if she desires by removing a particular piece of clothing that allows her to swim through the deepest and coldest waters. To the north, it's said that the merrow wears a seal-skin cloak, but in the south it is a unique red cap made of feathers. The clothing is a merrow's weak point; if she takes it off and doesn't hide it well enough, it can be stolen from her and she can be forced into marriage with a mortal. Even if the merrow manages to fall in love with their human mate, finding their clothing leads them back into the water, often never to be seen again.

Puca

While most creatures of Celtic lore can definitively fall under the categories of 'good' or 'evil,' the puca was seen as both a good and bad omen, depending on it's mood. Even in appearance, the puca was a shapeshifter, sometimes appearing as a creature covered in white fur, other times being seen as a black creature. They might take the shape of various animals, ranging from farm beasts like horses and goats, or domesticated pets like dogs, cats, and rabbits. They sometimes took on a human form, but they could be found out easily, as the puca typically keep some animal features, like a tail. They are very capable in speaking to humans, but find it fun to twist the truth. The puca, like many other creatures of Celtic lore, delights in causing mischief, but they appear to have a soft spot for farmers, often doing what they can to help the farmer find financial success.

Selkie

A selkie isn't overly different from the merrow faery. When a selkie is in its watery habitat, it takes on the form of a seal. As a selkie comes onto the land, it sheds its seal skin, which needs to be hidden away well. For it to regain its seal shape, it must put back on its sealskin. Much like the merrow, should a mortal get ahold of the selkie's skin, they could control the creature.

A selkie tends to be more benevolent than its merrow counterparts. While a merrow seeks to kill, toy with, and eat its prey, a selkie is content with dancing in the moonlight, searching for love. The selkie maintains a 7-year cycle where it can walk on mortal shores unless, of course, someone manages to steal their seal skin. Selkie women are said to be incredible wives and mothers, as long as they never find their skin. They will still long for the sea, but they love their husbands and children dearly. Should the selkie find her skin, she returns immediately to the water, never to see her husband again. If she has children, she can sometimes be found playing with them in the waves or watching them from afar. If she chooses to remain with her mortal family, typically by destroying her seal skin, she is forbidden from returning to the sea, just as she's banned from the human realm if she puts her skin back on.

CHAPTER 5

The Mythological Cycle

The first of the mythical cycles we encounter in the creation of the Celtic belief system is the Mythological Cycle. While most belief systems feature a creation of the world story, such as the Book of Genesis in the Christian Bible or the giant Ymir in Norse mythology, the Celtic mythology instead focuses on how the people of Ireland are 'the people who have come from far away.' The Mythological Cycle features a series of invasions of the island of Ireland, by those ranging from traditional humans, like Cesaire and Parthalon, to the otherworldly gods of the Tuatha dé Danann and demonic beings of the Fomorians.

The Book of Invasions

Cesaire

The first person to walk the land of Ireland was Cesaire, the granddaughter of Noah, so right away we see how Celtic mythology and Christianity intermix. Her father had been forbidden to get onto the ark, but luckily, Cesaire was skilled and had a plan. She built three arks of her own, each one with 50 women. She told her father, Bith, that if he agreed to forsake the God of Noah, that he would have a place on her boats. Aside from the women, the only men she brought were her father, her husband, her brother, and Ladra the pilot.

As the flood happened, Cesaire travelled the world in search of Inis Fail or 'the land of destiny,' later known as Ireland. Along their travels, two of the three ships were lost. Finally, they saw Ireland, docking their ships in Kerry. Cesaire, as the leader, was the first to walk on what is now considered Ireland. Her husband, Fintan Mac Bochra, was the first man. The rest of the crew landed safely, except for Ladra who had wounded his thigh on his oar. With so few people and the need to populate the island, the three men divided the 50 women among them. Bith took 16, as he was aging, while Fintan and Ladra took on 17 each.

Bith became the first death in Ireland; his 16 women were then divided between the remaining two men. Soon Ladra succumbed to the wound on his thigh, and Fintan became the sole man on the island to help the 50 women repopulate. Fintan, overwhelmed with the responsibility imparted upon him, fled to the hills to hide. Cesaire was deeply in love with Fintan, and to watch him with 50 other women tortured her, and after Fintan fled, she died on the island of a broken heart. Fintan hid in the caves of a high mountain, and as he hid the great flood came, killing all the women but one. Banba was a great warrior woman, and seeing the flood, she'd ventured high into the mountains to survive.

Fintan had hidden deep in his cave, and as the waters rose, he dreamed that he was a salmon. When he woke, he found the waters had flooded his cave, but he'd taken the form of a salmon. He swam through Ireland for 300 years until the waters finally receded. He went to sleep as a salmon, dreaming that he was a hawk, and when he woke, he was indeed a hawk, flying above the island, seeing all that happened. He lived as every animal on the island of Ireland, providing counsel to many of the men who made their way to Ireland over the centuries. Fintan became the great sage of Ireland, having collected knowledge for hundreds of years as various animals of Ireland.

Fintan and the Manor of Tara

The High King of Tara was in charge of setting a feast for all of his people every 3 years. The feast would run for 7 days and 7 nights, and had become a beloved tradition. King Diarmait became concerned by the cost of the feast, and looked out into the green land, wondering how he might put it to use for the sake of a profit.

His guests arrived for the feast, each receiving a portion of the feast. The High King mentioned his concerns, and that he might repurpose the manor of Tara, causing his people great concern. Each refused to eat until the matter was settled. Unsure of how to handle this type of decision alone, King Diarmait sent for Fiachra, the wisest man that he'd ever met. Fiachra refused to answer the question, calling for a man even wiser than he. He sent for Cennfaelad, but he too wouldn't answer. He called his five elders, the five oldest and wisest people in all of Ireland. When they arrived, they refused to answer unless their own senior agreed that it was right. And so, they sent for Fintan Mac Bochra.

When Fintan arrived, the people all rejoiced. They offered him the judge's seat, but he wouldn't take it until he knew the question. Instead, the people asked him for stories of invasions and battles, and he happily told them stories hundreds of years old. Finally, King Diarmait asked him what he should do with the Manor of Tara, and if it would be right to partition it for more profitable use. In answer, Fintan told him a story of a great giant visiting an old king. The giant had helped to divide Ireland into five provinces, declaring the island to remain the way it had been arranged.

Fintan and the Hawk of Achill

Fintan Mac Bochra had lived for over 5,000 years as all the animals of Ireland. One day, he met a hawk flying from the island of Achill. It was old, and commented on how withered Fintan looked. Fintan told the hawk that for all the children he had fathered, his favorite son had recently died. He wondered how he was still alive despite his broken heart. The hawk said he knew of Fintan, and had lived as long as he had, but stayed on Achill Island. He asked Fintan to tell him of all the things he'd seen in his lifetime, whether of greatness or evil.

So, Fintan told him of all the first deaths of Ireland, the great flood, and turning into a salmon. He told him of freezing in the river of Earne, how he tried to jump over a great waterfall and was plucked from the water by a hawk that claimed one of his eyes. The hawk admitted that it was he who had taken Fintan's eye. Fintan demanded compensation for the lost eye, but the hawk said he'd rather take Fintan's other eye if it would provide a meal. Fintan told him he was a harsh beast, but he was gentle, so they may as well continue to talk.

Fintan told the hawk of the first battle of Moytura, siding with the Fir Bolg in battle. The hawk remembered the battle, telling him he'd witnessed the death of Fintan's 12 sons, and had taken an eye, hand, or foot from each of them out of respect for Fintan. He told Fintan of the giant arm he'd gotten that day, the severed arm of Nuada, which fed his family for 7 years. Fintan returned with a story of the great giant Trefuilngidh, who provided him with the seeds to plant all over Ireland.

The hawk then returned with a story of Connor Mac Nessa, and the warriors of the Red Branch, who had provided him with many years of sustenance. He told of the warrior Cuchulainn, who had provided him many a meal, and that when he found Cuchulainn tied to a stone dying, how he'd try to take his eyes. Cuchulainn still had too much life to him, and speared the hawk through the breast; he'd barely made it home to Achill alive.

They exchanged many stories of the kings they'd witnessed and the battles that fed them. Finally, the hawk told Fintan that he knew that tomorrow he'd die, and was concerned for what lay beyond life for him. Fintan assured the hawk that he would fly in the clouds of the heavens, and that he would meet Death *with* the hawk to assure he didn't go to any form of hell. Together, they spent the night trading stories, and when morning came, they died together.

Parthalon

Parthalon was a giant Greek man who was heavily involved in war. He committed an atrocity—killing some of his family—and as such he'd been cursed. Nothing he ever endeavored to achieve would be successful. In his best effort, Parthalon gathered his wife and three sons, as well as all of their remaining family, and ran to Ireland, hoping to outrun his curse. When they arrived, there was a single plain that was habitable, the area that is now Dublin. They travelled all over the island, creating three more plains. When they reached what is now Donegal, they encountered the Fomorians, fearsome, magical pirates who had come from the Island of Tory (some legend says they were descendents of Fintan and Banba).

It took no time for Parthalon's people to realize there would be no harmonious living with the Fomorians. They engaged in a magical battle, standing on one leg, with one arm behind their backs, and one eye closed. This was how they would access the power of the Otherworld, and after a long battle, Parthalon's people won the battle.

Parthalon's people went to work establishing themselves on the island. Fintan Mac Bochra appeared to them, becoming an advisor to them, as nobody knew the island like he did. For a short while, the people were prosperous on the island. One day, Parthalon left for a hunt, leaving his wife and servant alone together. While he was gone, they lay together, then shared a drink between them from Parthalon's cup. When he returned, he could taste the two of them on the cup, and in a fit of rage he murdered the servant. The family lived together for another 30 years, before Parthalon was claimed by a plague. Parthalon's people lived on the island for 500 years, their populations reaching thousands of people, until another plague arrived, wiping them all out within a single week.

Nemed and the Fir Bolg

The next leader of Ireland was Nemed. When he arrived on the shores, he came with 30 ships, each manned by 60 people. When they arrived, they had to battle the Fomorians. When Nemed's people won the battle, the land accepted them, and the Nemedians were able to convince the Fomorians to build them a great fortress. The fortress was so magnificent that the Nemedians killed the craftsmen so that they could never again replicate the beauty of the fortress.

A great plague swept over Ireland, killing Nemed. The Fomorians took their opportunity, seizing control over the Nemedian people. They taxed them heavily, demanding two-thirds of all of the Nemedian children as sacrifices every 7 years. Conditions became so bad that the Nemedians rebelled against the Fomorians, seizing their home island of Tory. Being sea pirates with a magical connection to the sea, the Fomorians sought revenge by having the ocean flood the island. Thirty of the Nemedians managed to escape the flood, while the remainder perished. The 30 Nemedians scattered: some to Scotland, some to the North, and others to Greece.

After many years, the Nemedians of Greece returned to Ireland. They were treated terribly in Greece, oppressed and enslaved, and became known as the Fir Bolg. When they returned to Ireland, they again had to battle the Fomorians, again winning the land and becoming the rulers. They divided the island into five provinces. The one in the center became known as Uisneach, where the people of the remaining four provinces could come to settle their disputes on land that belonged to all. But even though they were sensible, good, and hard working, the reign of the Fir Bolg only lasted for 37 years.

Battles of Moytura

First Battle of Moytura

On the day marking the 37th year of ruling by the Fir Bolg, a great and heavy mist descended over the island, lasting for 3 days and 3 nights. With it came boats carrying the Tuatha dé Danann. They had descended from the Nemedians, who had traveled North when escaping the Fomorians. They'd lived and traveled through the four great cities of magic and science: Falias, Findias, Gorias, and Murias. Learning all they could, the Tuatha dé Danann returned to Ireland to reclaim their birthright, at the instruction of their goddess, Danu.

The Tuatha dé Danann brought four magical treasures with them. First was the cauldron of Dagda, which could feed as many as were seated before it. It would remain full, even after the last person with a full belly left it. The second treasure was a sword whose blade would never dull, no matter how many battles it was brought into, and no matter what it struck. The third was the spear that would never miss its intended target. The fourth and final treasure was the Lia Fail, the stone of destiny, which would sing when the rightful King sat upon it.

Among the Tuatha dé Danann were many great and mythical beings: the Mórrígan, who was the Goddess of War; Daghda, who knew no sense of entitlement and was the most generous being to walk the earth; Aengus Og, the God of Love and Happiness; as well as

Danu, who walked with her people as a Mother Goddess. They brought many others with them.

The Fir Bolg watched, completely astonished, as these tall, beautiful beings walked through the mists and onto the Irish shores. To their dismay, they watched as the Tuatha dé Danann set fire to their ships, letting the Fir Bolg know that they were here to stay. A bright and magical fortress sprang up from the mist overnight, and in their amazement, the Fir Bolg came near to examine it. A group of Tuatha dé Danann came out to greet them, introducing themselves and making pleasantries. As a show of friendship and kindness, they exchanged weapons; the weapons of the Tuatha dé Danann were light, sharp, and bright, whereas the weapons of the Fir Bolg were heavy, unwieldy, and blunted from use. The Tuatha dé Danann suggested to the Fir Bolg that the island be divided equally between themselves and the Fir Bolg, seeing no point in fighting over it, The Fir Bolg told them that they would need the night to think and consult with one another.

That night, the Fir Bolg met to talk about the offer the Tuatha dé Danann had made. After all they had overcome, and for how hard they'd fought for their land, they had no desire to allow someone else to come along and simply take half of the land they'd earned. They came to the conclusion that they would fight for the land.

The first day of battle happened on the Plains of Moytura. Despite their vigor in battle, the Fir Bolg suffered massive casualties. When the fighting was done, the Tuatha dé Danann again made their offer to the Fir Bolg to split the land in half. The Fir Bolg were ever stubborn, refusing the offer, going to battle again the next day. This time, they found a moment of victory, cutting the arm off of King Nuada. Because he could no longer be considered perfect and whole, the Tuatha dé Danann were left without a leader, but on the third day they came together all the same, defeating the Fir Bolg in battle.

Despite their clear victory, the Tuatha dé Danann extended a hand of friendship, allowing the Fir Bolg to claim one province as their own. They chose the province of Connaught and the Tuatha dé Danann claimed the rest of Ireland.

Cian and Eithne

Even after the Tuatha dé Danann defeated the Fir Bolg, they still had to contend with the Fomorians. Among the Fomorians was a man named Balor, the most powerful man among them. As a young child, he'd passed a house, hearing the chanting of the Druids inside. Even though he knew that one should never look in on Druids in the midst of casting their spells, he couldn't resist, seeing the window cracked open a bit. He peeked in, and as he did so a plume of smoke darted free from their cauldron and hit him directly in the eye. He let out a shout and the Druids ran out. They had been working with death spells, and seeing his eye, they knew he could now kill anyone he looked at. From that day forward, Balor kept his eye closed. Once he walked onto the battlefield, he'd simply open his eye and look at his enemy, causing them to drop dead before him.

As the years passed and Balor aged, the eyelid over his evil eye grew heavier, drooping to cover the eye. It came to the point where the Fomorians had to construct an iron ring with ropes and pulleys so that it took 10 men to lift the eyelid open, and 10 more to prod the eye into position with lances and spears!

Balor had been given a prophecy that he would die at the hand of his grandchild. Given that he had none, he didn't fear death, making him a menace on the battlefield. He eventually had one child, a daughter named Eithne. Despite her beauty, he locked her away in a glass tower so that he would never have to fear death. He placed 12 women in the tower with her as her handmaidens, but they were sworn to never speak of a man, as she was forbidden to ever know what a man was. As Eithne grew, she would sit atop her tower, watching as boats came and went, seeing creatures on them that she'd never seen before. She would ask her handmaidens about them, but they stayed silent. At night, she would dream the same dream of a beautiful face with features unlike herself and her handmaidens. Eithne described the face to her handmaidens, but they maintained their silence, knowing that she was describing the face of a man.

At this point, there was a man of the Tuatha dé Danann named Cian, who was one of the many lords. He possessed a treasure that Balor was desperate to own: a cow he called Glas Gaibheann that would never dry, no matter how much it was milked. The cow was so precious that Cian brought it with him everywhere attached to a leash, knowing well that many would try to steal her from him.

One day, Cian met with his brother Samthain, intending to visit their brother Goibniu, who was a smith, so that they could have new swords made. Cian left Samthain to guard his cow, going inside to see his brother. Balor saw he finally had a chance, and disguised himself as a red-haired child. He asked Samthain if he was having a sword made today, and he replied yes, he had already brought in the steel to his brother. Balor replied that he'd overheard the brothers inside talking about how they now had two magnificent swords, but there would be no more for a third. In a rage, Samthain threw the leash at the child, charging into the workshop to confront his brothers. As soon as Cian saw his brother come through the doors, he knew that he'd been tricked, and ran out. It was too late, and Balor was already gone with the precious cow.

Cian went to a Druid, determined to get his cow back. The Druid told him that there was no way to retrieve the cow while Balor was still alive. Frustrated, Cian visited another Druid, Birog of the Mountain, who was the wisest of all Druids. She knew of the prophecy against Balor, and told Cian that, while what the other Druid had said was true, there was another path he could take, as long as he helped her. Cian agreed, and with that, Birog transformed Cian into a woman.

Birog summoned a magic gust of wind, dropping her and Cian at the base of Eithne's glass tower. Birog shouted to the women that she had a Tuatha Queen who required shelter. Eithne directed the women to let her in immediately. Once Birog and Cian were inside, Birog cast a sleep spell on the 12 women, removing the disguise from Cian, sending him up to Eithne. As he reached the top of the stairs, he laid eyes on Eithne, falling in love with her sadness and beauty. When she turned, she fell in love, recognizing the face she'd spent her life dreaming of. They made love in the tower then and there. Cian begged Birog to bring Eithne with them to Ireland, but she refused, terrified of what Balor would do. She called up another magic wind, whisking her and Cian away, leaving Eithne behind in the tower.

Eithne grieved her lost lover, but was filled with delight to find out that she was with child. She gave birth to a baby boy, fastening a cloak around the baby with a pin. Balor took the child, throwing him into the waves, intending to kill him, but the pin came loose, and the child rolled into the waters. While the Fomorians thought the child dead, Birog had been watching, gathering the baby from the water and giving him to his father. Cian was overjoyed to see the child, naming his Lugh, and raising him with every advantage so that he would go on to fulfill the prophecy, eventually slaying Balor.

The Daghda's Harp

The Daghda possessed many beautiful possessions, but of the many, his most prized was his harp. He would play the harp to summon the changing of the seasons and to encourage his people to be fearless in battle. He would play it again after the battle to ease the grief of fallen friends. The Fomorians thought to themselves that stealing the harp would deal a heavy blow to the Tuatha dé Danann. They waited until Daghda was in battle, his home left unsupervised, so that they could break in and steal the harp. The Fomorians who stole the harp ran as far as they could with their families, hoping that it would help their people win. However, before long the Fomorians arrived, having been defeated, taking solace in the fact that they'd taken something precious from the Tuatha dé Danann.

Upon returning from their victory, the Tuatha called for Daghda to play his harp to celebrate their victory. Even after a hard battle, when Daghda found his harp missing he leapt up, calling to his people to help him retrieve it. Lugh of the Long Arm and Ogma the Artificer stood immediately, ready to dive back into Fomorian territory. They traveled far searching for the harp, when they found the encampment where the Fomorians were staying, and saw through the open window where the harp was hung on the wall. Peering through the window, Ogma saw the masses of Fomorians lying asleep, but still vastly outnumbering the three of them. He wondered out loud to his companions how they would retrieve the harp but before he could start to consider a plan, Daghda held out his arms, calling his harp to come to him. It sprang from the wall, flying to his open hands.

The sound woke the Fomorians, and seeing their foes outside, they sprang from their beds and drew their weapons. Lugh suggested to Daghda that it was likely a good time to play his harp. Daghda, with his harp in hand, played the Music of Mirth, and despite their rage, the Fomorians began to laugh. Their weapons fell to the floor, and the Fomorians began to dance. Daghda stopped playing, and the Fomorians gathered their weapons again to advance on the three men. Ogma told Daghda to play again, and this time, he played the Music of Grief. The Fomorians broke into deep sobs, but once again, when Daghda stopped playing, they drew their weapons again, preparing to advance. Daghda played his harp so softly that it could almost seem that there was no music being played. He played the Music of Sleep, and the Fomorians fell into a deep, restful sleep, and the three men of Tuatha dé Danann quickly escaped into the night. The harp of Daghda was never again stolen from him.

Second Battle of Moytura

After the first battle of Moytura, the Tuatha dé Danann had suffered a great blow; their king, King Nuada, had lost his arm, making him unable to continue on as king, despite the physician, Dian Cecht, making him a new arm of silver. This left the throne empty, the people without a leader. Deciding on a new king, the Tuatha dé Danann chose Breas, a strong and capable warrior of dual lineage: one of his parents was of the Fomorians, the other of the Tuatha. They chose Breas in hopes of bridging the gap between the two groups, potentially uniting them.

Unfortunately, Breas was not a good king to the people. He imposed heavy taxes, treating the people like slaves, even allowing the Fomorians to impose their own taxation on the Tuatha. He did all he could to oppress them, but the worst of his crimes in their eyes was how unbelievably cruel he could be. When a traveling bard arrived, he had expected hospitality. Instead, he was given a cold room, left alone with no fire, and given mere scraps to eat while he sat. This led the bard to compose Ireland's first piece of satire, all about the mean king of the Tuatha dé Danann. The people were so disgusted by Breas' representation of them as their king that they rose up, dethroning Breas. From that point forward, all kings of Ireland were very careful to respect the bards who visited them.

Upset by his loss of power, Breas ran to the Fomorian people, asking for an army so that he could reclaim his seat as king. At the head of the army was Balor, with his evil eye. Although he was very old and required the help of several men to lift the drooping lid of the eye and direct it, he was their best chance at being victorious However, they were not aware of the prophecy of Balor being killed by his grandson. He was also not aware that his grandson, Lugh, would be one of the great warriors of the Tuatha dé Danann people.

Hearing that the Fomorians were gathering an army, the Tuatha dé Danann began to organize themselves for battle. Lugh traveled to the army in Tara, in hopes of joining their forces. The guard at the door was under strict orders to not let through any stranger, in case it may be a Fomorian spy. The only way in was if the man possessed skills that might be useful to them in battle. When Lugh arrived at the door, he knocked. The gatekeeper asked him what skills he possessed. Lugh told him first that he was a magician, and was told that they already had magicians. So, he told the gatekeeper that he was a cook, but again, they already had a cook. Finally, he told the gatekeeper he was a smith. Again, he was refused; they already had a smith. He went on and on with the gatekeeper, listing his skills and being refused. Frustrated, he told the keeper to go ask if there was any one man in their battalion who could do all the things that he could, and finally, he was let in.

One of the strongest warriors of the Tuatha dé Danann decided that he needed to know what Lugh could do, challenging his strength. He gathered up a flagstone larger than 10 men with one hand, holding it high in the air, and carried it to the next hill over. Lugh walked quietly to the hill, lifted the same flagstone, and threw it back to where it had been to begin with. Proving his strength without having a confrontation with the man was how he gained the approval of the Tuatha. Lugh continued to entertain the people, performing all types of feats while showing off his marvelous skills. The people were so pleased, Lugh was named a leader of an army, which proved wise.

Daghda went on his own way to help secure victory. First, he visited the Mórrígan, the Goddess of War. Seeing him arrive and knowing his reputation for seducing women, the Mórrígan stood with one leg on either side of the river, doing her best to prevent Daghda from swaying her. Nonetheless, Dagdha was still so effective in his seduction that she gave in to him, and after they'd had a good romp, she agreed that she would join him in battle.

Next, Daghda attempted to visit the Fomorians, hoping to mediate the situation so that there wouldn't be a fight at all. Instead, they played pranks on Daghda, filling a large hole with meat, porridge, and other assortments of things, telling him to eat it. He brought out his giant spoon, emptying the contents of the hole, even scraping up some of the dirt. His belly was so heavy that it would drag on the ground, and so he left, upset that they could ridicule and abandon hospitality in such a way. As he made his way back to the Tuatha dé Danann, Daghda encountered a beautiful Fomorian woman, but she ridiculed his giant belly dragging behind him. He left, throwing up the contents of his belly, then returned to her and succeeded in seducing her. He pleased her so well that she chose to join him in supporting the Tuatha dé Danann in battle.

By the next day, the Tuatha dé Danann were fully prepared for battle. The Fomorians arrived, Balor standing at the head of the army. As his men began to haul back the lid of his evil eye, Lugh placed a stone in his sling and fired it at Balor. It hit him in his evil eye so hard that it rolled back to look at the Fomorian army, turning all of the warriors to stone, and securing victory for the Tuatha dé Danann.

After defeating the Fomorians, the Tuatha still had to decide who would be their new king. After the first battle, their original king, Nuada, had been dethroned by losing his arm. The physician, Dian Cecht, had created him a prosthetic, but his son, Miach, was an even better physician, restoring the arm he'd lost to health, then reattaching it so that Nuada was once again whole, and could reclaim the throne. At this, Dian Cecht flew into a murderous rage, killing his Miach. His daughter, Airmed, was so heartbroken that she kneeled over her brother's grave, and for each tear that fell, another healing herb would spring up from her brother's grave. The plants whispered their secrets to her, and Airmed, organized the herbs over her cloak so that she could track the purposes of the various plants. Seeing this, Dian Cecht was again overcome by jealousy, tossing the herbs from the cloak, sending them to every corner of the earth. This is why nobody could know the healing purposes of every plant.

Amairghin and the Sons of Mil

During the rule of the Tuatha dé Danann, Ireland was a prosperous and bountiful land. After many generations of kings, a High King died without choosing his heir, leaving his three sons to choose among themselves who would be the new king. They fought over it, nearly causing a civil war among the people of the island.

An old man named Ith came to Ireland, after having seen it from a tall tower in Spain and wanting to know of the island, because his people had constantly said he was just seeing clouds in the distance or simply a mirage. Ith gathered some men onto his boat, setting sail for the island he was sure he was seeing. When he arrived on Irish shores, he was struck by the beauty, but encountered the three brothers fighting and arguing about how to divide the land among themselves. Because he was an ancient man, they decided to ask Ith what to do with the land. He advised that they follow the laws that were set before them. After all, look at the beautiful land that had resulted. He praised the island so much that the three men became certain that he would attempt to conquer the land for himself, so without any threat, they killed him, sending the remainder of his men back to Spain to report his death.

When Ith's son, Mil of Ith, heard of his murder, he and his three sons resolved to go to Ireland and seek vengeance for the death. While Mil died on the journey to the island, his three sons made it to the shore. The one son, Amairghin, was a Druid, and sang songs to announce his arrival to the Tuatha dé Danann. He and his brothers went to the three kings, announcing to them their intention to seek vengeance, and the kings requested 3 days to make their choice; they needed to choose if they would abandon the island or fight for it. Amairghin agreed, and they boarded their ships, staying nine waves away from the island. The Druids of the Tuatha dé Danann were not so virtuous, stirring up a magical sea storm, hoping to rid themselves of the ships.

As the storm advanced on the ships, Amairghin was sure it was not natural. He sent a man up the mast to see if the storm came from above. While the man fell to his death, he managed to call out to Amairghin that the skies were calm above the storm. Amairghin, a Druid as well, countered the storm with his own songs, settling the storm. When the Milesians made landfall, they made their way to the Plains of Tailtiu, meeting the triple goddess Eriu and her sisters Banba and Fodla on their way. The goddess asked that the Milesians name the island after her, and she would help them win. The Milesians agreed, setting off to battle.

When the battle happened, the Milesians successfully slaughtered the three kings, taking many casualties with them. The Tuatha dé Danann couldn't recover from the sheer number of losses, retreating into the hills and taking their magic with them, rather than submitting to their conquerors. They lived the remainder of their lives peacefully in the faery mounds and hills of Ireland, while the Milesians became the final legendary 'people from away' to conquer and settle the island.

CHAPTER 6

The Ulster Cycle

The Ulster Cycle brings us away from the magic of the Tuatha dé Danann and into the tragic hero story centered around Cuchulainn. As an incredible and prominent warrior, Cuchulainn knew that his life would be cut short, but he knew greatness was promised to him in the end. The epic Irish warrior image finds some of its roots in these stories, from the conception, to the growth and adventuring of the warrior, all the way to the heroic death. Cuchulainn represents the undying spirit and warrior spirit of the fighting Irish.

Not only do we see the stories of Cuchulainn, but the stories that make and break these legends. The Ulster Cycle is the home of Macha, who is the namesake of Emain Macha, what is current known as the Navan Fort in modern times, as well as the story of Deidre of the Sorrows, who would result in the ultimate undoing of one of the greatest mythological groups of warriors in the Celtic Cycle mythologies.

The Birth of Cuchulainn

The story starts with his grandmother, Nessa. Once a gentle, pleasant woman, a group of raiders killing her family changed her entire life path. All softness was replaced with a taste for vengeance. Nessa became a powerful warrior, hunting down those who had torn her family from her. Coming into the court of Ulster, the King of Ulster, King Fergus Mac Roich, fell deeply in love with this powerful maiden. He requested her hand in marriage, to which she agreed, but with a catch: her son, Connor, (sometimes also called Conchobar) must be allowed to take the throne for a single year.

The King gathered his people, and it was agreed that the young man would take the throne; after all, the people knew who their true king was. Over the course of the year, Nessa guided Connor to become a great king, so much so that when the year was over and Fergus came back to reclaim his throne, the people objected to him, claiming that King Connor was a far better king than he. Fergus stepped aside, becoming a loyal retainer to the young king.

Nessa's daughter, Deichtre, was just as remarkable and powerful as her brother. It was decided, with Deichtre agreeing, that she should take a husband, and that she would marry Fergus's brother, Sulatim Mac Roich. The day of the wedding, Deichtre sat with her 50 handmaidens. When Sulatim came to fetch his bride, he made a horrible discovery: the bride-to-be had vanished without a trace, along with her 50 handmaidens. No matter how they searched, she could not be found. Little did the unfortunate bridegroom know, his bride-to-be decided that she needed a final grand adventure before settling into married life!

Deichtre vanished into the Otherworld with her handmaidens, who kept her company and tended to her needs. On a sunny afternoon, Deichtre sat on her balcony, enjoying a glass of wine when a mayfly flew into her cup. She unknowingly swallowed the fly and in that moment, a shining beautiful man appeared before her, introducing himself as Lugh of the Long Arm. He informed her that because she had swallowed the mayfly she would bear him a son. He offered that she stay in the Otherworld with him; because he was such a gorgeous man, Deichtre happily agreed.

Back in Emain Macha, the search for Deichtre continued for a full year, until finally, they held a feast to commemorate the year since the search had begun. As the feast began, a flock of 50 beautiful birds chained in pairs descended. They ate every last morsel of food, right down to every blade of grass. King Connor chased the birds with Fergus and nine of the warriors of the Red Branch, fearing the birds would eat Ulster into a famine. No matter how they tried to head them off, the birds couldn't be caught. After chasing them all over Ireland, they arrived in a strange land that none of them recognized.

Trying to find a place to stay, all that could be found was an ugly, decrepit hut. The man who owned the hut told Fergus that he would happily house the king and his companions. When Fergus returned to the group, a warrior named Bricriu the Bitter Tongue scoffed. A hut was no place for a king to stay! Fergus welcomed Bricriu to find something better. Bricriu took the challenge, searching high and low but finding nothing. He returned to the place Fergus had described, finding not a hut, but a glorious palace, seven pillars holding up a golden thatch roof, firelight glowing from around the door. Instead of being greeted by an old man, there was a beautiful shining man and the woman of the house, who greeted him by name.

After some discussion, Fergus came to realize that he was looking at Deichtre. She gave Bricriu a purple cloak to bring back to her brother. Bricriu rushed back to the party, but because he had a touch of mischief to him, he decided it would be far more amusing not to tell anyone that Deichtre had been found. His amusement grew as Fergus reminded King Connor that it was custom for the homeowner to show fealty to the king, as he was a king in a foreign land. It was also customary for the woman of the house to lay with the king that night.

Returning to the palace, the shining man informed the king that his wife had fallen to the pains of childbirth, and would not be available, but there were 50 beautiful handmaidens to choose from. The men feasted and drank late into the night, falling into the finest of beds with the women. When they woke, they were lying on a cold hillside. King Connor was surprised to find a woman lying in his cloak with him, holding onto a newborn. It was Deichtre, introducing him to his nephew.

She explained her time in the Otherworld, and how she'd decided that she wanted to raise her son in Ulster. Deichtre had sent her handmaidens as swans to antagonize the men into following the birds, rescuing her from the Otherworld. After a great debate over who would foster the incredible young man, it was agreed that Deichtre would raise the young boy with her husband, Sulatim, in Muirtheimhne until he was a suitable age, then would be brought to Emain Macha to be raised and taught by each of the great men.

Setanta Joins the Boy's Troop

Back in Ireland, Deichtre named her son Setanta. He was strong and clever, being educated in all things that would benefit the son of a warrior. Overhearing his mother talking about his uncle's day, Setanta learned of the Boy's Troop. He demanded more information, obsessed with the idea of the troop. She explained to him that King Connor had organized the Boy's Troop for the sons of the warriors of the Red Branch to learn how to battle, strategize, and become the absolute best warriors they could become. Setanta demanded to join, since Sulatim was a warrior of the Red Branch. Deichtre refused, telling him he was too young.

Setanta ran away to Emain Macha, finding the Boy's Troop. The group of 150 boys was playing hurling. Without a second thought, Setanta joined the game, taking the ball and scoring with no contest. The boys, unimpressed that a strange boy had interrupted and ruined their game, circled Setanta, attacking him. The commotion caught the king's attention, and he broke up the fight, recognizing Setanta. King Connor chastised Setanta, telling him he should have introduced himself to the boys, then ask for their protection. The troop would be honor-bound to never attack him. He did so, and was accepted by the troop. He then began to beat the boys, toppling each of them. When King Connor stopped him, asking what he was doing, Setanta stated that although he asked for their protection, it seemed it was *they* who needed protection from *him*. Each boy then introduced themselves, asking his protection. He accepted each of them, thus becoming the youngest boy to ever join the Boy's Troop.

Origin of Cuchulainn's Name

A year after Setanta joined the Boy's Troop, King Connor was called to the home of a great and talented smith. Before starting out, King Connor stopped to watch the boys playing their game. Game after game, Setanta could not be toppled or beaten. Impressed, King Connor asked Setanta to join him to visit Cullan the smith. Setanta complained that he was not done with his games, but he could follow the king's chariot tracks to the home of the smith after.

When the king arrived at the smith's home, he was welcomed to a lavish feast. Before they began, the smith asked the king if they were expecting anyone else, so that he would release his guard hound. He explained that he was not rich and only had a small piece of land, and everything on that patch of land represented his livelihood. This hound, almost the size of a pony, had been trained since he was a puppy to only recognize Cullan, and tear apart any intruder. Forgetting about inviting Setanta, the king told Cullan to release his hound so they could begin their feast.

Setanta finished his games, making his way to the smith's home with his ball and hurley. As he neared, he was spotted by the hound. The dog released a giant roar. The men in the house froze, the king remembering his invitation to Setanta. The men rushed out, expecting to find the dog standing over the boy's mangled body. Instead, they found that Setanta had kicked his ball down the hound's throat, grabbed him by the hind legs, and smashed the dog's skull open on a rock.

While the king and his companions rejoiced that the boy had survived the beast, Cullan broke down at the loss of his dear hound. The dog had been all that protected his livelihood; he could now lose everything. Because Setanta had killed the dog and felt guilty, he said he would become the guard of the land while Cullan trained a new hound. Every night, he would come to the smith's home, lay on the front step, and sleep with one eye open to protect the property.

The king's Druid, Cathbad, told Setanta that his new name would be Cuchulainn, meaning "Cullan's hound." Setanta protested, saying he liked his original name. Cathbad told him that he had prophesied that one day the name Cuchulainn would be spoken and remembered by all men. Setanta agreed to the name change, and spent the next year guarding Cullan's property.

Cuchulainn: Taking up Arms

A year after Cuchulainn killed the smith's dog, he was in lessons with the Boy's Troop. He attended a lesson with Cathbad, covering prophecy and poetry. The Druid taught them to read thrown sticks or rods as prognostication. Upon throwing the sticks, he read that today would be a fateful day: any boy who took up arms on that day would live a short but glorious life. Though the man would die young, his name would live on forever and his glory would never be matched. Many of the boys, despite being nearly of age to take up arms, took Cathbad's words as a warning. Glory and fame was not worth the early death.

Cuchulainn instead sprinted to his uncle, demanding a set of arms from the king. King Connor refused at first because of the boy's young age. Cuchulainn spoke in half truth, telling him that Cathbad had been the one who had suggested the idea, omitting the early death indicated in the prophecy. Hearing that the Druid had given his blessing, the king brought Cuchulainn the first set of arms. Cuchulainn tested the weapons, but shattered them. The King brought out multiple sets of arms, each shattering under Cuchulainn's strength. Finally, King Connor gave Cuchulainn his own set of arms, which finally withstood the boy's strength.

Cathbad entered, horrified at what he was seeing. King Connor stood confused, as the boy had the Druid's blessing. The Druid explained the extent of the prophecy, that it was a warning and not a blessing. Despite King Connor's fury with the young man, it was too late. The King decided that if the boy was to take up arms, it would be wisest to arm his nephew with all the best, giving him his own chariot and charioteer, Ibar, hoping that Ibar would keep Cuchulainn out of trouble and maybe make him more cautious.

As per custom, Cuchulainn and Ibar set out to leave Emain Macha. They passed by the Boy's Troop, who saluted the new warrior as Cuchulainn showed off his new arms and chariot. From there, they went to visit Cuchulainn's foster brother, Conal Cearnach, who was guarding a pass outside Ulster. Conal was stunned to see his foster brother in his kingly arms and chariot. Cuchulainn announced his intentions to draw his first blood and establish himself as a warrior. At that, Conal said he would escort Cuchulainn outside the boundaries of Ulster, because if something happened to him, it would be on Conal's head. Knowing that Conal would never allow him to battle should the opportunity arise, shortly after leaving the pass Cuchulainn shot the shaft of Conal's chariot, breaking it in half and sending Conal sprawling and breaking his arm.

Despite Ibar's constant requests to turn back, they soon found themselves coming into the land of the Sons of Nechtain. These brothers were the most powerful and fearful warriors in the land, impossible to beat. They'd killed as many Ulstermen as lived today. The youngest, Fannall Mac Nechtain, was the most skilled swimmer in Ireland, fighting every battle in the water undefeated. The next, Tuachell Mac Nechtain, was the fastest warrior in Ireland. Opponents only had a single chance to kill him, or he would easily overtake and instantly kill them. The eldest, Foill Mac Nechtain, could not be pierced with any sword or blade.

Cuchulainn chose a field to rest in, Ibar watching over him. Sure enough, Foill arrived to investigate. Ibar tried to talk him out of fighting Cuchulainn, saying he was just a foolish young child, not a true warrior. Cuchulainn sprang to his feet, not to be persuaded out of the fight. Knowing that Foill could not be pierced by a blade, Cuchulainn gathered a large stone in his slingshot, sending the stone flying into the warrior's skull, bashing it open. The second brother, Tuachell, came out to see what the commotion was. Knowing his speed, Cuchulainn gathered King Connor's spear and hurled it at the warrior. The spear entered one side of the warrior's chest, exiting the other side and dropping the fearsome man. Finally, Fannall came out, challenging Cuchulainn to battle in the river. Cuchulainn agreed, successfully wrestling the man under the water, beheading the man with King Connor's sword.

Cuchulainn carried the head from the water, then gathered the heads of the other two brothers, hanging them from the rim of the chariot. They made their way back to Emain Macha, and in his battle fury, Cuchulainn ran down two stags, roping them to run behind his chariot. He knocked a flock of swans from the sky, tying them by the necks to the chariot to fly as though a white cloud of feathers and honks. The people of Emain Macha saw the chariot coming, the stags and swans announcing Cuchulainn's presence. They saw him standing proudly, the heads of the Sons of Nechtain swinging behind him. His battle fury was clear, and the people knew there was a choice to make. Either the men battle him, and lose their greatest warrior, or they could let him destroy the town.

The women of Emain Macha were the solution, hiking up their skirts over their heads, walking out half naked before him. When Cuchulainn shut his eyes, hiding his face. The people rushed him, forcing him into a vat of cold water. The first vat burst into steam, the second vat boiled instantly. They shoved him into the third vat, and the water only warmed as Cuchulainn finally calmed from his battle-frenzied state.

Cuchulainn: The Wooing of Emer

Cuchulainn had developed a great reputation as a warrior, as well as being a beautiful man. The people of Emain Macha had come to the conclusion that it was time for him to marry, so that the women and wives could stop fawning over him every time he went by, and more importantly, so that he could have a son who would inherit his many talents. The only problem was that Cuchulainn would not marry a woman who was not his equal.

There was a single woman who could interest him, named Emer. He and his best friend Laeg came to find her where she was teaching a class, and spoke to her in riddles and puns. Nobody around them could understand what they were speaking of, but she happily spoke back to him in kind. At one point, he peeked down the top of her shirt, commenting on how he was pleased by the sight. She presented him a challenge: that no man would experience the pleasures of her flesh unless he could leap three walls and kill three groups of nine men with a single blow, leaving just one of each group alive. Then he must slay 100 men at each ford between her home and Emain Macha.

Laeg, not understanding the conversation the pair had been having thought that things had not gone well, and tried to console his friend. Instead, Cuchulainn said that they'd been speaking in riddles, and that she had given him the tasks that would help him earn her hand in marriage.

Emer's father, Forgall, found out about the exchange, and flew into a rage that a madman from Ulster would try to court his daughter. He disguised himself as a trader from Gaul and visited King Connor. He spoke to the king, expressing shock that with the great warriors among his people, none had trained with Scathach, the warrior woman who trained on the island of Skye in Scotland.

Forgall's plan was to have the King send Cuchulainn on the long dangerous journey to Scathach, hoping it would kill the warrior. Even if Cuchulainn made it, Scathach's training was incredibly difficult and had often killed those she trained. She was also in the middle of a war with another warrior woman named Aoife, and they'd been claiming each other's students in their battle. Forgall's plan was that even if Cuchulainn survived, he'd be gone for years, giving Forgall years to safely marry off his daughter to Lugaid, the King of Munster.

While Cuchulainn was away, Forgall quickly arranged the marriage. When Emer met her bridegroom, she refused to marry him, proclaiming her love for Cuchulainn and that should Lugaid force her into marriage, Cuchulainn would surely seek vengeance. Despite her father's protests, Lugaid left without the bride.

Of course, as soon as Cuchulainn finished his training, he returned to Emer. Her father, still hoping to kill the warrior, built three walls, with one of his sons commanding each. This was no issue for Cuchulainn, who hopped the walls and took out eight of the nine warriors in a single strike, leaving Emer's brothers unscathed. Forgall, convinced that Cuchulainn would kill him, lept over the wall to his death in an attempt to escape. Cuchulainn gathered his bride-to-be and her weight in gold, easily scaling the walls once again. At each ford on their way back to Emain Macha, Cuchulainn had to stop, slaying 100 men at each one.

Cuchulainn: Training with Scathach

When Emer's father disguised himself as a merchant, suggesting training with Scathach, Cuchulainn jumped at the opportunity, never satisfied with his skills. Two other warriors, Laoighre Budhach and Cuchulainn's foster brother Conal, agreed to go with him to pursue training. They left to begin their long journey, but soon the two were so overcome with homesickness that they turned back, leaving Cuchulainn to travel alone.

In the plains, he was met with a beast that looked like a lion. Each way he turned, it blocked his path until he leapt onto its back. They travelled that way for 4 days and 4 nights, until a group of youths ridiculed Cuchulainn for riding such a ridiculous beast. He continued on foot from there, until he came upon a home where a woman called him by name. She was a king's daughter who had stayed with Cuchulainn's family when she was young. She warned him of the traps set out for him by Forgall, and provided him with the safe path forward.

Able to avoid the traps, Cuchulainn made it safely to Scathach, meeting four friends from Emain Macha upon his arrival. They had a fantastic reunion, and after the reunion, Cuchulainn was told that he must cross an enchanted bridge. The bridge arched high in the middle, and when someone would step upon it, it would stretch, shrink, and buck to try to remove the person crossing it. Three times Cuchulainn attempted to get over the bridge. The fourth time, Cuchulainn leapt as a salmon to the middle of the bridge, then once again to the other side of the bridge. Scathach's daughter watched, enamored with the beautiful man leaping over the bridge. She met with him, welcoming him with food and drink, telling him exactly how to secure his place in training with her mother.

Cuchulainn arrived where Scathach was training her sons. In a swift ambush, he managed to pin her with his blade between her breasts, demanding to be trained. Impressed, Scathach agreed to take him on. He proved himself to be an incredible pupil, learning everything she had to teach him with ease.

At this point, Scathach was in a war with another warrior woman named Aoife. One day, Scathach's three sons met Aoife's three greatest champions on the road. In a wave of fear, Scathach sent Cuchulainn to their aid. He sprang ahead of her sons, easily beheading the three champions before him. When Aoife heard of the death of her champions, she flew into a fury, challenging Scathach to a duel, which Cuchulainn would fight for her as her champion. He asked her what Aoife's pride and joy was, to which she responded, her horse and chariot.

The day of the duel, the two stood, swords drawn. Cuchulainn shouted out that Aoife's chariot was going over the cliffside. When she turned to look, he charged, throwing her over his shoulder, carrying her to Scathach's fort, throwing her to the floor, and demanding that she surrender, his sword pointed at her chest. Aoife agreed, and she and Scathach made peace. For the remainder of Cuchulainn's stay, he and Aoife were lovers. As he prepared to return to Ireland, Aoife informed him that she was with child, and she was certain that it would be a son. Cuchulainn was ecstatic at the news, giving Aoife a red-gold ring to give to the child, asking her to name the child Connla. He was to be raised as a warrior. When he was old enough to wear the ring on his thumb without it falling off, Connla would come to Ireland to find his father. With that, Cuchulainn left for Ireland, finding Emer, and making her his wife.

Cuchulainn and the Champion's Portion

One of the warriors of the Red Branch, Bricriu the Bitter Tongue, was known for his bitter disposition in everything he did. This was largely because of a javelin accident that damaged his kidney. He could take no joy in a feast, as he was limited to bland, plain food. His bitter tongue became such an issue among the ranks that King Connor had to ask him to leave Emain Macha and stay in his own area.

To occupy himself, Bricriu built himself a great hall, the greatest in all of Ireland. The hall had 12 houses to represent the 12 branches of the Red Branch. Everything was to the highest standards possible in Ireland, even with an elevated seat for the king to sit on during feasts. Once the hall was complete, Bricriu sent out an invitation to the king, as well as all of his warriors. The king readily accepted, but Fergus had trepidation and said no. He was certain that if they all went, many of them would die because Bricriu would stir up trouble. Bricriu threatened that if they did not come, he would cause even more chaos than they could even imagine.

The king met with his council, and it was suggested that they all go, but with conditions. Bricriu happily accepted the conditions as laid out: that he would have a guard of eight men, that he would leave the hall when the feast began, and he would not return until the feast was done. Still, Bricriu had gone to work already, buttering different warriors, approaching Conal, Cuchulainn, and Laoighre to tell them that it seemed odd that they each didn't get the champion's portion at every feast for his great deeds and accomplishments. He spoke of the delicacies that would be his champion's portions and told each of them that the champion's portion should be claimed by their charioteers for each of them and them alone.

Once the feast began, Bricriu declared that it was time for the champion's portion to be claimed. At that point, the charioteers of each of them stood to claim the champion's portion for their warrior. The three warriors leapt to their feet and a battle ensued. Finally, King Connor stood, marching between the fighters unarmed, so that none could continue fighting without harming their king. The fighting ended, and the champion's portion was divided equally between the three, much to Bricriu's discontent.

So, since he failed with the men, Bricriu targeted the wives of the champions he had riled up. He told each of their wives as they left for a walk that the first woman who reentered the hall should be considered the First woman of Ulster, the queen before all others. As they returned from the walk, each picked up their speed until they were running with their skirts hiked around their waists. Sencha recognized that there would be a battle if the women made it to the door, and so they slammed the doors shut. He suggested that, should there be a battle, it should be a battle of words.

The battle of words escalated to a battle of fists by the men until the hall was shaken and battered. Beams were punched from the walls, and an entire wall raised to allow the women in to participate in the battle. The battle destroyed the hall, sinking it into the ground. Bricriu was flung from his seat in the balcony and placed a gaes (a curse or taboo) on all in attendance that not another bite of food or sip of drink would be had until his hall was righted. Try as they could, nobody could get the hall straight. With everyone tired, the champions agreed to settle the champion's portion another day.

Part 2

After the fiasco of the feast, it still needed to be decided who should receive the champion's portion. King Connor and his steward, Sencha, decided to bring the matter to King Ailil of Connaught and his wife, Queen Maeve. The three competing warriors set off to Connaught first, followed by the king and the other warriors of the Red Branch. For 3 days and 3 nights, they feasted and enjoyed their festivities. By the end of the third night, King Ailil finally asked King Connor what had brought him and his warriors to Connaught.

King Connor was honest with King Ailil, saying that he could trust no other with the choice of which of his three warriors should be the champion. King Ailil grumbled that it would be no easy task, but agreed, requesting 3 days and 3 nights to make the decision. The rest of the men of Ulster went home, aside from the three warriors in question, who stayed in their own houses.

The first night, Queen Maeve tested the men by opening the side of a faery mound, releasing three cat-like monsters. The monsters entered each of the warrior's homes. Laoighre and Conal each jumped to the rafters, staying there the full evening as the monsters did as they pleased, eating up the food and destroying the rooms. Cuchulainn saw a monster enter his room and immediately struck it over the head with his sword. The sword had no effect, bouncing off the monster as if Cuchulainn had struck a stone. They stared each other in the eye, unblinking, until morning when the monsters returned to their home in the mound.

Queen Maeve told King Ailil that the choice was clear, but the king wasn't keen on making a choice. No matter who they chose, they would make an enemy of the other two, or they wouldn't accept the choice. Maeve told him to leave it to her. To Laoighre, she gave a bronze cup with a small silver bird on the bottom. She told him to say nothing to the others, and to present the cup when the time came for the champion's portion selection. To Conal, she gave a silver cup with a red-gold bird at the bottom. To Cuchulainn, she gave a red-gold cup with a jeweled bird.

On their return to Ulster each warrior presented their cups at the next feast. Laoighre proudly presented his bronze cup, stating that Maeve declared him the Champion of Ulster. Conal already had his silver cup ready, showing that he had been determined above Laoighre as champion, and was prepared to claim the champion's portion. As the pair argued, Cuchulainn raised his red-gold cup, declaring that the champion's portion was rightfully his. The trio again nearly came to blows again, as Laoighre claimed that the cup had been bought. Sencha broke up the fighting again, deciding on a final route to decide.

Part 3

Sencha brought the great magician Cu Roi Mac Dara to help make the final decision. The three warriors were sent to Cu Roi, arriving at his home while he was away traveling, but welcomed warmly by his daughter, Blathnaid. She had been instructed by her father what should be done to test the warriors.

Cu Roi had a special enchantment that helped to keep the fort safe. As the sun went down, the fort would spin around, hiding all entrances to the fort until the sun rose again. At the top of the fort was a single seat for a warrior to stand guard. Each of the warriors would stand guard for one night.

Laoighre was the first to stand guard, settling into his seat as the entrances to the fort concealed themselves. From the stillness of the ocean rose a giant carrying stripped oak trunks. The giant began throwing the tree trunks at Laoighre, who managed to dodge them.

He threw his spear at the giant, missing him. After trading missiles for a while, the giant reached over, picking up Laoighre and throwing him over Cu Roi's fort. Inside the fort, they could not see the battle, but they heard the warrior land. They assumed that he'd leapt over the fort, showing off for those inside the fort. When he came inside in the morning, he didn't disagree with them.

The next night, Conal took the watch. The giant again rose from the ocean, having the same battle with Conal as he had with Laoighre. Conal met the same fate, being thrown over the fort by the giant, but not correcting anyone inside who thought that he had merely leapt over the fort.

The third night, Cuchulainn took his turn to guard the fort. Unlike the others, he watched nine warriors approaching the fort, each guided by a torch. Looking out at the lights, he called out a warning to them; if they were friends, they should stop where they were or turn back. If they were enemies, they were welcome to meet their end by his hand. The nine warriors attacked and he killed each of them, making a pile out of their heads. This happened two more times before the giant finally rose from the water to challenge him. They battled as the giant had battled Conal and Laoighre, except when the giant reached to grab Cuchulainn, he sprinted up the giant's arm, chopping off his head with his sword. Determined to show that he was equal to the other warriors, he leapt at the fort. He fell multiple times, only getting halfway up the wall. Finally, he threw himself with his great salmon leap, flinging himself over the fort.

In the morning, Blathnaid declared that it was Cuchulainn who had earned the champion's portion. The others refused to accept this decision, saying that he had to have had help from those he knew in the Otherworld. With this, they returned to Emain Macha, still not satisfied with the verdict.

Later on, there was a great feast in Emain Macha. A stranger entered the hall, introducing himself as Uabh. He stated that he was in search of the most honorable man in Ireland, but he'd yet to find him. The challenge was simple. The man must cut off his head with his axe, but with the agreement that he must then allow the man to cut off his own head the following evening. Laoighre jumped at the opportunity, volunteering himself. Uabh passed him the axe, laying his neck on the cutting block. Laoighre brought the axe down on the man's neck, deep into the wood beneath him. To everyone's shock and horror, Uabh stood up despite the gushing blood, gathered his head, and replaced it on his neck. He gathered his axe and left.

Laoighre in all his fear of facing this man ran away before nightfall. When Uabh returned, Laoighre nowhere to be found, he mocked and scorned the men of Ulster, laughing at them as they must be the greatest cowards. Conal took great offence to this, rising to the challenge Uabh had put forth. Uabh passed him the axe, laying his neck on the chopping block. Conal brought the axe down on Uabh's neck, then again on his head, chopping the head in half. Despite this, Uabh still stood again, gathering the pieces of his severed head and replacing them, leaving with his axe.

The next morning, Conal had vanished, hiding from the supernatural stranger. Uabh returned the next night, laughing and mocking the men of Ulster yet again. Cuchulainn had enough, this time stepping up to the challenge. One more time, Uabh passed the axe to his challenger, and Cuchulainn beheaded the man, throwing the severed head high into the rafters. Despite this, Uabh once again rose, collecting his head and his axe, leaving for the evening.

The next morning, Cuchulainn sat in sadness. He had no desire to die, but he would not let the stranger frighten him away. The people of Ulster were terribly upset, urging him to please run and hide, as they couldn't bear to lose their greatest warrior. Cuchulainn was determined to keep his word. Uabh returned to the feast hall that night, asking Cuchulainn if he was ready to keep his word. Cuchulainn knelt at the chopping block, when Uabh told him to stretch out his neck a little more. Cuchulainn bit back at him to stop teasing and tormenting, and just get it done. Uabh lifted the axe high, bringing it down with all of his power. To the shock of all around them, Uabh brought the axe down on the blunted side, thudding the axe into the ground next to Cuchulainn. When Cuchulainn raised his head in confusion, he looked to see that Uabh was actually Cu Roi.

Cu Roi announced to the people that this had been the final test to find who was worthy of the champion's portion. The victor was clearly Cuchulainn, and his wife was the First woman of Ulster. He assured the people that anyone who challenged his ruling would have him to fight, and that if anyone were to challenge Cuchulainn or attempt to take what was rightfully his, they would be killed.

Deirdre of the Sorrows

When King Connor Mac Nessa was still a young king, he and his Red Branch warriors were invited to feast with Filimid the Harper. Filimid was in a wonderful mood, as his wife was very close to giving birth to their child. In his excitement, he asked the king if he was willing to have his Druid, Cathbad, to offer a prophecy about what lay ahead for the child. It was agreed and Cathbad laid his hands over the woman's womb. He decried that the child was a girl, and would be the most beautiful who had ever walked the Earth, and that she would be named Deirdre. However, her beauty would be her curse, so much so that it would divide the Red Branch into two.

The warriors of the Red Branch demanded that the infant be put to death so that she could never have the opportunity to destroy them in such a way. Being a new king who wanted to be known as wise and merciful, King Connor refused. He would not allow for an infant to be killed in their father's home. Instead, when the child was born, she was raised in secret by his nurse, Leabharcham. If she was so beautiful as Cathbad had claimed, he would simply marry her himself, and keep the prophecy from being fulfilled.

The nurse then whisked the child away to be raised in the valleys. King Connor would come to check in on the child, and as prophesied, Deirdre was as beautiful as Cathbad had said. However, despite the fact that King Connor was a very attractive man, she held no affection toward him.

Leabharcham became extremely protective of the girl as she grew; aside from King Connor, she would allow nobody into the valley to visit except for a mute old man. He could not tell a soul about the exceptional beauty living in the valley, making him the only help that she would accept. One day, the nurse requested that he slaughter a calf for herself and Deirdre. As he cut the calf in half, the blood spilled out onto the fresh winter snow and a raven descended to eat the fresh blood. Deirdre gasped, fainting when she saw the scene. Leabharcham rushed to her, thinking her to be upset by the death of the calf. Instead, Deirdre told her that she had just fallen in love. She would love no man unless he had hair as dark as a raven's wings, cheeks as red as fresh blood, and skin as pale as new snow.

Deirdre demanded of Leabharcham if she knew of a man who fit the description she gave. The nurse didn't want to answer, but could not deny this treasured child the information she wanted. She said that yes, there was a warrior of the Red Branch who fit that description, by the name of Naoise. Deirdre demanded to see this young man, but Leabharcham wouldn't allow it, saying she would see him eventually when she became the king's wife. Deirdre wouldn't drop it, continuing to pester her caretaker until finally, Leabharcham relented, allowing Deirdre to see Naoise.

Leabharcham came up with a plan. She told the warriors of the Red Branch that she had seen great hunting in the valley she was living in, and that they should see what they could hunt. She told Deirdre that she could spy on the men, but she must stay out of sight. Naoise arrived with his brothers, Arden and Ainnle. The moment that Deirdre saw Naoise, she knew that he was the one that she wanted to spend her life with. She moved swiftly past Leabharcham, stepping into view of Naoise. She flirted with him as only a woman could, before asking him to run away with her. He recognized who she must be, knowing that she was reserved for the king, and refused. She put him under a gaes so that he had to leave with her.

Having no choice, Naoise realized he had to take Deirdre as far away from Emain Macha as he could manage. His brothers refused to be away from him, so together the four of them ran away, making their way to Scotland, where they served the King of Scotland, joining his army. However, they never stayed in the camps with the rest of the army; each night they would disappear into the woods. Having his suspicions as to their loyalty to him, the King of Scotland sent a spy after them the next time they vanished into the trees. When the spy returned, he told the king of the most beautiful woman he had ever seen. She was caring for the men, feeding them fine food, and seeing to all of their needs. Hearing of this woman, the king wanted to keep her for himself. However, the brothers were sworn to him, meaning he could not kill them. So, to try to speed up the process, the brothers were always put on the front lines, in hope that they would die quickly in battle, but they were too powerful to fall.

Deirdre realized that the King of Scotland was trying to kill the brothers, and insisted that they leave. They fled deep into the wilds, stopping near to the remote island where Scathach trained her warriors. Deirdre made a home for the four of them, where they were able to live comfortably for many years.

Back in Emain Macha, Fergus had never let the subject of the brothers go. He was fond of the brothers, and despite the rage of King Connor when the subject of the brothers was brought up, he continued to fight to get the king to forgive them for their betrayal. After so many pleas and arguments from Fergus, finally King Connor agreed that they could come back, but only if Fergus put them under his own protection. With that, Fergus ventured out to Scotland, searching for the brothers. When he reached the far shore, he let out a great shout. Naoise had been seated with Deirdre playing chess when he heard the shout. He stood, telling her that he'd heard the shout of an Irishman. Deirdre insisted that it couldn't be, it must be a Scotsman. Again, Fergus shouted from the shore, and again, Naoise stood. He told her that it wasn't just an Irishman, that it was a man from Ulster. Deirdre insisted again that it wasn't. He sat again, until Fergus cried out once more from the shore. He stood, declaring that it wasn't just any Ulsterman, that it was Fergus Mac Roich. Deirdre again tried to convince him that it was simply a Scotsman, but he wouldn't be persuaded otherwise.

Naoise demanded to know why she was lying to him and she caved, telling him of the dream she had the night before. She had seen a raven fly from Ireland to Scotland carrying three drops of honey in its beak. When the raven landed, the honey was no longer honey, but instead blood. The brothers were thrilled that Fergus had tracked them down, and in their excitement they dismissed her prophecy, rushing to the shore to see Fergus. Fergus told them of the agreement with King Connor, that they were to be forgiven for their transgression against him, and that they were welcome to return to the Red Branch. They vowed that they would neither eat nor sleep until they were home in Emain Macha, but as they sailed away from the shores of Scotland, Deirdre sang a sorrowful song for leaving the only home where she'd had found happiness.

When they landed in Emain Macha, a man came to Fergus, inviting him to a feast in his honor. The feast had been requested by King Connor, who wasn't so ready to forgive the brothers as he'd led Fergus to believe. Being a member of the Red Branch, it would be breaking a gaes to refuse the invitation of a feast in your own honor. Fergus agreed to attend, despite Deirdre pleading with him not to abandon the brothers. To ease her pleas, Fergus left the brothers under the protection of his son, Fiachu.

King Connor had refused to greet the men when they landed in Emain Macha, instead sending Leabharcham in his place. She told Naoise that he must hide Deirdre's face, and brought them to the Speckled House, the house where members of the Red Branch hung their weapons and stacked the heads of enemies they'd taken from the battlefield. They were fed and enjoyed drinks, and Deirdre passed the time with Leabharcham playing chess.

King Connor was undecided when it came to forgiving the brothers. On the one hand, he knew it made him look bad to continue holding onto a grudge the way he was, but on the other, every thought of Deirdre escaping with Naoise infuriated him. He went to Leabharcham, asking her if Deirdre was still the beauty that he knew her to be. Leabharcham lied, saying that the wilderness had destroyed her beauty, that she looked like a hag now, her teeth yellowed and her hair coarse and ugly. This eased the King's jealousy, and for a moment he considered welcoming the brothers back. When he gave it another thought, he wondered if he could trust Leabharcham to be impartial, and so he sent a servant out as a spy to report back to him. Naoise spotted the man peeking through the window, and tossed a chess piece at him, blinding him in one eye. When the servant returned, he reported that he would gladly be blinded in the other eye if it meant he was able to take another glimpse of Deirdre.

The King flew into a rage. He ordered the Red Branch to descend upon the Speckled House. Half would not attack their brothers in arms; the other half followed the order as instructed. As the attack began, the three brothers made a circle, shoulder to shoulder, shielding Deirdre behind them. Fiachu fought the king's son in one-on-one combat, and seeing the king's son in battle, Conal flew into the battle, beheading Fiachu. Once he realized whom he'd killed, he raised his blade to the king's son, stating that there should be one king's son for the others, beheading King Connor's son as well.

Watching over the battle, King Connor could see that neither side was advancing. He called for his Druid to help him. Cathbad told him that he would only help him if he didn't kill the brothers, which the king agreed to. He claimed to only want an apology, and all could move on. With that, Cathbad cast a spell, surrounding the brothers with a black sea; despite standing on dry land, the brothers swam away from their foes, Deirdre riding on Naoise's shoulders. They swam until they were exhausted, which was when they were captured by the king's men.

Seeing the brothers captured, King Connor informed them that he could not kill the brothers, but there was a great reward to anyone who did slay them. None of the Red Branch was willing to do it except for one, a man named Maigne Rough Hand who'd been the son of the King of Norway. Naoise had killed his family, so he would happily kill him now for the king. The youngest, Ainnle, pleaded to be the first killed, as he'd never known a life without his brothers. Arden begged to be the first killed, as he could not bear to watch his brothers be killed. Naoise raised his sword, stating that it would cut whatever was before it.

He suggested that all three die at once. Maigne agreed, and the three brothers knelt before him, and with a single swing, all three were beheaded.

At this point, Fergus returned from his feast. He looked around, seeing the brothers dead, and the body of his son lying not too far away from them. He burned all that he could of Emain Macha, then gathered the half of the Red Branch who wouldn't attack the brothers, leaving Ulster to pledge service to Ulster's greatest enemy, the Queen of Connaught.

King Connor now had his captive bride. He filled her home with all the finest things, but her hatred of him and what he'd done never abated. If he sang to her, she would shut the window, complaining of the awful noise. If he gave her the finest gifts, they were tossed aside. After a year of this, King Connor had enough of being disregarded by the maiden. He came to her, asking her if there was anyone who she hated more than him, for how great her hatred for him was, it seemed unlikely. She answered that she hated Maigne Rough Hand more than anything on the Earth, because he took from her the deepest love by killing Naoise. He told her that she would be given to Maigne Rough Hand to do with as he pleased for a year, and they would see if her heart would soften to him.

He sent for Maigne, who arrived with his chariot. As they rode off in the chariot, with each man on either side of her. The king made jokes that she was helpless, but as they went over a road where the cliffs hung over the road, she pushed her head through the chariot window, smashing her own head open.

Deirdre was buried in Emain Macha, near her beloved Naoise. King Connor couldn't stand the idea of them touching in life, much less in death, and so he drove two stakes between the graves. To his dismay, the stakes rooted, and together two trees grew together intertwined.

The Curse of Macha

There was a man living in Ulster by the name of Crunden. He had gone through a great loss; his wife had died, leaving him to care for their three children on his own. He knew little about cooking or cleaning, much less about caring for and raising children. Every day he had to get up, leaving his home and children alone in the field, as it was the only way that he could provide for them, and at the very least, keep them alive.

One day, coming home from a long day of working, he opened his door and stood stunned. The house was clean and neat, the children tidy and cared for. A fire was roaring, the most beautiful woman he'd ever seen standing over it cooking the supper. She informed him that her name was Macha, and she'd decided that she was now his wife. Not one to look a gift horse in the mouth, he accepted this, and from that point on, he decided to enjoy his good fortune.

Crunden knew that his wife had to be of the Otherworld; yes, she kept the house perfectly and the children never lacked for anything they needed, and they were deeply loved by her. She cared for her husband perfectly in all the ways that she should. But when she ran, she moved with such speed that her feet didn't seem to touch the ground. Despite this, he never made a fuss over it, and neither did Macha. She simply went about her duties as wife and mother.

Upon purchasing a brand new set of carriage horses, King Connor sent out an invitation to all of his subjects for a celebratory feast. Crunden was thrilled to join in the feast, but Macha gave him a warning: he should not speak of her, nor boast of her in any way. Doing so would doom their home and their family. He gave her his word, then left for the feast.

The horses were perfect; they were a gorgeous shade of grey. They were swift and beautiful and the feast was a wonderful representation of the king's generosity, as it was plentiful in food and drink. It wasn't long before the men began to boast. While they boasted of the beauty and cooking of their wives, Crunden stayed quiet. But then the king began to boast of the speed of his new horses, how there was nothing in all of Ireland faster than his new pair of horses. After having had several drinks at this point, Crunden could no longer contain himself. He bragged to the king that his beautiful wife was so fast, she could easily beat the king's horses in a race. King Connor didn't take kindly to this, having the men seize

Crunden, telling him to fetch his wife. Crunden was told that if this was not true, the punishment for his lie would be death.

Macha was brought before the king and she begged him to postpone the race; she was heavily pregnant with twins, but she would happily race him when she'd recovered from the birth. After Crunden's bragging, the king's ego was bruised, and he refused her request. She turned to the men of the kingdom, reminding them that each of them came from a woman. For them to force her to race like this was wrong, but none would step forward to plead or speak on her behalf. They had been drinking, and after Crunden's bragging, they wanted to see if she was truly faster than the king's horses.

The king must have lost some of his confidence upon seeing Macha, because before the race, he and Deichtre, his sister and charioteer, stripped all that he could from his chariot until there was nothing more than a plank to stand on, and wheels to help propel him forward. He removed his heavy armor and cloak, stripping down to the lightest of his tunics. He made sure that the race would be held on the flattest and most perfect grass so that his horses wouldn't be hindered, and dismissing Deichtre to man the reins himself, he gave the horses the lightest chariot possible to pull.

The race began, and the horses ran perfectly; to King Connor, he could have been flying, for that's how he felt. The horses were so fast, they were like the wind. However, if the horses were the wind, Macha was even faster. Her feet moved so fast that nobody could see her feet touch the ground. As she ran, she felt labor pains beginning and she screamed in pain and anguish, still continuing to run. The men of the crowd began to feel uncomfortable; while they expected to be entertained, a woman in agony was not the entertainment they wanted. Macha screamed through the entire race, finishing the course with her belly ahead of the horse's noses. She collapsed in the grass, technically victorious, but howling in the deepest pains. She gave birth to her twins in the grass, but neither survived.

Macha picked up her dead twins, looking out at the crowd of men, cursing them all. For refusing to use their strength to stand up for her and protect her, their strength would be useless to them, failing them when they needed their strength the most. For standing by and doing nothing while she howled in anguish, each of them would know 9 days and 9 nights of the pains of labor and childbirth. This would last for nine generations; as soon as their sons could grow a beard, they would be subjected to the pains. Holding her twins tight to her chest, she leapt over the crowd of men, disappearing. This is how Emain Macha, the fort of the King of Ulster, got it's name: the Twins of Macha.

Ferdia at the Ford

As the men of the Red Branch suffered the curse of Macha, Queen Maeve of Connaught was attempting to invade to steal the Brown Bull of Cooley. Cuchulainn, having not been at the feast, was the only man fighting at the ford. Being the greatest warrior of Ulster, he was a terror to Maeve's men; he raided their encampments every night, disrupted their deliveries of supplies, killing many of the men she sent to invade. The toll on Connaught grew too great, and Queen Maeve arranged a negotiation with Cuchulainn. She would call for the army to halt at the ford by the river, if he would only challenge one champion of Connaught each day. Cuchulainn was happy to agree; after all, it made it easier for him, and he knew that after a few more days, the curse of Macha would end and he would have the other warriors of the Red Branch to help him push back and defeat the invading armies.

Each day, Cuchulainn tossed aside each of her champions as if they were dolls or children. There was only one champion who could stand a chance against Cuchulainn: his brother in arms and closest friend, Ferdia. They were so close, they had even trained under Scathach together. Queen Maeve knew that she would struggle to convince Ferdia to battle Cuchulainn, but he was her only chance.

That evening, she invited him to a great feast, sitting him next to her daughter, Finnavir. They fed him good food and wine, Finnavir flirting and whispering into his ear the entire time. Once he was in high spirits, Queen Maeve asked Ferdia if he knew why she had invited him to the feast. He said it was because he was the greatest warrior of Connaught. Why shouldn't he be celebrated? Queen Maeve agreed, but also extended an offer: he could have all the best land, the best herds of cattle, the golden ring she wore on her thumb, her daughter's hand in marriage, a life without ever paying tithes or taxes, and all of her own love. Hearing the grand offer, Ferdia became sad, knowing what was coming; she would ask him to fight his closest friend. He refused her offer outright. Even being on opposing sides, he wouldn't break the bond he'd formed with Cuchulainn.

With that, Queen Maeve knew she'd have to manipulate him. She sighed, telling him she should have believed Cuchulainn. She claimed to have spoken to him, and that he'd told her that Ferdia wouldn't battle him. Not because of their bond, but because he knew that he was no match for Cuchulainn. This enraged Ferdia, that Cuchulainn would say such a thing, and he vowed that the next day he would take on Cuchulainn.

Cuchulainn and Ferdia met at the ford the next morning. Cuchuliann's heart broke upon seeing Ferdia. Overcome by sadness, his feet froze to the ground and he would not fight his friend. He spoke of their time together, and though Ferdia was moved by his friend's words, he threw it all back at him until Cuchulainn finally moved forward to fight. For 4 days, the pair fought. They were evenly matched, knowing each other's every move and not truly involved in the fight. They fought from sunrise to sunset, each night binding the others wounds, sleeping with their backs to each other.

The defining factor in the fight was Cuchulainn's refusal to use his weapon, the Gae Bolga, the spear made from the bones of a horrendous sea monster. If thrown, it would seek out the most vulnerable point of the opponent's body, exiting out of the body in 50 places.

The third day of fighting, something changed. The pair knew that they would have to truly battle each other, and so that night they slept separately. Fearing Gae Bolga, Ferdia tied a stone between his legs, hoping to block his most vulnerable point. The pair became grim, and they prepared for the next day. Waking on the fourth day, Cuchulainn could no longer hold off his battle fury. Each time Cuchulainn would leap at Ferdia, he would be flung into the water. Finally, he was overcome by the fury, doubling in size. The two pushed against each other, evenly matched until Cuchulainn went to deal a death blow to Ferdia. Yet Cuchulainn hesitated, seeing his friend through the battle fury; Ferdia didn't hesitate, seeing his opportunity and thrusting his blade into Cuchulainn's chest over and over.

Seeing Cuchulainn falling, his charioteer threw Gae Bolga into the river to float down to Cuchulainn. Ferdia had great fear seeing it heading towards him, and for a moment, he dropped his shield. Cuchulainn took the opportunity to plunge a javelin through his friend's chest. Gae Bolga came closer, and with his toes, Cuchulainn flung the spear into his friend. It destroyed the stone, and the spear splintered into a million pieces within Ferdia. Cuchulainn and Ferdia cried together, lamenting the treachery of Queen Maeve. Cuchulainn carried his friend to the Ulster side of the ford so that he may pass on land not poisoned by Queen Maeve's presence, holding Ferdia until he took his final breath.

Cuchulainn's Son

While training with Scathach, Cuchulainn had an affair with a woman named Aoife, just before marrying Emer. Aoife had told him just before he returned to Ireland that she was with child, and Cuchulainn had instructed her to name their son Connla, giving her the red-gold ring from his finger to give to his son.

Word had gone back to Aoife about Cuchulainn's immediate marriage to Emer, and she flew into a rage. She realized he must have known this woman and loved her far before he had met Aoife, and that he must have been thinking of Emer every time they'd made love. She was so enraged, she decided to use their son as a plot for revenge. She raised Connla as a warrior, giving him every last morsel of information that a warrior should know, sending him to train with Scathach as soon as he came of age.

Once the young man was grown, he prepared to set off to Ireland. Before he left, Aoife gave him three gaesa that he must follow. The first was that he must never step aside for another man. Second, he must never give his name before the other person. Third, he must never turn down a fight, even if he thought it may be the death of him. Connla agreed and set off.

Connla arrived in Ireland dressed in full warrior's regalia, landing in Baile's strand. King Connor was attending a ritual with his men and spotted the young man arriving. He sent a messenger to greet the man, asking his name. Connla refused to give his name, and when the messenger returned to the king, he was largely offended. Who did this young man think he was to refuse the king his name? So, King Connor sent a warrior, Conal, to get the man's name by force. Conal approached the young man, demanding his name. Again, Connla wouldn't back down and wouldn't give his name. The two men fought, Connla eventually overpowering the king's warrior.

Cuchulainn watched as Connla stripped Conal of his great reputation, taking the man's weapons as victory. Cuchulainn approached, begging Connla to tell him his name as he didn't want to fight the young man, he was too fine of a warrior to be killed. Connla explained that he was under gaesa to not speak his name first and never turn down a fight. Seeing Cuchulainn, Connla desperately wanted to speak his name, but couldn't. With the honor of King Connor on the line, Cuchulainn had no choice but to battle the young man.

The two battled like no other men could, knowing each move the other would make before he thought of it, evenly matched. The battle fury took over Cuchulainn, and in that moment, the two men called for their spears. Laeg passed Cuchulainn Gae Bolga as his hero light began to shine around his head. Connla recognized who Cuchulainn must be, and though he had his spear before Cuchulainn, he purposefully missed. Cuchulainn, not knowing his son, did not miss. As the spear splintered apart within Connla, he raised his thumb, showing Cuchulainn the red-gold ring that had been given to him. In that moment, Cuchulainn knew who he was fighting, cradling his dying son in his arms, and together they cursed Aoife for using Connla against him.

All of the men of Ulster and the Red Branch were called down to where Cuchulainn held his dying son so that they could introduce themselves to his son. After each of them had introduced himself to Connla, Cuchulainn slit his son's throat, putting him out of his misery. Worried that Cuchulainn would go into a battle fury over his grief for his son, King

Connor asked Cathbad for help. The Druid cast a spell on Cuchulainn so that for 3 days and 3 nights, instead of battling the men of his company, he battled the waves of the strand until he could no longer stand.

Cuchulainn's Illness

The people of Ulster, along with the men of the Red Branch and their wives, gathered in Emain Macha to celebrate Samhain. As per tradition, the men told stories of their bravery; since the Otherworld was so near during Samhain, if a man spoke a lie, his sword would sing, outing him for his dishonesty. While waiting for the rest of the Red Branch to arrive, Cuchulainn sat with Sencha, enjoying a game of chess. The women present saw a beautiful flock of white birds land in the water, and each of them was overtaken with the desire to have one. None of the men could capture one.

Emer stood, saying that if she asked, Cuchulainn would be able to get them the birds. As soon as she spoke, he threw his sword through the air, knocking the birds out of the air, not killing any. Each woman, apart from Emer, was able to have a bird for each shoulder, but Emer said it was fine. She was the one to request his service and so it was her gift to the women. Cuchulainn was determined that he would find his wife the most beautiful birds, and with that, two lovely birds linked by a chain of red gold flew over the lake.

Sencha recognized that these birds were enchanted and told Cuchulainn to leave them alone, but he wouldn't listen. He flung a stone from his sling, and to his surprise, missed the birds. Emer told him to let the birds be, as they clearly weren't of the human realm, but he dismissed her, determined to give her these beautiful birds. He flung a second stone, grazing the wing of one bird, but they kept flying. This upset Cuchulainn; he never, ever missed a shot, and now here he was, missing two. He lay down by the lake and went to sleep.

As he slept, Cuchulainn had a strange dream. Two tall women approached him, one of them sobbing. The other smiled, whipping him. The first woman then smiled, and the two continued to beat him with whips. When he was an inch from death, they stopped, happily walking away.

When Cuchulainn woke, he was battered from head to toe. He had to be carried away to his sickbed, where he stayed for a full year recovering. This sent Emer into a rage. She went to the king furious; after all, if this had been any other warrior, each of them knew that Cuchulainn would not have rested until he found a cure for them. But here they sat, a year later, feasting and sitting about as if nothing was wrong. She returned to her husband's bedside, reminding him of all his great feats, singing a song of his friends and their great adventures. Her song helped fortify him, and he found the strength to get out of the bed and tell Cathbad about the vision he'd had before he fell to his illness.

Hearing the vision, Cathbad concluded that the women must have been faery, and he must have struck one when they flew by as birds. He would have to return to where he struck the woman, hoping to bargain with them to regain his health. He returned to the pillar where he'd slept by the lake a year prior and had another vision. A woman, Liban, one of the women who had beaten him,approached Cuchulainn. She told him about Fand, who had been the wife of Manannán Mac Lir, but she had fallen in love with Cuchulainn, and Manannán had left her behind. The women had been heartbroken and so insulted by his throwing stones at him that they'd put him to his sickbed. However, she did have a deal for him: if he helped her, she would lift the illness that ailed him for the last year.

Her husband, Labraid the Sword-Wielder, was about to face a battle that he wasn't likely to win. She wanted Cuchulainn to come to her home in the Plain of Light and win the battle for her. If he could do this for her, not only would he have the illness lifted, but he could also have Fand for a wife. Though he was suspicious, Cuchulainn sent Laeg with her to confirm her story. Laeg returned, telling him the wonders of the Plain of Light and how beautiful Fand was. With that, Cuchulainn agreed to help her. The faery men laughed as he arrived, thinking he had to be a fool to challenge them. Instead, he shocked them all by defeating not only their king but also over 30 of their champions, winning the challenge for Labraid.

Cuchulainn spent a month in the Plain of Light, keeping Fand as his wife. When the month was over, she told him that he could choose any place in Ireland, and she would meet him there, running away to spend their lives together. They arranged to meet by a yew tree along Baile's strand. Emer had found out about this plan and flew into a blind rage. She gathered 50 women, all armed with knives, setting off to Baile's strand to put a stop to her husband's plan to abandon her.

When she arrived, Fand and Cuchulainn were already getting into the chariot. They argued, Fand and Emer screaming threats at each other. Cuchulainn begged for Emer to stop, as Fand was under his protection and he didn't want to fight her or harm her. After many harsh words, he realized the pain he was causing Emer, and agreed to set Fand aside. Fand wailed, now being left by two men whom she had loved. Hearing her wail, Manannán mac Lir realized he still loved her, returning to her and asking for her forgiveness. She agreed and the two vanished into the Otherworld.

While Fand and Manannán had resumed living happily, Emer and Cuchulainn were not so happy to be back together. Cuchulainn was heartbroken over his loss of Fand, as he'd fallen deeply in love with her. Emer was just as deeply cut by his betrayal, and the two were so miserable that their misery began to affect the people of Ulster. The Druids had to take action, brewing a potion to help them forget, and after consuming the potion, they were able to return to their happiness as they had been before.

Cuchulainn's Death

While Cuchulainn had been champion of Ulster, he had taken on many men, killing each man who dared to challenge him. Unbeknownst to him, one man whom he had killed had been a powerful sorcerer, Catalan, leaving behind a pregnant wife. She had been pregnant with six children: three boys and three girls. They were all raised to be powerful Druids and sorcerers, all spending their lives with a single goal: to avenge their father by killing Cuchulainn.

King Connor discovered the plan in place as the six siblings came of age. He chose to distract Cuchulainn with feasts and sports, knowing that if they managed to kill his best champion his kingdom would fall. For 3 days and 3 nights, the king did his best to keep Cuchulainn from discovering that he would be challenged, but the children of Catalan stirred up all of the noise of war. As the sounds threatened to catch Cuchulainn's attention, the king had his men bring Cuchulainn to the Valley of the Deaf, a place where no noise from the outside could penetrate.

When the children of Catalan realized that Cuchulainn wouldn't be drawn into their trap, they switched tactics. One of the daughters disguised herself as one of Cuchulainn's best friends, telling him he was needed in battle. Cuchulainn rushed to his horse, ready to jump into battle. He tried three times to hitch his chariot to his horse, but she danced away from him, showing him the white of her eyes. He berated her, telling her that they'd never shied away from battle before, and they wouldn't be starting now. This time she allowed him to hitch the chariot, but she cried tears of blood. He called to Laeg, who promptly grabbed the reins. Deichtre, Cuchulainn's mother came to him with a cup of wine, wishing to give him blessings in the coming battle. Each time Cuchulainn would raise the cup to his lips, the wine would turn to blood, no matter how often she refilled it. After three tries, he gave up and left for battle.

As he travelled, Cuchulainn passed by many omens of his death. First, an old woman was doing the washing in the river, telling him she was washing the armor of Cuchulainn, who was slated to die in battle. Next, he passed three hags who were roasting a hound. As he greeted them, they invited him to eat with them. He was under a gaes to never eat the flesh of a hound, as he was named for a hound, but they jeered at his refusal. His oath as a warrior gave him no way to refuse, and so he took a small piece in his left hand. He bit into the meat and the strength of his left hand faded. The meat fell onto his left thigh and the strength vanished from the left leg. Half of his strength was gone, rendering Cuchulainn no more than a regular man. He did not realise that the three women were actually the Mórrígan, who had felt slighted by him after offering him her love and being refused. Now, she'd exacted her revenge.

The three sons of Catalan stood in the way of the road with the son of Cu Roi. They had been told that the first three spears thrown by Cuchulainn in this battle would take the lives of three kings, and so they sought to take them. When the first son requested the spear, he threatened to smear Cuchulainn's name. Cuchulainn narrowed his eyes, telling him to never second guess his generosity, throwing the spear through his head. Cu Roi's son pulled the spear out, throwing it at Cuchulainn and missing, instead killing Laeg, a king among charioteers.

The second son asked for the spear, threatening to smear the name of Ulster. Cuchulainn would not have his people lose their honor over him, and he threw the second spear, the spear going through the second son's head. Cu Roi's son again pulled out the spear, again attempting to throw it at Cuchulainn and missed, killing his horse. Cuchulainn fell to his knees to cry over his horse, a king of horses.

The third son requested a spear, threatening to ruin the name of Cuchulainn's family. He would not allow him to bring dishonor to his family, and threw the spear through the third son's head. Again, Cu Roi's son pulled the spear free, this time spearing Cuchulainn through the stomach. Cuchulainn crawled to the water's edge, gravely wounded. The water helped him, but then he realized that he would die. He couldn't bear to die on the ground as though he were an animal, and crawled to a standing stone, tying himself to it so that he would die on his feet. As he breathed his last breaths, a raven walked by, tripping over his intestines. Cuchulainn laughed, dying as he did so. He stood for 3 days after he died, as none of his enemies believed him to be dead. The Mórrígan took the shape of a raven, settling herself on his shoulder, and when he didn't respond, they knew him to be dead. And thus died Cuchulainn, the king among the warriors.

CHAPTER 7

The Fenian Cycle

If Cuchulainn is considered the warrior hero of the people, the Fenian Cycle represents the outlaw heroes of the mythology. The Fenian Cycle follows the story of Finn, a man who, along with the rest of the Fianna, was willing to reject the comforts of civilized living, building a life for themselves as warriors and heroes who lived from the land. The outlaw nature of these myths brings light to the age of heroes, the roaming warriors who fought for the land without any care for creature comfort, and instead fought for honor and justice. Even though there is a heavy focus on Finn, the warriors of the Fianna, especially while divided, give representation to the wild, free, fighting spirit that can be found in Irish culture and mythology.

The Birth and Childhood of Finn

Long ago, there was a group of young men who had given up their societal ties. They were a group of fighters living off the land, hunting and foraging in the summer months so they could feast and celebrate through the winter. They'd given up their ties to their family, thrown aside their roles within their community, and taken up a set of mottos that they abided by in the woods: may their limbs be strong, may their hearts be pure, and may their words and actions always match. These men called themselves the Fianna.

The Fianna were well known for their generosity, and had no real attachment to ownership of land or material possessions. Their generosity was unending, and so there was a degree of hospitality that was expected by them. There wasn't a door in all of Ireland that wouldn't open to the Fianna. The land was their maiden, and they knew all her secrets, from the paths of the animals to the patches of food to the most comfortable sleeping areas. They knew the ways into the Otherworld, and were respected for their knowledge. While the Fianna took to the land to hunt and live in the summer, in the winters they would stay with noblemen. In exchange for their hospitality, the Fianna would provide feasts and entertainment with the finest poets and bards, sharing their own tales of the hunt, and when necessary, acting as mercenary warriors to any nobleman who needed them.

The Fianna were divided into two main groups within themselves: Clan Baiscne and Clan Morna. From the Clan Baiscne was the leader of the Fianna named Cumhaill. He was a great warrior, blessed with a magical item called the Oxter Bag. Made from the skin of a stork, this bag held whatever Cumhaill needed at any moment. While he was greatly respected for his prowess, skill, and intelligence, and easily recognized by the Fianna as their collective leader, one man would constantly challenge Cumhaill.

The man's name was Goll Mac Morna, from the Clan Morna. No matter what Cumhaill said or did, Goll would defy him in small ways, never enough to erupt into a war, but just enough to be a thorn in Cumhaill's side. Goll would always step down should tensions grow too high, until finally the tension became too much and two clans of the Fianna divided for the winter. Clan Morna went to stay with the King, Conn Cead Cathach, while Clan Baiscne went to stay with the Druid Tadhg.

While staying with Tadhg, Cumhaill fell in love with his daughter, Muirne. Cumhaill asked Tadhg for Muirne's hand in marriage, but Tadhg refused. In his defiance, Cumhaill gathered Muirne with him, stealing her away, hoping to bring her back when she had agreed to marry him. But when Tadhg realized that his daughter had been taken, he went straight to the king, demanding that he send his armies after Cumhaill to retrieve his daughter and kill the Clan Baiscne. With this, the king sent the Clan Morna to battle the other half of the Fianna.

In the battle, Goll was able to take leadership of the Fianna; he killed Cumhaill, but in the chaos of battle, Cumhaill's treasured Oxter bag was lost. Much to Tadhg's dismay, Muirne had conceived a child with Cumhaill, and in his anger, he threatened that he would kill his daughter for it. Muirne's sister, Bodhmall took her away, bringing her to Slieve Bloom so that she would be protected from their father. The child was born, and Muirne named the boy Deimne. Together Muirne and her sister raised him for 6 years in Slieve Bloom. He learned from his mother, who was a deer woman, to run with the deer, and even faster than the deer, earning his name, which meant "Little Stag." His aunt was a powerful warrior woman who had trained many of the Fianna, and so she taught Diemne all of the fighting skills of Ireland.

When Deimne was 6 years old, news of his birth and where he was staying with his mother and aunt reached Goll Mac Morna. Goll decided that he would kill the boy and his mother. His aunt dressed him in rags, sending Deimne to travel with a group of poets. They nicknamed him Finn for his golden hair, and brought him all over Ireland, teaching him all of their poems and stories. Finn travelled with them for a year, and as his year came to a close, he met a woman who had lost her son, and knowing the importance of the bond between mother and son, Finn vowed to avenge her son's death. He found the warrior, challenged him, and easily killed him. From his body, he took a bag made from stork skin: the Oxter bag his father had lost when he was killed. Finn didn't understand what it was that he had found, but he brought the bag with him.

Finn continued his journey, meeting an old Druid named Aengus. The Druid had dedicated Finn's entire lifetime to sitting over the riverbank, attempting to catch the salmon of knowledge as it swam to and from the Otherworld to eat from the Tree of Life. If he could catch the salmon, the Druid said, he would be able to have all of the knowledge in the world. By the time Finn came to him, Aengus was wasting away, refusing to leave the riverbank, in case he should miss the salmon on it's journey. Finn made a deal with the Druid: he would hunt and care for the Druid if Aengus would teach him all he knew. Finn helped Aengus to rebuild his health and strength, and in exchange, Finn learned the arts of composing poetry and before long, Aengus had his success: he'd caught the salmon of knowledge.

He gave the fish to Finn to cook, telling him not to take so much as the tiniest nibble of the fish, as the knowledge was for Aengus, and Aengus only. Finn agreed, setting off to cook the fish. As it cooked, a small blister rose up on the fish's skin. Finn popped the blister, burning his thumb in the process. He put his thumb to his mouth to soothe the pain, and when it was done cooking, he brought the salmon to Aengus. The Druid took a bite and asked Finn if he'd eaten the fish, because the knowledge was gone from it. Finn objected, saying he knew not to eat the fish. They went back and forth, until Finn finally revealed the blister on his thumb, proving he hadn't eaten the fish. Aengus sighed, saying Finn may as well just eat the fish himself, because he now had the salmon's knowledge. Finn said that he didn't think so, because he felt no different from when he'd started cooking the fish. Aengus instructed him to put his thumb between his teeth, and going forward, this is what Finn did if he needed knowledge or to see the future.

Finn and the Fianna

Now that Finn possessed all the knowledge in the world, he decided that it was time to find his father's brother. His uncle stayed with the remaining members of Clan Baiscne, now nothing more than hunters living off the land, no longer considered Fianna. Finn was able to find them without trouble, introducing himself as Cumhaill's son. They were ecstatic to meet him, and even more thrilled to see that he had his father's Oxter bag. It was decided among the men that this boy needed to take leadership of the Fianna as his father had, and so they set off to see the High King in Tara.

They arrived on Samhain Eve, as the High King was preparing the feast for the following evening. The king's feast had been plagued for several years by the same tragedy: each Samhain, the men of the table would fall asleep, and when they woke the hall was on fire. Finn decided that he would stay up that evening to figure out why such a thing would keep happening to the High King. He stood, instead of sitting at the table, leaning against his spear so that if he should drift to sleep, the point of his spear would wake him.

A sweet, eerie song rose through the night, causing all the men within the hall but Finn to fall into a deep sleep. He looked out the window, watching as the hillside opened up, and a great faery creature rose up from the opening. It breathed fire as it approached Tara, singing it's slumber song. Finn muffled it's fire with his cloak, ready to fight it. The creature tried to retreat, but Finn was able to cut the creature's head off.

When the people of Tara woke in the morning, they saw that for the first time in many years the High King's hall had not been engulfed in flames. They saw Finn standing over the slain creature, and with much celebration, the king praised Finn. It was this way that Goll stepped aside and Finn became the leader of the Fianna. Finn decided that things within the Fianna needed to change. While the tests of the Fianna were difficult already, he increased the difficulty, so that only the best of the warriors could join them. The Fianna became the greatest defenders of Ireland under Finn's leadership, protecting the weak and the poor.

Caoilte's Rabble

Caoilte Mac Ronan was the best runner in all of the Fianna and a wonderful hero to them. He was so fast that when the King had asked all the fastest runners in Ireland how long it would take them to gather sand from all the beaches of Ireland, they answered that it would take them months, weeks, or even days. When the king finally reached Caoilte, he gave the king a grin, holding up a bag. He told him that it was already done while they were all busy chatting.

At one point, the Fianna had started a rebellion with the people of Ireland, putting themselves in the crosshairs of the High King. The High King didn't want a war with the Fianna, but he knew he had to act, and so he requested that Finn come to him as a willing hostage while the problems were resolved. Finn agreed, peacefully joining the High King. The problem was, Caoilte wasn't present when the deal was made between the High King and Finn. He heard nothing of the peaceful agreement, only that his friend and leader was now the king's hostage. Caoilte set off on a vengeful, destructive rampage, destroying all in his path until he reached Tara.

Arriving in Tara, Caoilte stole the clothing of a doorkeeper. He slipped into the king's hall, trading the king's sword for his own, which had been worn down to resemble a blade of grass after decades of battle. He found his place behind the king, holding just a candle in his disguise.

Word of Caoilte's rampage had found its way to the High King, and he grew nervous. Finn dismissed the king's fears, saying that Caoilte was of a high mind, and wouldn't resort to slinking through Tara with a candle. The king's nerves settled, until he had his servant pass him a cup of wine, saying that he could smell Caoilte on the glass. Caoilte revealed himself, demanding to know how he could free Finn. The king considered his demand; it wasn't that he wanted to keep Finn as a hostage, and having to look over his shoulder for a madman was driving him crazy. So, he told Caoilte that he wanted to see a pair of every animal in Ireland at once. He figured it would give the rebellion time to settle, and so he sent Caoilte off on his task.

Caoilte managed to bring all the animals to the King, but he had done so too quickly. He arrived in the evening with the herd of animals, and so the king sent a servant down to say the king wanted to see the animals in the daylight. Caoilte herded the animals into a particular house with nine doors, but all night, he had to run round and round the house to keep the animals from escaping. He did so all night, and when the sun finally rose that morning, he brought all the animals to see the High King. The noise was so much from the animals that the herd came to be known as Caoilte's Rabble. The king looked over the herd, pleased with his plan. He'd bought himself enough time to settle the rebellion, and what a gift he'd received, to have a pair of every animal in his kingdom in one place! He released Finn from being held hostage. As soon as Finn was free, Caoilte stopped herding the animals in place. They shot off in all directions, the result of the High King's demands being a single look at the herd.

The Hostel of the Quicken Tree

The Fianna were once called to defend Ireland's shores from invasion. The King of Lochlann had sent his troops into battle, but the Fianna had found victory when Finn killed the invading king and his sons, breaking the will of the army and sending them to return home. The only son Finn didn't kill was the youngest, named Miadach, who he brought with him as a hostage. Finn decided he would foster the boy with his other fosterlings.

Finn treated all his fosterlings with kindness, holding no grudges for their upbringing. Miadach didn't feel the same, wanting revenge against the man who'd killed his father and brothers. He never let his hatred of Finn show, smiling sweetly and behaving kindly through the years until he came of age. Finn gave him a plot of coastal lands, but Miadach left Ireland without ever looking back.

Years later, the Fianna were tracking a wild boar through the woods, to their surprise finding Miadach in the road. Finn greeted him with kindness and warmth, and by all appearances, Miadach was pleased to see the Fianna. He invited them to join him at the Hostel of the Quicken Trees for a drink, and Finn was delighted to accept his invitation. One of the Fianna, Conan Maol Mac Morna, protested the invitation, saying that Miadach had never held this kind of kindness or generosity for Finn, so he didn't believe they should accept the invitation. He didn't feel Miadach could be trusted, but Finn chastised him for his rudeness, and off they went.

Despite reprimanding Conan, Finn heeded the warning. To be safe, he brought with him Conan and his brother Goll, sending his own son and the other young warriors to wait for them with the rest of the hunt. They followed Miadach into a beautiful hostel, admiring the tapestries and floor coverings, sweet smoke emerging from the fires, the furniture, beautiful and luxurious. They were so distracted by the beauty of the hostel that none of them noticed that Miadach hadn't entered the hostel with them. When they turned to look for Miadach, the hostel had changed. The windows that had given them such a lovely view were now boarded with planks. The tapestries and floor coverings were gone, the walls and floors bare.

The sweet fires were no longer burning, each grate sitting cold. The lavish furniture they'd sat down on was gone, and the men found themselves sitting on cold dirt. The hostel had vanished, and instead they were sitting in a hut.

Each of the warriors attempted to stand, finding that they couldn't. The more they fought against the bind keeping them to the floor, the more they were stuck in place. Conan cursed Finn for not listening to his warning better. Finn bit the thumb he'd burned on the salmon of knowledge, seeing the plans Miadach had set in place. He saw that they were in grave danger, as Miadach had brought the armies of the King of Torrents, and they were quickly approaching. The spell keeping them in place could only be broken with the King of Torrent's own blood. In their panic, they sounded the battle cry of the Fianna, summoning two of the young warriors.

Conan yelled at the young men not to come in, and Finn told them what was about to happen. The young warriors decided that they must fight, finding a ford that any army would have no choice but to cross to get to the hostel where their leader was held captive, deciding to take their stand there.

That evening, a chieftain decided that he wanted the glory of killing Finn to himself. He brought his part of his army along with him, coming over the ford where the two young warriors were waiting. The battle was long, but the young men succeeded, except that one had fallen to his wounds. The brother of the chieftain decided he too wanted the glory of killing Finn to himself, taking his army to the ford. They found the surviving young man surrounded by the dead of the last army and retreated. Miadach, however, stepped forward to challenge the warrior.

The other warriors who had been waiting knew nothing of what was happening with the ford or their leader, returning to find one warrior dead, and the other in battle with Miadach. Miadach had managed to gravely wound the young warrior, and at that point, Diarmuid and Folda had found the battle, Diarmuid running in and slaying Miadach. The young warrior died of his wounds. Finn's son, Oisin, went to fetch the rest of the Fianna while Folda and Diarmuid held the ford against any approaching armies. Diarmuid brought the head of Miadach with him, telling of the stories of their fallen, showing Finn that they'd been avenged.

Diarmuid returned to the ford, and Folda collapsed into an exhausted sleep. Diarmuid held off the armies until Folda woke, and the two of them worked to fight the armies back. They managed to kill the three sons of the king, rushing back to the hut to bathe the stuck men in the blood. Diarmuid first doused Finn in the blood, releasing him, and then Goll. When he reached Conan, almost all the blood had run out, and his back remained stuck to the floor. Finn and Goll grabbed Conan by the arms, wrenching him from the ground. He should have been in agony, but Conan continued to shout at them to pull harder until finally he came loose from the floor, leaving all the skin of his back behind. Finn saw a black sheep in the near distance, killed the sheep, and brought it back to Conan. He skinned the sheep, and used magic of adhesion that remained from the floor to secure the sheep's skin to Conan's back. It began to grow as though it belonged there, allowing Conan to recover. The Fianna finally arrived, massacring the opposing armies. From that point on, each spring Conan had to be sheared of the wool he'd grown.

Diarmuid and Grainne

One of the most famous warriors of the Fianna while Finn was leader was Diarmuid O'Duibhne. He was born to a man named Donn, raised alongside his half-brother, who was born of a man named Roc. One day, Diarmuid's half brother found himself frightened, running to hide behind Donn's legs. Seeing his opportunity, Donn crushed the boy between his legs and left him dead. When Roc discovered his son, he performed a ritual to bring his son back to life in the body of a great boar. He gave the boar a gaes that he must kill Diarmuid. He knew that Diarmuid had his own gaes: he could not pierce the skin of a pig, leaving him defenseless should the boar find and attack him.

Diarmuid grew to become an incredible warrior, passing the tests of the Fianna. He had the most respect for Finn, but he was known for more than just his skills in battle. He was born with a love mark on his forehead that could make any woman fall in love with him if they saw it. Knowing the trouble it could cause, Diarmuid grew his hair long over his forehead to keep the mark hidden.

Finn, by that time, was aging. While he was still the greatest warrior of the Fianna, he knew that someday someone would need to replace him as the head of the Fianna. Every year on his birthday, he leapt across a great chasm; in his mind, it was better to die in the fall than to live while his strength vanished from his body. As he aged, it was agreed that he lived too long without a wife, and so the men of the Fianna agreed the only woman worthy of him was the daughter of the High King, Grainne.

Grainne was known to be the most beautiful woman in all of Ireland. However, trouble struck when she was 12 years old, watching a boys' match of hurling. One of the boys playing had his hair blown back in the wind, and she noticed a spot on his skin. From that point on, she was hopelessly in love with him, refusing the advances of any and all men who asked for her hand. Upon hearing that Finn was requesting her hand in marriage, she decided she may as well marry him, because she couldn't find the man with such a strong hold on her heart.

A great feast was held to celebrate the upcoming marriage. Grainne hid behind a curtain, peeking out to catch a glimpse of who her husband would be. She saw Finn seated with his son, Oisin, and wondered why Finn would want to marry her, rather than marry her to his son; after all, Oisin was much younger than his aging self, and she began to regret her decision. At that moment, Finn moved aside, and she spotted Diarmuid. Immediately she realized she couldn't marry Finn, having finally found the boy who'd stolen her heart all those years ago.

Sitting down to feast, Grainne passed around a cup of wine that she had tampered with to put all the men to sleep. In turn, she asked each leader of the Fianna to run away with her, each refusing. When she came to Diarmuid, she put him under a gaes that he must leave with her. Diarmuid struggled with this. He had never betrayed Finn, nor would he ever want to, but he could not break the gaes put on him by a woman. She told him she would be readying herself in her chambers, and while she was gone, Diarmuid spoke with the other leaders of the Fianna; they all agreed that he had no choice, he had to leave with her, he couldn't break the gaes.

Very upset, Diarmuid left with Grainne. She quickly tired, asking him to carry her. He refused, hoping she would tire out and return to Finn, but instead she put him under another gaes to supply them with horses. He had no choice, and so they went looking for the horses. On their travels, they met Aengus Og, the God of Love. He was thoroughly pleased by their coupling and told them they could never sleep in a cave with a single opening, a home with a single door, or under a tree with only one branch. They could not eat the meal where it had been cooked, nor could they sleep where they had eaten. They would need to keep moving to avoid the Fianna pursuing them.

When Finn woke the next morning, his heart broke over Diarmuid's betrayal. He resolved that he must get revenge, setting out to pursue them. He chased them over the land for a long time. In each nest that Diarmuid made for Grainne, he left behind a piece of raw fish or meat, leaving it as a message to Finn that he'd not touched Grainne. One day as they crossed a ford, a wave splashed Grainne, wetting her thigh. She lashed out at Diarmuid, saying that no matter how fearless he was in battle, a simple splash of water on her thigh had more courage than he did. With that, he gave into the shame and lay with Grainne, making her his wife, leaving no more meat for Finn as they travelled.

The Fianna finally caught up with them one evening as they stayed in a home with seven doors. Each door was guarded by a member of the Fianna. Aengus Og came to them, offering to take them both to safety, but Diarmuid refused, sending Grainne to safety with the God. He went to each door, the warrior guarding each door offering to let him free. He refused, and finally opened the door that Finn guarded. Finn told him in his anger that if

Diarmuid came out the door, he would kill him. Diarmuid took the fight, and once the Fianna surrounded him he leapt high over their heads, escaping to join Grainne in safety.

A year later, Diarmuid gained permission from a giant to hunt on his land, as long as he didn't eat the magic berries of the rowan tree. Grainne, large in her pregnancy, craved the berries, and so Diarmuid killed the giant, bringing Grainne up the tree so that they could feast on the sweetest berries. It was at this time the Clan Morna decided to make peace with Finn, hoping to rejoin forces with him. They were told they could bring him Diarmuid's head or the berries of the magic rowan tree. Figuring the berries would be easier, they went to the giant's tree, finding the giant dead, and most berries missing. They reported their finding to Finn.

Finn knew that there was only one man who could slay the giant. Having a sneaking suspicion that Diarmuid was still in the tree, he sat beneath it with Oisin, playing a game of chess. Each time Oisin would move in a way that Finn could beat him, a rowan berry would fall on the board where he should move. This led to him beating Finn for the first time, causing Finn to fly into a rage. There was only one man in Ireland who could beat him at chess, and that was Diarmuid. Diarmuid leapt from the tree to safety as Aengus Og yet again spirited Grainne away to safety.

After running for many years, Grainne and Diarmuid decided that they were tired of running with their four sons. They sought to make peace with Finn. Finn agreed, arranging a feast for them, and began rebuilding his lost friendship with Diarmuid. Years later, the pair went for a hunt and came across a wild boar. The boar charged at Diarmuid; it was the son of Roc. Finn reminded him of his gaes to never pierce the skin of a pig, and as the boar drove through him with its tusks, he slammed the hilt of his sword over its head, killing it. But, it was too late. Diarmuid begged Finn for a drink of water from his hands, as Finn's hands could restore any man to health. Finn agreed, but at the last moment, he remembered his hatred for Diarmuid's betrayal, letting the water fall from his fingers. He then had a change of heart and gathered more water, but again, his anger took over and he dropped the water. He tried a third time, bringing the water to Diarmuid, pouring it over his lips, but Diarmuid was already dead.

Oisin

Finn loved nothing more than a hunt with his men and their dogs. One day, he was on a hunt, when his dogs caught the scent of a doe. They chased after her, but instead of playing with the doe, she led them on the chase, stopping on the hillside for Finn to catch up to her. The doe became a beautiful young woman and revealed herself as the daughter of his enemy. Her name was Blaith Dearg, and she invited Finn to lie with her that evening. He did, and when he woke the next morning, she was nowhere to be found. He searched for her, but no matter where he looked, he could not find her.

A year later, they went on a hunt again, and again, the dogs went chasing after a scent. They found a child sitting beneath a tree, and as he bent down to see the child, Finn saw the flash of a doe's tail in the trees. Finn realized the child was his, gathering his son to raise him. The baby was named Oisin, meaning 'little deer.' Over time, Oisin trained to become a great warrior, passing the tests of the Fianna, and becoming a leader of one of the clans of Fianna.

One morning, Oisin sat by the beach. He had a vision of a road forming over the water and a beautiful woman riding a white horse towards him. She sang to him in the most wonderful voice. She told him that her name was Niamh Chinn, and she'd come from the Land of Promise. She'd heard of him, and wanted him for herself, asking for him to follow her to live in the Land of Promise as her husband. He agreed, leaping onto the horse with her and they had three sons in the Land of Promise. Each time Oisin would find himself homesick, she would arrange a hunt or a feast for him, distracting him from his grief.

After what seemed like 3 years, Oisin begged Niamh to go visit his comrades. She told him that time passed slower in the Land of Promise, and the world he knew no longer existed. Oisin's heart broke, but he insisted on seeing for himself. Neamh agreed, warning him that if his foot touched the land of Ireland, he would never be able to return to her and their sons.

Oisin left on Niamh's white horse, and as he rode into Ireland, he recognized nothing about the land before him. He asked the people he encountered about Finn and the Fianna, but each of them ridiculed him for believing in stories from hundreds of years past. He felt his heart weep for the men he'd known, now only known as legends and stories. He turned the horse around, ready to return to the Land of Promise when he spotted four men struggling to move a boulder. He approached, leaning forward to move the boulder, when the saddle strap snapped and he landed on his back in the dirt. The moment he hit the earth, the hundreds of years aged him all at once, his hair turning white, and the teeth falling from his mouth. He told the people who stood in awe watching him age about Finn and the Fianna. They couldn't decide if he spoke the truth or if he was just insane, so they brought him to Saint Patrick.

The Saint recorded all of Oisin's stories, then told him of Christianity. Oisin couldn't fathom the rules of the Christian God, and when Saint Patrick offered to baptize him, he asked if Finn would have been baptized. The Saint replied no, as a Pagan he was surely burning in hell. Oisin dismissed him, saying that Finn wouldn't be held anywhere he didn't want to be, and he would rather die a Pagan as his father did so that they may be together. He died, unbaptized, then buried by Saint Patrick.

CHAPTER 8

Cycles of the Kings

The Cycles of the Kings follow the inherent tie between the quality of the king who led the realm and the health and prosperity of their land and people. Gaesa are heavily featured in these stories, promises that represent the sacred bond between the king and his people. These stories follow the successes and failures of semi-historical Kings of Ireland, and the impact they had on their people by the quality of their leadership.

Cormac Mac Art

Before Cormac's conception, there were two men; Cormac's father, Art, and Art's brother, Logaid. Their father was king, and they argued over who should claim the throne, as they were both entitled to it. After many arguments, they decided the only way to resolve the issue was to battle to the death at Maigh Mucruimhe.

Before the battle, Art paid a visit to the wise smith, Olc Acha. After telling him the story of why he was going to fight his brother, Olc scolded Art for choosing to fight his brother over such a decision. He and Logaid had equal rights to the throne, but surely there was a better way to handle the situation than dying. Art dismissed Olc's advice, insisting that he must fight for his throne. Resigned to Art's decision, Olc asked him how many children he had to carry on his lineage. Art told him that he had none, so Olc took his daughter aside to forge a plan.

When they approached him again, Olc told Art that since he seemed determined to die in battle for no good reason, Art should first lie with Achtan, his daughter. She would conceive that night so that, should he fall. Art would have an heir who could be raised away from the throne until they were of age to claim it. Of course, Art agreed with this plan and lay with Achtan that evening.

As a daughter of a great smith, Achtan was wise and intuitive. That night, she had a prophetic dream; she was beheaded, but a massive tree began sprouting from her neck. The branches of the tree reached far, covering Ireland. As the tree branches continued to spread, a gigantic wave rose from the ocean, sweeping over her, knocking the tree from her shoulders. Achtan woke suddenly, asking Art to interpret the dream for her. Art believed that since the husband is the head of the home, Achtan being beheaded would indicate his death today. The tree growing from her was for the son that she would bear. As the branches spread, their son grew, his control of the land growing, and he would never be defeated in war or battle. The final wave knocking the tree over pointed to their son dying by choking on a fishbone.

As predicted, Art was slain by Logaid that day. Not long after, Achtan discovered that the conception was successful; she was carrying Art's child. Olc offered the child protection by drawing four circles over Achtan's stomach, offering protection from wolves, drowning, battle, and fire. To keep Logaid from discovering the child, Achtan went to stay with close friends of Art's at the House of Lugna.

As they entered the Lugna property, the labor pains began. Achtan got out of the carriage, lying in a bed of ferns to birth the child. At the moment the child was born, a boom of thunder roared across the sky. From inside the house, Lugna told his people that thunder like that meant the birth of a king.

Lying in her fern bed, Achtan told her handmaiden to keep watch over the child while she got some rest. As Achtan rested, so did the handmaiden, and they woke to the horror of the baby missing. As they'd slept, a she-wolf had stolen the child. Achtan was devastated, and they rushed to the House of Lugna to seek help in finding the child. Despite the search, the child wasn't found.

Returning to the World of Men

Several years later, a huntsman had been tracking a she-wolf. She led him back to her lair, and there he discovered not only her litter of pups but a healthy, bubbly boy. Scooping up the boy, the huntsman rushed to the House of Lugna, remembering the lost boy. The hunter told Lugna about where he'd found the boy living with the wolves.

Lugna took him in and named him Cormac. He raised the boy alongside his two sons. As far as Cormac was concerned, the House of Lugna was all he knew, so Lugna must be his father. The idea came crashing down on him when he'd gotten into a fight with his brothers, and the older boy mocked him, claiming it was a shame to have been knocked down by a boy who didn't have a father. Cormac demanded the truth from Lugna, who finally explained to the child his origin. After finding out that he was the blood of High Kings, Cormac demanded that they go to Tara so that his family could finally know him and claim what was rightfully his. Lugna agreed, and they set off.

When they arrived, Logaid was settling a dispute between his wife and an old woman. The lady was poor, with little to her name except for her small flock of sheep. Her sheep had gotten loose, and one had eaten the queen's woad, a plant that she used when dyeing fabrics. The queen had demanded justice, and to satisfy his wife, Logaid decreed that the woman should give the queen her sheep.

Cormac spoke, his voice ringing through the room. This wasn't a fair judgment since the woad would grow back. He claimed that a just king would decree a shearing for a shearing. The old woman would give the queen the shearing of the sheep that had eaten the queen's woad, and they would be even. The room murmured in agreement with Cormac, and at that moment, the very land beneath Logaid's feet sank several feet into the Earth. The people dethroned Logaid peacefully, and Cormac became the new king.

A few years into his reign, it came time for Cormac to take a wife. Working on the roadside, he noticed a beautiful woman named Eithne. He was enamored by how hard she worked and how striking she was. He wasted no time in asking her foster father, Buacha, for her hand in marriage. He'd once been a wealthy man, but Eithne's brothers had taken advantage of his kindness and generosity until they'd taken all of his wealth. He left with his wife and Eithne, now living in poverty. Eithne never complained about working for her foster father, and she did so diligently.

Buacha told the king that he would love to see Eithne marry him, but she wasn't his to give away. So instead, Eithne and Cormac eloped. When they returned to Buacha's home, they'd already conceived a child, so it would be too late to protest the marriage. Cormac restored Buacha's fortune as a bridal price, paying him enough to pay for seven kings' daughters. Over time they had a son and a daughter together.

The Silver Branch

On an early May morning, Cormac sat on the hillside. An unbelievably tall and beautiful man approached him, clad in a green cloak held together by golden brooches. Golden circlets were on his head and wrist, but it was what was in the stranger's hand that caught Cormac's attention: a silver branch with perfect tiny golden apples. The stranger explained that the branch would put all who heard it into an enchanted sleep that could heal all of their wounds when the branch was shaken. The stranger asked Cormac if they could become friends, which Cormac eagerly agreed to. He immediately asked the stranger if he could have the stick, to which the stranger agreed to if he could have three promises in exchange. Cormac quickly said yes, happily accepting the stick.

The stranger gave him his first wish: he would leave with Cormac's daughter, Alba. Cormac had to maintain his honor, and Alba left that day with the stranger. The people of Tara grieved for Alba, but the king shook the stick, casting the people into a deep, healing sleep. One year later, the stranger returned, this time claiming Cormac's son Cairbre. They left, and again, Cormac shook the sick for his people. In another year, the stranger returned, gathering Cormac's wife.

The Land of Promise

Cormac no longer had anything left to lose, now that he was without his wife and children. He gathered his warriors, taking off to chase after the stranger. While they crossed the plains, a thick fog rolled in, and when it lifted, Cormac found himself alone in a strange land.

Cormac walked until he found a beautiful home, seeing many strange sights along the way. Two of the most beautiful people he had ever seen, a man and a woman, welcomed him into the house, leading him to the table. They presented him with a pig, an ax, and a log. The pair explained that as long as the pig was killed by that ax and burned on that log, all would be whole again tomorrow. All that needed to happen for the pig to cook was to speak four truths over it, and it would roast to perfection. The three of them told four true stories about themselves and the pig cooked.

King Cormac had one issue; as king, he couldn't eat without his men. The man shrugged, obliging the king by summoning the king's men, who appeared suddenly. Once they were all around King Cormac, the man identified himself; he was the beautiful stranger, also God of the Sea, Manannán Mac Lir. He had brought King Cormac the branch, giving it as a test, meant to draw him into searching for wisdom.

He presented King Cormac with a golden cup. Manannán Mac Lir explained that when a lie was told over it, the cup would shatter into three pieces. With three truths, it would repair itself. Sure enough, he told a lie, and the cup split into three. Manannán brought King Cormac's wife and children to the table. He told King Cormac that the three of them had been unharmed while in the Land of Promise. He then said that King Cormac's wife and daughter had not seen or lain with a man and that his son had not been with a woman. The cup jumped up, repairing itself. He handed King Cormac the cup, telling him to keep the cup and branch, but on one condition. When the king died, the cup and branch had to be returned to the Land of Promise. King Cormac accepted, and from that day forward, his kingdom was prosperous. There was never an empty belly or an unsatisfied home. King Cormac lived to old age until choking on a salmon bone, just as his parents had predicted.

Conaire Mor

If you were a King of Ireland, it was typical that you'd marry the most beautiful woman in the land. Unfortunately for the kings of the time, if you married the most beautiful woman you've ever seen, it was likely that she wasn't entirely human. This was the case for King Eochaid and his wife, Etain. Neither he nor Etain knew of Etain's faery lineage when they married and had a child, a beautiful baby girl. A few years into the baby's life, Etain's faery husband, whom she'd been arranged to marry, came to retrieve her from the mortal realm, leaving behind her daughter to stay with King Eochaid.

The young girl was beautiful, and for as much as the king loved his daughter, he couldn't bear to look at the child. She looked too much like her mother. King Eochaid issued orders to his men to take the girl away and kill her. The king's attendants intended to follow the king's orders, bringing the child to a well. With a single giggling smile, the young girl melted their hearts, and neither could bear to be the one to kill such a beautiful child. Instead, they brought the child to a cowherd to rear. The young girl was given the name Meas Buachalla. Fearing that she might be discovered, the cowherd built her a small home without windows or doors, leaving half the roof open so that she could still feel somewhat free. As she grew, she became just as beautiful as her mother had been.

Years later, the High King of Ireland sought to marry. He called for his Druid, requesting that he tell him who his wife would be. The Druid prophesied that the king would find the most beautiful wife in all the land but warned that she would be of unknown race. Unsure what to make of this warning, the king sent his men to scour the land for the woman his Druid had seen.

During their travels, two of the King's men came across Meas Buachalla's tiny home, at first mistaking it for a storage shed. Peering through a crack in the wall, they saw the most beautiful woman that either of them had ever set eyes on, and they rushed back to the High King to deliver the news. The king thought about it, deciding this had to be the woman his Druid had seen and sent for the woman to be collected for him.

The same night that the High King sent his men, Meas Buachalla was visited by a strange guest. A giant bird descended through the hole in her roof, and as she watched in wonder, the bird dropped its feathers, revealing a gorgeous man standing before her. They lay together that night, and when they were done, he revealed that he was the Bird King. He told her that she would bear his son but that she would soon marry the High King of Ireland and that all would believe the child to be the king's. The Bird King instructed that she was to name his son Conaire and that the child would become king one day.

As predicted, the king's men arrived, whisking away Meas Buachalla to marry the High King, and in time she bore the Bird King's son. Everyone accepted the boy as the High King's son and he was celebrated as such. Meas Buachalla loved her son so much that she chose three foster brothers for him to grow alongside as company.

The four boys were inseparable. They dressed in the same colors, even riding horses of the same colors. If four plates were set for them, they would eat from one, splitting everything equally between them. When he was born, Conaire was given three gifts: the gift of sight, the gift of hearing, and the gift of judgment. So strong was his love for his brothers that he gave each of them one of his gifts.

Hunting was a common sport for the boys. During one hunt, they spotted a massive flock of birds and pursued the flock. Each time they got close, the flock would up and fly away. If a spear was thrown, it was always just out of range, and if they managed to get close, the birds always seemed to be a step ahead of their hunters. This led the boys to the water's edge.

The very same day the boys went hunting the birds, the High King of Tara died. To be High King of Tara, you couldn't inherit the throne. Instead, there was a Bull Feast ritual. A bull was killed, the blood drained into a barrel. The town would roast and feast on the bull while a Druid would consume the entire barrel of blood as the townspeople danced and celebrated. The Druid became drunk off the blood, sleeping to have visions about who the new High King would be. The Druid woke, telling the people that he'd had a vision of a young man walking into Tara completely nude. As they continued the celebration, the people of Tara anxiously watched for their new High King to arrive.

The Bird King's Gaesa

At the water's edge, Conaire was in for a surprise. He'd finally managed to line up the perfect shot to hunt one of the birds. As he drew back his spear, he watched the entire flock rise, the feathers of the birds dropping. Several striking yet visibly annoyed men stood before him. The most beautiful of all of them came forward, sternly addressing Conaire. He approached, asking Conaire if he'd forgotten his gaesa never to hunt or kill a bird? His father had been a Bird King, after all. Stunned, Conaire told the man that he knew no such thing; he'd never been told but promised he'd never hunt another bird.

Understanding that Conaire knew nothing of his history or future, the man revealed Conaire's prophecy: he would become the High King of Ireland. If he wanted the prophecy to come true, he must strip down and walk to Tara naked and alone. His reign would be prosperous, but he had several gaesa that needed to be kept.

The first, Conaire knew, was never to harm a bird. Conaire must be careful to never travel clockwise around Tara, nor should he travel counterclockwise around Breaga. While traveling, he could not spend more than nine consecutive nights outside of Tara. He must never hunt the crooked beast of Cearna, and should he ever see firelight through the spokes of a cartwheel, he could not sleep in that house that evening. He should also never enter a home if three reds entered before him. Wherever he stayed, he could not allow for a single man or woman to enter any place he was staying after sunset. Finally, as High King, Conaire could not allow pillaging, and if there was ever a dispute between two of his subjects, it was not for him to settle the dispute. Conaire agreed to each gaes, promising to obey each when he became the High King.

With the blessing of the Bird King, Conaire stripped from his clothing and walked the entire journey to Tara nude. When they spotted him, the people rushed to clothe him in purple cloaks, rushing him to be crowned. Some subjects saw his youth, hesitant that he may not be a good king. He promised them that he would always seek counsel from the wise men of the kingdom, and with that, he was crowned the High King of Ireland. As predicted, his reign was prosperous, his people fed and well cared for.

Conaire's Foster Brothers

With Conaire gone as the new High King, his brothers were left to their own devices. They grew bored with hunting, deciding to seek excitement with other young men who felt bored and mischievous. There was one farmer in particular whom the boys loved to harass. Each year they stole from this farmer one pig, one ox, and one cow. At first, the farmer didn't want to bother the High King with such petty thievery but soon grew tired of the boys pillaging his animals. He finally brought the issue to King Conaire.

King Conaire wasn't sure of what to do. The punishment for pillaging was death, but he couldn't bear to put his brothers to death. Of the group they were with, all men were decreed to be killed by their fathers, except his brothers, who were exiled to Britain.

Arriving in Britain, the brothers quickly found a new group of men to pillage with and made quick friends with a local king. They agreed with the king that they could plunder as they desired, as long as they would one day do him whatever favor he asked.

Broken Gaesa

This marked the first of the gaesa that King Conaire would break. Shortly after his brothers' exile, the king was told of two subjects to the South who were in such a dispute that it threatened to turn to warfare. The king chose to visit the men to settle the problem between them. He spent the first five nights with the first man while resolving the discourse. While he prepared to leave, he realized he would have to spend an equal amount of time with the second man so that the dispute wouldn't restart over perceived favoritism, so the king stayed away from Tara for 10 consecutive nights. On his return to Tara, he could hear the hoofbeats and sounds of the underworld warriors, having visions of faery fires burning. King Conaire knew he was in danger after breaking a gaes. Trying to avoid the threat led him to travel clockwise around Tara first, then counterclockwise around Breaga.

The deep fog began to cover the road as the king attempted to return to Tara. They could see a beast running ahead of them, and King Conaire threw his spear at the creature. He discovered with horror that his spear had slain the crooked beast of Cearna. The fog continued to thicken with each broken gaes, the sounds of underworld hordes growing louder. Soon only one road could be seen, leading to Da Derga, a friend of the king's. As they approached the hostel, the king could see that they were following three men; all with red hair, red cloaks, riding red horses. Try as he may, the men wouldn't allow him to pass them, and so they entered the hostel ahead of the king. Resigning himself to another broken gaes, King Conaire dismounted from his horse, falling to the ground. He looked up, seeing the firelight within the house through the spokes of a carriage wheel, but with nowhere else to safely go, the king entered the hostel.

Unbeknown to the king, his brothers returned from Britain with their band of outlaws, the King of Britain, and his warriors. They'd returned to pillage and plunder Ireland and saw the faery warriors outside of the hostel. Recognizing the king would be in the hostel, they chose to join the faery horde. To keep track of how many were lost in the battle, each threw a stone on a pile, to be later picked up on their way out. They sat back, waiting for the fight to begin.

After sunset, King Conaire heard a knock on the door. He opened the door to see an ugly, aged hag standing before him, begging to be let in to escape the horrible weather. At first, the king asked her if she was sure that there was nowhere else for her to go, but she scorned him for being a king willing to allow his subjects to suffer. With this, he let her in, and she hugged him in delight. She told him that though he was a good, hospitable king, he would leave the hostel in no larger a piece than a bird could carry in its talons.

King Conaire understood he'd been tricked. The faery hordes came crashing through the door of the hostel, and he fought bravely against them, no matter how futile a battle. At the peak of the fight, he was overcome by a powerful thirst, but the water would escape him each time he reached for a drink. His son, Ferfla, and his servant, Mac Cecht, left, seeking water to return to the king. Knowing their intent to quench the king's thirst, the water escaped them as well, with Ferfla dying on the servant's back as the water in his body escaped as sweat. Mac Cecht found a single lake that allowed him to gather water in his cupped hands, bringing it carefully back to the king.

Mac Cecht returned to the king in time to see the faery horde beheading his beloved king. Determined to fulfill his king's request, he poured the water into King Conaire's mouth and then over the stump of his neck. King Conaire's head spoke to him in gratitude. Before returning to Tara, Mac Cecht found all of the pieces that he could of the High King to be buried when he returned.

Niall of the Nine Hostages

After losing Etain, King Eochaid, the High King of Ireland, and his new wife, Mongfind, had four sons: Fergus, Fiachra, Ailil, and Brian. On the surface, the family was wonderfully happy, but behind the scenes, the High King was in love with a hostage. The hostage was named Caireann. Because of the king's affections, Mongfind despised the hostage. Her hatred meant heavy manual labor for Cireann, fetching water for the entire house on her own.

Eventually, they found out that Caireann was pregnant with King Eochaid's child. With that, Mongfind began working her even harder, hoping that she would lose the child in pregnancy. However, Caireann was strong and carried the baby to term. She went into labor one day as she ventured to the well, giving birth in the grass. Fearing what the queen would do, Caireann left the child in the grass. The others feared Queen Mongfind as much and wouldn't so much as touch the child to provide comfort.

Torna, a great poet and Druid, spotted the child in the grass. He picked him up, having a vision that the child would be the greatest king Ireland had ever known. Even those descended from the child would become great kings, and the child would gain the throne unopposed. After having the vision, Torna chose to raise him in secret, away from the hateful queen. The child was named Niall, and Torna taught him all that he could. He refused to allow Niall to be in Tara until he was of age to claim the throne.

Returning for His Throne

When Niall was of age, he returned to Tara. Upon his return, he found that his mother was still serving the king and queen, fetching water for the household while dressed in rags. Niall went to her, telling her that this would not do. Against her protests, he took her away from her duties, dressing her in exquisite purple robes.

King Eochaid was delighted to see his son return, as were the subjects of Tara, despite the fury of Queen Mongfind. Niall had become an athletic, kind, and educated young man and a perfect candidate for the throne. The queen realized that Niall had been too happily accepted by the people, meaning she could only sit back and watch as his return was celebrated.

The Druid's Test

Since Mongfind couldn't directly go after Niall, she decided to weaponize his father against him. She told the king that he would have to choose an heir out of his sons, thinking he would undoubtedly choose Brian as the best candidate. Instead of making a choice himself, the king tasked the Druid Sithchean to test the five men to see who would be the best king.

Sithchean fashioned a test, sending the five men into a forge with instructions to construct a weapon. The weapon they forged would determine who would win the throne. Once the five men entered, the Druid locked them inside, setting the place ablaze. The true test was to see what the men rescued on the way out of the blaze.

First out of the forge was Brian, carrying an armload of hammers. This pleased Sithchean, indicating his strength; he would be an excellent fighter for his people. Next was Fiachra, who brought with him a great case of beer. Again, Sithchean was pleased; this meant that he would care for sciences, arts, and beauty among his people. Third from the forge was Ailil, carrying a massive chest of weapons. Sithchean was delighted by this; he would avenge his people whenever necessary. Fourth from the forge was Fergus. In his arms were large bundles of kindling. Sithchean was less impressed by this and prophesied that he would be impotent and without children. Finally, Niall emerged from the forge, hauling an anvil behind him. Sithchean proudly declared that they'd found their king. Niall would be a great king and anvil to the people of the kingdom.

The queen was displeased. She tried to turn her sons against Niall, telling them to stage a fight. When he attempted to break the fight, they were to kill him. When the fighting began, Niall stepped forward to stop them, but Torna stopped him in his tracks. He told him they must resolve their own issues.

Securing the Throne

After the Druid's test, the five sons of Eochaid decided to go for a hunt. They went far out of their home territory, and that evening made a fire together, and after feasting on what they'd killed. But then they realized that none of them had brought even a single drop of water with them, so they began to search for water to quench their thirst.

The youngest, Fergus, went to search first. He looked all over, finding nothing until discovering a well. A hideous hag blocked passage to the well. He asked if he could get past her to gather water for him and his brothers. She agreed, but only if he would kiss her. He refused, returning to his brothers, saying he couldn't find anything.

Each brother took their turn searching for water. Each found the hag and was given the same condition: they could gather water, but only if they kissed her. Ailil and Brian both refused, returning empty-handed. Fiachra summoned enough courage to give the hag a

330

slight kiss on the cheek. While she was pleased with his effort, she would not allow him water but informed him that two of his descendants would one day be kings.

Finally, Niall went searching for water, finding the hag at the well. She told him the condition: in exchange for a kiss, you can have all the water you'd like. He told her he would do more than kiss her, but he would lie with her as well. He whisked her off her feet, and as he lay her in the grass, she transformed into the most beautiful woman. This thrilled her, and she told him that not only would he be the king, but so would all of his descendants. He gathered the water for him and his brothers, but before Niall left, she gave him one final condition: his brothers could not have even a drop of water unless they swore allegiance to him and allowed him to take the throne unchallenged.

Upon returning with the water, Niall kept his word to the hag. None of the brothers could have a drop of water until they renounced their right to the crown, promising never to challenge Niall's position on the throne. As they renounced their claim to the throne, each received a drink of water.

The group traveled back to Tara. As they entered, the brothers hung their weapons, with Niall hanging his weapon a hand's length higher than the others. When they sat at the table, Niall claimed the seat at the head of the table. Eochaid and Mongfind came to sit with the men, asking how the hunt had been. Niall spoke for them, but Mongfind interrupted him. She claimed it was inappropriate for him to respond in place of his elder brother. He explained that his brothers had given him dominion over them and that none would challenge his throne, despite her attempts to manipulate the heir to the throne.

Once Niall took his throne, he conquered each of the nine provinces of Britain, Scotland, and Ireland. Instead of ruling over these places himself, he took a hostage from each region, ensuring his safety from revolt or rebellion. This is how he earned the name King Niall of the Nine Hostages.

Mongan

Two kings once ruled the kingdom of Ulster, a pair of cousins named Fiachra Finn and Fiachra Dubh. Each year they would rotate who sat on the throne, while the other would be free to travel and do as they pleased for the year.

During a year away from the throne, Fiachra Finn chose to visit the King of Scandinavia. While he was there, the Scandinavian King fell ill from a curse. The only way to break the curse was to consume the meat of a cow that was all white, except for red ears. Finn took it upon himself to search for the cow. He searched the entirety of Scandinavia until he finally found a single cow matching the description.

A widowed black hag owned the cow. She owned nothing else of value, sustaining herself on the cow's milk and butter, selling whatever excess she had to keep herself afloat. Finn went to her, first offering her another cow in exchange for this one, but the hag was too attached to her cow and would not trade it. Then Finn told her that the Scandinavian King would give her a cow for each hoof of her prized cow. She considered it, then agreed, but only if Finn could vouch that the king would hold up his end of the bargain. Finn was confident that the king would ensure that she received her cows, so he promised her, leaving with the cow. He brought the cow to the Scandinavian King, and upon eating the cow, the King was restored to health and vigor, and Finn returned home to reclaim his throne.

A year later, the hag found Finn. She told him that she had never received her four cows and that despite her cow saving his life, the King of Scandinavia had left her destitute. Horrified and feeling responsible for the hag's predicament, Finn offered her 40 cattle to return home with. She told him she didn't care for cattle or gold; she wanted revenge.

Mongan's Conception

Finn gathered his troops, setting off to Scandinavia once again. He was stunned when they reached the shore; waiting for them was an army that dwarfed their own, along with a herd of vicious sheep with giant heads and gnashing teeth. Finn knew they stood no chance against this army and its terrors.

The wall of sheep and soldiers parted, suddenly revealing a tall, beautiful man in a green cloak. The cloak was held closed by golden brooches, and there were silver circlets on his head and wrists. It was the God of the Sea, Manannán Mac Lir. He offered Finn a trade; if he could have a single night with Finn's wife, he would even the playing field and ensure Finn's victory on his current battlefield.

Finn wasn't sold on the idea, but he knew he could not win this battle otherwise. Seeing his apprehension, Manannán promised that when he saw Finn's wife, he would take on Finn's appearance so that she would be none the wiser, and he would perform in a way that would make Finn proud. The only catch would be that she would then conceive a child with the god. Finn agreed, and with that, Manannán killed 1,000 men and produced a hound from his cloak that chased away the sheep. Once Finn won the battle, he awarded the hag with seven castles and 200 sheep.

When Finn returned home, his wife was already pregnant. When she gave birth, the child was covered in hair, and so they named him Mongan, meaning 'hairy beast.' The same night that Mongan was born, two others were born; Finn's manservant had a son, and Fiachra Dubh had a daughter named Dubhlacha. The two boys were baptized together to be bound as brothers, and Dubhlacha was betrothed to Mongan. Soon after the birth, Manannán returned, claiming his child to be raised in the Land of Promise. Mongan grew up learning prophecy, poetry, and shapeshifting until he could return to Ulster.

Mongan's Return

Mongan returned to Ulster when he turned 16, finding that Dubh had murdered Finn. He had grown tired of sharing the throne. Dubh was stunned when he saw Mongan, never considering that he would someday return from the Land of Promise to claim the throne. Thinking quickly, he made a deal with Mongan to share the throne the way Dubh had shared it with Finn. Mongan agreed, and with that, Dubhlacha was given to him to marry, his foster brother becoming his manservant. His manservant married Dubhlacha's handmaiden, and together the foursome lived happy lives.

Soon after, Manannán Mac Lir came to visit his son. Seeing the situation, he admonished Mongan for not avenging his father and choosing to rule with his murderous uncle rather than exacting revenge. Mongan agreed, slaying his uncle and claiming the throne for himself.

Now that he was the sole king on the throne, Mongan took a journey throughout Ireland to get to know his kingdom better. During his travels, he visited King Brandubh, the King of Leinster. While Mongan stayed with the fellow king, he fell in love with the cattle he owned, all white with red ears. Brandubh said that if Mongan wanted the cattle, he could have them, but only if they began a friendship where Mongan would never refuse his requests. Eager to have the herd, Mongan agreed.

Many years later, King Brandubh came to visit Mongan. Reminding him of his promise, Brandubh requested Dubhlacha's hand in marriage. Mongan didn't want to lose his wife, nor did she want to leave her husband. She told him that he must allow it to happen to honor his word. Dubhlacha made a deal with Brandubh that she would go with him, but only if he promised that he would not touch her or force her to marry him for an entire year. Once he gave her his word, she went with him to Leinster, bringing her handmaiden with her.

Mongan and his manservant now found themselves without their wives. The manservant became a miserable mess, constantly complaining to Mongan that he missed his wife and her womanly comforts. The longer he went without his wife, the more personal the attacks became against Mongan. He told him that his time learning in the Land of Promise had been wasted, as he knew nothing useful if he couldn't get their wives back. As far as he was concerned, Mongan had been coddled, learning nothing but creature comforts.

Retrieving Their Wives

Mongan decided it was time to take matters into his own hands, and so traveled to Leinster with his manservant. They encountered two monks of the House of Leinster, redirecting them into the river. Mongan shapeshifted himself and his manservant to take the appearance of the monks. When they arrived to see King Brandubh, they were warmly welcomed, and they said they were there to take the king's future wife's confession. They were given privacy with her and her handmaiden.

Once they were alone, Mongan revealed their true form, and they spent time with their wives. The King's monks arrived during that time, causing confusion as they'd just been welcomed into the home. Mongan again assumed the form of a monk, telling the guards that the two at the door must be Mongan trying to trick the king of his future wife. They believed him, chasing off the real monks. Mongan and his servant visited this way three more times until the year drew to a close, and Brandubh began making arrangements for the wedding.

On the day of the wedding, Mongan and his manservant attended the festivities, assuming the form of other nobles. They encountered a hag on the way to the wedding. Mongan asked her to attend the wedding, and with the promise of fine food, she agreed. He shapeshifted her into the form of the most beautiful woman in Ireland, and the trio made their way.

Upon arriving, King Brandubh spotted the hag in her shifted form, forgetting all about Dubhlacha. He offered Mongan all of the riches and luxuries he could, even offering him spells that could cure him of any illness, but Mongan refused it all. Brandubh pleaded with him that he had to have this beauty for a wife, and feigning reluctance, Mongan gave in. He gathered Dubhlacha and her handmaiden, bringing them home with him and his servant. Brandubh married the hag, and in the morning, woke in horror. Beside him was not the beautiful maiden that he'd lain with the night prior, but instead a hideous hag.

Labhraidh Loingseach

Once, two brothers served as Kings of Ireland: Cobhthach, who served as King of Leinster, and Laoghaire, who served as High King of Ireland. Cobhthach was an incredibly jealous man, especially when it came to Laoghaire. If Laoghaire was successful, it was a slight against Cobhthach. His jealousy was so intense that it made him physically ill, his skin becoming sallow and thin, festering with his jealousy. He began to waste away, his people naming him Cobhthach Caol, meaning 'Cobhthach the miserable.'

Laoghaire came to visit his sick brother. During the visit, he accidentally killed a single chicken, stepping on it and breaking its neck. This was all it took to make Cobhthach feel vindicated in his hatred of his brother. He told his people to send a message to his brother that he had succumbed to his illness. He was to be lain on a funeral bier with a knife hidden in his hand. When Laoghaire arrived to grieve his brother, he threw himself over what he believed to be his brother's corpse, sobbing for his lost brother. Cobhthach stabbed his brother, finally having his way. Without Laoghaire to stand in his way, Cobhthach took the seat of High King of Ireland.

Despite finally having his way, Cobhthach still saw Laoghaire's son as a threat to his throne. He invited Laoghaire's widow Aine, Laoghaire's son Allile, and their young son to supper with him. The young family arrived for the feast, but instead of festivities, Cobhthach killed Allile, his nephew. He cut the man's heart from his chest, forcing his young boy to eat his father's heart, as well as forcing him to swallow a mouse whole, tail and all. Overcome by grief, horror, and disgust, the boy fell mute. This was pleasing to Cobhthach since a mute could never be a King in Ireland. The boy took the name Maol, meaning 'mute.'

Reclaiming His Voice

As a man, Maol began attending hurling matches. One day, he became so excited by the game that a shout escaped his lips, exciting those around him. They began shouting

"Labhraidh," meaning "He speaks," and from that day forward, his name became Labhraidh Loingseach.

Aine was terrified for her son; now that his voice had returned, his uncle may find out. Her son could be in grave danger. She advised Labhraidh to leave Ireland. Shortly after, he and some of his comrades left Ireland together, heading for France.

Labhraidh in France

Once they arrived in France, Labhraidh wasted no time in telling the King of France that he, Labhraidh, was of royal descent, saying that Labhraidh's grandfather was the High King of Ireland. The King of France put Labhraidh in charge of one of his armies, and Labhraidh did so well in command that he garnered the admiration and respect of the French people. Stories of Labhriadh's greatness traveled far, so much so that the daughter of the King of Munster, Moiriath, fell in love with him from afar.

Deciding that she had to have him, Moiriath sought out Craiftine, one of Ireland's greatest bards and poets. Together they crafted a love-lay for Labhraidh, and once it was complete, Craiftine left for France with the song and gifts. Labhraidh was delighted by the gifts, and even more so by the love-lay, especially once he discovered that Moiriath had written it herself. He was enraptured by her and returned to Ireland immediately to meet this incredible woman.

The people of Munster greeted Labhraidh with great enthusiasm, and they had a fabulous feast. Once he laid eyes on Moiriath, Labhraidh fell hopelessly in love with her. Despite the respect he garnered, Moiriath's parents also knew how exceptional their daughter was, refusing to allow her to be seduced by just any man. The king kept the pair occupied, and once guests began heading for bed, the queen took to bed outside her daughter's bedroom. She slept the first half of the night with the left eye open, the second half with the right open.

Craiftine decided that he would help the young pair find privacy. He warned Labhraidh to cover his ears, then played a beautiful sleep melody on his harp. All who heard it fell asleep, and those who were already asleep fell even deeper into sleep. Labhraidh snuck into Moiriath's room that night, and they spent a lover's evening together.

When everyone woke in the morning, the queen immediately knew there had been a man in her daughter's room. She and the king demanded that their daughter tell them who she had been with so that he could be killed for defiling her, but she held her silence. Labhraidh stood and admitted that he had been the one to spend the night with their daughter and had fallen in love with her. The queen and king were relieved that it was him. They gave their blessing that Labhraidh may have their daughter to marry.

Returning to Leinster

After marriage, Labhraidh realized that he no longer had to fear his uncle. He was a respected military leader with no shortage of followers through France and Ireland. This led him and Moiriath to move to Leinster and take the throne.

Cobhthach Caol wasn't pleased to hear that his nephew had returned to the crown but couldn't do anything to Labhraidh without it being a declaration of war. He went to work to find an angle that could help him remove his perceived threat, while Labhraidh quietly went to work with his people. Gathering all the iron supplies they could, they went to work creating iron nails, hinges, bricks, and doors. They held such secrecy that nobody knew who was making what pieces of their new king's plan, even among friends and family.

Together, the community of Leinster helped Labhraidh to build an entire house of iron, layering wood on the exterior to disguise it into looking like a regular house. With the building complete, Labhraidh invited his uncle to feast with him. Cobhthach had his suspicions, and so to ease his mind, Labhraidh told him to bring as many of his guards as he needed to feel comfortable; he wanted to make peace. His mind at ease, Cobhthach agreed to come to the feast, bringing his entire army with him.

Arriving at the iron house, Cobhthach was impressed by the lavish feast. However, his suspicions returned when he looked into the house, seeing that none of Labhraidh's people were inside. He refused to enter for fear of being attacked.

Aine and Labhraidh exchanged a look as she nodded to him, silently telling him that she understood the plan and for him to continue, with her in the house. Feeling assured that nothing would happen with Labhraidh's mother present, Cobhthach and his army filled the house. As the last man entered, the doors were closed and barred behind them. Labhraidh's men arranged piles of wood around the house, then lit them on fire. Everyone inside the iron house, including Aine, suffocated and died in the heat. Labhraidh's father was finally avenged with his mother's sacrifice, and Labhraidh went on to take the throne of High King, becoming a king of great dignity, grace, and respect.

Conclusion

Celtic mythology as a whole is full of mystery, leaving us with many questions. Their oral traditions mean that much of the rich, incredible history of these peoples were easily altered by those who tried to record them, or, as in this case of the Christians, twisted to be given a more Christian slant in an effort to convert the Pagans to the new religion. There were even more that could have been not only misinterpreted, but also lost to time if not recorded, as oral traditions waned. As the ancient Druids of old died away, so did the beauty of the old myths and the pantheon within them. Thankfully, because of the Romans, who recorded what they could from the stories, poems, and songs of the bards and Druids, we are able to turn our eyes to the histories and understand what and who it was that the ancient Celts worshiped, even if the true origin of it's people are unknown.

The type of history that comes with Celtic mythology is one of gods, heroes, warriors, and fantastical creatures of great power and mischief. This reflects on the people who worshiped these beings: unconquerable people who fought with passion and vigor, who had a deep respect for those who battled with all they had, and the kings who put their people above all else. The work put in by the Romans who encountered the ancient Celts, as well as the Christian people who met them in the Middle Ages, means that even if the information were altered to suit their purposes, whether comparing the Celtic pantheon to that of the Romans, or joining the Celtic Pagan religion with Christianity, we can still access who these people were, as well as what they stood for. Looking back at the songs, poems, and stories gives us a connection to people long lost, and a glimmer of understanding of what the world looked like to these ancestral people. We turn back to these stories to empower us, to embrace the fighting passion within ourselves, and bring out heroic champions within us when we battle in our own lives.

What is most appreciated within these stories is the timeless manner in which they translate to our current lives; we may not be traversing lands on foot or steed to become the ultimate champion of the land, but we are still fighting to be the best we can be and at times battling the demons within us, such as rage, jealousy, envy, and pride. We may not be High Kings of Tara, but we still learn to honor our promises as the kings and warriors held firm to their gaesa, and to protect and fight for our loved ones as if our home is our kingdom. When we turn to the Tuatha dé Danann in the legends, we find ourselves within the gods and goddesses; they are still depicted with human flaws, giving in to passion and jealousy, even if their power could flip an entire city on its head. In turning to these ancient stories that were passed through the generations, we see not only the world through the eyes of the ancients, but a way to examine ourselves, and the way we can develop into a stronger version of ourselves.

Despite the loss of information that left this earth with the Druids who taught it, we can still find the wonder of ancient mythology. Modern pagans still worship as best they can over the course of the eight festivals. We can experience the power of locations like Stonehenge, the Navan Fort, the castles and forts that still line the hilltops of the Celtic countryside of Wales, Ireland, Scotland, and Britain. We can still visit the stone that contains the Abhartach in Slaghtaverty, or the Lia Fáil that still stands proudly on the Hill of Tara in County Meath. These memorials of the ancient peoples and the mythologies they represent give us a timeless connection to the warriors, kings, and deities that we can no longer see, and experience the magic of the Celtic majesties with our own eyes.

A Short Message from the Author

As a small author, reviews are what help me out the most! It would mean so much if you could please leave a review of the book.

If you enjoyed reading this book and it left an impact on you leaving a review would help me reach more readers.

It won't take more than a few seconds and will help me out tremendously.

Thank you, I can't wait to read what you thought of my book!

References

10 Celtic deities you should know. (2018, December 24). Learn Religions. https://www.learnreligions.com/gods-of-the-celts-2561711

Arawn: The Welsh ogd of the afterlife. (2020, November 2). Symbol Sage. https://symbolsage.com/arawn-the-welsh-god/

Belenus Celtic deity. (n.d.). Encyclopedia Britannica. https://www.britannica.com/topic/Belenus

Brent, H. (2019, August 22). *Exploring Irish mythology: Clurichauns*. The Irish Post. https://www.irishpost.com/life-style/exploring-irish-mythology-clurichauns-170462

Butler, C. (2015, October 1). *Druids, filid & bards: Custodians of Celtic tradition*. Irish News. | https://irishempire.org/news/travel-roots/druids-filid-bards-custodians-of-celtic-tradition/25

Caer Ibormeith. (2019, July 31). Wikipedia. https://en.wikipedia.org/wiki/Caer_Ibormeith

Cartwright, M. (2021, November 23). *The ancient Celtic pantheon*. World History Encyclopedia. https://www.worldhistory.org/article/1715/the-ancient-celtic-pantheon/

Celtic otherworld. (2020, November 13). Celtic Life. https://celticlifeintl.com/the-celtic-otherworld/

Cernunnos. (n.d.). Encyclopedia Britannica. https://www.britannica.com/topic/Cernunnos

Cian. (2021a, February 11). Bard Mythologies. https://bardmythologies.com/cian/

Connor (2019, December 1o). *The Dullahan of Celtic mythology*. The Irish Place. https://www.theirishplace.com/heritage/the-dullahan/

Danu. (2021b, February 11). Bard Mythologies. https://bardmythologies.com/danu/

Donnelly, D. (2020, May 23). *Abhartach the Irish vampire: Irish folklore & ghost stories from Ireland.* Your Irish Culture. https://www.yourirish.com/folklore/abhartach-irish-vampire

Eithne. (2021c, February 11). Bard Mythologies. https://bardmythologies.com/eithne/

Far darrig. (2021, May 23). Wikipedia. https://en.wikipedia.org/wiki/Far_darrig

Fenian cycle stories. (2021, April 12). Bard Mythologies. https://bardmythologies.com/fenian-cycle-stories/

Fields, K. (2020, January 7). *Celtic goddess Brigid: How to work with the Irish triple goddess.* Otherworldly Oracle. https://otherworldlyoracle.com/celtic-goddess-brigid/

Forsyth, S. (2021, November 1). *Legend of the banshee.* Celtic Wedding Rings. https://www.celtic-weddingrings.com/celtic-mythology/legend-of-the-banshee

Garden, G. (2018, December 17). *The Celtic goddess Cerridwen.* The Goddess Garden. https://thegoddessgarden.com/the-celtic-goddess-cerridwen/

Gill, N. S. (2019, July 30). *A list of Celtic gods and goddesses.* ThoughtCo. https://www.thoughtco.com/celtic-gods-and-goddesses-117625

History.com Editors. (2020, April 15). *Who were Celts.* History. https://www.history.com/topics/ancient-history/celts

Irish fairies: Merrows. (n.d.). Ireland's Eye. http://www.irelandseye.com/animation/explorer/merrows.html

Irish legends: Aengus Og: The love god of ancient Ireland. (n.d.). IrelandInformation.Com. https://www.ireland-information.com/irish-mythology/aengus-og-irish-legend.html

isleofman.com. (n.d.). *The myth of Manannan Mac Lir*. IsleofMan.com. https://www.isleofman.com/welcome/history/mythology-and-folklore/manannan-mac-lir/

Johnson, B. (2017, August 26). *The kelpie, mythical Scottish water horse*. Historic UK. https://www.historic-uk.com/CultureUK/The-Kelpie/

Johnson, H. (2021, May 17). *The Morrigan goddess: Goddess of death*. Order of Bards, Ovates & Druids. https://druidry.org/resources/morrigan

King cycle stories. (2021, April 12). Bard Mythologies. https://bardmythologies.com/king-cycle-stories/

Maccrosan, T. (2002, May 29). *Oral tradition and the Druidic class*. Llewellyn. https://www.llewellyn.com/encyclopedia/article/186

Macha. (2021d, February 11). Bard Mythologies. https://bardmythologies.com/macha/

Mandal, D. (2019, October 25). *15 ancient Celtic gods and goddesses you should know about*. Realm of History. https://www.realmofhistory.com/2018/07/02/ancient-celtic-gods-goddesses-facts/

Midir. (2021e, February 11). Bard Mythologies. https://bardmythologies.com/midir/

Muldoon, M. (2021, May 1). *The eight sacred Celtic holidays of the year*. IrishCentral.Com. https://www.irishcentral.com/roots/history/sacred-celtic-holidays-ireland

Mythological cycle stories. (2021, April 12). Bard Mythologies. https://bardmythologies.com/mythological-cycle-stories/

OBrien, C. (2010, September 3). *Irish mythology: The merrow (sea fairies)*. Irish Celtic Jewels. https://www.irishcelticjewels.com/celtic-wedding/2010/09/irish-mythology-the-merrow-sea-fairies/

O'Hara, K. (2021, January 13). *The Morrigan: The Story of the Fiercest Goddess in Irish Myth*. The Irish Road Trip. https://www.theirishroadtrip.com/the-morrigan/

Perkins, M. (2019, December 29). *Irish mythology: Festival and holidays*. ThoughtCo. https://www.thoughtco.com/irish-mythology-festival-and-holidays-4779917

Pinto, E. M. (n.d.). *Áine: The Irish sun and moon goddess*. Celtic Sprite. https://branawen.blogspot.com/2012/07/aine-irish-sun-and-moon-goddess_18.html

Rafferty, R. (2021, May 30). *The myths and legends of Ireland's hound of deep, the Dobhar Chu*. IrishCentral.Com. https://www.irishcentral.com/roots/irelands-hound-dobhar-chu

Sullivan, M. (2021, February 3). *The enduring traditions of St. Brigid's Day*. IrishCentral.Com. https://www.irishcentral.com/roots/st-brigids-day-traditions

The kelpie: Scottish mythological creature. (2021, June 11). Symbol Sage. https://symbolsage.com/the-kelpie-scottish-mythology/

Ulster cycle stories. (2021, April 12). Bard Mythologies. https://bardmythologies.com/ulster-cycle-stories/

West, B. (2020, January 30). *Eriu: A rggeat oddess of the feminine trinity of ancient Ireland*. Projeda. http://www.projectglobalawakening.com/eriu/

Who were the Celts? (n.d.). National Museum Wales. https://museum.wales/articles/1341/Who-were-the-Celts/

Winters, R. (2016, August 8). *Legends of the selkies, hidden gems of sea mythology*. Ancient Origins. https://www.ancient-origins.net/myths-legends/legends-selkies-hidden-germs-sea-mythology-006409

Wright, G. (n.d.). *Celtic gods*. Mythopedia. https://mythopedia.com/celtic-mythology/gods/

UNCOVERING EGYPTIAN MYTHOLOGY

A Beginner's Guide into the World of Egyptian Gods, Goddesses, Historic Mortals, and Ancient Monsters

LUCAS RUSSO

Introduction

When it comes to ancient Egyptian culture, there are things probably everyone—or almost everyone—recognizes. The pyramids and the mummies; Cleopatra and King Tut; ancient curses and a lot of golden decorations. Movies such as *The Mummy* (1999) or *The Night at the Museum* (2006) conditioned us to associate ancient Egypt with all things mysterious, esoteric, and perhaps even dangerous. And indeed, any time I visited a museum that had even the smallest section devoted to ancient Egypt, my feeling was that this culture had been so vastly different from everything that came after: more colorful (with special attention to gold) but also more hierarchical and even, at times, stiff. It overwhelmed me with the near-unimaginable vastness of its time span, but it also fascinated me with its cult of sacred animals, sophisticated rituals around death, and engineering ingenuity. Being an engineer myself, I could only admire the Egyptians' genius in constructing the pyramids.

So I decided to dig deeper. There must be more to this fascinating civilization than just the question of Cleopatra's beauty or King Tut's curse. And indeed, there was: I discovered a fascinating world of gods, goddesses, and monsters, far surpassing my expectations of Egyptian culture. I delved into the world where a woman could become a pharaoh, where time was cyclical and tied closely to nature, and where cats received their due attention as divine beings. A mythology where death didn't mean the end, but a new beginning. A hierarchy and tradition that kept one civilization in power for thousands and thousands of years.

Now, I'd like to invite you into this world. This is going to be a truly epic journey: from the intricacies of the historical civilization to the world of immortals and legends; from what is seen to the unseen; from the beginning of the world to its very end. Prepare to discover the story behind a god who needed to be killed and reborn in order for the universe to fall into its place; of mortal men who were deified after their death; and of powerful women whose weapon wasn't just their beauty but also their brilliant minds.

Be prepared to be swept away by the uniqueness that was ancient Egypt.

CHAPTER 1

Ancient Egypt

We tend to think about ancient Egypt in terms of a singular entity—but in fact, it was a civilization spanning thousands of years. For us, it's hard to imagine a political entity that would change so little over so many centuries, but it's my hope that after reading this chapter, you might understand better why it was so.

It is also my wish to introduce the ancient Egyptian culture to you in a way that will help you grasp the most important concepts in the mythology of this rich civilization. No mythology exists in a vacuum, and the stories that we have preserved from ancient Egypt reflect the beliefs that the Egyptians held in their day-to-day lives. In this chapter, you will learn about the organization of the kingdom, its pharaohs, their pyramids, and the societal structure and diversity of the ancient Egyptians.

Chronology

The moment we look closer at the chronology of the ancient Egyptian civilization, it makes our heads spin. The date of 3600 B.C.E. might feel abstract to us until we realize that this was actually the time when the last mammoths roamed the Earth! The gap between what we know as prehistory and "proper" history is not as big as we might think: the last mammoths roamed the Siberian wildland just as the Egyptians were starting to build a rapidly advancing civilization.

Now, let us see how it all started.

Early Dynastic Period

Around 3150 B.C.E., the kingdoms of Upper and Lower Egypt unified under the banner of the pharaoh Menes. Already at that time, there were diplomacy and alliances, along with symbolic imagery tied to them. The division of Egypt into the Upper and Lower kingdoms follows the course of the river Nile: that source of Egyptian bounty and a metaphorical spine on which the civilization grew. Lower Egypt lay to the north, around the Nile Delta, while Upper Egypt was located in the south, stretching as far as the modern-day city of Aswan (ancient Swenett). The symbol of Upper Egypt was a plant, and its titular goddess was Nekhbet, the vulture deity—while a bee was the symbol of Lower Egypt, and its titular goddess was Wadjet, the cobra. The ritual unification of the two lands earned many depictions on the walls of Egyptian buildings and in the documents—and from that point in history, the rulers of the unified lands wore a double crown, consisting of the white conical crown of Upper Egypt and the red crown with a likeness of a cobra, the symbol of Lower Egypt.

A political unification such as this doesn't emerge out of nowhere. The land of Egypt had been occupied for the last million years, and the last phase of the prehistoric period saw an already rather refined civilization of Naqada, with the first hieroglyphic writing, multilayered tombs, board games, and even cosmetics. But the unification brought additional resources and expanded the power of Egypt. From that point in history, the counting of the Egyptian dynasties begins with the First Dynasty being founded by the semi-legendary Menes.

After the unification, a new capital was established: Memphis, positioned on the doorstep of the Nile Delta. Menes was believed to have diverted the course of the Nile with dikes, protecting the city from yearly floods. In later periods, Memphis would become a true cultural hot spot and would see the development of wonders in terms of architecture and engineering.

The Early Dynastic Period encompasses the First and Second Dynasties of pharaohs, and it lasted until ca. 2686 B.C.E. when a new stage of development saw the emergence of the Old Kingdom.

We have no major cultural landmarks from the Early Dynastic Period, but it was a time when the later, characteristically Egyptian art, architecture, and mythology took its shape. It was a time when the cult of the famous gods such as Set and Horus emerged and the first step tombs, called *mastabas*, were built—precursors to the pyramids. The foundations for one of the most powerful civilizations in the whole world were placed.

Old Kingdom

The Old Kingdom (ca. 2700–2200 B.C.E.) is famously known as "the Age of the Pyramids." It reached over the life span of four dynasties, from the Third to the Sixth, and it left perhaps the most iconic landmarks in the Egyptian landscape. The first known pyramid was a step pyramid ordered by pharaoh Djoser of the Third Dynasty (ca. 2691–2625 B.C.E.), in Saqqara near Giza. The name of the construction stems from its structure: Rather than the later iconic, perfect pyramid shape, it was built through layers upon layers of decreasing surface, forming steps.

We will delve deeper into the pyramid construction in the latter part of this chapter; for now, let us focus on chronology. After the pyramid of Djoser, the most famous Great Pyramid of Giza, ordered by pharaoh Khufu (or, as we know him today, Cheops), was built between 2589 and 2566 B.C.E. during the Fourth Dynasty. Additionally, another iconic Egyptian landmark, the Great Sphinx of Giza, was built either during the reign of Khufu himself or one of his sons, Djedefre or Khafre.

The period of the Old Kingdom ended with the Sixth Dynasty and the increasingly weakening power of the pharaoh, punctuated by internal strife between the high ruler and the governors of the provinces. The last known pharaoh of the Sixth Dynasty was Pepi II (2278–2184 B.C.E.), after whose reign the kingdom was sucked into decades of famine and strife, known as the First Intermediate Period, which comprised the Seventh, Eighth, Ninth, Tenth, and a part of the Eleventh Dynasty. Not much is left from this unstable time, and we only know that several regional centers were warring for dominance, and many temples and palaces were pillaged and vandalized. In the end, the conflicted Upper and Lower Egypt were reunified by the pharaoh Mentuhotep II (2060–2009 B.C.E.) from the Eleventh Dynasty, whose rule started the period of the Middle Kingdom.

Middle Kingdom

The Middle Kingdom (ca. 2040–1782 B.C.E.), lasting over the Eleventh and Twelfth Dynasties, was marked by the reunification of Upper and Lower Egypt. The unifier, Mentuhotep II, hailed from the city of Thebes (also known as Waset; not to be confused with Thebes in Greece), which would become the capital of the kingdom during the reign of the Eleventh Dynasty and would gain prominence from that point onward.

The Middle Kingdom is known as the second "golden" era in ancient Egyptian history. The kingdom reached its peak in the Twelfth Dynasty under the pharaoh Senusret III (1878–1839 B.C.E.), who expanded the realm through a series of conquests and implemented administrative reforms.

Furthermore, the Middle Kingdom saw the first female pharaoh, Sobekneferu, the last ruler of the Twelfth Dynasty. Contrary to any previous women from the pharaoh's family, Sobekneferu didn't rule as a regent in a male heir's stead but was a pharaoh in her own right. She died without leaving any heirs, though, and so the rule passed to the Thirteenth Dynasty.

The first pharaohs from the Thirteenth Dynasty saw the steady decline of the Middle Kingdom when several provinces of Egypt proclaimed their independence and the pharaohs were unable to hold the whole kingdom together. The Second Intermediate Period (ca. 1650–1550 B.C.E.) was, yet again, marked by Egypt's fracture, with the dynasties from the Fourteenth to Seventeenth being unable to gain control over the entirety of the land. It was a period marked by unease and characterized, for the first time in Egyptian history, by the rule of foreign pharaohs. Egyptologists refer to them as Hyksos and suppose that they most likely originated from the Levant (the eastern Mediterranean).

At last, the arrival of the Eighteenth Dynasty under the rule of pharaoh Ahmose I saw the expulsion of the Hyksos from Egypt and the establishment of the New Kingdom ca. 1550 B.C.E.

New Kingdom

The New Kingdom of Egypt (ca. 1550–1069 B.C.E.) spans the Eighteenth, Nineteenth, and Twentieth Dynasties and marks the peak of the power of ancient Egypt. It is also a time of the rule of perhaps the most famous pharaohs that we know. After Ahmose I, the Eighteenth Dynasty saw rulers such as Hatshepsut, the second female pharaoh; Amenhotep III the Great, during whose rule Egypt reached the peak of its artistic achievements; his son, Akhenaten, who started perhaps one of the most mysterious cultural revolutions in human history; and Akhenaten's son, Tutankhamun, known as King Tut, who brought back order, even though he died young. Tut's tomb remains one of the most tantalizing and magnificent monuments of ancient Egyptian culture. We will talk at length about all these rulers in the chapter devoted to Egyptian mortals.

The Nineteenth Dynasty saw the veritable peak of Egypt's military power. Under Ramesses I and II, also known as Ramesses the Great, Egyptians defeated the Libyans, Syrians, and Nubians; the power of the kingdom spread far beyond the valley of the Nile. Ramesses II is also the most likely candidate for the pharaoh depicted in the biblical book of Exodus, as the man who forbade the Jews to leave Egypt and was punished with 10 plagues.

But the immense power of Egypt waned with the advent of the Twentieth Dynasty. During the reign of Ramesses III, the Sea Peoples—a confederacy of seafarers whose identity is, to this day, shrouded by mystery—invaded Egypt. Although the invaders were initially defeated, the warfare weakened the kingdom considerably, which resulted in famine. This was heightened by adverse meteorological conditions when a volcano eruption (most probably Hekla 3 in Iceland) caused air pollution and a bad harvest.

After Ramesses III died, his heirs fought for the crown. Egypt entered its Third Intermediate Period (ca. 1069–ca. 664 B.C.E.), the longest of the three. It coincided with the collapse of many civilizations of the Near East and the Mediterranean of the time, known as the Late Bronze Age Collapse.

Not much is known about this period. Egypt saw several dynasties, from the Twenty-first to the Twenty-fifth, many of which included foreign rulers from Libya or Nubia. The Nubian kings of the Twenty-sixth Dynasty, however, managed to reunite Upper and Lower Egypt and guided the kingdom toward a new era of prosperity, known as the Late Period. Unfortunately, a new power was growing to the east—the Persian Empire—that would finally prove Egypt's undoing.

Late and Ptolemaic Period

The Late Egyptian Period (ca. 664–ca. 332 B.C.E.) follows the rule of the Twenty-sixth to Thirty-first Dynasties. Of them, the Twenty-sixth Dynasty was the most powerful. In 525 B.C.E., Egypt was conquered by the First Persian Empire, and the Twenty-seventh Dynasty effectively consisted of Persian emperors during a time when Egypt became a satrapy, or regional province. In 404 B.C.E., Amyrtaeus, the prince of Sais, successfully rebelled against the Persians, instating the Twenty-eighth Dynasty. His and the following two other dynasties were the last independent dynasties that ruled Egypt. In 343 B.C.E., the kingdom was re-annexed by the Persian Empire. The Thirty-first Dynasty, yet again, consisted of Persian emperors.

But the new times were coming. Macedonian-Greek ruler and conqueror Alexander the Great defeated the Persians in 305 B.C.E., taking over not only the vast areas of the original empire but also the conquered satrapy of Egypt. The Ptolemaic period of ancient Egypt, named after Alexander's companion Ptolemy I Soter, lasted from 305 to 30 B.C.E. and was marked by heavy Hellenistic (Greek) influences.

It is this era that saw the rule of the most famous female pharaoh, Cleopatra (51–30 B.C.E.). She was also the last ever ruler of Egypt before the land became a part of the Roman Empire. Her entanglement in the Roman civil war finally brought the end to the ages-old line of pharaohs. After Rome conquered Egypt, the new province was ruled by governors although no decision was made to replace the Greek officials with Roman ones. The Romans also respected Egyptian religion and customs—but its influence and practice waned anyway, already heavily influenced by Greek culture and, now, by the Roman cult of the emperor.

The Roman rule of Egypt would last all the way until 641 C.E. when the area was conquered by the Muslims. By that time, not much was left of the ancient worship and culture.

So there we have it: over 3,000 years of rule, expansion, strife, and re-establishment of peace. Over 3,000 years of the development of civilization and culture that would forever influence people's imagination, even to this day. Now, let us delve a little deeper into the main characteristics of this civilization. It was a civilization and culture that remained surprisingly traditional throughout the ages—but that doesn't mean there was no change at all.

Pharaohs and Their Pyramids

A pharaoh wasn't only a title that the kings of ancient Egypt adopted. It was a political office, of course, but it was also a highly religious one. A pharaoh not only owned the whole land of Egypt, enacted laws, oversaw conquests, and commanded the army—his (or her) responsibility was also to erect new temples and officiate religious mysteries. He was to maintain order: not just political and social but also cosmic. The Egyptian idea of Maat is a fascinating one, and we'll look at it closely in the chapters relating to the goddesses and the afterlife.

The pharaoh wore the double crown of Upper and Lower Egypt, but he also held numerous other regalia. Scepters were a sign of authority and varied in stature. But the most iconic crowns and headdresses that we often associate with the depictions of pharaohs on their sarcophagi were the Nemes headdress—the piece of striped cloth worn over both sides of the head—and the uraeus, a likeness of a cobra and a symbol of the goddess Wadjet, often affixed to the middle of the pharaoh's forehead. Apart from these attributes, the pharaoh would also often wear the divine beard—an elongated fixture worn over one's chin, symbolizing divinity.

The pharaoh's official name was always adopted upon his ascension to the throne. It was called their Horus name—as the god Horus was supposed to have been the first pharaoh and a patron of all rulers—and was later written in hieroglyphs on a special square frame called the cartouche. The best way of distinguishing a pharaoh's—or a god's—name from the crowd of hieroglyphs in any inscription is to look for symbols that are surrounded by a frame. The respect for the figure of the pharaoh was so great that even their name deserved a special distinction.

The pharaoh was a semi-divine figure. He was supposed to be a deputy between the people and the gods, practically a god on Earth, and when he died, he joined the gods, passing from the protection of Horus to that of Osiris. It is no wonder that a ruler whose significance was so great would receive as monumental a tomb as a pyramid.

The Construction of Pyramids

A pyramid's shape was highly symbolic: It represented a primordial mound from which, according to ancient Egyptian beliefs, the whole world was created. Another symbolic value would be to represent the sun's rays falling from the sky to the earth. A pyramid was a literal gateway to the heavens, pointing to the center of the sky. It's entirely possible that both the exterior and the interior of a pyramid, with its burial chamber and conjoining shafts, were a means to launch the pharaoh's soul directly to the sky.

But symbolism aside, construction-wise, a pyramid was a marvel of ancient engineering. As already mentioned, the earliest pyramids evolved from the bench-like *mastabas* and were step pyramids, likely also influenced by the *ziggurats* of Mesopotamia. But the Fourth Dynasty perfected the shape, creating the "true pyramid" that we all know today.

The construction of the pyramids is a subject of much debate. The extraordinary achievement was viewed as so marvelous that it gave way to various conspiracy theories, even those involving aliens. It's quite extraordinary that we are so unwilling to believe in the ingenuity of our ancestors that we'd rather have an extraterrestrial civilization interfere… but that is a subject for a different book.

The common myth is that the pyramids were built by slaves. But most likely, at least the biggest and most well-known Great Pyramid of Giza, were built by a crew of skilled workers whose recompense was a tax relief. Many of the unskilled laborers who worked under them might have been volunteers. Egyptologists surmise that the Great Pyramid of Giza required a workforce of between over 14,000 to 40,000 (Lehner, n.d.). Additionally, staggering amounts of stone had to be used. In 2013, a bundle of papyri (ancient Egyptian writing material) known as the *Diary of Merer* was discovered. It contains notes from an inspector who oversaw the transportation of white limestone blocks from the quarry in Tura (halfway between modern-day Cairo and Helwan), through the Nile to the building site in Giza. The diary describes how up to 200 blocks of limestone were shipped every month for the pyramid (Stille, 2015). It is the greatest archaeological discovery connected to ancient Egypt in recent history.

As we can see, the construction of a pyramid was an enormous enterprise. There are various theories as to how those structures were built; already in ancient times, this was a bit of a mystery. Most likely, the stones were lifted by wooden ramps combined with levers, but it's uncertain how big exactly and what shape they were. In 2018, remnants of a 4,500-year-old ramp were discovered by a team of archaeologists. It was composed of a central ramp and two staircases, and it most likely allowed the builders to pull up stone blocks on very steep slopes. Since the ramp dates back to the times of Khufu, it's entirely possible that it was used in the building of the Great Pyramid of Giza.

Hieroglyphs

The famous Egyptian hieroglyphs are our window to this ancient civilization. For centuries, the clue to their decryption had been lost, and any attempts to decipher them led nowhere. The main reason for this was that most scholars assumed the hieroglyphs represented ideas, not sounds—where, in fact, this had been a system of writing that combined the logographic (a symbol represents a word), syllabic (a symbol represents a syllable), and alphabetic (a symbol represents a single sound or phoneme) elements.

The breakthrough came when, during Napoleon's invasion of Egypt in 1799, the Rosetta Stone was discovered. It was a stone with a decree inscribed on it, and it contained a version in hieroglyphs alongside a version in ancient Greek. It was an immense discovery—practically like a dictionary to the mystery language. Still, it took several attempts before the stone was finally deciphered in the 1820s. From then on, the study of ancient Egyptian took off.

Of course, the hieroglyphs changed over thousands of years of use. The earliest forms of this system of writing can be dated from around 4000 B.C.E. before the first unification of Upper and Lower Egypt. However, the best-documented variant of the hieroglyphs is the Middle Egyptian, which developed around 2000 B.C.E. and was in use for around 700 years. Around 1350 B.C.E., Late Egyptian emerged; it was the language of the New Kingdom.

During the Late Period, a new version of the script was developed. It's called the Demotic script, and it was developed from a northern variety of the hieroglyphs. It was simplified, much more resembling an alphabet we are used to seeing than the Egyptian pictograms. The last evidence of the use of the Demotic script comes from 452 B.C.E.

During the Ptolemaic period, a Greek-based new alphabet started circulating in Egypt: Coptic. The hieroglyphs were slowly forgotten, even though some version of the late Egyptian survived. The Coptic language and script survive to this day in the liturgical use of the Coptic Orthodox Church and Coptic Catholic Church.

The hieroglyphs were a highly complex writing system. There were hundreds of signs, and their mastery required time and skill. It is no wonder that an Egyptian scribe—a literate man who was capable of writing down official and legal documents as well as literature—was highly esteemed in ancient Egyptian society.

The Mummies

We have talked about two of the most iconic elements associated with ancient Egypt—pyramids and hieroglyphs—and now, it's time for the third one: mummies and the process of mummification. The Egyptian rituals and cult surrounding death have given rise to many spooky stories and mysterious theories. We will talk at length about the Egyptian descriptions of the afterlife in a separate chapter, but for now, it is worth mentioning that the ancient Egyptian belief was that if the body was preserved in a lifelike form after death, then the spirits of the underworld would be able to recognize it and the dead person would be allowed to live again.

Looking at the matter from a more practical standpoint, mummification was most likely developed because of the dry Egyptian climate. The first mummified bodies were most likely accidental. But around 2600 B.C.E., the intentional process started developing.

The mummification process was a long and costly one. Hardly any common man or woman could afford it; in practice, only the pharaohs, high officials, and the nobility were mummified. Occasionally, the bodies of animals would also undergo mummification: This was tied to the Egyptian beliefs in sacred animals, which we'll talk about in the chapters devoted to gods and goddesses.

Mummification took 70 days. It was performed by several priests who acted as embalmers, reciting prayers and performing the necessary acts. A detailed knowledge of human anatomy was crucial to the process. That's why in ancient Egypt, not only the dead but also the living received unprecedented medical care: Surgeries were common and performed with precision, and knowledge of the functions of the human organs was surprisingly vast and accurate.

But let us come back to mummification. The knowledge of anatomy was crucial since the first step of the process was to remove all parts of the body that might decay quickly: internal organs. The brain was removed with hooks through the nostrils—a complicated process that required precision—and the organs from the chest and abdomen were accessed and removed through cuts. They would be later preserved in special boxes and buried with the mummy.

The heart was left in place: It was believed to be the center of being and a source of intelligence, much as today we know the brain to be. After the other organs were removed, the body was covered with natron, a special type of salt that helped draw all moisture from the body. When the body dried out, the natron was removed.

Now, the mummy was very dry, but the body was still in a recognizable human form. Artificial eyes were added to make the image more lifelike. Then, the wrapping began.

Hundreds of yards of linen were used to wrap a single body. This was a process that required the most rituals: Amulets were placed on various parts of the body, and prayers were uttered in order to preserve them.

When the mummy was complete and ready to be placed in the tomb, the burial chamber was furnished with numerous objects that the person might need in the afterlife: furniture and little statuettes representing everyday objects. When everything was ready, a ritual was performed by the tomb's door. It was called the "Opening of the Mouth" and consisted of the priests touching various parts of the mummy in order to "open" the person's senses so that they could enjoy the afterlife. Following this, the mummy was finally placed into a coffin (or multiple coffins), which was then sealed in a tomb.

The Egyptian climate preserved a lot of mummies, most of them from the New Kingdom. The care that the Egyptians placed upon mummification means that, at least in early

Egyptology, most of the study of ancient Egypt came through the mummies and their tombs, and it created the image of ancient Egypt as highly death-centered.

But this culture was as much about life as it was about death. After all, eternal life was the main reason for mummification. Now, let us discover some of the aspects of Egyptian society that went beyond death. Let's talk about daily life.

Egyptian Society

Egyptian society was highly hierarchical. Most of the population consisted of farmers (who were also obliged to work on irrigation and construction projects), but officially, all land and produce were owned by the pharaoh and the nobility. Farmers were the lowest class— unless we assume that the ancient Egyptians kept slaves. There is no consensus among historians when it comes to this.

Above the farmers were the artisans, to which class we'd count both the artists and the craftsmen. They were highly controlled by the state that paid them because their workshops were, for the most part, attached to the temples.

The scribes and officials were the upper class. Literature was seen as a form of display of one's status—the nature of the hieroglyphic writing required it. The scribes wore white, bleached linen garments and were, therefore, known as the "white kilt class."

Above the scribes were all specialists in the most sophisticated areas of knowledge: priests, engineers, and physicians. The study of their craft took years, and their knowledge was essential to the process of pyramid-building, embalming, and worship. The functions of a priest and a physician were often combined as we have seen in the example of the mummification process.

On the very top of the social ladder was the nobility, with the pharaoh and his or her family above everyone else. This class practically owned all of Egypt. The highest state official was the vizier; he often came from the royal family and was appointed directly by the pharaoh.

His duties could be compared to that of a modern prime minister. He would oversee the running of the whole country and receive reports from tax collectors, scribes, and other officials. He administered the palace's treasury, storage, and granaries, and he oversaw the construction of any major engineering projects. He also heard petitions from the common people, and, at least in theory, everyone could be admitted before a vizier to plead their case.

Women's Rights

One of the rather extraordinary features of Egyptian society and law, at least in comparison to other ancient societies of the region, was the relative freedom enjoyed by the female part of the population. We have already seen the emergence of female pharaohs—and it wouldn't have been possible without the way Egyptian society functioned.

In the face of the law, men and women were equal. Women had the right to own and sell property, and in the case of married couples, the husband and the wife owned their house jointly. Moreover, women could plead their cases in court, marry of their own will, as well as divorce, receive inheritance, and make any legal contracts. Marriage contracts were frequently drawn upon entering the union, in which a husband's financial obligations toward his wife and potential children were specified in case of the end of the marriage— much as it happens in many countries today. All in all, the legal rights and protection of women in ancient Egypt not only surpassed ancient standards but would hold up to scrutiny even in the modern world.

Women could also become priestesses. For example, the cult of the god Amun consisted mostly of women, and the high priestess of Amun was called "God's Wife of Amun." She held considerable political power.

The Egyptian Ethnicity

Before we delve into the world of gods and goddesses, there is one other issue that needs to be discussed. The question of the ancient Egyptians' ethnicity has been one of considerable controversy. In the past decades, we have grown used to seeing pharaohs in movies being played by white actors—but were the ancient Egyptians White? Or, maybe more resembling the people from today's Middle East? Or, were they Black?

The question of Egyptian ethnicity is heavily charged by the modern issues surrounding race. Many people are trying to find a simple, definitive answer to the question, but the truth is, it depends on the dynasty and historical period. If we look at Cleopatra's likeness, we'll see a woman of, at least in part, Greek and Macedonian heritage. But if we look at the pharaohs from the Twenty-fifth Dynasty during the Third Intermediate Period, there is no doubt that they came from Nubia and were Black. Today, although many controversies still arise, it's mostly accepted that the population of ancient Egypt was ethnically diverse, consisting of people from the sub-Saharan region, as well as Semitic people and North African people. Upper Egypt was most likely more Black than Lower Egypt, and undoubtedly, the culture of Black African kingdoms such as Nubia and Ethiopia (back then called the Kingdom of Kush), as well as the peoples from the Horn of Africa, influenced Egyptian culture, not only in the Late Period but also in the very beginnings of the Egyptian civilization.

All in all, ancient Egypt was diverse. Whitewashing and linking ancient Egyptians to modern Europeans is definitely not the way to go. Rather, it seems that ethnicity should be established on an individual, case-by-case basis, whenever it is possible. At the same time, it's worth remembering that the ancient Egyptians didn't have the same notion of race that we, in our Western postcolonial societies, have. On the contrary, the question of skin color didn't seem to be important to them at all.

CHAPTER 2

Creation Myth

Now that we've gotten to know the Egyptian civilization a bit better, it's time to finally delve into some myths. As with most mythologies, we'll start from the very beginning: the creation of the world. The ancient Egyptians didn't have one coherent creation myth; instead, we now know about four major ones (and some varieties thereof), associated with four religious and cultural centers: Heliopolis, Hermopolis, Memphis, and Thebes.

The Myth of Heliopolis

Heliopolis (or, rather, the ancient Egyptian Iunu) was one of the oldest cities of ancient Egypt, reaching back to predynastic times. Located in the Nile Delta, it was a bustling city, especially during the Old and Middle Kingdoms. Sadly, today, it's mostly destroyed—but its importance is preserved in records. Consequently, the creation myth from Heliopolis is the best known one.

And this is how it goes: In the beginning, there were only primordial waters called Nun. They were represented by two pairs of gods, each of whom symbolized different aspects of the primordial chaos. There was the Invisibility and the Infinite as well as the Lack of Direction and Darkness.

But from these waters emerged a primordial mound called Benben, which was a prototype for all pyramids. There are two versions for what happened later. Some said that on top of Benben, a blue lotus flower sat from which blossomed the king of all gods, Ra, the sun. Others identified Ra with Atum, who was worshiped profusely in Heliopolis, a city whose name could be translated as "The City of the Sun." Atum is said to have created himself out of the force of his will and by uttering his own name. Other versions of the myth talk about Atum-Ra being birthed by the goddess Neith, the goddess of the sky and primordial waters, the true first being and the creator of everything, including Nun. But if Neith gave birth to Atum, she then wasn't involved in the act of creation any further.

After his creation, Atum became the king of heavens and earth and wore the double crown of Upper and Lower Egypt. His symbol became the *ankh*, a hieroglyphic symbol representing life: a key to life itself.

Like every Egyptian after him, Atum's soul and body consisted of many parts. There was *khet* (the physical body), *sah* (the spiritual body), *ren* (name or identity), *ba* (personality), *ka* (vital essence), *ib* (heart), *shut* (shadow or silhouette), *sekhem* (form or power), and lastly, *akh* (intellect).

Atum's *ba* had the form of a Bennu bird—a heron or a phoenix that was capable of rebirth. It was this bird that flew over the waters of Nun and landed on Benben. From there, he gave a mighty call, bringing the world forth to creation. Then, he was consumed in flames and reborn again.

The first deities that Atum gave birth to were the god Shu, the god of lions, peace, air, and wind and the goddess Tefnut, the deity of moisture, mostly in the form of dew and rain. Atum held in himself both the male and female elements and, therefore, was capable of creation. Some sources said that he spat out, or sneezed, Shu and Tefnut; others, that the pair of deities were created by the act of Atum's masturbation, in which the hand of the god represented the female element.

Shu and Tefnut then coupled and produced offspring: Geb, the earth, and Nut, the sky. Now, the primordial waters receded, and Atum-Ra finally had a place to rest.

Geb and Nut produced their own children, ones that are probably the most familiar Egyptian gods to us. Nut gave birth to Osiris, the god of fertility and regeneration; Set, the ambiguous god of chaos; Isis, goddess of motherhood; and Nephthys, the goddess of protection. Atum and his children, grandchildren, and great-grandchildren became known as the Ennead, the group of higher gods. We will talk about their stories and properties in the later chapters of this book.

The myth of Heliopolis explains the creation of the universe with all its coexisting and contrarian aspects: earth and sky, dryness and moisture, chaos and order, femininity and masculinity. Atum, or Ra, identified with the sun, is the source of all life.

The Myth of Hermopolis

Hermopolis's Egyptian name was Khemenu. It lay on the border between Upper and Lower Egypt and was a provincial capital since the times of the Old Kingdom. As a town located between the two parts of Egypt, it saw a vast exchange of goods and people and was, therefore, a very opulent and rich place.

The Hermopolis creation myth doesn't focus so much on the creation itself, but rather, on the nature of the world before the creation. The ancient Pyramid Texts (funerary texts) from the region of Hermopolis describe a group of primordial deities. They are called the Ogdoad, a name that denotes their number: eight. They are grouped into four male-female pairs.

The members of the Ogdoad are as follows. First are Nu and Naunet, water and sky, representing the primordial waters. Then come Ḥeḥu and Ḥeḥut, personifications of infinity, whose names mean "flood," yet again harking back to the primordial water theme. The symbol of male Ḥeḥu is a frog and of female Ḥeḥut—a snake. The frog head represents fertility and creation.

Next, come Kekui and Kekuit, night and day. Kekui bears the head of a serpent, while Kekuit has the head of a cat. The pair of deities is closely tied to ka, the part of the human soul that contains the vital essence of a person.

The last pair of gods is shrouded in mystery. Their names seem to be Qerḥ and Qerḥet, but they are sometimes mentioned as Amun and Amunet. Both are important deities: Amun is an aspect of the sun-god Ra, and Amunet might have been another personification of the night. Both names mean "the Hidden Ones" but can also mean inactivity, or rest. It seems the ancient Egyptians didn't have clear concepts when it came to this pair of deities.

All the eight deities, however, were regarded as aquatic. Their convergence, or coupling, produced a great upheaval in the primordial waters; from it arose the Benben, the mound which we are already acquainted with. The mound, in turn, produced the sun-god Ra.

The Myth of Memphis

Memphis was a city in Lower Egypt and was said to have been founded by the legendary King Menes. It was positioned strategically on the Nile Delta, and its port saw a large influx of goods. As a result, the city abounded in workshops, factories, and warehouses, and the craftsmanship produced there circulated throughout all of Egypt. It was a bustling city throughout the Old, Middle, and New Kingdoms. It is no wonder that a manufacturing city such as this would take as its patron the god Ptah, the deity of craftsmen.

And it is also Ptah that plays a major role in the Memphian myth of creation. Every craftsman has the ability to see the finished product in their mind's eye, to envision their creation. In a similar way, Ptah created the world. It wasn't a physical but rather an intellectual act. The world was created in Ptah's heart—for ancient Egyptians, a center of thought—and came into existence when Ptah named its elements. It is a very beautiful myth emphasizing the power of creativity and language.

Later, the Memphian myth was combined with the Heliopolitan one, and Ptah was said to have created Atum and the Ennead. He was also said to have been responsible for the creation of the primordial waters and the mound as well as the mound's guardian, the god Tatenen, who would later become the patron of all pyramids.

The Myth of Thebes

We have already briefly mentioned the city of Thebes in Upper Egypt (not to be confused with a city of the same name in Greece). For long periods during the Middle Kingdom and New Kingdom, it was the capital of Egypt and one of the most venerated cities. Due to its location close to the kingdom of Nubia, many trade routes led through the city, which controlled valuable mineral resources coming from the desert.

The Theban creation myth is focused on Amun, who the Thebans didn't regard as merely a member of the Ogdoad but as a creator of everything. He was supposed to encompass all characteristics of the primordial deities but also transcend them. He was separate from the world, and nobody, not even the gods, could understand the full extent of his nature.

Amun's act of creation was likened to a call of a goose who circled over the primordial waters. Through this call, the supreme god brought into being all the members of the Ogdoad and the Ennead: They were all only aspects of Amun himself.

Other elements of the creation—the lesser gods' genealogy, for instance—were similar to those described in the myths coming from Heliopolis and Hermopolis.

In time, due to Thebes's importance, Amun became the chief deity of ancient Egypt. We will talk more about his cult in the next chapter, but here, it's worth noting that although he was a chief of a vast pantheon of gods, his attributes such as transcendence and practical omnipotence are slightly reminiscent of a monotheistic deity, such as the Jewish God.

Now that we have told the stories of creation, let us dig deeper into the world of Egyptian gods and goddesses. Let us meet the Ennead as well as the lesser gods.

CHAPTER 3

Gods

Let's start our journey through the Egyptian pantheon with the male gods. Their cult shaped Egyptian worship and theology. It is with figures such as Ra, Amun, Osiris, or Horus that we find the most important legends and myths that were crucial to the organization of Egyptian society.

Familiar Male Deities

Ra, Osiris, Horus, Set—those are probably the names most of us recognize when thinking about Egyptian mythology. The first part of this chapter will be dedicated to them and their intertwining stories.

Between Ra and Amun

Ra of the Sun

Depending on the time and place, Ra took multiple forms. The god of the sun, he was practically the most important in the Egyptian pantheon, and whenever any other god rose to higher prominence, he would become described as an aspect of Ra, or conflated with him (such as Amun-Ra, about whom we'll talk in a bit).

We have already seen Ra as the creator. As a personification of the sun, he represented life and growth. Atum from Heliopolis was his nighttime form, while a lesser deity called Khepri, a scarab-god from the Egyptian desert, represented the rising sun. He was even sometimes conflated with Horus because they were both often depicted as humanoid gods with a face of a falcon. But on top of Ra's head lay a red disc, surrounded by a cobra: the eye of Ra that saw everything that happened on Earth.

But the sun could be equally a source of growth and death. It had its punishing aspect, too. The humans were created from its tears, but one day they decided to rebel against it. So Ra transformed the fire in his eye into the goddess Sekhmet, a warrior goddess. She was ruthless and sent solely to punish mankind. She sent scorching heat on the Earth and the rebellion was quenched.

Sekhmet was one of the three daughters of Ra. The other two were Bastet and Hathor, both of whom were more nurturing and forgiving. We will talk about them in the next chapter.

As the sun, Ra was also connected to the Egyptian underworld. His journey through the sky led him through the hours of the night as well as the hours of the day. He traveled on two solar barques: the one he used during the day was called Mandjet and the nighttime one Meseket. According to the Egyptians, there are 12 hours that belong to the day and 12 hours that belong to the night. During his nighttime journey, Ra was said to visit 12 minor deities guarding the gates of the underworld, each of them representing one hour.

So each night, Ra descended into the underworld in the form of Atum, bearing a ram's head. There he battled with various monsters, accompanied by the other gods who aided him in his fight. The god of chaos Set and the serpent-god Mehen were some examples, but Ra was also accompanied by various minor deities that were personifications of the aspects of his nature. To them belonged: Sia (perception), Hu (command), and Heka (magic power). With their help, Ra was capable of combating Apophis, a giant serpent that tried to stop his boat every night. And each night, although the battle was fierce, Ra was victorious and rose in the sky again in the morning.

The journey of Ra represents one of the most important manifestations of the rather popular motif of rebirth that we can find in Egyptian myth. The other manifestation of that motif will be shown in the story of Osiris.

Heliopolis was the main center of Ra's worship. Its Greek name, meaning "the Sun City," owes its name to him. The beginnings of Ra's cult reach as early as the Second Dynasty, but it was the pharaohs of the Fourth Dynasty that started seeing themselves as manifestations of Ra on Earth. Pyramids, obelisks, and temples would be built in the god's honor, and he became the state deity.

Amun-Ra

Initially, Amun had been one of the members of the Ogdoad and, with his wife Amunet, was worshiped from the times of the Old Kingdom. During the First Intermediate Period, Amun became the chief deity of Thebes. There, he had his own temple built at Karnak, which to this day is one of the most monumental temple complexes preserved from the ancient Egyptian civilization.

But his national importance only came fully into prominence by the end of the Second Intermediate Period. By this time, the foreign pharaohs from the Seventeenth Dynasty were defeated by Ahmose I, who was from Thebes. Ahmose would found the Eighteenth Dynasty, under which Egypt achieved the peak of its power. And throughout that period (with the exception of the rule of Akhenaten, of whom we'll talk in Chapter 6), Amun was effectively the most important deity of the Egyptian pantheon.

As a champion of the rebels who expelled the pharaohs from the Seventeenth Dynasty, Amun became a patron of true justice and those suffering from misfortunes. He was identified with Ra, the sun, but also with Min, the god of fertility. Most importantly though, he protected the poor. Before praying to him, it was crucial to confess one's sins—after all, Amun was the patron of Maat, justice and order. But he also seemed to be quick to forgive.

Sometimes, Amun was depicted with a ram's head or ram's horns. This was most likely an influence of the Kingdom of Kush, which was partly conquered by Egypt during the New Kingdom. The Nubians had worshiped a ram-headed solar deity for centuries.

The worship of Amun was extremely important to the Egyptian social structure. The high priest of Amun, called the First Prophet of Amun, was the highest-ranking priest in the kingdom. At the time of the Twentieth Dynasty, the priests of Amun possessed two-thirds of the temple lands in Egypt. Their hold on the economy was so strong, and they sometimes exercised greater power than that of the pharaoh himself.

Similarly, there also existed the already mentioned female order of Amun priestesses, with the God's Wife of Amun being the leader. She would, in most cases, be also a wife of the ruling pharaoh, ensuring that their offspring would be seen as half-divine. She also exercised political power over the priesthood.

Amun's cult was so prominent that it influenced other cultures of antiquity. He was worshiped in Nubia and Sudan, and even in Greece, where he had his temples and sometimes gave some of his attributes to Zeus. He is also mentioned in the Hebrew Bible.

Osiris

After Ra, Osiris is perhaps the most important—and recognizable—deity in the Egyptian pantheon. The god of agriculture and fertility, on one hand, and the afterlife and death, on the other, he represents rebirth and resurrection, which is exemplified in the myths preserved about him. The earliest version of the Osiris myth can be dated as far back as the Fifth Dynasty, around 2400 B.C.E.

Osiris and his siblings were born from Geb and Nut, heaven and earth. Osiris was the eldest, and thus, he ruled Egypt with Isis, his sister, as his queen. But Set, his brother and the god of chaos, had a grievance against him. Some sources state that he was resentful of a kick Osiris gave him one day, others that he was jealous because Osiris had intercourse with Nephthys, Set's consort. However it was, Set decided to murder Osiris.

No text describes Osiris's death in detail. It's most probably because the ancient Egyptians believed words had the power to become reality and feared disrupting the balance of the world.

After the deed was done, Set cut Osiris's body to pieces and scattered them around all the 42 provinces of Egypt. Thus, the true king of Egypt was tied even stronger with his land. Following the murder, Set assumed the kingship.

But Isis, Osiris's inconsolable wife, never stopped looking for him. Assuming a likeness of a falcon and with the aid of her sister Nephthys, she traveled across the land. The two goddesses also called on the help of other gods, including Thoth, the god of healing, and Anubis, the god of funerary rites. At last, they found all the scattered pieces, and Anubis put them back together, performing the ritual of embalming. Thus, Osiris became the first mummy and a source of all mummification rites.

In one version of the myth, Isis found all the pieces of Osiris's body save for the penis, which had been eaten by a fish in the Nile, so she had to restore it with magic. This served as a basis for the Egyptian cultural taboo around eating fish.

Set and his followers tried to damage Osiris's body, but Isis protected him. At last, he became whole and revived. Then, Isis gave birth to Horus, her and Osiris's son.

Osiris's revival seems to never have been permanent: from now on, he became the king of Duat, the underworld, while his son and rightful heir, Horus, assumed the kingship of Egypt. The spirit of Osiris lived in him.

Osiris is a classic god of rebirth. In some versions of his story, his cyclical death symbolized the yearly flood of the Nile, with the waters of the Nile being the mixed bodily fluids of Osiris and Isis's tears. Osiris's death then became an ambiguous event, being both a disaster and a life-giving occurrence, after which Egypt's vegetation grew with renewed force. This cycle also represented continuity and stability.

In worship, Osiris was often depicted as a pharaoh, with the double crown of Upper and Lower Egypt on his head. Sometimes, the personality aspect of his soul, the *ba*, was worshiped in its own right. It was called Banebdjedet and took on the form of a ram. This was most likely an effect of the fact that in ancient Egyptian language, the word *ba* meant both a soul and a ram.

Many prayers uttered over a mummy during the embalming process were dedicated to Osiris. Additionally, yearly fertility rites were held in his honor. These rites were highly androgynous in nature: Osiris's castration and reassembly by the female Isis were emphasized. At the hour of their death, both men and women were able to identify with Osiris.

The Osiris myth seems to have been very popular among the common people of Egypt. Its religious meaning was that any person, no matter the rank, could achieve a pleasant afterlife, and so even those who couldn't afford the costly process of mummification seemed to have been included. Another source of the myth's popularity was its depiction of the strong love between Osiris, Isis, and Horus.

Horus

Horus, Osiris's and Isis's son, was primarily the god of kingship and the sky, but he also served many other functions. The first record of Horus's name comes from the city of Nekhen, or Hierakonpolis, the capital of Upper Egypt in prehistoric Egypt and the Early Dynastic Period. There, a pharaoh is likened to Horus in life, as he is to Osiris in death.

Horus plays a very important role in the continuation of the Osiris myth. When Isis was pregnant with him, she is said to have hidden from Set in a thicket of papyrus in the Nile Delta. There, she gave birth to him, so the place was called "the nest of Horus" and was frequently depicted in Egyptian art.

Then, something extraordinary happened: Isis set out to travel all around the kingdom in disguise, asking various people and gods to protect her son from all manners of evil. This is an unusual occurrence since in Egyptian mythology the gods and humans are commonly very separate. Isis was, however, guarded by seven minor scorpion deities.

One wealthy woman refused to give help to Isis. For that, the scorpion gods stung her son. But the goddess was more merciful than her companions: She healed the child who had not been to blame for his mother's actions. This event is one of the examples for the Osiris myth's appeal to the common and the poor. It illustrated how the poor could be more virtuous than the rich. It, moreover, emphasized Isis's compassionate nature. We will come back to it in the next chapter.

Now, Isis had to protect her son from all manner of bodily ailments. He was a sickly child and had to be healed from simple stomachaches as well as scorpion stings and snakebites. The hostile creatures had been sent by Set, but Isis managed to repel them and to heal her son with spells. The incantations that she was reported to have used have been preserved in Egyptian medical texts. It was the belief that Isis's power in healing Horus could be extended to mundane patients, too.

Years passed, and Horus grew up. At this time, Set was still the king of Egypt, having usurped the throne after the death of his brother. Horus then went to Set's throne and challenged his claim before the whole Ennead. The gods assembled under the command of Geb, with Thoth acting as a conciliator and Isis as an advocate for her son.

The conflict between Horus and Set was long and complicated. Most of the story as we know it today has been written down as *The Contendings of Horus and Set* at the time of the Twentieth Dynasty, ca. 1100 B.C.E.

First, both gods asked other deities to plead on their behalf and engaged in physical contests. They organized a boat race, and Horus won. They changed into hippopotami and fought; yet again, Horus was victorious. Now, it seemed like the contest was won because most of the gods were on Horus's side. But Ra favored Set, and so, the conflict dragged on for 80 years.

And it became much broader than a single combat between two gods. Other deities got involved, too. A battle started. At some point, Isis thrust her spear at Set but tragically missed and hit Horus instead. Horus, full of battle frenzy and unheeding of his surroundings, cut off his own mother's head.

Luckily, Thoth replaced Isis's head with that of a cow. It would, from now on, become her iconic attribute.

The deciding part of Horus and Set's contest took part in the realm of sexuality. According to some accounts, Set sexually abused Horus, but according to others, it was consensual intercourse between the two gods, with Set receiving pleasure in exchange for lending Horus some of his power. In the latter part of this chapter, we will talk about Set and his connection to sex as well as homosexual desire.

But in the Egyptian tradition, semen was regarded as partly poisonous. Horus needed to be careful, for if Set's semen entered him, he would become sick. So he thwarted Set and caught the semen in his hands. Isis then put it on lettuce leaves which Set ate, thus becoming "impregnated," as the semen appeared on his forehead in the shape of a golden disk. Set's defeat became apparent.

But this was not the end. The gods still battled. Horus managed to cut off Set's testicles, but Set gouged Horus's eye out. Horus's Eye was an important symbol in Egyptian mythology. It represented the moon, and the theft, therefore, became the first moon eclipse. Horus managed to retrieve his eye with the help of Isis, restoring the moon.

In the end, the conflict between Horus and Set ended with a truce. The gods divided Egypt between them, with Horus receiving the fertile part around the Nile Delta and Set being given the harsh desert. Thus began the division into Lower and Upper Egypt.

Horus was given the throne of the kingdom as the rightful heir of Osiris. As a punishment, Set was ordered to carry Osiris's body to its tomb, where Horus performed the funerary rites and helped his father become the rightful king of the underworld.

It is worth emphasizing that, even though Set was the aggressive party in the conflict with Horus, he was still viewed as an inevitable part of the natural order. We will come back to him and the development of his figure.

As can be seen from the story about the Eye of Horus, this god not only became to be venerated as the patron of pharaohs but also as the god of the sky. His right eye was the sun, while his left one was the moon, and every day and night, he flew across the sky in the form of a falcon.

The Egyptians celebrated Horus in a yearly festival. It was called The Festival of Victory and was celebrated in the temple at Edfu in Upper Egypt. It included a sacred drama—a re-creation of the conflict between Horus and Set. The pharaoh himself would play the part of Horus, while Set would be represented by a hippopotamus. The striking of the animal by the pharaoh's spear would mark the symbolic victory of Horus over Set.

Set

We have already met Set, the Egyptian god of chaos, destruction, and mischief, but we haven't been properly introduced. Now, it's finally the time to meet him: the god of deserts, storms, chaos, violence, and, interestingly, foreigners.

He was represented by his totemic animal *sha*. The interpretations of this creature's nature vary. It might be a jackal, a wild dog, or a hyena, but most likely, it's a creature that never existed in an actual Egyptian landscape. The symbol itself is very ancient, dating from the times before the unification of Upper and Lower Egypt.

Despite his aggressive nature and his rivalry with Ra, during most of ancient Egyptian history, Set wasn't regarded as a demon figure. For example, during the Old Kingdom, Horus and Set both were seen as defenders of the god Ra and depicted as brothers (sometimes even twins), instead of an uncle–nephew duo. They would be seen on illustrations depicting the anointing of the new pharaoh, standing on both sides of him, equal and in agreement.

Set's role as the defender of Ra was very important. During each excursion of Ra's sun barque through the waters of the night, Set fought the sea serpent Apep, or Apophis, thus allowing the sun-god to cross the waters safely and reemerge on the sky in the new sunrise.

Set's role in the conflict with Horus, especially during its sexual phase, is a debated subject among Egyptologists. As previously mentioned, there are conflicting accounts as to Set's motives: Some regard the intercourse between Horus and Set as a consensual transaction, others as rape. In the version with rape, Set's desire to have intercourse with Horus stemmed from his jealousy and hatred of the young, handsome, and beautiful god, and he tried to get him drunk and seduce him. But Horus only feigned drunkenness, and when Set attempted to rape him, he caught his seed in the manner previously described. The mere fact that there exist conflicting accounts as to the incident points to some ambiguity there, but it's difficult to interpret it. Ancient Egyptian views on homosexuality remain unclear, even though some depictions of same-sex relationships have been found. There are no texts or laws condemning same-sex desire, from which we might conjecture that it was mostly tolerated.

During the Second Intermediate Period, Set became worshiped as a chief deity. The Fifteenth Dynasty, known as the Hyksos, chose him for their patron since he was the god of foreigners and bore some resemblance to the Sumerian god Hadad. Even after the overthrow of the Fifteenth Dynasty, the New Kingdom pharaohs merely overtook the cult of Set instead of extinguishing it.

There are many preserved temples of Set. Most notably, the temple complex in Sepermeru in Middle Egypt contains a very grandiose set of buildings dedicated to Set, dating from the Ramesside period during the New Kingdom. The location of Sepermeru was not accidental: It was viewed as a "gateway to the desert" and, therefore, fitting as a place of worship for the desert god.

So when did Set become what he is associated with today: the demon god, the root of evil? It seems to have happened quite late during the Third Intermediate and Late Periods. The attitudes of Egyptians toward foreigners had changed with the growing oppression at the hands of foreign empires, such as the Persians. Thus, the patron of foreigners also came to be despised. Moreover, the influence of other mythologies and religious systems on the ancient Egyptian religion became apparent, for example, the Greeks identified Set with Typhon, a serpentine giant who attacked Zeus. Set's attack on Osiris was seen in a similar light.

As a result of this shift, many temples of Set were destroyed or overthrown. But he was still worshiped in some outlying towns, where he was regarded as a "Lord of the Oasis," a source of life in the desert landscape.

Other Male Deities

Many Egyptian gods attained and lost their importance over time. In this section of the chapter, we'll talk about gods who might be a bit less familiar to you but who were very important to the Egyptians at one point in history or another.

Anubis

Anubis, or Anpu, the god who performed the funerary rites over Osiris's body, is the god of mummification and embalming. Before Osiris came to be worshiped as the king of the underworld in the times of the Middle Kingdom, that role had been reserved for Anubis. But even after Osiris took over, Anubis retained his role as a god who granted entry for a soul into the underworld. In the Late Period, he would also perform a very important role of weighing the soul of the dead in order to see how well it performed justice during its life and to determine its fate.

Anubis was depicted with the head of a jackal. It's possible that this choice stemmed from the fact that in the cemeteries where the common people were buried, the graves were shallow and the jackals, being scavengers, often hunted for bodies. In the principle of "fighting like with like" then, the divine jackal was supposed to protect the bodies from predators.

Anubis's parentage and familial ties are unclear. Initially, he had been worshiped as son of Ra, but in later versions of his myth, he became a bastard son of Osiris and Nephthys, Set's wife, for which Set hated him.

Even though Anubis is a very ancient deity, worshiped even during the reign of the First Dynasty, there are no extensive myths pertaining to him. He preferred to stay in the shadows, performing the vital rites of the dead.

Thoth

We have already met Thoth in the Osiris myth when he accompanied Anubis in the embalming process and later when he mitigated the conflict between Horus and Set. But he played many more important roles in Egyptian myth: the god of the moon, learning, hieroglyphs, science, magic, and judgment, among other things. In a way, he was the source of all wisdom.

He was often depicted with a head of an ibis. This sacred animal, whose beak resembles a crescent moon, was connected to that celestial body, which, in Egyptian theology, was the main source of time. Thoth was credited with inventing the calendar. It's worth mentioning that it's the Egyptians who first used a 365-day calendar. According to the myth, in the beginning, the year was supposed to have 360 days, during which Nut, the sky, was supposed to be sterile. But Thoth gambled with the moon for a part of its light and won, so during the remaining five days, Nut gave birth to Osiris, Set, Isis, and Nephthys.

In accordance with the Egyptian belief that words held the power of creation, Thoth, as the one who conceived the hieroglyphs, was immensely powerful. Some versions of the Osiris myth say that it was Thoth who gave Isis the right words that allowed her to restore her husband to life. As the developer of the writing system, Thoth was also the inventor of spells and all manner of scientific disciplines: astronomy, astrology, mathematics, geometry, medicine, botany, theology, and others.

Thoth was said to be married to Maat, the personification of justice. As such, he accompanied Anubis in judging the deceased souls. He had his own creature in the underworld, a dog-headed ape (or a baboon) called Aani, who represented equilibrium.

Thoth doesn't appear to have any parents. He might have created himself, and, in some accounts, he also calculated all the proper distances between the heavens and the Earth.

The main place of Thoth's cult was Hermopolis, especially during the Late Period. There, many ibis mummies were discovered, most likely buried to honor him.

Ptah

Ptah, the master craftsman and the creator god, took on many forms. The most common one was as a man with green skin, the divine beard, and a scepter shaped in the sign of *ankh*, the symbol of life. The color of Ptah's skin might have also represented life.

As one of the creator gods, Ptah was often linked with the sun. Thus, he was sometimes depicted with a solar disc and linked with fire that resides in the center of the earth. That was his link to metalworkers and craftsmen who used fire in their furnaces.

The cult of Ptah was very important. His high priests would be chief architects and royal craftsmen, and it would be their responsibility to work with the vizier and plan out the construction and inner decoration of royal temples and pyramids. Imhotep, the chancellor to the pharaoh Djoser from the Third Dynasty (both of whom we'll talk about in Chapter 6), was famed to have been the son of Ptah. The primary center of Ptah's cult was in Memphis, but later, also in Deir el-Medina, an extraordinary village inhabited solely by workers who worked on the tombs in the Valley of the Kings from the Eighteenth to the Twentieth Dynasties. There, the image of Ptah had been carved repeatedly into the walls, often depicted with large ears to symbolize a god who listens to the prayers of the people.

Apis and Serapis

In comparison to other gods we've already talked about, Apis is a bit unusual. Instead of being a humanoid god with an animal head, like most of the Egyptian pantheon, he is fully animalistic: a sacred bull, son of the goddess Hathor, of whom we'll talk in the next chapter. He often served as an intermediary between the higher gods and the people.

Most notably, he was the herald of Ptah, or sometimes, even his manifestation. As such, he was worshiped in Memphis, where a search for a calf that could be considered Apis incarnate was incessant. Such a calf had to meet several requirements in order to be considered sacred: It needed to have a white triangular marking on its forehead, an outline of a wing on its back (symbolizing the wing of an Egyptian vulture), a crescent moon shape on its right flank, and a scarab-shaped mark under its tongue.

If an extraordinary calf like that was found, it was then brought to the temple of Ptah and given a harem of cows. It was worshiped as an aspect of Ptah, and after its death, both the calf and its mother would be buried with a special ceremony. Then, a search for a new calf would begin: an ever-present cycle of death and rebirth.

In time, a special section of the temple complex in Memphis became dedicated solely to the burials of the sacred bulls. This would later be known as the Serapeum of Saqqara and was a vast underground complex, which was in use from the times of Ramesses II into the reign of Cleopatra.

Over time, as foreign influences on Egypt increased, other aspects of Apis's nature were added to the god until he became fully transformed. He was favored by Alexander the Great when the ruler conquered Egypt, and after his death, Ptolemy I Soter, the founder of the Ptolemaic Dynasty, sought to find a deity that could unite the ancient Egyptian religion with Hellenistic views. A human-like figure was created that was said to bear the name of Osiris-Apis, which would later become Serapis. This god was supposed to look like the anthropomorphic Greek gods but, at the same time, represent the Egyptian ideals of the divine. He was created to resemble Hades, the Greek god of the underworld, and his attribute was a serpent, resembling the Egyptian uraeus.

It seems that the cult of Serapis didn't so much catch on just in Egypt but rather spread over other parts of the Hellenistic world. There are accounts of the cult of Serapis in the Middle East, in Babylon, as well as in Greece, and later, even Rome. Serapis's temple in Alexandria became renowned, though, and it would only be destroyed by the Christians in the 4th century A.D.

Atum

We have already mentioned Atum as the creator god of Heliopolis and the father of Shu and Tefnut. It is said in one of the Heliopolian myths that when his children were born, they both became very curious about the primeval waters and wanted to explore them. But they quickly got lost in the darkness. Atum couldn't bear that loss. He sent his eye, the sun—in Heliopolis identified with the Eye of Ra—to search for his children. When he finally found them, he shed tears of joy. From them, the first human beings were created.

This myth, along with the aforementioned myth of Shu and Tefnut's birth via spitting or masturbation, exemplifies the gender ambiguity surrounding Atum. As a self-created god and the first being, he encompassed both the male and female elements, being a father as well as a mother to his children.

Atum's cult in Heliopolis was a very important one—but sadly, only one monument of this cult, a large obelisk, remains to this day. It was built during the times of the Twelfth Dynasty, and it weighs over a hundred tonnes.

Geb

Geb, the god of the earth and member of the Ennead from Heliopolis, was an important deity in the Egyptian pantheon, even if in time, he was replaced, giving way to Osiris, Horus, and the others. Son of Shu and Tefnut, and grandson of Atum—or, according to other versions, Ra—he was the personification of earth itself. His laughter was said to provoke earthquakes, and he was also supposed to be a father of all snakes living in the ground. One of them, Nehebkau, became revered as a snake-god connected to the afterlife, who judged the dead and distinguished them from the living.

On a more benevolent side, he blessed the crops and allowed them to grow.

Since the dead were symbolically swallowed by the earth when buried, Geb also became associated with the underworld. It was said that he could swallow the wicked people before their time.

Geb's wife is most often Nut, the sky, but according to some, it's Renenutet, the goddess of harvest. It's with her that Geb was supposed to conceive Nehebkau.

We have one important myth involving Geb, and it contains jealousy and rivalry.

It is said that after Geb and his sister Nut were born, the god of earth became instantly enamored with his sister. But this angered his father, Shu, the god of the air, and he wedged himself between the siblings in order to separate them, just as they were in the middle of coupling. Geb, enraged by his father's entitlement, then took and imprisoned within him his mother, Shu's sister-spouse Tefnut, who is the goddess of moisture. The myth explains the order of the universe: The earth and the sky are separated by the air, and the earth, in its turn, takes the moisture inside and gives back fertile crops.

Some myths associated with Geb credit him with giving birth to a goose that circled the primeval waters and laid an egg from which the whole world sprung up. We have seen the goose as a metaphor for Amun's act of creation in the Theban version of the creation myth; Geb's candidature for the association with the goose might stem from the fact that his name in the ancient Egyptian language was similar to that of a goose.

During the Ptolemaic period of ancient Egyptian history, Geb became associated with the Greek chthonic, or underworld, deity Cronus. Both gods were fathers to a whole pantheon of deities, and both were associated with earth. The priests of Geb during the Hellenistic times often referred to themselves as the priests of Cronus in Greek texts.

Shu

Now that we have repeatedly mentioned him, Shu also deserves his own section within this chapter. This god is not only the deity of wind but also peace due to the wind's cooling, or pacifying, tendencies, especially in the hot Egyptian climate.

Fog and clouds were considered parts of Shu and often described as his bones. The god's symbol was a feather, standing for lightness and emptiness. He was often depicted as a man bearing that single feather in his headdress and holding the sign *ankh* in his hand. Sometimes, he was also depicted holding the sky up above his head, like the Greek Atlas.

We have seen how the organization of the world was explained through a story of conflict between Shu and his son Geb, but sometimes, the ancient Egyptians would also explain natural disasters in this manner. At the end of the Old Kingdom period, some terrible meteorological disaster touched Egypt, possibly a severe heat wave combined with a drought. It resulted in a composition of a story in which Shu and his wife Tefnut argued over the fact that their children and grandchildren were receiving higher worship than them. Tefnut then left Egypt for Nubia with all of her moisture. Shu immediately missed her and tried to get her back, but she was angry and transformed into a vicious cat, attacking and killing anyone who dared to approach.

It is told that in the end, the god Thoth managed to convince Tefnut to come back to Egypt. He was in disguise, and he referred to Tefnut as honorable, a title that flattered her, so she agreed to bless Egypt again with her moisture.

Shu was worshiped mainly in Heliopolis, where he was revered as part of the Ennead.

Sobek

Sobek is a complicated deity. In simplest terms, he is the crocodile god worshiped to protect from the dangers of the Nile. But the history of the myths surrounding him and his cult is full of contradictions and ambiguities.

Sobek had been worshiped in Egypt since the times of the Old Kingdom. Faiyum, a city located south of the Nile Delta, also known as "the Land of the Lake" for its location within an oasis and near Lake Moeris, was the main center of his cult. It flourished especially during the time of the Middle Kingdom when Sobek took over some of the characteristics of Horus and Faiyum became known as Crocodilopolis. But many other towns and cities in the surrounding area had their own temples and their own versions of Sobek. Similarly to Apis, Sobek's cult was also centered on the reverence of sacred animals; crocodiles were reared and mummified in his honor.

Sobek's character had always been ruled by an ambiguity: a protector of the Nile, on one hand, but an aggressive and very animalistic deity, on the other—just like a crocodile whose head he bore. In early accounts, Sobek was known as a robber or as a god who killed the ones with whom he mated. But after his association with Horus, he started to be known as one of the healers of Osiris and a deity that united his mutilated parts and helped to bring him back to life. As such, Sobek became to be known as a healing and protective deity. He was supposed to be as fierce a protector as a crocodile mother was for her young.

Interestingly, the first female pharaoh adopted a name connected to Sobek upon her ascension to the throne: Sobekneferu. She was the first pharaoh to do so, but it's not entirely clear why it happened.

Anhur

Anhur was the god of war. Married to a goddess Mehit from Nubia, he was often depicted as a war general, wearing a fake beard and a headdress with four feathers and holding a lance in his hands. Sometimes, he would also be depicted as a man with a lion's head.

Anhur's main center of worship was in Abydos, one of the oldest cities in Egypt, in Upper Egypt. His cult was especially important during the times of Egypt's expansion because he was the patron of the Egyptian army. Sometimes, he was equated with the god of wind Shu, as his name could also mean "Sky Bearer." In the Ptolemaic era, the Greeks often equated Anhur with Ares, the Greek god of war.

There are no known stories pertaining to Anhur.

Kek

In the cosmogony of Hermopolis, Kekui and Kekuit were a pair of male-female gods who represented primeval darkness and were a part of the Ogdoad. Kek could be interpreted either as another name of the god Kekui or as a name for the pair, a representation of darkness itself.

As the male god, Kek was often represented by a frog. Not much is known about him, but he seems to have been responsible for the thickest darkness just before dawn as he is sometimes referred to as "the bringer of the light." Light doesn't exist without darkness, and vice versa.

There are no accounts of Kek's worship outside of Hermopolis.

Khnum

Khnum is one of the oldest gods in Egyptian religion. And no wonder—he's the patron deity of the source of the Nile. Since the Nile's origin didn't lay within ancient Egypt's borders, the river's life-giving presence was shrouded in mystery and could seem like an effect of divine intervention.

Khnum was often depicted as a divine potter because the Nile waters brought clay. According to early sources, Khnum was credited with creating the first humans from the clay by the Nile's riverbank. Some later accounts also acknowledged him for creating the gods.

Khnum was often depicted as a humanoid god with a head of a ram and accompanied by small figures that represented human children made of clay.

Khnum's main places of worship were Elephantine and Esna, two riverside cities in Upper Egypt. In Elephantine, he was more often solely referred to as the god of the Nile, while in Esna, he was credited with being a creator god.

We don't know any myths associated with Khnum.

Khonsu

Khonsu was the god of the moon. His name means "traveler," as he traveled through the sky every night, marking the passage of time. It was believed that he was the son of Amun and Mut, a mother goddess, and as such, he was worshiped in Thebes. He was often depicted as a mummy or as a human child: a mysterious, ambiguous nature, most likely linking his nature as a perpetual child with his nightly associations connected to the afterlife.

Khonsu was said to watch over the people who traveled at night. He was to repel the evil spirits as well as to heal those who were sick. During the New Kingdom, the cult of Khonsu rose in prominence, and he was referred to as one of the greatest gods.

Min

Min is one of the oldest Egyptian gods we know about. His cult reaches way back to the predynastic period. Later, he would sometimes be conflated with Horus, but generally, his worship survived for thousands of years.

Min was the god of fertility. He was often depicted as a Black man with an erect penis and a flail (an ancient agricultural tool) in his hand. His cult was centered around Upper Egypt, where numerous festivals would be held in his honor, some of them possibly orgiastic in nature. Naked games were also organized, some of which consisted of climbing an erect pole.

Min's ties to agriculture and life gave him a special popularity among the people, especially men. It was chiefly them that worked as farmers in the fields. His symbols were, among others, sacred white bulls and lettuce leaves, which at the time were considered to be an aphrodisiac.

During the Middle Kingdom, Min was worshiped as Min-Horus, and thus, he became the god of fertility and kingship at the same time. At that time, this previously fatherless deity was also given Horus's parents: Osiris and Isis. By the New Kingdom, there was a special coronation ceremony in which the new pharaoh had to plant a seed in honor of Min in order to ensure the yearly flooding of the Nile. It is generally believed that these were literal plant seeds, but some have suggested that the king was expected to ejaculate. In general, in the worship of a male fertility deity, we can observe that ancient Egyptians didn't tie fertility solely to women—on the contrary, men were also credited with the concept, and even expected to participate in childbirth, something that lay in stark contrast with other ancient cultures at the time.

Aten

The last god I wanted to talk about in this chapter is a very unique one. The story of his worship is strongly tied to a singular incident in Egyptian history: a religious reform, or, rather, a revolution, conducted by the pharaoh Akhenaten.

Initially, Aten was only one of the names for the sun disk of Ra. During the time of the Middle Kingdom, a dying pharaoh was sometimes described as uniting with the sun disk, which was deified in that depiction. By the time of the Eighteenth Dynasty and the New Kingdom, Aten grew to a rank of a god—one of many aspects of Ra. His popularity was growing.

But the true revolution came when the pharaoh Amenhotep IV changed his name to Akhenaten and announced a new state religion in which Aten would be worshiped as the creator of everything. A creator god wouldn't be so surprising by himself—but what was more astonishing was the abandonment of all the other gods. From now on, Egyptian religion was supposed to be monotheistic.

The basis of the new religion, called Atenism, can be found in a long poem attributed to Akhenaten himself. It's called the *Great Hymn to the Aten*, and it describes the sun-god as the creator of everything. Night is depicted as a time of fear and evil, and the sun makes any endeavor better. The poem enumerates everything that Aten has created: the Nile and the animals within, the people, and nature. It bears some resemblance to the psalms from the

Hebrew Bible, and possible connotations between the two are a subject of much academic debate.

Since in the new religion only Aten was god, the pharaoh now named himself the son of Aten but without assigning a divine status to himself. Similarly, the all-powerful god was no longer a personal, human-like deity, but rather, he transcended all creation and could be found anywhere.

The cult of such an extraordinary god could only be extraordinary, as well. Akhenaten built a new city, Amarna, close to the border between Upper and Lower Egypt to be the center of his new cult. The temple of Aten was starkly different from the temples of the other gods. Instead of being a closed-off building, it had an open roof to allow the sunrays to permeate the place. No statues or likenesses of Aten were permitted. Much as in the ancient Hebrew religion, they were seen as idolatry. However, unlike the Hebrew tradition, the depictions of mortals praying to Aten were permitted—and as a result, the walls of Amarna were covered by decorations depicting Akhenaten and his family praying to the sun disk that represented the new god.

And these were extraordinary depictions. They veered away from all the canons and precepts of traditional Egyptian art. The symbolic depictions of people with solemn expressions gave way to faces with realistic expressions, portrayed smiling—an unthinkable thing for earlier Egyptian art. People, animals, and plants were now rendered in motion, conveying action. The convention was, especially with the depictions of Akhenaten and his family, to show elongated faces and skulls and to portray the pharaoh as rather androgynous-looking. This has led to a lot of speculation among historians: Did Akhenaten have some genetic disease? An illness? Was the reason behind the revolution something more mundane than a religious conviction? We will discuss these theories in Chapter 6 in the section dedicated to him.

The Atenist revolution was short-lived. Akhenaten's son, the famous Tutankhamun, brought the old ways back, and all of Akhenaten's edicts ordering the destruction of the temples and depictions of the old gods were overturned. The last pharaoh of the Eighteenth Dynasty and Tutankhamun's successor, Horemheb, dismantled Aten's cult entirely.

The cult of Aten is an interesting example of a religion that we know more from the Hebrew tradition, and later, from the Christians. Having told numerous stories about the Egyptian versions of cosmogony and various gods' attributes, we can see that Aten's cult didn't come completely out of nowhere, though. Already before, there have been gods who were said to have created themselves or who, like Ptah, seemed to be omnipotent, at least to some degree. But only Aten's cult seemed to conflict with the worship of all other deities—and that, in the end, proved too much for the ancient Egyptians. Akhenaten's social and theological experiment failed.

CHAPTER 4

Goddesses

We have seen the rich world of Egyptian gods. But we have also observed how this world cannot exist in isolation. The goddesses—Isis, Nephthys, Tefnut, and others—have already appeared in our stories, and in very important roles, too. Let's now delve deeper into their world.

Familiar Female Deities

Isis

The wife-sister of Osiris and the one who brought him back to life, Isis was the mother goddess. Along with her husband, she was the most revered deity not only in ancient Egypt but also in the ancient Greco-Roman world. She was considered to be a symbolic mother of every new pharaoh and was said to aid Osiris in his rule of the afterlife, as well as in healing. Often depicted with a symbolic, throne-shaped hieroglyph on her head, she would also sometimes bear cow horns with a sun disk between them—a symbol that she took over from another goddess, Hathor.

Isis's cult reaches back to the times of the Old Kingdom. Her figure as a mourning wife and, later, a mother, was a popular one among the people of Egypt. In the myth in which she searched for Osiris's body parts and restored breath to his body with magic and love, she is portrayed in a very human, emotional manner. It was Isis's love that was capable of restoring Osiris to life as the king of the underworld but also of producing his heir, Horus, who would later carry his father's spirit within himself.

Isis's role as a helper in the underworld was similar to what she did for Osiris: She restored human souls to life—to the very specific type of afterlife, to be more precise. She would provide nourishment to the souls and welcome them as their mother. Some Egyptian funerary texts also suggest that she might have chosen some female souls to be her attendants in the afterlife.

As a mother goddess, Isis was especially lauded for her protection over little Horus: her quest for help to hide her son, her brave fight with all the beasts, and her protection from Set's attempts at killing him. These actions represented Isis's more warlike features and made her the protector of kingship—Horus was, after all, the original pharaoh.

But Isis was also sometimes credited with being a mother to other, lesser deities, especially those related solely to the afterlife, which we will talk about in Chapter 7. Isis was also venerated as the mother of Min, the fertility god, who would often be conflated with Horus. From time to time, she was even seen as a goddess accompanying humans at the beginning of life as well as the end: She would be capable of seeing a person's future and preside at the hour of their birth, predicting their fate.

Sometimes, Isis was also linked with the rain that falls from the sky and with floods. This was most likely due to the many tears she shed after Osiris's death.

Isis's cult practically erupted in the Ptolemaic times. She was adopted by Greeks and Romans and was lauded as the universal goddess of the entire cosmos: kingship, weather, nature, and life itself. She would become a creator goddess in a similar way that Ptah had been before. She was supposed to bring the whole world to life through her words. In this role, she was venerated on the small island of Philae in the Nile Delta.

All in all, Isis was perhaps the most powerful goddess in the whole of the Egyptian pantheon.

Nephthys

Nephthys, the last of the four siblings and children of Geb and Nut, was a sister-wife to Set. Despite her marriage, she helped Isis find the parts of Osiris's body and mourned him along with her. For that, she was often venerated as the goddess of mourning. But she was also connected to night and death, as well as several other concepts. Depicted with a headdress in the shape of a house on her head, she was known as "the Helpful Goddess." Given that she often appeared as a helper of Isis, she was regarded as a goddess of nursing and was said to nurse every new pharaoh.

According to tradition, she was Anubis's mother, who she conceived with Osiris, betraying Set. She is said to have tricked Osiris into sleeping with her by impersonating her sister Isis. Set's wrath, however, focused on Osiris, not on Nephthys herself.

As a wife of Set, Nephthys only seemed to have accompanied him when he was conforming to the more benevolent aspects of his nature, such as healing or fighting the primeval snakes during the night. There are no negative, or destructive, elements to Nephthys's nature. On the contrary, she seems to be one of the more benevolent and gentle goddesses in the Egyptian pantheon. As such, she was especially worshiped during the times of the New Kingdom and Ramesses II.

As the goddess of mourning, Nephthys was often seen as a patroness of embalmers. In Abydos, she was especially venerated alongside Isis, as one of the two mourners of Osiris. During a yearly festival in honor of them, two priestesses would assume the roles of Isis and Nephthys and perform elaborate mourning songs with the accompaniment of tambourines, known as the "Lamentations of Isis and Nephthys." The songs told the story of Osiris's mutilation and return to life, as well as contained litanies to the gods.

But Nephthys was also revered in a more cheerful context. As the goddess of night, she was connected to darkness and everything that was obscure. By association, she became to be known as a protective deity of a delirious state and a goddess of beer. Lavish beer offerings were given to her, and the pharaohs prayed to her to give them the joy of drunkenness without the pain of the hangover.

Bastet

Bastet was a cat goddess, and originally, also a lioness goddess who had been worshiped in ancient Egypt from the times of the Old Kingdom. The main center of her cult was the city of Bubastis in Lower Egypt, where she was worshiped in a temple standing in the middle of a small island, which served as a symbol of the sun disk.

Bastet was the daughter of Isis and Ra and a wife of Ptah. Initially a warrior goddess, she later became associated with the slightly less fierce members of the feline family, becoming the goddess of pregnancy and childbirth. She was also seen as a defender of Ra and the pharaoh, as she was one of the deities accompanying Ra on his nightly journey through the dark waters.

The reverence that the ancient Egyptians held toward cats is a well-known one. As we have seen, they weren't, by far, the only sacred animals in Egyptian theology, but they definitely occupied a special place. As predators for mice and other vermin, among them snakes, they were especially useful for farmers. The cats' fierce protectiveness and tenderness toward their young also made Bastet a perfect candidate for the goddess of childbirth.

We don't have any extant myths involving Bastet. However, the Greek historian Herodotus (ca. 484–ca. 425 B.C.E.) described a festival dedicated to Bastet and held in the city of Bubastis, and he claimed it was one of the most important festivals in the whole Egyptian calendar. The festival involved sacrifice, drunkenness, song, and dance and attracted hundreds of thousands of visitors of both genders. In fact, there might have been as many as 700,000 of them (Herodotus & Blakesley, 2012).

Hathor

Hathor is a very important goddess. As a wife of Horus, she was a sky deity and, along with Isis, a symbolic mother of the pharaohs. She was depicted with the sun disk on her head, and she was revered as the Eye of Ra, the feminine aspect of the sun-god. Along with Bastet and Sekhmet, she was one of the three daughters of Ra.

But she was also associated with cattle and depicted as a cow. This ancient cult reached predynastic Egypt, and it's possible that the earlier, different goddess had been conflated with a later figure of a different kind. As a result, Hathor was granted many areas of expertise besides the sky and the sun. In fact, some historians believe that the name Hathor didn't apply to one goddess, but rather, to a category of goddesses or semi-divine beings, much as nymphs and muses are categories in Greek mythology. Some Egyptian texts speak of seven Hathors, or even 362 of them (Bleeker, 1973). It's possible that the figure of a Hathor represented every area of life that the ancient Egyptians associated with femininity as such.

So, what were the different functions played by Hathor?

As the sky goddess, some versions of the creation myths put Hathor even before Ra in the creation chain, describing her as a celestial cow who birthed Ra and put the sun disk between her horns. But more commonly, she was depicted as the wife or the daughter of Ra, and she was said to accompany him on his solar barque. This uncertainty as to Hathor's exact familial tie to Ra might represent different phases of the sun: at the dawn, Hathor as the sky gave birth to the god; at midday, she was his consort; at sunset, he gave his power back to her as if birthing her.

In the funerary text known as the *Book of the Heavenly Cow*, Ra wanted to punish humans who rebelled against him. I have mentioned this event before, remarking that it was Sekhmet who Ra sent to punish humans. But in that story, Sekhmet was only a mask, so to speak, that Hathor put on her face, transforming herself from a mild and benevolent goddess into a destructive warrior. It is said that as Sekhmet, Hathor didn't want to stop her revenge, until even Ra was terrified, so he ordered all beer in Egypt to be tinted red and poured all over the land. Sekhmet, mistaking it for blood, drank it until she was full. Inebriated, she went to sleep and, then, turned back into the benevolent Hathor.

But Hathor rebelled against Ra again, this time, not out of fury, but out of joy. She went away to roam the deserts and lands of Nubia and Libya, curious of their charms. Ra missed his Eye and called after her, but she didn't want to come back. So he sent Thoth who, through trickery, brought her back to Ra, who then married her. We have already seen this myth—only, with Shu and Tefnut in the main roles. It seems that the pair of Ra and Hathor is a repetition of the tale about the primeval gods.

Because of the joyful part of her nature, Hathor became the goddess of music and dance. In ancient Egyptian belief, all the joys of life, including music, dance, incense, and alcohol, were the gods' gifts to humanity, and Hathor was the main patroness of them. The happy, loud, and rowdy celebrations of Hathor venerated her both as the joyful goddess and thanked her for ending the destruction of mankind. The redness of wine and red-tinted beer were likened to blood, and prayers were uttered for the presence of the former liquid rather than the latter. It was said that music had to be played to Hathor by the gods in order for her not to descend into rage again.

Moreover, Hathor's joyful side also made her the goddess of love, beauty, and sexuality. When in the Heliopolian creation myth Atum produced his children, Shu and Tefnut, by the act of masturbation, some versions of the story likened his hand to a feminine element and personified it as Hathor. She also appeared in many folkloric tales and short stories, many of them rather bawdy and heavy in sexual themes. In one of them, Hathor motivated a tired Ra, who decided not to get up and ride through the sky, by lifting up her skirt and exposing her genitals. This made Ra laugh and lifted his spirits, arousing him.

Hathor could appear to common men in the form of an alluring woman with luscious long hair or as a dangerous beast. If the latter occurred, the humans' task was to pacify her with gifts. Hathor's hair was an important part of her allure, and losing a lock of it by the goddess was likened to a castration.

There is one other interesting aspect linked to Hathor's association with sexuality: the afterlife. Ancient Egyptians believed in a form of reincarnation where sex enabled the rebirth of the deceased souls. Thus, Hathor was venerated as the goddess who made this process possible, rousing the dead to a new life. She never became a major goddess associated with the afterlife, but nevertheless, she played a major part in it.

Hathor was also the goddess of motherhood. In the story of Isis and Horus, she acted as a foster mother of sorts, healing Horus from various ailments inflicted by Set through the power of gazelle milk or a milky sap of the sycamore tree—both of which became her symbols. In the Late Kingdom, she was often portrayed as Horus's wife, however, and thus, she was a mother to all manners of lesser deities considered to be offspring of Horus at various times. As a mother figure, she was also connected to fate, presiding over the birth of an infant and predicting their life.

Another area of Hathor's specialty was trade and travel to foreign lands. It is most likely because as a sky goddess, she was the patroness of navigation. This attribution resulted in various goddesses from other cultures with which the Egyptians were trading—such as Canaan and Syria—being likened to foreign versions of Hathor.

Other Female Deities

Sekhmet

We have met Sekhmet already—in some versions of the myth, a vicious aspect of Hathor, in others, a separate goddess. She was portrayed with the head of a lioness and was a goddess of war as well as healing. She was said to breathe fire and to bring plague—but she also protected the pharaohs, especially on war campaigns. As the goddess of healing, she had both the power to bring the disease and to end it.

In some myths, it was Sekhmet, not Bastet, that was the wife of Ptah. With him, she was supposed to have had Nefertem, a personification of the lotus flower that grew on Benben at the beginning of the world.

Sekhmet's worship was mostly conflated with the worship of Hathor: that loud and rowdy yearly celebration that was supposed to placate both goddesses. Thousands of people attended, and thousands of people got drunk. The temples of Sekhmet had special porches only for drunk people.

Heqet

Another goddess sometimes identified with Hathor, Heqet was the patroness of fertility. She was represented by an image of a frog since for the ancient Egyptians, a frog was related to the flooding of the Nile that brought fertile crops. She was considered to be the wife of Khnum, and her cult was very old; she was supposed to have helped this ancient god to form humans on his potter's wheel.

Heqet was also associated with birth. She was said to have breathed the first breath into Horus's lungs and to do this for every child since. Hence, women who were going through childbirth often wore amulets with an image of a frog, praying to Heqet to deliver the child fast and without complications.

Because of Osiris's rebirth, Heqet also became associated with resurrection and reincarnation.

Amunet

Amunet, the female counterpart of Amun and a member of the Ogdoad of Hermopolis, was a truly ancient goddess, whose name appears in the oldest Egyptian religious texts.

Initially, Amunet was considered a very powerful goddess and worshiped as the patroness of night and a deity from before all time. But by the Twelfth Dynasty, her power receded and was given to a new deity adopted from the Kingdom of Kush: Mut. Amunet's cult became localized, mainly to Thebes. She still played an important part there, being invoked in the rites of the pharaoh's coronation, but she was no longer the ruler of the whole universe. Her role was to protect the new pharaoh in his capital, and as such, she was sometimes depicted together with the god of fertility, Min.

We don't know of any stories related to Amunet.

Maat

When talking about Maat, we are going not only to refer to the goddess but also to the concept of justice in Egyptian society. We have already mentioned how crucial Maat was to everyday life in ancient Egypt, so now, let's look closer at this idea.

As a goddess, Maat was depicted as a young woman with wings or with an ostrich feather in her headdress. It was against this feather that a deceased person's heart would be judged in the afterlife. She looked over a pharaoh, making sure that the ruler of Egypt upheld justice. The pharaohs, in turn, would dedicate votive statues to her as proof of their adherence to cosmic harmony.

Maat was the daughter of Ra, placed by him upon the world in order to repeal chaos. According to some accounts, she was also the wife of Thoth, the patron of science and scribes—and we will soon see why.

There are no mythological stories about Maat—but conversely, Maat as a concept in Egyptian society deserves a more thorough explanation.

Maat didn't only mean justice or order as we would today recognize it, linking it to the judicial system of a well-functioning state. Instead, the concept encompassed all life: from the orderly way the universe was organized, with the movements of stars, the flooding of the Nile, and the passage of night and day, to the daily life of every Egyptian citizen. Egypt, as we have already mentioned, was a diverse place inhabited by many people with sometimes conflicting interests. The obligation to uphold Maat was a necessity for an efficient functioning of the society, so everyone needed not only to conduct themselves with honesty and justice, treating everyone equally in interpersonal interactions but also observe the religious rituals and honor the gods. Just as an imbalance in the state of the cosmos could bring about a disturbance in society, an irregular behavior by an individual could disturb the order of the world. For example, a pharaoh who was impious could bring about a plague or a famine.

It's also for this reason why Egyptian society and culture were so staunchly opposed to change, and instead, relied on conforming to a tradition that lasted for thousands of years. It's not difficult to see how Akhenaten's religious reforms and a reorganization of the society could have been perceived as an utmost threat to Maat.

The cast of scribes, whom I have mentioned in our introductory chapter, was the main force behind upholding the Maat. During their training, they would be tested repeatedly not only for their knowledge of the law but also for their ethical bearing. They started their training when they were five to ten years old, and it lasted for several years, including a four-year preliminary course and a couple more years of apprenticeship.

The scribes' responsibility was to hold important positions in the country, so it is no wonder that they needed to know the ins and outs of justice and order. And they weren't only employed by the rich—every village would need to have a scribe that could put the poor, illiterate people's plights into letters and intercede on their behalf to the authorities. Those letters needed to be written in a high rhetorical fashion since adherence to Maat was seen as adherence to the rules of flowery speech. But they also needed to embody Maat in spirit, to argue for the right cause. Crucial to our understanding of Maat is the fact that despite the hierarchical structure of Egyptian society, it was believed that any individual, no matter the rank, deserved justice.

In Chapter 7, dedicated to the Egyptian afterlife, I will go into more detail concerning the specific rules that an Egyptian had to adhere to in order to preserve Maat. For now, let us come back to the goddesses.

Mut

Originally from the Kingdom of Kush (or Nubia; present-day northern Sudan), Mut was the mother goddess that in time took over some of the characteristics of Amunet, Hathor, and Sekhmet. The new wife of Amun, she was the patron of the pharaohs during the Middle and New Kingdoms, for which she was revered in Thebes, along with her son, Khonsu, a local variation of the god of the moon.

She was depicted as a young woman with the double crown of Egypt on her head—but in Upper Egypt, she would also often be portrayed as a lioness goddess, like Sekhmet, or as a cat, cobra, or cow. The latter depiction would honor Mut as the heavenly goddess, like Hathor.

Mut's worship became widespread in the later eras of ancient Egypt. Apart from being revered in Thebes, she had a temple in Karnak, where she would be revered daily; the queen of Egypt would often be the presiding chief priestess in these rituals. If the pharaoh was female, the role of the priestess would be taken over by her daughter. The records show that Mut was highly favored by women in power. It was the second female pharaoh, Hatshepsut, who brought her cult to the forefront and promoted it.

Neith

Neith was another warlike deity, a tutelary goddess of Sais in the Nile Delta right from the predynastic times. In fact, she's one of the oldest known Egyptian deities.

Similarly to Hathor and Mut, Neith was also worshiped as a creator and a sky goddess who gave birth to the sun every day. As such, she was on par with other Egyptian deities, such as Atum, who were capable of giving birth without having a partner. It has been, therefore, suggested that there was something androgynous in Neith's nature, especially so Neith's act of birth seemed to be described without any sexual imagery whatsoever (in contrast to Atum and his symbolic act of masturbation).

Neith's warlike nature was represented by her affinity for arrows, with which she was often depicted. She was not only a warrior, but she also made weapons for the fighting soldiers and protected them during battle. She shot her arrows at the enemies, which, by proxy, also made her the goddess of death, responsible for guiding the souls of the deceased from the world of the living to the afterlife. She was often referred to as the one who opened hidden paths.

In addition to being the mother of the sun, Ra, Neith was also sometimes depicted as an ancient chthonic deity who gave birth to Nun, the primordial waters, and the water snake Apophis. Other times, she was also seen as a goddess of waters and the mother of Sobek, the crocodile god. As such, she would become the wife of Khnum, instead of Mut.

She was also the goddess of weaving, and some said that it was through that act that she brought forth the universe. For her association with both war and weaving, Neith would later become revered by the Greeks since these were the attributes that they associated with their own goddess of war, Athena.

In some versions of the myth about Horus and Set's rivalry, it was Neith that ended their fight and decided that Horus should rule Egypt.

Neith was celebrated yearly in a festival that the ancient Greek historian Herodotus described as the Feast of Lamps. The people would burn hundreds of lamps and lanterns under the open sky and dedicate them to the goddess.

Nut

Nut, similarly to Neith, is the goddess of the sky, and she was sometimes depicted as a young woman with blue skin and stars all over her body, crouching over the earth like the sky dome. The daughter of Shu and Tefnut, she was the sister-wife of Geb, from whom she had been separated by her father.

The most important myth concerning Nut was that of her conceiving the four most important Egyptian gods: Osiris, Isis, Set, and Nephthys. I have already touched upon it in the section on Thoth—but here, it's worth recounting in full.

At the time when the world was young and the year had only 360 days, the sun-god Ra decreed that Nut shouldn't give birth to any god or creature and, instead, remain sterile.

Ra's word was like law itself, and so, nothing could seemingly be done. But Nut spoke to Thoth, the god of wisdom—if anyone could have a solution to this, it was him.

So Thoth instructed Nut to gamble with Khonsu, the god of the moon, for his light that rivaled only that of Ra. The plan was for Khonsu to lose so many times that it would buy Nut a lot of additional light—meaning, additional days of the year that she could use to her advantage.

It wasn't difficult to win when the god of wisdom himself oversaw Nut's moves. Khonsu lost enough of his light that it formed an additional five days. This was a loophole: Those days weren't part of the year, so Nut could bear her children during them. On each day, she gave birth to a different child: According to this version of the legend, Horus was also among these children.

But the fury of Ra was great. In this story, it was his wrath, and not the jealousy of Shu, that separated Nut and Geb forever—Shu was only executing that decree. But it was too late, and the gods had already been born, and Nut never regretted her rebellion.

As the goddess of the sky, Nut was believed to separate the orderly world from the forces of chaos. The heavenly bodies coursed through her own divine body, and when they disappeared from the sky, it was believed that she swallowed them, and they would be reborn in their next cycle.

Nut also became the patroness of astronomy. The ancient Egyptian astronomical texts that we know today are called *The Book of Nut*.

Renenutet

Renenutet was the goddess of nourishment and harvest. She was depicted as a woman with the head of a cobra—a symbol of protectiveness. She was said to be the patroness of nursing and to nurse the pharaoh throughout his or her life.

As the goddess of harvest, she was connected to the Nile, whose yearly flooding provided the Egyptians with nourishment. Thus, she was often perceived as the wife of the crocodile god Sobek. She gave birth to Nehebkau, a supernatural snake, of whom we'll speak in the next chapter, which she had conceived with Geb, the earth. Sometimes, she was also depicted as a mother to Neper, a minor god of grain.

The main center of Renenutet's cult was Terenuthis, or Tarrana, in the Nile Delta, but from there, it spread all over Egypt.

Serket

Serket's specialty was very specific: She healed venomous bites. Originally, she was the personification and deification of a scorpion in accordance with the rule of fighting like with the like. When she became a goddess, she also gained divine parentage. She was revered as the daughter of Neith and Khnum and the sister to Sobek and the serpent Apophis.

Serket's power was both to sting and to heal the bite. She could constrict her victim's throat—a symptom of being bitten by a scorpion—but also open it to breathe again. Since so many scorpion and snake bites were fatal, Serket also became associated with the world of the dead. She was said to be a patron of the embalmers and to protect the canopic jars, the small jars into which the intestines of the deceased were put.

Wadjet

Initially, Wadjet had been only a minor local goddess of the city of Dep, also known as Buto or Per-Wadjet, in the Nile Delta. In time—and it was a very ancient time, before the unification of Upper and Lower Egypt—Wadjet became the protector of Lower Egypt. After the unification, she joined the patron goddess of Upper Egypt, Nekhbet, in their joint enterprise of protection of the new political structure.

As the patron goddess of Egypt—we remember the uraeus symbol of the pharaohs—Wadjet was depicted as a woman with green skin and a head of a cobra, similar to Renenutet—or, sometimes, as a full cobra. Sometimes, Wadjet's snake would be depicted entwined around a staff—a secret symbol that would later be known as the caduceus. Sometimes, she would also be shown twining around a papyrus—a symbol of Lower Egypt.

According to some accounts, it was Wadjet who was Horus's nurse when he was a child. As a cobra with a highly protective nature, she fought off the monsters and dangers sent by Set. For this, she also became a patron of women in childbirth.

Nekhbet

Just as Wadjet was the patron of Lower Egypt, Nekhbet was a titular deity of Upper Egypt. Initially only a local goddess of the city of Nekheb, her influence grew rapidly as Upper and Lower Egypt unified. She was depicted as a vulture, often clutching a ring in her talons. It was called the *shen* ring and represented eternal protection.

After the unification, Nekhbet and Wadjet were often shown together and referred to as "Two Ladies." Their friendship symbolized the unity of Egypt; they were heavily referenced in texts and symbolism. I have already talked about the double crown of the Egyptian pharaohs and the name every ruler of Egypt adopted upon the ascension to the throne. Well, the double crown consisted of the cobra and the vulture symbols and represented the two goddesses—and the adopted name was the *nebty*, a dual noun that was supposed to represent the unity of Nekhbet and Wadjet.

With Wadjet, we close our overview of the goddesses of ancient Egypt. As I hope you have noticed, the ancient Egyptians attributed great power and importance to their female deities. They might not be the kings of the universe like Ra, but they were connected to its very beginnings, and in many cases, it was believed that the universe wouldn't have existed without them. They were also numerous and represented both a benevolent as well as a fiery nature.

In the next chapter, we will visit the versatile and fascinating world of Egyptian monsters. We will meet the sphinxes—but not only them. Let's get ready for the next step in our journey.

CHAPTER 5

Monsters and Creatures

Most gods and goddesses in Egyptian mythology combine the human and animal elements and, therefore, are "monstrous" to some degree. However, there are also creatures in Egyptian myth and folklore whose provenance is solely the world of monsters. In this chapter, we will meet them all: the dangerous, the benevolent, and the ambiguous.

Egyptian Demons

Egyptian mythology has its demons. They are, of course, not to be confused with the Judeo-Christian image of a demon, but they are, nonetheless, terrifying, even if not all of them are essentially evil.

Ammit

Ammit's identity is somewhere between a goddess and a monster. She was female, even though she only appeared in the form of a lion-crocodile-hippopotamus hybrid. Known as the Devourer of the Dead, Ammit played an important role in the afterlife.

After death, the soul of every person was weighed against Maat's feather. If it was found unjust and inadequate, it was devoured by Ammit—a terrible fate since it meant a second death and a lack of chance for reincarnation. A devoured soul would become eternally restless, or according to a different tradition, it would be destroyed forever.

Ammit's physical form is the best attestation to how much she was feared. Lions, crocodiles, and hippopotami were the largest and most dangerous predators in Egypt. To combine three of these greatest threats into one creature was to give it the utmost power of destruction.

Apophis

I have mentioned Apophis, or Apep, numerous times throughout this book. He was the giant serpent that Ra had to battle every night during his travels in the sun barque, aided in this task by Set and other gods. Son of Neith and Khnum, Apophis was the personification of chaos, called Isfet, and, therefore, the very opposite of justice, Maat. But some said he didn't have a mother and a father but, instead, was born from Ra's umbilical cord.

It is very telling that in either version of Apophis's birth and parentage, he's not a primordial being, connected to the creation of the world. This stands in stark contrast to snake or dragon figures from other mythologies that seem to emphasize the presence of evil in the world from the very beginning—or even from before the beginning. Instead, evil in Egyptian theology seems to be a result of an individual's own actions. Apophis is born either as a child of two responsible beings or emerges symbolically from Ra's own birth, just as when every human child is born, they are born with the ability to do good as well as evil.

Apophis was big, though not supernaturally so. He was supposed to be 16 feet long and have a head made of flint. He would wait for Ra every night though someone said that he waited for him just after dusk, others—just before dawn. When he moved, earthquakes erupted, and he had the power to render his foes helpless by the fire in his eyes. In the end, only Set was capable of battling him, and that strife often caused storms and lightning during the night.

That divine battle was a source of the Egyptians' worship. It was widely believed that there were prayers and rituals that could help Ra defeat Apophis and keep the monster from entering the daylight world. Additionally, there was a yearly celebration during which the priests would build an effigy of Apophis, designed to contain all of his evil powers, and then burn it or defile it in other ways, for example, by spitting at it or running it through with a lance. This could be done at a temple as well as in private homes.

Babi

Babi was a deification of the baboon. The ancient Egyptians believed that the baboons were the incarnations of the dead, and thus, Babi became one of the patrons of the underworld. Like Ammit, he devoured the souls of evil people, feasting on their entrails—a characteristic that was derived from a baboon's aggressive and omnivorous nature. As the important guardian of the underworld, in time, Babi became known as a son of Osiris, the god of the dead.

Another important area of Babi's expertise was the dead's virility. Baboons have high libido and visible erections, so that aspect of their nature became deified, too. Babi was often portrayed with an erection. It is probably a bit counterintuitive to us now, but the Egyptians believed that the dead were capable of having sex in the afterlife.

Bes and Beset

Bes—as well as his female counterpart, Beset—occupy a liminal space somewhere in between gods and monsters. They were protective deities guarding homes, mothers, children, and childbirth, but their depiction differed significantly from that of other Egyptian gods and goddesses. They were shown as stunted, almost dwarfish figures with fearsome, slightly grotesque features: huge noses, bushy eyebrows, and significant beards. But despite their unbecoming appearance, they were predominantly good spirits, and during the New Kingdom, they became defenders of households from everything that was bad and threatening.

There was also one other significant difference between the depiction of Bes and other Egyptian deities. Where the vast majority of the gods were presented in profile, Bes was always shown forward-facing. The most probable reason for this was that he was supposed to look angry and always ready to launch an attack on an evil force.

Bes and Beset would fight both physical and supernatural threats. They would protect the household, especially children, from venomous snakes as well as from evil spirits. People would keep their figurines in their homes. Since Bes was the patron of all that was good, he became associated with dance, music, and sexual pleasure—and thus, his face would be worn as a mask during celebrations as well as be tattooed on the dancers' legs. In some homes, special chambers were discovered with depictions of Bes and Beset on the walls. It is believed that those might have been healing chambers, or places designed to cure infertility.

In the later periods, Bes became popular amongst many foreign nations, especially the Phoenicians. Interestingly, one of the Phoenician colonies—the island of Ibiza—derives its name from Bes.

Nehebkau

Offspring of Renenutet, Nehebkau was a primordial snake-god, initially a demon. In time, he came to be associated with the afterlife.

His role in the realm of the dead was important. He was tasked with judging them and providing them with *ka*, their vital essence, which was essential for rebirth because it distinguished the living from the dead.

In a way, Nehebkau was a mirror image of Apophis. A beautiful snake tied to protection, he often accompanied Ra on his voyages and was sometimes even believed to have existed before Ra. It seems though that over time, this being, who first appeared in ancient texts as a devouring monster of chaos, became more benevolent and god-like. In fact, numerous depictions of Nehebkau have been found on protective amulets.

Nehebkau had his own center of worship in Heracleopolis near the Nile Delta, where a festival was held in his honor. He was prayed to as a deliverer from snake and scorpion bites.

Nehebkau is sometimes depicted as a snake, but more often, he is shown as a human-snake hybrid or as a snake with human legs.

Sphinxes

Rather than being a singular creature, sphinxes—these iconic monsters well-known from the Egyptian landscape—were a category of beings. They were shown as creatures with the head of a human (most commonly a man), the body of a lion, and the wings of a falcon. In the Egyptian tradition, sphinxes were ferocious and sometimes dangerous as a consequence but still mostly benevolent beings who ward off the forces of evil. They also might have been associated with Sekhmet, the lioness goddess.

But the figure of a sphinx was borrowed from Egypt to Greece rather early. The Greeks created their own lore around it: The Greek sphinxes were always women and always malicious. Today, the only mythological story we know about a sphinx comes from Greek mythology, and it's a story of how Oedipus saved the city of Thebes (in Greece; not to be confused with Thebes in Egypt!) from a malicious man-eating sphinx by solving its riddle. Since it's the most well-known sphinx story, I will tell it here, but it's worth remembering that the Greek sphinx is a slightly different being than the Egyptian one.

Oedipus and the Sphinx

Oedipus is one of the most well-known tragic heroes of ancient Greece. His life was spent trying to avoid a prophecy about his fate (saying that he would kill his father and marry his mother), but everything he did brought the fulfillment of the said prophecy.

It is when Oedipus learned about the prophecy and tried to escape it that he chanced upon the sphinx. He was fleeing from the city of Corinth where he had grown up, convinced that the king and queen of the city were his real parents. Of course, he didn't know that he had been adopted and that his actual parents were from Thebes.

At the moment when Oedipus met with the sphinx, he had already killed a man on the road who he thought was a complete stranger but would turn out to be his father. Our hero then heard about Thebes, a beautiful city that was terrorized by a ferocious sphinx who killed all the travelers trying to get inside. The creature would ask them riddles and, when they couldn't give it a correct answer, kill them. A prize had been instituted for the one who could solve the sphinx's riddle: the throne of Thebes and marriage to the recently widowed Queen Jocasta.

Oedipus decided to take on the challenge. The sphinx's riddle was: Which creature, though it only has one voice, is four-footed in the morning, two-footed during the noon, and three-footed in the evening?

For Oedipus, this was easy. He responded: This was a man. A human crawls on all fours in the first years of their life (the morning), walks on their two legs in the prime of their life (the noon), and needs the support of the walking stick in the last years of their life (the evening). Upon hearing the right answer, the sphinx threw itself off a precipice and died.

Now, Oedipus took his reward. He became the king of Thebes and married Jocasta. He didn't know that he was marrying his own mother. Years later, when a plague would attack Thebes and a prophet would say that it was all Oedipus's fault, the hero would learn the terrible truth—and he would gouge his own eyes out in sorrow.

Hieracosphinx

But let us come back to ancient Egypt. Ironically, we have no tales involving sphinxes in Egyptian mythology—but we know of at least one variety of sphinx that distinguished it from the others. Hieracosphinx, instead of having the face of a human, had a head of a hawk, the likeness of Horus. As such, it was Horus's symbol. The name itself was coined by the Greek historian Herodotus, who wanted to distinguish this particular type of sphinx from other types, including Criosphinxes—sphinxes with a head of a ram.

In time, the hieracosphinx became a symbol in European heraldry. We might know its slightly modified version under a different name: a griffin.

Famous Depictions of Sphinxes

There are some well-known depictions of the Egyptian sphinx with which you may be familiar. Most of them were probably created as protective figures.

There is, of course, the iconic Great Sphinx of Giza, which we probably all have in mind when we think about a sphinx. It was built during the Old Kingdom, and its face most likely depicts the pharaoh Khafre from the Fourth Dynasty, son of the famous Khufu (Cheops). It's been a symbol of Egypt from the moment of its creation. Throughout the centuries, it inspired awe even though for most of history, its body was covered by sand and only the head peeked out. The first partial excavations of the sphinx's body took place in the 19th century, with the 20th century seeing the complete uncovering of the whole statue.

It still, famously, misses its nose, though. Recent findings have concluded that it hasn't fallen off by accident. Instead, it was intentionally broken off with chisels, sometime between 3rd and 10th century C.E. (not shot off by Napoleon's soldiers as popularly assumed). The missing nose hasn't been found, and the motives for its destruction aren't known either, although it might have been an attempt to destroy a "pagan idol" by the Muslim inhabitants of Egypt.

Other known Egyptian depictions of a sphinx are nowhere near as monumental as the Great Sphinx of Giza. The Great Sphinx of Tanis, most likely created at the same time as its counterpart from Giza (or a couple of dynasties later), is a big statue that would take the larger part of a room but seems tiny in comparison to the 240-foot-long (73 meters) sphinx of Giza. It is now in the Louvre in Paris.

The Sphinx of Memphis, the third best known sphinx, is located near the ancient ruins of that city. It was most likely created during the New Kingdom in the times of the Eighteenth Dynasty. Its facial features are ambiguous and could either depict the female pharaoh Hatshepsut, Amenhotep II, or Amenhotep III. It's made out of alabaster and 26 feet (8 meters) long.

Other Mythical Creatures

There are many creatures in Egyptian myth and folklore that aren't easy to classify. As I've already mentioned, even the so-called demons can't really be equated with the demons of the Western European tradition, and matters become even more complicated with the creatures I am about to describe here. But maybe classification and definitions aren't too important. Maybe going with the flow of imagination will give far better results.

Aani

Aani is Thoth's sacred animal and, similarly to Sha, it's not a creature that can be found in the real world. Contrary to Sha though, Aani is a very clear hybrid between two real animals: a dog and an ape. Alternatively, it can be interpreted as a baboon.

Representing the god Thoth, Aani was a sign of wisdom and equilibrium.

Abtu and Anet

Both Abtu and Anet were sacred fish. They were supposed to guide the barque of Ra on its nightly travel through the dark waters. It was said that Abtu's role was to alert him of an upcoming danger, while Anet fought off the unidentified monsters. Abtu was golden, while Anet was red.

There are hypotheses claiming that the goddess Isis herself once transformed into Abtu, giving the fish its sacred role. In that guise, she was supposed to have swallowed Osiris's penis when Set mutilated his body, presumably to prevent Set from finding it. She would then restore the penis with magic.

Bennu Bird

Bennu, apart from being considered a part of Ra or Atum (his *ba*, or personality), can be regarded as a separate creature. He was a heron who created himself and who flew over the primordial waters, sat on a rock, and uttered a cry that called forth the whole universe.

Bennu is tied to the sun and rebirth. That's why he can be regarded as the ancestor of a phoenix. The concept of a phoenix is Greek, but Bennu shared enough characteristics with it that Herodotus, when the people in Egypt described the bird to him, recognized it as an Egyptian version of a phoenix.

Bennu's likeness was often carved on amulets entombed with mummies. As a symbol of rebirth, it was this bird's task to ensure a soul's reincarnation.

Medjed

Medjed's status is ambiguous. He's mentioned in The Book of the Dead as a god and depicted there as a ghost-like figure, one which looks a bit as if a person put on a sheet with two holes cut out for eyes for a modern Halloween party.

Medjed is a mysterious creature. Not much is known about him apart from the fact that he's supposed to shoot sunrays from his eyes and that his name means "smiter"—possibly because he smites the dead with his power? Nothing more is known. But, surprisingly—and rather hilariously—this slightly funny-looking creature has recently found its way to Japanese culture, especially to anime.

Serpopard

Serpopard was known both in Egypt and Mesopotamia and is a very ancient creature. Its depictions date as early as the predynastic period. Essentially, it was a leopard with the neck and head of a snake. Serpopards were often depicted in pairs with their necks intertwining with each other. They were also shown restrained—their necks were kept on leashes by people.

The symbolic meaning of this creature isn't clear, but it has been suggested that it might be a symbol of chaos reigning outside the borders of Egypt, represented by two of the most violent animals. As such, it could also be a manifestation of chthonic, ancient powers.

Sha

Sha is the already mentioned totemic animal of Set. But unlike other sacred Egyptian animals, this one can't be easily identified with an animal from the real world. At first glance, it looks like a greyhound or a jackal, and yet, upon further inspection, it doesn't represent either of them. However, it is possible that Sha is simply the Persian greyhound, or saluki, which is one of the earliest domesticated breeds of dog. Sha's ears reach upwards, which resembles the saluki mid-run.

What is interesting, is that when the Greeks came to closer contact with Egyptian myth, they clearly identified Set with a figure from their own mythology: Typhon, a serpentine giant and an agent of chaos. By association, Sha became known as the "Typhonic beast."

Sha closes our overview of Egyptian fantastical creatures. In the next chapter, we will delve more into the world of history–but as we'll see, the stories of mortal men and women of Egypt are often surrounded by their own set of myths.

CHAPTER 6

Mortals

Most probably, when I described ancient Egyptian chronology, you already noticed how many fascinating historical figures hide on the (papyri) pages of the history of this civilization. In this chapter, we're going to look closer at these figures. We'll see the fascinating history behind the pharaohs such as Akhenaten, Hatshepsut, and Cleopatra, and we'll try to solve some mysteries. Why did Akhenaten start his religious revolution? Was there really a curse connected to King Tut's tomb? And why was Cleopatra's beauty legendary? Let's find out.

Djoser and Imhotep

We'll start our journey with the Old Kingdom and the time of the oldest pyramids. As I've already mentioned in Chapter 1, Djoser was the pharaoh from the Third Dynasty who ordered the construction of the first known pyramid. Imhotep, in turn, was the pharaoh's vizier who oversaw its construction and, most likely, also designed it.

Djoser was the founder of the Third Dynasty and, at the same time, the first ruler of the Old Kingdom, inaugurating one of the first periods of Egypt's prosperity. He most likely reigned for 28 or 29 years and undertook several construction projects during that time, as well as subdued the inhabitants of the Sinai peninsula. But it is his project of the step pyramid that brought him the most fame.

The pyramid was made of limestone and contains an enormous maze underneath. Apart from Djoser's own burial chamber, there are separate galleries with symbolic burial chambers of his ancestors from the First and Second Dynasties as well as real burial sites of the members of Djoser's immediate family, which include his wife (or one of his wives) Hetephernebti as well as his daughter Inetkawes. All in all, the tomb complex contained over 40,000 objects, such as vases, bowls, and other vessels, as well as a majestic statue of Djoser himself (Bard, 2015). It is the first known ancient Egyptian construction built entirely out of stone. The scale of the enterprise is enormous.

Imhotep the Superhero

During his life, Imhotep was Djoser's vizier and chancellor and, most likely, oversaw the construction of the pyramid. But apart from that, very little is known about his mortal life. However, after his death, he was deified, and over the centuries and millennia, his figure was shrouded in all kinds of legends. Apart from his political position, he was granted to be an author of many wisdom texts and a formidable physician. Because of this, he became glorified as the god of healing and, in time, even equated with Thoth himself. When the Greeks came into contact with the Egyptian religion, they equated Imhotep with their own mortal-turned-god healer, Asklepios.

Various divine parentages were attributed to Imhotep over the years. He was seen as a son of the goddess Sekhmet and the god Ptah, or of a mortal woman called Kheredu-ankh who, in time, also attained a status of a semi-goddess.

Imhotep's cult survived even to Ptolemaic times. Legends from that period include a story of how he managed to end a famine that erupted during Djoser's reign. He was supposed to explain a dream to the pharaoh, telling him that the god Khnum had promised that the Nile would flood the fields soon.

As we can see, there must have been something extraordinary about the real Imhotep's life to grant him his supernatural status. Most probably, the construction of an unprecedented project, which was Djoser's pyramid, gave the vizier more than enough credit. It is interesting, though, that there is completely no evidence as to the historical Imhotep's connection to medicine, the discipline that later became his divine specialty.

Khufu, or, Cheops

Cheops is the Greek equivalent of Khufu's name. It is not surprising that this pharaoh's fame reached so far and wide that the Greeks gave him their own name—he is the instigator behind the most magnificent, most monumental, and most iconic architectural project that Egypt had ever seen: the Great Pyramid of Giza.

The second pharaoh of the Fourth Dynasty, Khufu reigned between ca. 2589–2566 B.C.E. Not much is known about his rule beyond the overseeing of the pyramid project and most historical sources that mention him come from roughly 2,000 years after his death. We do know, however, that his name was derived from the god Khnum and that Khufu might have propagated his cult.

But Khufu's reign was almost completely overshadowed by the Great Pyramid. This was an endeavor that must have been the talk of the whole country—and what is more, whoever was capable of working on the project, probably did. In Chapter 1, in the section about pyramids, I have mentioned a recent discovery of Merer's diary, a day-by-day report by an inspector who oversaw the transport of huge limestone blocks from Tura near the Red Sea to Giza. This unique document proves that the commotion and action connected to the Great Pyramid weren't only contained to the building site. Thousands of people could see and get involved in the works.

In the end, the pyramid they built was enormous: The base measured 750 x 750 feet (230.4 x 230.4 meters) and was 481 feet (147 meters) high (Lehner & Hawass, 2017). Today, the structure is a bit shorter since the tip has been damaged due to erosion, and the pyramidion—the topmost, highly decorated fragment of a pyramid—was lost due to grave robbery.

The pyramid has three inside chambers. The topmost one is the burial chamber of the king, the middle one contains statues, and the lowest one is a symbolic underworld chamber that is unfinished. A grand arched gallery, over 28 feet (8 meters) high, leads to the king's chamber (Smith & Hawass, 2018). It's an impressive structure built within such a massive heap of stone.

Initially, the pyramid was surrounded by a vast funerary complex—a veritable necropolis. A wall was built around the pyramid, and Khufu's temple, the complex's most prominent feature, faced the pyramid from the eastern side. The necropolis contained the mastabas (proto-pyramids) of princes and princesses from Khufu's entourage and extended family. Interestingly, there were also pits in which full-size solar barques for Khufu were buried, in order to serve as a means of transport for the pharaoh into the afterlife. One of the barques has been excavated, and it's the world's oldest intact ship. It's a mastery of workmanship at 142 feet (43.4 meters) long (Jenkins, 1980).

The Great Sphinx of Giza is also a part of Khufu's funerary complex although it was possibly built by one of his successors. It is possible that its function was to guard the cemetery.

Like other pharaohs, Khufu was deified after his death, but his cult became especially popular. In the Old Kingdom, by the end of the Sixth Dynasty, Khufu had at least 67 priests—more than any pharaoh from that period. His cult only continued into the Middle and New Kingdoms, and he became a character in several stories featuring magic and prophecies. There, he was characterized in a contradictory way: on one hand, an almost ruthless tyrant, on the other—generous and merciful. He was, it seems, a rather mysterious character.

When Khufu's fame reached the Greeks, they depicted him as a rather cruel tyrant. The tradition of showing Khufu as a ruthless man who ordered thousands of slaves to work in backbreaking conditions in order to build the Great Pyramid for him originated with Herodotus. And to this day, it's a story that many people believe in. But as we have seen, the people employed in the construction of the pyramid were most likely qualified workers receiving compensation.

Still, while remembering Khufu, it's also worth remembering all the people that were living during his reign: those who oversaw the project of the pyramid and those who worked on it in the lowest positions. An endeavor such as the Great Pyramid of Giza would have been impossible to create if it was only a vision of one man. Instead, let's think about it as a nationwide achievement.

Ahmose-Nefertari and Amenhotep I

Queen Ahmose-Nefertari and her son, the pharaoh Amenhotep I from the Eighteenth Dynasty, the first dynasty of New Egypt, are two other examples of rulers who became deified and enjoyed a considerable cult after death. As we'll see shortly, the Eighteenth Dynasty is perhaps one that consists of the most widely known pharaohs and the most powerful ones besides, so it's only right that we talk about its first rulers.

Ahmose-Nefertari was a sister and a wife—as was not uncommon in royal dynasties at the time—of Ahmose I, the founder of the Eighteenth Dynasty. Their reign marked the end of the Second Intermediate Period in Egyptian history and the definite expulsion of the Hyksos, the foreign rulers of Egypt. Ahmose-Nefertari's whole family, and especially her husband, dedicated themselves to this task and to reuniting Upper and Lower Egypt once again.

Ahmose-Nefertari bore many children and was known as the royal mother. Her preferred title was, however, "God's Wife." She was a powerful, matriarchal figure. It has been suggested that this model of feminine rule had been adopted by her from ancient Nubia, whose influences were rather strong at the time. Her husband died while her son, Amenhotep I, was still very young, so she might have ruled as a regent in his stead. She seems to have outlived her son and died during the reign of her possible grandson Thutmose I when she was in her 70s.

In time, Ahmose-Nefertari became known as a grandmother of the whole Eighteenth Dynasty and perhaps one of the most venerated mortal women in ancient Egypt. She was deified as a sky goddess.

Ahmose-Nefertari was often depicted with black skin. Although some of those depictions might have been more symbolic than realistic (black being the color of the soil and symbolizing fertility). However, some features of the queen's remains suggest that she might have had Nubian heritage.

Amenhotep I wasn't expected to inherit the throne. He had at least two older brothers; however, they both died, and Amenhotep became the crown prince at a young age. His policy was one of domination: Even his royal name meant "he who inspires great terror." He defeated the Nubians and led several other military campaigns. But he was also known for the cultural development accomplished during his reign, especially for the founding of a village built purely for artisans, Deir el-Medina. Also, important texts about the afterlife were written during his reign as well as some medical treatises. The first water clock, or a clepsydra, was invented at that time. It was a time of great power and progress.

Amenhotep didn't have any children. His successor, Thutmose I, was either his unknown son or his military general. Upon his death, Amenhotep was deified and made a patron of his artisan village Deir el-Medina, where many feasts were held in his honor. He was worshiped as a god of prophecy, and oracles would be built in his name, where people asked questions about their fate.

Ahmose-Nefertari and Amenhotep were just the beginning in a veritable succession of famous and fascinating rulers of the Eighteenth Dynasty. Let us now see the other ones.

Hatshepsut

Hatshepsut wasn't the first female pharaoh—that title goes to Sobekneferu from the Twelfth Dynasty of the Middle Kingdom—but before Cleopatra, she was definitely the most famous one.

Initially, she was only the queen of the ruling pharaoh, Thutmose II, who was also her brother. Thutmose's son with another woman, Thutmose III, was declared heir to the throne, but he was only two years old when Thutmose II died. Hatshepsut stepped in, but instead of ruling as a regent in Thutmose III's stead, she assumed the role of a pharaoh, claiming that she had always been intended for the throne by her and Thutmose's father. She reigned for about 20 years.

Hatshepsut seems to have been a bit of an innovator. First, she managed to assume the throne in the stead of a male heir who wasn't her own son, something that up to this point was unthinkable. She was also very vocal when it came to celebrating her female reign: She constructed numerous temples with her likeness, thus making the Egyptians accustomed to an image of a woman in such a high position. All the while, she used her connections to powerful men in court in order to elevate her position and presented herself as demure and sincere, gaining supporters for her reign. She was the only female pharaoh to reign during a time of prosperity and power.

And she left Egypt even more prosperous than she found it. Many trade routes, disrupted during the reign of the Hyksos, were reestablished during Hatshepsut's reign. She oversaw countless building projects from temples that celebrated her as a pharaoh and God's Wife of Amun, through monuments at the temple in Karnak, to obelisks and her own mortuary temple (a temple adjacent to her own tomb), which was a marvel in construction, with a grand colonnade and a series of terraces covered by extensive gardens. These buildings were not only testimonies to Hatshepsut's power, but they also contributed to advancement in architecture.

In time, some legends arose around Hatshepsut's life—they might have been circulated to further her claim to the throne. In one of them, it was the god Amun that was the real father of Hatshepsut, and he fathered her when he came to her mother in the form of Thutmose II and placed the *ankh*, the symbol of life, on her nose. Then, Hatshepsut's soul and body were created by Khnum, and Heqet attended the birth of the little girl. Hatshepsut was then referred to as Amun's favorite daughter.

After Hatshepsut's death and toward the end of the reign of her successor, Thutmose III, curious and alarming procedures were taking place. Hatshepsut's statues were ordered to be destroyed and buried, her name erased from the records and the temple walls. It's not entirely clear why it happened, but one of the hypotheses is that Thutmose III was resentful for having been ousted from the throne by Hatshepsut for many years. However, this seems a bit simplistic, and besides, the shocking change only took place in the last years of his reign. Another hypothesis is that at the time, Thutmose III was already old and susceptible to influence and that his future successor, Amenhotep II, ordered the erasure of records. He was supposed to do it in order to usurp some of the achievements of Hatshepsut's reign because his own position as a pretender to the throne wasn't very strong.

There have been also other, more feminist-aligning theories, such as that the successful and prosperous reign of Hatshepsut was seen by Thutmose III and Amenhotep II as a threat to the future of Egypt, where women might realize that they didn't need to limit themselves to the roles of royal wives and mothers only. Maybe the kings thought that her reign disrupted the Maat and, therefore, needed to be erased from memory.

However it was, the destruction of Hatshepsut's name and images wasn't very systematic. We still have many statues and documents preserved, and they allow for a rather accurate reconstruction of her reign. Still, the erasure attempts caused Egyptologists to wrongly assume for years that Hatshepsut was only a regent and not a pharaoh in her own right.

Hatshepsut's reign is a very interesting case study of the position of women in ancient Egypt. On one hand, as I've already mentioned in Chapter 1, women in Egyptian society enjoyed far more privileges than their contemporaries from other cultures. At the same time, female pharaohs were extremely rare—though still not impossible, as they would have been in other countries. Moreover, there seems to have been a difference between a female pharaoh who assumed power in times of strife or decline, in an act of patriotic duty to Egypt—and a female pharaoh who ruled during a time of prosperity and had the courage to appear strong and unwavering. There are still many mysteries surrounding Hatshepsut's reign, and it seems that not all of them can be resolved in an easy and straightforward way.

Akhenaten, Nefertiti, and Tutankhamun

The story of Akhenaten's religious reform and the subsequent return to the "old ways" by his son Tutankhamun is a long one. I have already hinted at it numerous times when we talked about the Egyptian gods. Now, we'll look at the whole revolution from a less theological angle, and a more historical and human one. What might have been the possible reasons for Akhenaten's radical disruption of Maat? Was he a visionary, or mentally unstable? What was the role that his wife, Nefertiti, played in all this?

Let's start from the very beginning.

Akhenaten Assumes Power

Akhenaten was the son of pharaoh Amenhotep III of the Eighteenth Dynasty, who reigned in the 1300s B.C.E. His birth name was Amenhotep, too. Little is known about his life as a prince; however, one of the few facts that we do have is that he had an older brother and wasn't initially considered for the throne.

Akhenaten married Nefertiti likely shortly before he assumed the throne. She wasn't a member of his immediate family but, instead, a daughter of one of the highly ranking officials. Together, the couple had at least six children, most of them daughters, but there was also a son, Tutankhamun.

It's highly probable that, for at least the first couple of years of Akhenaten's reign, he shared his power with his father who was still alive. He came into his own around 1353 or 1351 B.C.E. Initially, he continued all the long-established traditions of his ancestors, worshiping all the gods and taking part in festivities. This suggests that Akhenaten didn't assume the throne with a clear plan for a revolution in mind.

But, while he continued to revere other gods, Akhenaten built considerably more temples of Aten than of the other deities during the first years of his reign. And there were some unusual features in the way his royal wife, Nefertiti, was depicted. She appeared on reliefs almost more often than her husband and seemed to have assumed roles reserved only for the pharaoh. For example, she was depicted smiting the enemies of Egypt, a role that would normally be only given to a conquering pharaoh.

The Revolution

Everything changed, though, between the fourth and fifth year of Akhenaten's reign. First, the capital of Egypt was moved to the city of Akhenaten (modern-day Amarna); then, the name change for the pharaoh occurred and the new exclusive cult of Aten was proclaimed and established. The role of the pharaoh changed completely, and Nefertiti assumed more and more powerful roles as the priestess of the new religion. She also changed her name to Neferneferuaten-Nefertiti.

Some historians describe the cult of Aten as purely monotheistic, while others say that it was monolatry, which means that the existence of other gods wasn't denied, but they were simply deemed not nearly as important as Aten. Even in that latter version, the change to what had been an established religion before couldn't have been more radical. It has even been proposed that the similarities between the cult of Aten and the Hebrew traditions might mean that Atenism was practically an ancestor of Judaism.

There are countless theories and speculations as to the reasons for the revolution. Judging by the radical difference between his depictions and the depictions of the pharaohs before him, it has been theorized that Akhenaten might have suffered from some genetic abnormality that manifested in an elongated skull, pigeon chest, and a more feminine appearance; there have even been propositions that he might have been intersex. According to these theories, the change of style in Egyptian art might have been a celebration of Akhenaten's unusual features.

However, judging this solely on his depictions is to ignore artistic license and the fact that, even though the artistic style of the Amarna period steered more toward realism, it was still highly symbolic, and Akhenaten's androgynous appearance might have symbolized the androgyny of Aten, one god who encompassed both masculinity and femininity.

Or, maybe, Akhenaten suffered from epilepsy, which would explain his religious visions. That is, however, impossible to prove.

But Akhenaten was also recognized as the first man to follow his individualistic desires in a time when people revered age-old traditions. Is it possible that the changes he adopted were purely a result of a whim, or to put it more kindly, of some individual religious experience that he felt he must share with his subjects? We will probably never know.

The Power of Nefertiti

Cleopatra might be the most famous female name associated with ancient Egypt, but it is Nefertiti's face that most people would be able to recognize, even if they don't realize it belongs to her. She is the famous brown-skinned beauty with striking, slender features, as depicted on her bust, which followed the new, realistic Amarna style. But it's more than possible that she wasn't only a pretty presence at Akhenaten's side. Perhaps her thought and influence also stood behind the religious revolution—in any case, the adoption of the cult of Aten meant also her elevation in status.

Judging by her depictions, especially from the later years of Akhenaten's reign, it's more than probable that she was elevated to the status of coruler by the pharaoh. She is often shown assuming the king's role: smiting the enemies and worshiping Aten just as a pharaoh would. And if her elevation to the status of a pharaoh really happened, then it would have been natural for her to assume the throne after Akhenaten's death. And that leads us to another interesting hypothesis.

Akhenaten wasn't directly succeeded by his son Tutankhamun. Instead, a pharaoh of an unknown origin, Smenkhkare, assumed the throne. He followed the religious and cultural changes instituted by Akhenaten, but his reign didn't last longer than a year. A thoroughly mysterious figure—mostly because the later rulers and historians tried to erase the Amarna period from Egypt's memory—he might have been a member of Akhenaten's family.

Or… he might have been Nefertiti herself. Various theories on this topic have been proposed. One of them was that Nefertiti ruled Egypt for three years after the death of Akhenaten and was then succeeded by Smenkhkare—but perhaps, it was her that disguised herself as a male pharaoh? There is definitely too little evidence to know anything for sure.

It's not entirely clear either what Nefertiti's outlook was toward Atenism in the last years of Akhenaten's reign and after his death. Was she trying to desperately uphold the new religion, or was she gently trying to minimize the "damage" and slowly revert to the old ways? Did she teach her son Tutankhamun about the old gods?

It's hard to decide on that either. But whatever Nefertiti's influence on her son might have been, it would be him that would put an end to the brief but fascinating Amarna period in Egyptian history.

Tutankhamun Reverts to the Gods

Tutankhamun, commonly known as King Tut, was the last pharaoh of the Eighteenth Dynasty. He was a child when he assumed the throne—between eight and nine years old—and he was still very young when he died, around eighteen. He most probably suffered from a physical disability, which required him to use a cane while walking. Over the years, Egyptologists have tried to diagnose him with many possible genetic disorders, which he may have inherited from his father, but so far, only some physical ailments have been proven after the examination of his mummy.

Tutankhamun was tutored throughout his reign by his vizier, Ay, who would later become his successor. It's possible that Tut's harsh stance toward Atenism was partially the result of Ay's influence.

Straight after his crowning, Tutankhamun reinstated the priesthoods of the other gods and endowed the previously neglected temples. He changed his initial name from Tutankhaten to Tutankhamun, and he removed his father's mummy from Amarna and placed it in the Valley of the Kings, just like the pharaohs of old.

But Tut's changes weren't only religious. Akhenaten had neglected diplomatic relations with other countries, whether because he was a lover of peace or too engrossed in domestic reforms is not entirely known. Tutankhamun sought to restore those relations and end the period of unrest and economic instability within the kingdom.

He couldn't, however, conduct extensive changes before he died. It seems that his death was unexpected; this is, at least, judged by his famous tomb, which, despite containing unimaginable riches, is very small for a tomb of a pharaoh. It's possible that the structure initially intended for Tutankhamun had not been completed before he died.

And this brings us to the far more recent times and perhaps the most famous story in the whole of Egyptology: the discovery of Tutankhamun's tomb.

Curse or No Curse?

Tutankhamun's tomb was discovered in 1922 by Howard Carter and his patron, George Herbert, 5th Earl of Carnarvon. It was an unprecedented find. Most tombs of the pharaohs have been discovered and plundered throughout the centuries, but King Tut's tomb was hidden and, therefore, intact.

The discovery gave Egyptologists a clear idea of how rich the pharaohs' tombs really had been. There were over 5,000 objects in Tutankhamun's burial chambers (Carter & Mace, 2012): gilded furniture, trinkets, vases, symbolic objects needed in the afterlife… and there was also, of course, the famous golden mask covering the pharaoh's mummy.

The excavation process was torturous and extremely difficult. Many objects were fragile, and the archaeologists had to contend with moisture and limited access to the burial chamber. The process of excavation was highly publicized, and the photographs of the found objects circulated the world, starting a fad for Egyptian-inspired art and fashion. The native Egyptians were given a sense of their national pride, drawing their lineages back to the ancient pharaohs. The whole public opinion was in a frenzy.

And then, curious things started happening.

Not long after the tomb goods were excavated and the chambers were closed again, Carnarvon accidentally cut open a mosquito bite while shaving; a wound that would then become infected. He died of blood poisoning and pneumonia. Despite the fact that Carnarvon had been in poor health previously, rumors started circulating that his death might have not been accidental. At the time, already many novels with ancient Egyptian themes were circulating in which the dead pharaohs enacted their revenge for disturbing their tombs. Combined with the highly fashionable use of mediums and psychics at the time, this made for an atmosphere of hysteria. Odd signs were reported to have been observed just before the tomb was found, and people would later conveniently "remember" the words of a curse written over the tomb's entrance.

Now, any further deaths, even slightly related to the men who excavated the tomb, were interpreted as a result of the curse. Aubrey Herbert, Carnarvon's half-brother, died a couple of months later and so did George Jay Gould, a financier who had visited the tomb. Even the death of the Egyptologist Arthur Cruttenden Mace, six years after the tomb's discovery, was attributed to the curse, as were the deaths of Carnarvon's secretary in 1929 and the Egyptologist Arthur Weigall in 1934. From today's perspective, it's rather clear that there was no causation between these deaths, and the whole thing was more of a result of mass hysteria.

And so, the life of a disabled boy-king who turned Egypt back to its old ways was obscured by curses, mysteries, and sensationalist plots.

Ramesses II the Great

But let us come back to ancient Egypt—leaving the strife and uncertainty of the last rulers from the Eighteenth Dynasty and moving on to the Nineteenth Dynasty—we come upon a pharaoh that was, perhaps, the most powerful pharaoh to ever live. The New Kingdom was the most glorious period in Egypt's history, and the Nineteenth Dynasty was the most powerful dynasty of that period.

Ramesses's life and reign were marked by numerous military campaigns. He battled the neighboring Nubians and the troublesome sea pirates, but it was his Syrian campaigns against the Hittite Empire, originally from Anatolia, that brought him real fame. The most famous battle of Ramesses's rule was the Battle of Kadesh, which was inconclusive but famous for the enormous military effort that the pharaoh put into organizing his army. Proto-factories were built, which were capable of producing over 1,000 weapons in a week (Tyldesley, 2001).

In the end, Ramesses conducted three campaigns into Syria, which ended in a peace treaty in the 21st year of his reign. There, both countries and their respective gods were called for peace. There would be no further disturbances between the two empires.

Ramesses was one of the longest-ruling and living pharaohs. His reign lasted 66 years, and the pharaoh was aged about 90 when he died. His reign was truly an age during which he secured Egypt's borders and attained peace. It was also a time of significant cultural development. Ramesses used art as propaganda for his victories and campaigns, and his construction projects were the most ambitious since the time of the pyramids. He transformed the temples at Thebes and built new ones, and he instituted a new capital, Pi-Ramesses. The statues built in his honor were colossal. The biggest one weighs 83 tons and is now in the museum in Giza (BBC News, 2006).

Over the years, it became a popular hypothesis to assume that Ramesses II was the pharaoh depicted in the biblical Book of Exodus. The name Ramesses is mentioned in the Bible but not in connotation with him. Still, his reign was long and powerful, and it fits with the depiction. It's worth remembering, however, that Ramesses is only one of the many candidates for the figure described in Exodus.

Cleopatra

And now, finally, we reach Cleopatra, the last ruler of Egypt in the millennia-long succession of pharaohs and an extraordinary woman. In the common consciousness,

Cleopatra is presented as an epitome of an Egyptian queen, and is probably often confused with the likeness of Nefertiti. In reality, she was both a descendant of ancient Egyptian nobility and the Greek-Macedonian Ptolemaic dynasty, and her contemporary bust shows her looking like many Greek women of the era. She is also often presented within the context of the Roman men she got herself entangled with—Julius Caesar and Mark Antony—even though she was rather extraordinary in her own right. So, let us now set the record straight and possibly also dispel some myths.

Cleopatra was born around 69 B.C.E. and died in 30 B.C.E.: the final stage of the Ptolemaic period, which saw a rapid strengthening and the beginning of the Roman Empire's expansion. At the time, Egypt already was only semi-independent, being a client state to Rome since the Empire intervened in a succession crisis in 81 B.C.E.

Most of Cleopatra's Ptolemaic ancestors, even though they still got nominally crowned according to the ancient Egyptian rites, only spoke Greek and resided in Alexandria, a largely Greek city founded by Alexander the Great. But Cleopatra knew Egyptian and several other languages besides. She grew up, and most likely, also studied in Alexandria, which, at the time, was a veritable center of the world's knowledge. As a result, she was a highly educated woman, surpassing her male contemporaries.

Cleopatra's childhood was marked by unrest. Her father, Ptolemy XII, had to deal with a revolt, where some of the country's officials, as well as foreign powers, backed his other daughter Berenice IV for the throne. Ptolemy was exiled and spent some time in Rome, where he was most probably accompanied by an 11-year-old Cleopatra. In the end, he was restored to the throne with the help of the Romans. Ptolemy XII died around 51 B.C.E. and was supposed to be succeeded by two of his children, Cleopatra and Ptolemy XIII.

But Cleopatra didn't like this. She wanted to rule Egypt alone, even despite the difficulties she inherited from her father: a staggering debt to Rome; unrest caused by the former Roman troops who came to Egypt with Ptolemy XII and were now roaming without aim and causing unrest; and on top of everything, there was a famine.

And now, Ptolemy XIII wasn't taking kindly to being ousted from the throne and was amassing allies. By the end of 50 B.C.E., he had the upper hand in the conflict, and it seemed like his rule would start soon. Cleopatra was forced to flee from Alexandria to Thebes.

But the internal conflict was heightened when it got entangled with Rome's own unrest. Roman general Pompey had been engaged in a conflict with his former political ally Julius Caesar and sought help, as well as refuge, in Egypt. He was planning to retreat to Egypt and replenish his forces there after they were destroyed in the Battle of Pharsalus in 48 B.C.E.

But Ptolemy XIII didn't like the idea of Egypt potentially becoming a backstage for the Roman civil war. So a plot was concocted: Outwardly, Pompey was welcomed in Egypt, but when he arrived at one of the port towns, Pelusium, he was ambushed and stabbed to death. His severed head was sent to Caesar. But even though Ptolemy's rival, Caesar expressed his grief and outrage at this turn of events and soon arrived in Alexandria himself, calling for the ceasing of conflict between Cleopatra and Ptolemy XIII.

And this is when Caesar and Cleopatra's famous dalliance started. In truth, Cleopatra used her knowledge that Caesar liked having affairs with royal women and decided to come to Alexandria in person, dressed alluringly, and convince Caesar to back her. A semi-mythical account says that she was smuggled there inside a bed sack.

Hearing that his sister was consorting with Caesar, Ptolemy XIII attempted to start a riot in Alexandria. But he was quickly arrested and brought before Caesar, where the Roman general read the will of Ptolemy XII, once again naming Cleopatra and Ptolemy XIII joint rulers but clearly favoring Cleopatra. Ptolemy XIII, however, managed to escape and gathered his troops to lay a siege to the palace of Alexandria, trapping Caesar and Cleopatra inside.

After a few months, in the early 47 B.C.E., Caesar's reinforcements arrived. Ptolemy XIII was forced to withdraw to the Nile, where Caesar's forces pursued him, and as he tried to escape, he drowned. Cleopatra won.

Caesar was still unwilling to name her the sole ruler of Egypt, however (most probably because of the recent memory of Berenice IV's revolt), so she was proclaimed a joint ruler with her other brother, the 12-year-old Ptolemy XIV. This was an arrangement in name only; unofficially, Cleopatra continued to rule with Caesar. At the time, she was already pregnant with Caesar's son.

Caesar left Egypt in April 47 B.C.E. but stationed some of his legions for the queen's defense. Their son, Caesarion, was born in June the same year. The next year, Cleopatra visited Rome with Ptolemy XIV, was treated with all honors, and resided in Caesar's villa.

Caesar was, however, assassinated in March 44 B.C.E., but Cleopatra still stayed in Rome. Most likely, she was trying to have Caesarion recognized as Caesar's heir but without any luck. So a few months later, Cleopatra went for a radical move. She had her young brother poisoned and made Caesarion her coruler. Of course, in practice, it meant that she ruled alone.

After Caesar's assassination, the rule of Rome was taken over by the triumvirate of Octavian Augustus, Mark Antony, and Marcus Aemilius Lepidus. They were set on bringing Caesar's assassins to justice, and Cleopatra sided with them. This led to an invitation for Mark Antony to visit Alexandria in 41 B.C.E.—and to another famous relationship.

Despite later romantic legends, Cleopatra's choice of Mark Antony as the father of her future heirs was most likely calculated. He was, at the time, the most powerful Roman general. With his backing, Cleopatra could retake control over the terrains that were now under Roman rule.

And thus started their relationship, with Antony on and off in Egypt on his campaigns and Cleopatra sending her military aid. In 40 B.C.E., she gave birth to twins, Alexander Helios and Cleopatra Selene II, both of whom were acknowledged by Antony as his own children. Their names were symbolic: Helios and Selene in Greek mythology symbolized the sun and the moon, and it was a promise of rejuvenation of Egyptian society.

But in 39 B.C.E., Antony married Octavian's sister Octavia, a Roman noblewoman, which was more acceptable for him as a Roman leader than a dalliance with an Egyptian queen. The relations between Cleopatra and Antony soured, especially after Octavia gave birth to Antony's children. Still, Antony recognized Cleopatra's children and enlarged her domain. For a time, everything was triumphant, with Antony's further campaigns in Armenia bringing him victory and with Cleopatra naming their son the king of Armenia.

Perhaps the epitome of this short-lasting prosperity was the triumphant ceremony in which Cleopatra dressed as Isis and was called the Queen of Kings, while her nominal coruler Caesarion was declared King of Kings, with Alexander Helios being named King of Armenia, Media, and Parthia and Cleopatra Selene the Queen of Crete and Cyrene. It is even possible that during this ceremony Antony and Cleopatra were married.

But not all was going well for Antony. He was engaged in a long battle of wills and propaganda with his coruler, Octavian, who accused him of bowing to his Eastern queen and her customs and of endangering Roman freedoms. Antony's Roman wife, Octavia, backed Octavian as well. Soon, the two were not just rivals but enemies.

In 31 B.C.E., the forces of Octavian and the joined forces of Antony and Cleopatra met each other in the famous Battle of Actium. It was a naval battle, and Octavian won; Antony and Cleopatra were forced to escape mid-fight, and large numbers of their troops defected to Octavian's forces.

Antony took refuge in Alexandria, where he reportedly completely secluded himself. Cleopatra started grooming her son Caesarion to become the future sole ruler of Egypt. She also sent envoys to Octavian in hopes of winning him over, asking him to allow Antony to stay in Egypt as an exile. Octavian responded, but he urged Cleopatra to have Antony killed so that her life could be spared. Antony, however, learned of these plans and sent the envoys back to Octavian, presumably without consulting with Cleopatra. Now that the negotiations failed, Octavian invaded Egypt.

It was 30 B.C.E. Octavian's succession of victories in Egypt was quick and overwhelming. In August, Antony's fleet and cavalry surrendered to him. At any moment now, Octavian's troops would enter the palace.

Cleopatra hid in her future tomb and sent a note to Antony telling him that she had killed herself. In reaction to this, heartbroken Antony stabbed himself to death and was later embalmed and buried by Cleopatra. It was clear that she was still trying to play her own game.

When she was brought before Octavian, Cleopatra famously refused to be led in a triumph to Rome, stripped of her power and humiliated. But she soon learned that Octavian disregarded her wishes, and she was to be transported to the Roman capital with her children. She arranged for suicide.

Cleopatra took her own life on August 10, 30 B.C.E. Caesarion's death was ordered two days later by Octavian. The fate of Alexander Helios is unknown, while Cleopatra Selene survived and eventually married the king of Numidia in Western Africa.

Cleopatra was the last of the absolute monarchs of Egypt, who combined her knowledge of current politics and her Greco-Roman education with her desire to rule like the pharaohs of old. As we have hopefully seen, she was far from just a beautiful woman who fell in love with Roman generals, as the literary tradition (including Shakespeare) would lead us to believe. Nor was she a "man-eater." On the contrary, she was an ambitious, intelligent, and politically minded woman who tried to push her country onto the path of its former glory. Unfortunately, she couldn't compete with the growing power of the Roman Empire and chose the wrong ally in the end. But that, if anything, makes her an even more fascinating figure.

CHAPTER 7

The Underworld and the End of the World

Let's come back from the land of the living mortals to the land where they go after death—the Egyptian underworld, or Duat. In this chapter, we will see in detail how the process of judging the dead looks, which gods assist with it, and what the punishments are. We'll understand how the belief in the underworld ties in with the Egyptian idea of cyclical time.

And that, in turn, will lead us to Egyptian beliefs on the end of the world. Let us take the last part of this journey together.

Duat, the Underworld

Duat was the nighttime realm through which the barque of Ra traveled every night. Ruled by Osiris, it was full of odd creatures and demons—such as Apophis or Ammit—but that is not to say it was equivalent to a Christian Hell. Many gods apart from Osiris resided in Duat, too, among them Anubis, Thoth, Horus, Hathor, and, most crucially, Maat. For the ancient Egyptians, it wasn't the residence in the underworld that was the punishment of deceased souls—it was the denial thereof.

And that, at last, brings us to the ceremony of the weighing of the heart. It was impossible not to mention it in the previous chapters, but now, let us see in detail what happened with a mortal who got into Duat.

The Journey

When a pharaoh died, his or her soul reunited instantly with Ra, who was their divine father. But for more ordinary mortals, the judgment awaited, and they had to navigate the difficult landscape of Duat in order to get to the place where their destiny would be decided. For the pharaoh and the important officials, their means of transportation to the underworld was a royal barque, which would often be buried in the tomb with them. For more common people, their coffins would be such a means.

First, each soul had to pass several gates in order to get to Duat. They corresponded to the hours of the night and were guarded by minor deities. Knowledge of these deities was essential to passing through the gate. Some souls would pass unharmed, while others would suffer burning by fire.

All the gates are described in detail in one of the funerary texts from the New Kingdom called the *Book of Gates* as well as on the wall paintings in the Valley of Kings:

1. First gate: Guarded by Sia, an aspect of Ra corresponding to his perception, she unlocked the gate for the barque of Ra when it passed through the night, as well as opened the first gate for the dead.

2. Second gate: Guarded by a deity called the "Swallower of Sinners," it was preceded by a lake of fire, and presumably, some sinful souls were unable to pass it, while others became heavily burned.

3. Third gate: Guarded by a vicious snake but also by a goddess referred to as the "Mistress of Food," this was the place where Ra, during his nighttime journey, drew his first breath.

4. Fourth gate: Guarded by several deities whose names we no longer know, it was a gate where all the deceased from four corners of the world met. According to the Egyptians, there were four main ethnicities in the world: the Egyptians themselves, Levantines (the inhabitants of the eastern Mediterranean, including Palestine and Greece), Libyans (North Africans), and Nubians. They were all referred to as the "Cattle of Ra."

5. Fifth gate: Guarded by the goddess called the "Lady of Duration," this was the place where Apophis lived. It's implied that many souls wouldn't manage to escape his

devouring clutches, even as many deities tried to overpower him. He was constantly grinding those he caught.

6. Sixth gate: It is guarded by jackals.

7. Seventh gate: It is guarded by the goddess called the "Shining One" and other gods who held whips, whose symbolism is lost to us today.

8. Eighth gate: It is guarded by a flaming snake that burned Osiris's enemies.

9. Ninth gate: It is guarded by Horus and Set.

10. Tenth gate: Yet again, this was the gate where Apophis appeared, but this time he was chained and no longer dangerous.

11. Eleventh gate: With an enigmatic name "Mysterious of Approaches," this gate was guarded by a cat-headed minor god called Meeyuty.

12. Twelfth Gate: This is the last gate and was guarded by Isis and Nephthys. After passing through this gate, the souls went to their judgment, while the barque of Ra emerged into the day again in the form of the rising sun.

This succession of gates is the best described one. But there are also other versions of the passage of the dead in the funerary texts, some containing seven gates, others–twenty-one. The gods guarding these gates have very evocative names, referring to the presumed fate of the sinful dead. They evoke dread and fire but also cleansing.

The Judgment of the Dead

Now that the souls had passed all the gates, they would be led before Osiris, where their lives would be judged. The most extensive description of the judgment comes from *The Book of the Dead*, whose origins reach the Second Intermediate Period and which was developed throughout centuries.

Every deceased person was led by Anubis before Osiris, and their heart was put on a mighty scale. On the other side of the scale was Maat's feather, representing justice. Then, the deceased was compelled to recite a so-called negative confession, consisting of a list of 42 sins, which they denied committing because they wouldn't grant them a place in Duat. Some of the sins were rather intuitive, such as stealing, robbing people, and killing, as well as having intercourse with a married woman, cursing, and being violent or impatient. Other transgressions were more elaborate and less expected: destroying food offerings, disputing property, cursing a god, or stealing special cakes from the dead.

As the recitation went on, the heart was being weighed. A balance meant that the deceased was just during their life: Anubis would now lead them before Osiris, who would grant them eternal life in Aaru, the Field of Rushes. Aaru was an ideal version of the world as the Egyptians knew it: the idealized version of the Nile Delta.

But if the scales were out of balance, Ammit would devour the heart, either rendering the soul forever restless or ending its existence altogether.

A very important aspect of the beliefs surrounding the underworld was rebirth. The worst fate would be to be denied reincarnation and to perish forever. Those dead who withstood the weighing of the heart were given a chance for rebirth, when, after some time in Aaru, the mother goddesses would put their limbs and their breath back together and guide them back to the world of the living through their wombs.

The End of the World

As we have seen, cyclical time was crucial to what the ancient Egyptians believed about the universe. Just as the Nile undergoes cyclical floods, just as the day always follows the night, so the cycle of life and rebirth continues. It wouldn't be surprising, therefore, if the Egyptians believed that this cycle was eternal.

But it seems it was not so. Even though the ancient Egyptians didn't speak much about the end of the world—most likely in order not to make it happen—it seems that they believed that the cycle of the universe would one day end. In some passages from *The Book of the Dead*, Atum says that one day he will dissolve the whole world just the way he created it, and it will come back to its primeval state of chaotic waters. Only Atum, the creator, and Osiris will survive. It's not clear what will be the fate of the dead associated with Osiris, however.

Given that the universe won't dissolve into complete nothingness, but rather, revert to its original state, it's possible that it, like everything else, will be reborn again, and a new cycle of creation will begin. This, however, is unclear—and perhaps the ancient Egyptians didn't want to reach that far with their speculation. After all, those things were hidden and known only to the gods.

As we started our journey through Egyptian mythology—with the primordial waters from which the universe arose—so we will finish it. It's probably fitting given the nature of the civilization we've been talking about. I sincerely hope that this cycle of stories and discoveries was fruitful for you.

Conclusion

We have now ended our journey. It led us through a rich and vast world, encompassing unimaginable amounts of time, as well as marvelous amounts of space (especially in the case of the pyramids). I hope that you enjoyed the stories about the creation of the universe, gods, goddesses, and monsters. I also hope that you learned more about the mortal side of Egyptian history and culture and that it proved to be an entertaining piece of knowledge.

But this, by no means, is the end. I have presented the best known figures and stories from both Egyptian mythology and history, but, as you hopefully already realized, this civilization was so vast there will always be more to discover. So let this book serve as an invitation and a gate—almost like the gates to the underworld—opening before you, inviting you to explore. This exploration can take on many forms: more reading, but maybe a trip to the closest museum that holds relics from ancient Egypt? Or maybe a trip to Egypt itself?

The mysteries of Egypt await you—all you have to do is reach for them.

Glossary

Aani: Dog-ape, **Thoth's** sacred animal.

Aaru: Field of Rushes; paradise for the just dead.

Abtu: Sacred fish; guarded the barque of **Ra**.

Actium, Battle of (September 2 31 B.C.E.): Naval battle between the forces of **Octavian** and **Mark Antony**; won by Octavian.

Ahmose I (ca. 1550–1525 B.C.E.): Pharaoh, founder of the Eighteenth Dynasty (New Kingdom). Drove the **Hyksos** away from Egypt.

Ahmose-Nefertari (dates unknown): Wife of **Ahmose I**, mother of **Amenhotep I**. First Great Royal Wife of the Eighteenth Dynasty (New Egypt). Deified after death.

Ammit: Monster-goddess, lion-hippopotamus-crocodile. Devoured the souls of the unjust dead.

Amun: Chief god of Egypt, creator deity, sometimes conflated with **Ra**.

Amunet: Female version of **Amun**, primeval goddess.

Anet: Sacred fish, guarded the barque of **Ra**.

Anhur: God of war.

Ankh: Symbol of life in the Egyptian hieroglyphs.

Antony, Mark (83–30 B.C.E.): Roman politician and general, partner of **Cleopatra**, rival of **Octavian**. Committed suicide after the defeat by Octavian.

Anubis: God of the dead, mummification, and afterlife.

Akh: Part of the soul, intellect.

Akhenaten (1353–1336 B.C.E.): Tenth pharaoh of the Eighteenth Dynasty (New Kingdom). Instigator of the religious revolution of **Atenism**. Husband of **Nefertiti**, father of **Tutankhamun**.

Alexander Helios (40 B.C.E.–unknown): Son of **Cleopatra** and **Mark Antony**.

Alexander the Great (356–323 B.C.E.): King of Macedon, conqueror of Greece, Egypt, Persia, and other terrains in Asia, creator of an empire.

Alexandria: City port in Egypt, founded ca. 331 B.C.E. by **Alexander the Great**.

Amarna (1): City in Egypt, founded by **Akhenaten** in 1346 B.C.E., new capital of Egypt.

Amarna (2): Period in Egyptian art and culture during the reign of **Akhenaten**.

Amenhotep I (1525–1504 B.C.E.): Second pharaoh of the Eighteenth Dynasty (New Kingdom). Inherited the kingdom from **Ahmose I** and continued his policy. Son of **Ahmose-Nefertari**.

Amenhotep II (1427–1401 B.C.E.): Seventh pharaoh of the Eighteenth Dynasty (New Kingdom). Inherited the kingdom from **Thutmose III**.

Amenhotep III (1391–1353 B.C.E.): Ninth pharaoh of the Eighteenth Dynasty (New Kingdom). Brought prosperity to Egypt. Succeeded by **Akhenaten**.

Amyrtaeus (404–399 B.C.E.): The only pharaoh from the Twenty-eighth Dynasty (Late Period). His reign marked the last significant independence of Egypt.

Apep: see: **Apophis**.

Apis: Sacred bull from **Memphis**.

Apophis: Giant serpent, embodiment of chaos.

Armenia: In antiquity, kingdom from 321 B.C.E. to 428 C.E.

Aswan: City in southern Egypt.

Aten: God of the sun disk, the only god in **Atenism**.

Atenism: Religious system of beliefs introduced by Akhenaten, focused around the only god **Aten** who transcended everything.

Athena: Greek goddess of war and wisdom.

Atum: First god in the creation myth of **Heliopolis**.

Ay (1323–1319 B.C.E.): Vizier during **Tutankhamun's** reign and his successor. Penultimate pharaoh during the Eighteenth Dynasty (New Kingdom).

Ba: Part of the soul, personality.

Babi: Sacred baboon.

Bastet: Gentle cat goddess.

Benben: Mound that emerged from the primordial waters in the creation myth from **Heliopolis**.

Bennu: Supernatural bird; phoenix.

Berenice IV (58–55 B.C.E.): Princess and Queen of the Ptolemaic Dynasty, ruled Egypt during her father, **Ptolemy XII's**, exile. Sister of **Cleopatra**.

Bes: Dwarfish demon-god, protector of childbirth and mothers.

Beset: Bes' feminine counterpart.

Caesar, Julius (100–44 B.C.E.): Roman general, statesman, dictator. Partner of **Cleopatra**.

Caesarion (47–30 B.C.E.): Son of **Cleopatra** and **Julius Caesar**, co-pharaoh with **Cleopatra**, then briefly the last pharaoh of Egypt.

Carter, Howard (1874–1939): British archaeologist and Egyptologist, discovered the tomb of **Tutankhamun**.

Cartouche: In Egyptian hieroglyphs, an oval with a line indicating a royal name.

Cheops: see: **Khufu**.

Cleopatra (69–30 B.C.E.): Queen of the Ptolemaic Dynasty, last pharaoh of Egypt with her son **Caesarion**.

Cleopatra Selene II (40–ca. 5 B.C.E.): Daughter of **Cleopatra** and **Mark Antony**, princess and queen of Numidia.

Corinth: City in ancient Greece.

Criosphinx: Sphinx with a head of a ram.

Cronus: Greek god, leader of the older Greek pantheon.

Deir el-Medina: Ancient Egyptian village of workers.

Djedefre (ca. 2575 B.C.E.): Pharaoh of the Fourth Dynasty (Old Kingdom). Successor of **Khufu**.

Djoser (ca. 2686–2648 B.C.E.): First pharaoh of the Third Dynasty (Old Kingdom). Had a step pyramid built for himself.

Duat: Egyptian underworld.

Edfu: Ancient Egyptian temple on the west bank of Nile.

Elephantine: Island on the Nile and ancient Egyptian city.

Ennead: Group of chief deities in ancient Egyptian theology (**Atum, Shu, Tefnut, Geb, Nut, Osiris, Isis, Set, Nephthys**).

Esna: Riverbank city in ancient Egypt, place of worship of **Khnum**.

Exodus, book of: Book in the Hebrew Bible describing the exodus of the Israelites from Egypt.

Faiyum: City in Middle Egypt.

Geb: God of the earth.

Giza: City in Egypt, site of the pyramids and the **Sphinx**.

Gould, George Jay (1864–1923): American financier and railroad executive. Died after visiting the tomb of **Tutankhamun**.

Hathor: Sky goddess, wife of **Horus**.

Hatshepsut (ca. 1479–1458 B.C.E.): Fifth pharaoh of the Eighteenth Dynasty (New Kingdom). Second female pharaoh in history.

Ḥeḥu: Member of the **Ogdoad**, personification of infinity.

Ḥeḥut: Female counterpart of **Ḥeḥu**.

Heka: Aspect of Ra, magic power.

Heliopolis: Major city in Ancient Egypt.

Heqet: Goddess of fertility.

Herbert, Aubrey (1880–1923): British diplomat and intelligence officer. Half-brother of **George Herbert**, died five months after him.

Herbert, George, 5th Earl of Carnarvon (1866–1923): British aristocrat, sponsored the excavation of the tomb of **Tutankhamun**. His death caused rumors about the curse of Tutankhamun.

Hermopolis: Major city in Ancient Egypt.

Herodotus (ca. 484–ca. 425 B.C.E.): Ancient Greek historian and geographer.

Hetephernebti (dates unknown): Queen of the Third Dynasty (Old Kingdom). Wife of **Djoser**.

Hieracosphinx: Sphinx with a head of a hawk.

Hittite Empire (ca. 1650–1190 B.C.E.): Empire of the peoples from Anatolia.

Horemheb (1319/1306–1292 B.C.E.): Last pharaoh of the Eighteenth Dynasty (New Kingdom).

Horus: God of kingship and the sky, one of the most important gods in ancient Egypt.

Hu: Aspect of Ra, command.

Hyksos: Fifteenth Dynasty (Second Intermediate Period), foreign rulers of Egypt.

Ib: Part of the soul, heart.

Imhotep (ca. 27th century B.C.E.): Vizier to pharaoh **Djoser**, deified after death.

Inetkawes (dates unknown): Princess of the Third Dynasty (Old Kingdom), daughter of **Djoser**.

Isis: Goddess of motherhood, wife of **Osiris**, one of the most important goddesses in Ancient Egypt.

Iunu: see: **Heliopolis**.

Jocasta: In Greek mythology, Queen of **Thebes**, mother and wife of **Oedipus**.

Ka: Part of the soul, vital essence.

Kadesh, Battle of (May 1274 B.C.E.): Battle between ancient Egypt under **Ramesses II** and the **Hittite Empire**. Inconclusive.

Kek: Representation of darkness, or alternate name of **Kekui**.

Kekui: Member of the **Ogdoad**, personification of primordial darkness.

Kekuit: Female counterpart of **Kek**.

Khafre (ca. 2570 B.C.E.): Pharaoh of the Fourth Dynasty (Old Kingdom), successor of **Djedefre**, son of **Khufu**.

Khemenu: see: **Hermopolis**.

Khepri: Scarab god, representation of the rising sun.

Khet: Part of the soul, the physical body.

Khnum: God of the source of the Nile.

Khonsu: God of the moon.

Khufu (2589–2566 B.C.E.): Second pharaoh of the Fourth Dynasty (Old Kingdom). Ordered the construction of the Great Pyramid of Giza.

Kush, Kingdom of (ca. 1070 B.C.E.–ca. 550 C.E.): Ancient kingdom in Nubia.

Lepidus, Marcus Aemilius (ca. 89–13 B.C.E.): Roman statesman and a member of the Second Triumvirate with **Octavian** and **Mark Antony**.

Libya: In antiquity, a term referring to Northern Africa.

Maat: Goddess of justice, concept of justice in ancient Egypt.

Mace, Arthur Cruttenden (1874–1928): English archaeologist, member of the expedition that excavated **Tutankhamun's** tomb.

Mandjet: Solar barque of **Ra**, used during the day.

Mastaba: Early Egyptian tomb, proto-pyramid.

Media: Region in northwestern Iran.

Medjed: Ghost-like god.

Meeyuty: Minor cat god, guards one of the gates in **Duat**.

Mehit: Lioness goddess, wife of **Anhur**.

Memphis: Ancient capital of Lower Egypt.

Menes (ca. 3200–3000 B.C.E.): Pharaoh of the Early Dynastic Period, according to the legend united Upper and Lower Egypt.

Mentuhotep II (2060–2009 B.C.E.): Sixth pharaoh of the Eleventh Dynasty (Middle Kingdom). Reunited Egypt and ended the First Intermediate Period.

Merer (dates unknown): Middle-ranking official during the reign of Khufu, whose diary provides insight into the building of the Great Pyramid of Giza.

Meseket: Barque of Ra, used during nighttime.

Min: God of fertility.

Mut: Mother goddess.

Naqada culture: Archaeological culture of predynastic Egypt.

Naunet: Female version of **Nun**, member of the **Ogdoad**, personification of primeval waters.

Nebty: Royal name of the pharaohs.

Neferneferuaten-Nefertiti: see: **Nefertiti**.

Nefertiti (ca. 1370–ca. 1330 B.C.E.): Queen of the Eighteenth Dynasty (New Kingdom), wife of **Akhenaten**, possibly also a pharaoh.

Nehebkau: Snake-god, associated with **Ra**.

Neith: Goddess of fate, wisdom, and childbirth.

Nekhbet: Patron goddess of Upper Egypt.

Nemes: Headdress of a pharaoh.

Neper: Minor god of grain.

Nephthys: Goddess of darkness, childbirth, wisdom, magic, embalming. Wife of **Set**.

Numidia (202–40 B.C.E.): Ancient kingdom in northwest Africa.

Nun: Member of the **Ogdoad**, personification of primeval waters.

Nut: Goddess of the sky, stars, and astronomy.

Octavia (ca. 66–11 B.C.E.): Wife of **Mark Antony**, sister of **Octavian**.

Octavian August (63 B.C.E.–14 C.E.): Roman statesman, politician, general, and first Roman emperor.

Oedipus: In Greek mythology, a tragic hero who defeated the **Sphinx**, killed his father, and married his mother.

Ogdoad: Group of eight primordial deities.

Osiris: God of the dead, one of the most important gods in Egyptian mythology.

Parthia: Historical region in northeastern Iran.

Pelusium: Port city in eastern Nile Delta.

Pharsalus, Battle of (August 9, 48 B.C.E.): Battle between the forces of **Julius Caesar** and **Pompey**. Won by Caesar.

Pi-Ramesses: New capital of Egypt erected by **Ramesses II**.

Pompey (106–48 B.C.E.): Roman general and statesman. Assassinated in a plot by **Ptolemy XIII**.

Ptah: God of craftsmen, creator of the world.

Ptolemy I Soter (ca. 367–282 B.C.E.): First pharaoh of Egypt from the Ptolemaic Dynasty.

Ptolemy XII (ca. 117–51 B.C.E.): Pharaoh from the Ptolemaic Dynasty, father of **Cleopatra**.

Ptolemy XIII (ca. 62–47 B.C.E.): Pharaoh from the Ptolemaic Dynasty, brother and co-ruler of **Cleopatra**, died during the civil war.

Ptolemy XIV (ca. 59–44 B.C.E.): Brother and co-ruler with **Cleopatra**, poisoned by her.

Qerḥ: Member of the **Ogdoad**, represents night or inactivity.

Qerḥet: Female counterpart of **Qerḥ**.

Ra: God of the sun, one of the most important gods in Egyptian mythology.

Ramesses I (1292–1290 B.C.E.): First pharaoh from the Nineteenth Dynasty (New Kingdom).

Ramesses II The Great (ca. 1303–1213 B.C.E.): Third pharaoh of the Nineteenth Dynasty (New Egypt). Probably the most powerful pharaoh in Egypt's history.

Ramesses III (1186–1155 B.C.E.): Second pharaoh of the Twentieth Dynasty (New Kingdom).

Ren: Part of the soul, name or identity.

Renenutet: Goddess of nourishment and the harvest.

Sah: Part of the soul, the spiritual body.

Saqqara: Egyptian village in the region of **Giza**.

Sekhem: Part of the soul, form or power.

Sekhmet: Warrior goddess.

Serapeum of Saqqara: Burial place of sacred bulls dedicated to **Apis**.

Serapis: see **Apis**.

Serket: Goddess of healing scorpion bites.

Serpopard: Half-serpent, half-leopard, symbol of chaos.

Set: God of deserts, violence, and foreigners. One of the most important gods in Egyptian mythology.

Sha: Animal of **Set**.

Shen: Nekhbet's ring of eternal protection.

Shu: Primordial god of air and wind.

Shut: Part of the soul, shadow, silhouette.

Sia: Aspect of **Ra**, perception.

Sobek: Crocodile god.

Sobekneferu (mid-18th century B.C.E.): Pharaoh from the Twelfth Dynasty (Middle Kingdom). First female pharaoh.

Sphinx: Creature with a human head, a body of a lion, and wings of a falcon.

Tefnut: Primordial goddess of moisture and rain.

Thebes (Greece): City in Greece, in Greek mythology guarded by a **Sphinx**.

Thebes (Egypt): One of the main cities of Upper Egypt.

Thoth: God of wisdom, magic, science, and hieroglyphs.

Thutmose I (1506–1493 B.C.E.): Third pharaoh of the Eighteenth Dynasty (New Kingdom).

Thutmose II (1513–1499 B.C.E.): Fourth pharaoh of the Eighteenth Dynasty (New Kingdom). Husband of **Hatshepsut**.

Thutmose III (1479–1425 B.C.E.): Sixth pharaoh of the Eighteenth Dynasty (New Kingdom). Successor of **Hatshepsut**.

Tura: Quarry of limestone in ancient Egypt.

Tut, King: see: **Tutankhamun**.

Tutankhamun (ca. 1341–ca. 1323 B.C.E.): Pharaoh at the end of the Eighteenth Dynasty (New Kingdom). Son of **Akhenaten**, reversed his religious reforms.

Uraeus: Sacred cobra, symbol of pharaohs.

Wadjet: Protector goddess of Lower Egypt.

Waset: see: **Thebes**.

Weigall, Arthur (1880–1934): English Egyptologist.

Ziggurat: Pyramid-like structure in ancient Mesopotamia.

References

Allen, J. P. (2000). *Middle Egyptian: An introduction to the language and culture of hieroglyphs*. Cambridge University Press.

AncientHistory. (2014). *"Queen Nefertiti," the most beautiful face of Egypt (Discovery Channel)* [Video]. YouTube. https://web.archive.org/web/20170308132614/https://www.youtube.com/watch?v=7Kht878XLsg&gl=US&hl=en

Arab, S. M. (2017). *Medicine in Ancient Egypt: Part 1 of 3*. Arab World Books. https://www.arabworldbooks.com/en/e-zine/medicine-in-ancient-egypt-part-1-of-3

Ayad, M. F. (2013). *God's Wife, God's servant: The God's Wife of Amun (ca. 740–525 B.C.E.)*. Routledge.

Baker, R. F., & Baker, C. F. (2001). *Ancient Egyptians: People of the pyramids*. Oxford University Press.

Bard, K. A. (2015). *An introduction to the archaeology of Ancient Egypt*. Wiley-Blackwell.

BBC News. (2006, August 25). *Giant Ramses statue gets new home*. http://news.bbc.co.uk/2/hi/middle_east/5282414.stm

Billard, J. B. (1989). *Ancient Egypt: Discovering its splendors*. National Geographic Society.

Bleeker, C. J. (1973). *Hathor and Thoth: Two key figures of the ancient Egyptian religion*. Brill.

Boylan, P. (1979). *Thoth, the Hermes of Egypt: A study of some aspects of theological thought in Ancient Egypt*. Ares Publishers inc.

Boyle, A. (2013). *4,500-year-old harbor structures and papyrus texts unearthed in Egypt.* NBC News. https://www.nbcnews.com/science/cosmic-log/4-500-year-old-harbor-structures-papyrus-texts-unearthed-egypt-flna1c9356840

Breasted, J. H. (1908). *A history of the ancient Egyptians.* Charles Scribner's Sons.

Breasted, J. H. (1962). *Ancient records of Egypt: Historical documents from the earliest times to the Persian conquest.* Russell & Russell.

Burleigh, N. (2007). *Mirage: Napoleon's scientists and the unveiling of Egypt.* Harper Collins.

Caiger, S. L. (1946). Archaeological fact and fancy. *Biblical Archaeologist, 9.*

Canadian Museum of History. (2019). *Egyptian civilization–myths: Creation myth.* https://www.historymuseum.ca/cmc/exhibitions/civil/egypt/egcr09e.html

Carlos, J. (2013). *Ancient Egyptian administration.* Brill.

Carter, H., & Mace, A. C. (2012). *The discovery of the tomb of Tutankhamen.* Courier Corporation.

The Collector. (2022, February 9). *Were ancient Egyptians black? Let's look at the evidence.* https://www.thecollector.com/were-ancient-egyptians-black/

Cooney, K. (2020). *When women ruled the world: Six queens of Egypt.* National Geographic.

Cooney, K. (2015). *The woman who would be king: Hatshepsut's rise to power in ancient Egypt.* Oneworld.

David, A. R. (2002). *Religion and magic in ancient Egypt.* Penguin Books.

van Dijk, J. (1996). Horemheb and the struggle for the throne of Tutankhamun. *Bulletin of the Australian Centre for Egyptology, 29 - 42.*

Dodson, A. (2009). *Amarna sunset: Nefertiti, Tutankhamun, Ay, Horemheb, and the Egyptian counter-reformation.* American University in Cairo Press.

Dodson, A., & Hilton, D. (2010). *The complete royal families of Ancient Egypt.* Thames & Hudson.

Encyclopedia Britannica. (n.d.). *Did enslaved people build the pyramids of Giza?* [Video]. https://www.britannica.com/video/226777/did-enslaved-people-build-the-pyramids

Faulkner, R. O. (1936). *Egyptian texts: Songs of Isis and Nephthys.* Attalus.org. http://attalus.org/egypt/isis_nephthys.html

Fischer, H. G. (2000). *Egyptian woman in the Old Kingdom and of the Heracleopolitan Period.* The Metropolitan Museum of Art.

Fleming, F., & Lothian, A. (2003). *The way to eternity: Egyptian myth.* Barnes & Noble Books.

Forbes, D. C. (2005). *Imperial lives.* KMT Communications, Inc.

Frankfort, H. (1969). *The art and architecture of the ancient orient.* Penguin Books.

Gardiner, A. H. (1962). *Egypt of the pharaohs, an introduction.* Oxford University Press.

Gillam, R. (2001). Sobekneferu. In *The Oxford Encyclopedia of Ancient Egypt* (Vol. 3). Oxford University Press.

Grimal, N.-C. (1994). *A history of ancient Egypt.* Blackwell.

Gwynn-Jones, P. L. (1998). *The art of heraldry.* Parkgate.

Fairman, H. W. (1974). *The triumph of Horus: An Ancient Egyptian sacred drama.* Berkeley: U.C. Press.

Faulkner, R. O., & Griffiths, J. G. (1962). The conflict of Horus and Seth. *The Journal of Egyptian Archaeology, 48,* 171. https://doi.org/10.2307/3855805

Faulkner, R. O., Goelet, Jr, O., & Von Dassow, E. (2015). *The Egyptian book of the dead: The book of going forth by day: Being the Papyrus of Ani (royal scribe of the Divine Offerings), written and illustrated circa 1250 B.C.E., by scribes and artists unknown, including the balance of chapters of the books of the dead known as the Theban Recension, compiled from ancient texts, dating back to the roots of Egyptian civilization.* Chronicle Books.

Favard-Meeks, C. & Meeks, D. (1996). *Daily life of the Egyptian gods.* Cornell University Press.

Flamarion, E. (1997). *Cleopatra.* Harry Abrams.

Hart, G. (2005). *The Routledge dictionary of Egyptian gods and goddesses.* Routledge.

Herodotus & Blakesley, J. W. (2012). *Herodotus.* Hardpress Publishing.

Highfield, R. (2007). How Imhotep gave us medicine. *Telegraph.* https://www.telegraph.co.uk/news/science/science-news/3293164/How-Imhotep-gave-us-medicine.html

Hornung, E. (1999). *Akhenaten and the religion of light.* Cornell University Press.

Hornung, E. (1982). *Conceptions of God in Ancient Egypt.* Cornell University Press.

Hornung, E., & Lorton, D. (1999). *The ancient Egyptian books of the afterlife.* Cornell University Press.

Hussein, K., Matin, E., & Nerlich, A. G. (2013). Paleopathology of the juvenile Pharaoh Tutankhamun—90th anniversary of discovery. *Virchows Archiv, 463*(3). https://doi.org/https://link.springer.com/article/10.1007/s00428-013-1441-1

Jarus, O. (2018, October 31). *This 4,500-year-old ramp contraption may have been used to build Egypt's Great Pyramid.* Live Science. https://www.livescience.com/63978-great-pyramid-ramp-discovered.html

Jenkins, N. (1980). *The boat beneath the pyramid: King Cheops' royal ship*. Holt, Rheinhart, and Winston. http://www.gizapyramids.org/static/pdf%20library/jenkins_boat.pdf

Johnson, J. H. (2002). *Women's legal rights in Ancient Egypt*. The University of Chicago. https://fathom.lib.uchicago.edu/1/777777190170/

Jones, P. J. (2006). *Cleopatra: A sourcebook*. University Of Oklahoma Press, Cop.

Kemboly, M. (2010). *The question of evil in Ancient Egypt*. Golden House Publications.

Kemp, B. (2007). *Ancient Egypt: Anatomy of a civilisation*. Routledge.

Killebrew, A. E. (2013). The Philistines and other "Sea Peoples" in text and archaeology. *Society of Biblical Literature Archaeology and Biblical Studies, 15.*

Kuiper, K. (2011). *Ancient Egypt: From prehistory to the Islamic Conquest*. Britannica Educational Pub.

Kousoulis, P. (1999). *Magic and religion as performative theological unity: The apotropaic ritual of overthrowing Apophis. Ancient Egypt Magazine, 9(3).*

Lehner, M. (n.d.). *NOVA Online/Pyramids/Who built the pyramids?* PBS https://www.pbs.org/wgbh/nova/pyramid/explore/builders.html

Lehner, M., & Hawass, Z. A. (2017). *Giza and the pyramids: The definitive history*. The University Of Chicago Press.

Leprohon, R. J., & Doxey, D. M. (2013). *The great name: Ancient Egyptian royal titulary.* Society Of Biblical Literature.

Lichtheim, M. (2000). *Ancient Egyptian literature: A book of readings. The Old and Middle Kingdoms*. University of California Press.

Luckhurst, R. (2012). *The mummy's curse: The true history of a dark fantasy*. Oxford University Press.

Lutz, D. (2007). *Exploring Egypt: A traveler's view of an ancient civilization*. DIMI Press.

Mandal, D. (2022, August 10). *12 fascinating Ancient Egyptian mythological creatures*. Realm of History. https://www.realmofhistory.com/2022/08/10/egyptian-mythological-creatures/

Michaels, B. (1978). *Red land, black land: Daily life in ancient Egypt*. Dodd, Mead.

Moss, K. (2009). The Seth-animal: A dog and its master. *Ancient Egypt Magazine, 9*(6).

Najovits, S. R. (2003). *Egypt, trunk of the tree: A modern survey of an ancient land*. Algora Pub.

O'Connor, D. B. (2011). *Abydos: Egypt's first pharaohs and the cult of Osiris*. Thames & Hudson.

O'Connor, D. B., & Silverman, D. P. (1995). *Ancient Egyptian kingship*. E.J. Brill.

Palmer, D. (1993). *Science: Mini mammoths survived into Egyptian times*. New Scientist. https://www.newscientist.com/article/mg13718662-600-science-mini-mammoths-survived-into-egyptian-times/

Parkinson, R. B. (1995). "Homosexual" desire and Middle Kingdom Literature. *The Journal of Egyptian Archaeology, 81*, 57–76. https://doi.org/10.2307/3821808

Plutarch & Griffiths, J. G. (1970). *Plutarch's De Iside et Osiride*. University Of Wales Press.

Prof. Geller. (2016, October 8). *Geb: Egyptian god of the earth*. Mythology.net. https://mythology.net/egyptian/egyptian-gods/geb/

Rappoport, S. (2005). *History of Egypt Volume 12*. Www.gutenberg.org. https://www.gutenberg.org/files/17332/17332-h/17332-h.htm (Originally published 1906)

Redford, D. B. (2001). *The Oxford encyclopedia of ancient Egypt*. Oxford University Press.

Redford, D. B. (2003). *The Oxford essential guide to Egyptian mythology*. Berkley Books.

Robins, G. (2008). *The art of ancient Egypt*. The British Museum Press.

Robins, G., & Troy, L. (1990). Patterns of queenship in Ancient Egyptian myth and history. *The Journal of Egyptian Archaeology, 76*, 214. https://doi.org/10.2307/3822039

Roller, D. W. (2010). *Cleopatra: A biography*. Oxford University Press.

Rose, D., & Berninger, S. (2007, May 18). *The surprising truth about how the Great Pyramids were built*. Live Science. https://www.livescience.com/1554-surprising-truth-great-pyramids-built.html

Seawright, C. (n.d.). *Kek and Kauket, deities of darkness, obscurity and night*. Tour Egypt. http://www.touregypt.net/featurestories/kek.htm

Selden, D. L. (2013). *Hieroglyphic Egyptian: An introduction to the language and literature of Middle Egyptian hieroglyphs*. University of California Press.

Seton-Williams, M. V. (1999). *Egyptian legends and stories*. Barnes & Noble.

Shaw, I. (2006). *The Oxford history of ancient Egypt*. Oxford Paperbacks.

Singer, G. G. (2011). *Ahmose Nefertari, the woman in black*. Academia. https://www.academia.edu/414029/Ahmose_Nefertari_the_Woman_in_Black

Smith, M. (2017). *Following Osiris: Perspectives on the Osirian afterlife from four millennia*. Oxford University Press.

Smith, C. B., & Hawass, Z. A. (2018). *How the Great Pyramid was built*. Smithsonian Books.

Smithsonian. (2012). *Egyptian mummies*. Smithsonian Institution. https://www.si.edu/spotlight/ancient-egypt/mummies

Spence, K. (2011). *BBC–History– ancient history in depth: Akhenaten and the Amarna Period*. BBC. https://www.bbc.co.uk/history/ancient/egyptians/akhenaten_01.shtml

Statue colossale: Sphinx de Tanis. (n.d.). Musée Du Louvre. https://collections.louvre.fr/en/ark:/53355/cl010010062

Stille, A. (2015, September 22). The world's oldest papyrus and what it can tell us about the Great Pyramids. *Smithsonian Magazine*. https://www.smithsonianmag.com/history/ancient-egypt-shipping-mining-farming-economy-pyramids-180956619/

Strauss, B. (2019). *Bennu, the bird of fire, and other mythical monsters of Ancient Egypt*. ThoughtCo. https://www.thoughtco.com/egyptian-monsters-4145424

Stubby the Rocket. (2015, August 7). *Meet Medjed, the Egyptian God who's big in Japan!* Tor.com. https://www.tor.com/2015/08/07/medjed-obscure-egyptian-god-is-popular-in-japanese-culture/

Taronas, L. (2019). *Akhenaten: The mysteries of religious revolution*. American Research Center in Egypt. https://www.arce.org/resource/akhenaten-mysteries-religious-revolution

Taylor, J. H. (2001). *Death and the afterlife in ancient Egypt*. University Of Chicago Press.

Taylor, J. H. (2010). *Journey through the afterlife: Ancient Egyptian Book of the dead*. Harvard University Press.

Te Velde, H. (1967). *Seth, god of confusion* (G. E. Van Baaren-Pape, Trans.). E. J. Brill.

Tyldesley, J. A. (2022, July 28). Cleopatra In *Encyclopædia Britannica*. https://www.britannica.com/biography/Cleopatra-queen-of-Egypt

Tyldesley, J. A. (2001). *Ramesses: Egypt's greatest pharaoh*. Penguin.

University College of London. (n.d.). *Two ladies*. https://www.ucl.ac.uk/museums-static/digitalegypt//ideology/kingname/ladies.html

Wallis, A. (2010). *An Egyptian hieroglyphic dictionary: In two volumes, with an index of English words, king list and geographical list with indexes, list of hieroglyphic characters, Coptic and Semitic alphabets.* Cosimo Classics.

Wildung, D. (1977). *Egyptian saints.* New York University Press.

Wilkinson, T. A. H. (2005). *Early dynastic Egypt.* Routledge.

Wilkinson, R. H. (2003). *The complete gods and goddesses of ancient Egypt.* Thames & Hudson Inc.

Wilkinson, T. (2007). *The Egyptian world.* Routledge.

Zivie-Coche, C. (2004). Sphinx: History of a monument. *Internet Archive.* Cornell University Press. https://archive.org/details/sphinx00chri/page/16/mode/2up

UNCOVERING JAPANESE MYTHOLOGY

Exploring the Ancient Stories, Legends, and Folktales of the Land of the Rising Sun

LUCAS RUSSO

464

Introduction

Japanese mythology and folklore have been food for inspiration and fascination for years, if not decades. It was transmitted to the Western world through translations, books, anime, manga, and feature films. And yet, in the general consciousness, the understanding of Japanese mythology, folklore, and the system of beliefs that stood and still stands behind it, is still only perfunctory.

In this book, I want to show you not only a selection of the most fascinating stories from Japanese folklore—and there is no shortage of those—but also to acquaint you with the most important Japanese deities, and to help you understand the religious principles that stand behind the belief in many of the entities and supernatural creatures, as well as the Japanese philosophy of life. Culturally, Japan has been in a rather unique position in comparison to other civilizations from the region, and from the rest of the world: With its ages of political isolationism and its characteristic set of religious beliefs stemming from Shintoism and the Japanese version of Buddhism, it created a very particular climate for the development of myths and folktales. A climate that differs from the one we are used to with various mythologies originating in Europe. As a result, the mythology that stemmed from these specific cultural circumstances—and which will be the main focus of this book—is also highly original.

So let us begin our journey. First, we will try to understand Japanese religious beliefs and historical social structure better: The principles behind Shintoism and how Buddhism arrived in Japan; the divine status of the Japanese emperor, and the meaning of the social classes. But most importantly, we will explore the rich world of numerous Japanese deities, supernatural creatures, and heroes—and we will learn the stories pertaining to them. We will learn about the creation of the world and the islands in the Japanese archipelago; about the powerful Sun goddess and volatile gods of the storm; and finally, about regular, impoverished people who encountered supernatural beings in numerous Japanese fairy tales.

I hope that you will enjoy this rich world of myth that Japan has to offer. From the highest of gods to the lowest of people, there is something in this mythology for everyone.

CHAPTER 1

The Foundation of Myth

Shinto and Japanese Buddhism were two cornerstones upon which Japanese mythology was built, and they are crucial for its understanding. In this chapter, we will learn the principles standing behind each of these traditions. We will also explore Japan's historic political structure, as well as develop a basic understanding of the antiquity of Japanese tradition and how it changed throughout history—as a better understanding of the Japanese social structure might prove very useful in understanding the plot points of folktales. Treat this chapter as a compendium and an introduction: A guide that you will take on your journey.

Shinto—Religion From Japan

Shinto is a religion that differs a lot from the most popular monotheistic religions such as Christianity or Islam. First of all, it is polytheistic, holding a belief in many divine beings; but it's also animistic—meaning that it ascribes divine properties and spiritual essence to animals, places, and even objects. This special nature of Shintoism is also the most defining feature behind Japanese mythology: Although many Japanese gods can be distinguished as such, the line between a god and a spirit or a semi-divine being can be blurry. Additionally, the animistic aspect of Shinto means that everyday objects, places, and animals would acquire supernatural status—something that we will look at more closely in Chapter 6.

Moreover, Shinto has no single canon of texts and versions of beliefs; instead, beliefs vary and can often contradict each other. In this, Shintoism is similar to many decentralized polytheistic religions; but in contrast to many of them, the sheer number of mythical beings and gods in which the followers of Shinto could believe is much larger. It is not just that there are different versions of the same gods in different regions of Japan; it's also that some of the gods only preside over tiny dominions, in one or two regions only. In fact, the decentralization of Shinto is so great that the only unifying feature that could describe this religion as a whole is the belief in kami, or, supernatural entities (meaning both gods, spirits, and other, less specified powers) (Cali et al., 2013).

Some scholars have described Shinto as less of a religion, and more of a philosophy or a way of life (Picken, 1994; Cali et al., 2013). Unlike many modern Western religions, Shinto isn't exclusive and allows for the practice of other religious beliefs alongside it. Over the ages, many non-Japanese religious beliefs have infiltrated Shinto; Buddhism is perhaps the most prominent of these influences, but so are Chinese Confucianism and Taoism.

There are different types of Shinto, from the more official version centered around shrines to the more private one, practiced by individual people. Historically, there was also the official state version of the religion, emphasizing the divine status of the Japanese emperor and enacting financial control over Shinto temples. This, of course, is no longer the case in modern-day Japan.

Given that Shinto is so relaxed and decentralized, is there any set of beliefs, besides the broadest belief in the kami, that can be pointed out as characteristic of that religion? Perhaps the most defining feature of Shinto and one that can be found the most surprising to the Western mentality is the lack of clear division between good and evil. The kami can encompass both good fortune and destruction, and there is no reward for "good deeds" in the afterlife. In fact, Shinto is more concentrated on life rather than on what might come after it; some believers hold that the dead assist the living as ghosts, and others adopt more Buddhist afterlife beliefs (Littleton, 2002); but in any case, Shinto emphasizes life and adaptability to its ever-changing circumstances.

However, instead of good and evil, Shinto distinguishes between purity and impurity. Humans are considered intrinsically pure; however, they can become impure through contact with death or disease, or through practicing cultural taboos such as incest or bestiality; menstruation and childbirth can also cause impurity (Nelson, 2006). There are many rituals aimed at purification, and some of them are an imitation of the rites that some of the kami are believed to have undergone when faced with similar challenges.

Shinto does not have a single code of conduct. Some of the qualities that are emphasized as desirable for its followers include honesty and adherence to truth, frankness, hard work, and giving thanks to the kami (Picken, 2011). This list of precepts is general enough that historically, it could be applied to many varying social and political circumstances—and as we will see in later chapters, it also influenced the rather vague morality behind Japanese folktales.

Today, Shintoism tends to veer toward general conservatism and valuing Japan's national interests.

Japanese Buddhism

Buddhism first arrived in Japan around the 6th century C.E. The Silk Road—the trade route that connected India to China and Korea—had its extension in the maritime route between Japan and Korea and China. As such, the Japanese version of Buddhism was already filtered through the Chinese and Korean versions of the religion when it arrived on the archipelago. According to one of the chronicles of Japan, the *Nihon Shoki*, the Japanese emperor Soga no Iname (506–570) allowed only one Japanese clan (the Soga clan) to adopt Buddhism, in order to see how the worship would affect his subjects and if the Japanese kami would be furious (Deal & Ruppert, 2015).

As a result, the Soga clan became the staunchest champions of Buddhism, even though they initially faced a lot of opposition, and sometimes even outright hostility. Over the years and throughout the rule of different imperial dynasties in Japan, Buddhism was more or less accepted and endorsed by the state. Often, this was tied to general strong cultural influences from Korea and China, which, at various points in history, were considered more sophisticated; thus, Chinese technology and poetry found their way to Japan. Along with Buddhist practices, the art, and architecture tied to that religion were also introduced.

Fascinatingly, Buddhism became a religious vehicle for cultural exchange spanning thousands of kilometers: Some of the Japanese Buddhism iconographies can trace its roots as far as Hellenistic-Indian depictions, which allows us to find a common style between ancient Greek sculpture and Japanese sculpture (Tanabe, 2003).

But apart from artistic influences, what was the religious importance of Buddhism in Japan? Today, Japanese Buddhism mainly centers around one Buddha. But historically, as Buddha was a name applied to a category of those who have attained awakening or nirvana, rather than to a singular person, over 3,000 Buddhas were worshiped in Japan (Nukariya, 2016). This ties to the local Japanese Shinto traditions with its multiplicity of gods.

Moreover, the Japanese Buddhist pantheon was hierarchical. There were six levels of deities (the first level being the highest, and the sixth the lowest): The Buddhas (those who attained enlightenment), the Bodhisattvas (those who attained enlightenment but have chosen to stay on earth and spread the knowledge of Buddhism), Wisdom Kings (powerful gods who can influence reality), Heavenly Deities (gods who go through a cycle of rebirths and strive to attain nirvana, therefore try to help the followers of Buddhism), Circumstantial Appearances (protective forces which are mostly Shinto gods adopted for Buddhist purposes), and finally, Religious Masters (influential historical figures).

There are numerous schools of Buddhism in Japan, both historically and contemporarily. Although some of them are esoteric (based on hidden teachings), all emphasize attaining enlightenment, thus filling the gap in the Shintoist lack of belief in any form of afterlife. Moreover, they add new concepts and deities to the already enormous pantheon of Japanese gods.

Japanese State

Both Shintoism and Buddhism were religions used by the Japanese state to reinforce order and obedience to the emperor. But what was the societal structure of Japan? How did it change throughout the centuries? And, most importantly, how did it influence the Japanese system of beliefs?

Brief Chronology

Before we talk at length about the organization of the Japanese state, it's worth mentioning the chronology of Japan's history; after all, the culture hardly stayed the same throughout over 1,500 years of its development.

Jōmon Period (ca. 13000–1000 B.C.E.)

Although human activity on the Japanese archipelago reaches paleolithic times, the first signs of a complex culture can be dated to this period. The people of that time slowly changed from hunter-gatherers to a sedentary culture and started creating elaborately decorated pottery. Not much more is known about them, however.

Yayoi Period (ca. 1000 B.C.E.–ca. 240 C.E.)

The period is named after the Yayoi People, who migrated to the Japanese archipelago from China and Korea, transforming the culture that they encountered. Most prominently, they introduced the cultivation of rice, as well as bronze and iron weapons. Traditionally, the first legendary emperor of Japan, Emperor Jimmu, was believed to have ruled in this era, in the 7th and 6th century B.C.E.

Around 82 C.E., a Chinese chronicle called the *Book of Han*, was created; it contains the first known mention of Japan as an entity divided into as many as a hundred kingdoms. A later Chinese work, *Wei Zhi* from the 3rd century C.E., mentions that around 240 C.E., one of the Japanese kingdoms gained power over the others and the unification process began (Sansom, 1982). The kingdom's name was said to be Yamatai, and it was supposed to be ruled by a semi-mythical empress and shamaness, Himiko.

Kofun Period (ca. 250–538)

The first serious unification attempt arrived with the Kofun period of Japanese history when several previously independent kingdoms united under a single territory. The word *kofun* refers to a style of burial mounds that are most characteristic of this period. It also saw the development of the three oldest Shinto shrines in Japan: The Nagata Shrine, Hirota Shrine, and Ikuta Shrine.

Asuka Period (538–710)

The Asuka Period started what is known today as Classical Japan. Its most defining feature was the introduction of Buddhism by the Soga clan which then controlled Japan for much of this age. The clan was overthrown in 645 by the Fujiwara clan, who introduced extensive reforms to government, based on Chinese structures of power and on the spirit of Confucianism. Overall, the Asuka Period saw large Chinese cultural influences on Japan.

Nara Period (710–794)

The Nara Period was very important for the construction of Japanese mythology. During this time, two legendary accounts, the books of *Kojiki* and *Nihon Shoki*, were created; they describe the Japanese creation myth and explain the descendance of Japanese rulers from the gods.

Unfortunately, this period was also characterized by some natural disasters, including famines and disease, which led to a more forceful promotion of Buddhism as a way to appease the higher powers by increasing the piousness in the people.

Heian Period (794–1185)

The Heian Period was one of the most important in Japanese history. The government, controlled largely by the Fujiwara clan, wasn't the strongest at the time, with most land outside of the capital being controlled by private landowners; on the other hand, this period also saw major cultural and artistic developments at the imperial court. The Chinese influence declined and more sophisticated forms of Japanese script were developed.

The period ended with a succession dispute which then led to a civil war, a result of which was the seizing of power by the shogun Minamoto no Yoritomo. This marked the symbolic end of Classical Japan and the beginning of Feudal Japan, a time period that is perhaps the best-known to non-Japanese readers.

Kamakura Period (1185–1333)

This period was characterized by the consolidation of power and the rule of the military class (the shogunate) which would last for centuries to come. The hierarchical social structure, which we will talk about in a bit, was largely created during this time. The shogun, or the military dictator, remained practically the most important person in the country, and the principles of the samurai army were developed. Politically, this period saw two invasions of the Mongols, in 1274 and 1281, respectively. Although these invasions ended in an eventual Japanese victory, the wars exhausted the state's finances, leading to the discontent of the samurai who were poorly compensated for their fighting. This led to a series of rebellions which eventually resulted in the end of the Kamakura Period and the start of the Muromachi Period.

Muromachi Period (1333–1568)

The Muromachi Period saw the split between Southern and Northern Japan, as a result of a revolt and civil war. It was a period of violent strife and disobedience of the feudal magnates, called the daimyōs, to the shogunate.

But it was also the time when the first Europeans arrived in Japan. In 1543, Portuguese traders mistakenly set off course and arrived at Japanese shores. This would start a trade exchange which would also play a part in the period of anarchy; for example, European muskets would be introduced to the Japanese army (Farris, 2009).

But the Europeans also started missionary work. In the second half of the 16th century, the first Jesuits were allowed to settle in some Japanese villages and to convert their inhabitants to Christianity. However, Christian beliefs and missionary streak often clashed with Japanese culture, resulting in the Jesuits' expulsion from many areas.

Despite the civil war and anarchy, the Muromachi Period saw a large uptake in population and a flourishment of trade. Some of the most characteristic Japanese art forms were developed during that time, such as ink wash painting, the creation of the bonsai trees, and Noh, a type of a dance-drama (Perez, 1998).

Azuchi-Momoyama Period (1568–1600)

The relatively short Azuchi-Momoyama Period was characterized by the consolidation of power and the restriction put upon the daimyōs, as well as by persecution of the previously tolerated Christians. The most prominent ruler from this time, the warlord Toyotomi Hideyoshi, led many aggressive campaigns against Korea and China. However, the war ended right after his death, and, after some strife, the throne passed to Hideyoshi's former ally, the shogun Tokugawa Ieyasu, who started a new era: The famous Edo Period.

Edo Period (1600–1868)

The Edo Period was a time of peace and prosperity. The Tokugawa shogunate maintained social order and restricted the influence of the daimyōs, but often at a very harsh price: The death penalties were often very brutal (for instance, death by boiling). It was also during that time that the concept of seppuku, the ancient practice of suicide, was ritualized and presented as an alternative punishment for those belonging to the nobility.

It was also during that time when a new policy, that of Japan's isolationism, was implemented. After the times of unrest, all foreign influences were seen as a threat. Thus, effectively, foreign trade as well as sea travel were banned, and previous foreign influences were uprooted (Christianity was banned as a whole in 1638). The only exception to the foreign trade ban were the Dutch who were allowed to trade at Nagasaki (*Dejima Nagasaki*, 2013).

During the Edo Period, the population of Japan doubled, reaching thirty million (Totman, 2014). The capital of the country, Edo (modern-day Tokyo), was the largest city in the world (Henshall, 2012). It was also a time of the development of the merchant class which, having accumulated more and more wealth, became the patrons of the arts. Cultural concepts such as the haiku (a short form of poetry), and the institution of a geisha (a professional entertainer—not a prostitute!) were developed.

As the years went by and the Japanese society changed, the shogunate slowly declined in power. The merchant class was more and more prominent and the peasantry was growing discontent, especially after a series of famines in the early 19th century. Even the samurai slowly grew disillusioned with the rulers. At the same time, the only window that Japan had to the West—through the Dutch traders—brought new ideas and ideologies to the archipelago, sparking interest among the intellectuals.

In 1853, the American fleet commanded by Commodore Matthew C. Perry forcefully arrived at Japan's shores, aiming to end the country's isolationism. The ships were equipped with guns, against which the Japanese forces were helpless; in the end, the Americans forced the Japanese to agree to let them replenish their ships with provisions and to trade with the Americans in the future. It was a veritable cultural clash, and Japan was in turmoil.

Many Japanese people were angered by the shogunate's inability to repel the American 'barbarians.' Nationalistic sentiments grew, and in 1868, the young emperor Meiji was forced to end the Tokugawa shogunate.

Meiji Period (1868–1912)

The Meiji Period could be classified as the first period of Modern Japan. It was characterized by the rule of the oligarchs, with the emperor holding only nominal power. The oligarchs sought to transform Japan so that it could stand equal among the Western superpowers.

The class system was abolished and the daimyōs' domains were changed into prefectures; the ban on Christianity was lifted. Institutions for scientific research were established, and even in terms of clothing and hairstyle, the Japanese started following the Europeans. Western literary styles were adopted, which sparked a wave of prose writing. This allowed for the inventive and fascinating nature, merging of the traditional Japanese and Western storytelling practices. It was also a time of rapid economic growth.

The Meiji Period also saw Japan's military expansion. Through conflicts with Taiwan and Russia, the country expanded into the Japanese Empire.

Taishō Period (1912–1926)

During that short period, the importance of the Japanese Empire on the political map grew. Japan also adopted Western democratic institutions, although political dissidents would also be penalized harshly. In terms of culture, this was a time when Japanese prose was more and more widely read and further developed.

However, the death of Emperor Taishō marked the end of the period, giving way to the longest reign in Japanese history—that of Emperor Hirohito.

Shōwa Period (1926–1989)

The beginning of Emperor Hirogito's reign was marked by a growing popularity of nationalistic movements in Japan, which resulted in the country's turn to fascism—and in the end, with Japan's involvement in World War II on the side of Nazi Germany. Even before the war, Japan's expansionist tendencies resulted in some truly deplorable actions, such as the massacre of Chinese civilians in Nanjing during the Second Sino-Japanese War in 1937.

In 1945, after the lost world war and the absolutely disastrous consequences of the dropping of two atomic bombs on Hiroshima and Nagasaki by the Allies, Japan was in tatters. The Empire of Japan was dismantled in 1947, and from 1945 to 1952, the country was occupied by the Allied forces. Under their rule, Japan underwent drastic changes: Political power was decentralized; the country was demilitarized; and further democratic reforms followed. Emperor Hirohito was forced to denounce his divine nature in return for the allowance to keep his power. This was a massive cultural and religious shift in Japan's consciousness.

From the 1950s onward, Japan experienced rapid economic growth. Moreover, it remained an ally of the United States during the Cold War. Further cultural developments were made most notably, cinema flourished.

Heisei Period and Reiwa Period (1989–present)

The last two periods of Japan's recent history, marked by the reign of Emperor Akihito from 1989 to 2019 and Emperor Naruhito from 2019 to this day, saw further economic growth for Japan, despite a temporary setback in the 1990s. Culturally, it was—and still is—a time of development and thriving of Japanese popular culture, with its manga, anime, and video games—many of which use motifs from traditional Japanese folklore. Today, Japan is one of the technological champions in the world, even if some of its political decisions, especially regarding its relations with China in the past, remain controversial (Henshall, 2012).

All in all, Japan underwent an incredible journey: From the feudal society that it remained way into the 19th century, to the modern technological power. This change we'll later see reflected in its myths and folk stories, which carry on way beyond the end of feudalism and traditional values.

Traditional Social Structure

The traditional and most iconic social structure that we often have in mind when we think about historical Japan, is that of the Edo Period; and that is also the structure we will talk about here. This model of society will be later reflected in many traditional Japanese tales.

The social hierarchy during the Tokugawa shogunate somehow resembled a pyramid. The Emperor, of course, was on the very top of that structure; however, for most of the period, his rule was only nominal, even if he claimed descendance from the gods. The real ruler of Japan was the shogun—the military commander.

Yet still above the shogun were the kuge: The court nobility. They were civil servants whose positions were prestigious and held cultural significance, but similarly to the emperor, their power was very restricted. They would often be, however, patrons of the arts.

Below the kuge was the shogun—the actual ruler of Japan. He was de facto a military dictator who oversaw all comings and goings in the country. The title was hereditary, and it remained in the hands of the Tokugawa clan for the duration of the Edo Period.

Below the shogun were the already mentioned daimyō. They were magnates and landowners, responsible for the administration of their domains and being the most prominent members of the military class. They, in fact, controlled the vastest areas in the country.

Almost all the rest of the Japanese society was grouped below the daimyō and were divided into four groups: The samurai (warriors), peasants (or farmers), artisans, and merchants. The samurai were the most prestigious and highest-standing of these groups, and were considered nobles. They would be employed by their daimyō, and their warfare would be restricted by a number of honor-based rules, which often turned warfare into artform rather than simple skill. Among the samurai themselves, there were also ones of higher and lower standing.

Importantly, the peasants were esteemed in Japanese society. After all, they produced food and were the backbone of the country's proper functioning. However, the peasants were mostly tied to their villages and required a permit in order to travel outside. Still, they owned the land they farmed, even if it would often be taxed by the local daimyō.

Artisans, as the producers of non-essential goods, were placed below the peasants. They mostly lived in cities and produced items that would later be bought by the nobility.

Finally, the merchants were the lowest of classes—as those who traded, but they did not produce any goods. Like the artisans, they lived in cities, and would often be disregarded— however, as we have already mentioned, their numbers steadily grew during the Edo Period and as time passed, they gained more and more power, despite the laws that restricted them from displaying their wealth too overtly.

Below all the social classes was a group of people regarded as untouchable. Those were people who performed jobs in some way related to death—such as undertakers, butchers, or executioners—and therefore, according to the Shinto principles, were perpetually impure. Ethnic minorities were also excluded from the class structure. Those people would be actively discriminated against and live in their own ghettos, isolated from the rest of the population.

CHAPTER 2

The Origin Story

The Creation of Takamagahara

According to *Kojiki* and *Nihon Shoki*, the world was created from chaos. In the beginning, there was nothing but this chaos, and everything was silent. The chaos itself was a tangle of particles that finally started moving around, causing the lightest ones to float upwards and the heaviest to fall downwards.

The light was a result of the lightest particles grouping on top of the universe. Below, the heavier particles formed clouds which then created Takamagahara, "the High Plane of Heaven," which would later become the realm of all gods. The heaviest particles, for their part, fell way down, creating the Earth (Chamberlain, 2008).

The realm of Takamagahara was a sacred one. Later, it would be connected to the Earth by a special bridge, called the Ame-no-ukihashi ("the Floating Bridge of Heaven"). For now though, it gave birth to the first gods: The Kotoamatsukami, who would later disappear and not take part in any other myths and legends.

The first three deities who appeared from the Heavens were Amenominakanushi (Central Master), Takamimusubi (High Creator), and Kamimusubi (Divine Creator). After them, Umashiashikabihikoji (Energy) and Amenotokotachi (Heaven) appeared. None of these deities had a fixed gender or a partner, and their creation was spontaneous. Immediately after their emergence, they hid themselves from view. Those mysterious deities wouldn't be widely recognized, nor worshiped outside of the creation story.

The Emergence of New Gods

But then, new gods emerged from the universe. Later, they would collectively be known as Kamiyonanayo, or, the seven generations of the kami—the Shinto gods. They appeared in the following order:

First came Kuni-no-Tokotachi and Toyokumono. Like the older gods, those deities emerged spontaneously, and their appearance is likened to a reed growing out of the soil. They didn't have partners, either, nor did they have gender. They also hid themselves almost immediately.

Next came subsequent pairs of male-female gods who were consorts as well as siblings: Uhijini and Suhijini; Tsunuguhi and Ikuguhi; Ōtonoji and Ōtonobe; Omodaru and Aya-kashiko-ne; and finally, Izanagi and Izanami. It is that last pair that would play an important role in Japanese mythology: It is the pair of creator gods who gave birth to a number of other important deities, as well as organized the Earth, lifted it from the chaos, and created the Japanese archipelago.

How did Izanagi and Izanami achieve all this? When they were born, the Earth was chaotic and was drifting on the water like floating oil (Chamberlain, 2008). The gods were tasked with solidifying its shape. For this purpose, they used the Amenonuhoko, a spear laid with jewels. They stirred the chaos with the spear and gathered all the landmass together. The dripping matter that fell from the tip of the spear when the task was done, formed a small island called Onogoro. It was a mythical place where later, Izanagi and Izanami descended and erected a large stone pillar. They realized that their task was now to be married and to have children; so in the first-ever marriage ceremony, they walked in the opposite direction of the pillar, and got married when they walked around the whole island and met each other in the middle again. Later, Izanagi and Izanami would create a palace on Onogoro.

Then, they had their first child: Hiruko (or Ebisu), the God of fishermen and good luck. He was imperfect, born without bones. This was the result of an initial blunder between his parents during their marriage ceremony, Izanami spoke first, even though it was the man, Izanagi, who was supposed to have precedence.

So Hiruko was put on a reed boat and set afloat. Later, he would be washed ashore and would find foster parents, thanks to whom he would overcome his disability; we will talk about him in the next chapter.

But meanwhile, Izanagi and Izanami decided to repeat their marriage ceremony. This time, Izanagi spoke first and the union was successful. Several islands of the Japanese archipelago were born from it, including Awaji Island, Shikoku, Oki Islands, Kyushu, Iki, Tsushima, Sado, and Honshu. The next task was to beget the gods who would populate these islands. So, Izanami gave birth to three more children: The sun goddess Amaterasu, the moon god Tsukuyomi-no-Mikoto, and Susanoo-no-Mikoto, the contrary god of storms. Unfortunately, after giving birth numerous times, Izanami's body grew tired. She finally died giving birth to Kagutsuchi, the god of fire.

Izanagi couldn't bear the grief that this brought him. In his rage, he struck Kagutsuchi, beheading him, and then cut his body into eight pieces. The chunks of Kagutsuchi's body became volcanoes, from which emerged new gods, born of Kagutsuchi's remains mixed with Izanagi's tears: Watatsumi, the water dragon; Kuraokami, the ice dragon; Takemikazuchi, the god of thunder; Futsunuchi, the warrior god; Amatsumikaboshi, a malevolent trickster god; and finally, Ōyamatsumi, the god of mountains, sea, and war.

The death of Izanami marked the end of the creation process and was the first death of any being. Izanagi now descended into Yomi, a mythical island of the dead. He hoped to see Izanami again and, possibly, to resurrect her. There was only one condition, he couldn't look at her when he led her from the Underworld.

Unfortunately, Izanami had already eaten food that was served to her on the land, and therefore, couldn't leave it. When Izanagi heard of this, his anger grew and he broke the only condition set upon him. He lit his torch and raised it to see Izanami's face one more time... Only to drop it with horror when he realized that his wife was now a rotting corpse.

Horrified, Izanagi fled from Yomi. Izanami, ashamed of having been seen in such a decaying state, sent several gods of thunder after him, but Izanagi distracted them and fled. We will learn what happened to him later in the next chapter; for now, the history of the world's creation was finished, and the history of the world began.

Jimmu, the First Emperor

Even though the legend of Emperor Jimmu has no place in the story of the creation of the world, it's an important origin story of the Japanese state—and a legend that for ages has served Japanese emperors as the explanation of their legitimacy. The chronicles of *Kojiki* and *Nihon Shoki* cite the dates of his reign as 660–585 B.C.E.: Right in the middle of the Yayoi Period. Today, historians mostly agree that Jimmu was a legendary figure rather than a historical one; however, some of the events in which he was supposed to be involved might be a reflection of actual wars and migrations of peoples to the Japanese archipelago (Henshall, 2014).

According to the legendary accounts, Jimmu was the descendant of the gods: His father was Ugayafukiaezu, a god and a grandson of Ninigi-no-Mikoto, who had been sent to govern Japan by the sun goddess, Amaterasu, herself one of the numerous children of Izanagi and Izanami. In turn, Jimmu's mother was Tamayori-hime, also a goddess. Jimmu was then semi-divine, and his reign would mark the beginning of human history and the end of the gods' rule over the Earth.

Jimmu had three younger brothers: Hikoitsuse, Inai, and Mikeirino, and one older brother, Itsuse no Mikoto. They were all born on the island of Kyushu, the southernmost part of the Japanese archipelago. This was not a good strategic spot for ruling the country, however; so they decided to migrate.

Initially, Itsuse no Mikoto led the migration. The brothers traveled through the Seto Inland Sea, reaching Naniwa (today's Osaka). However, it was already occupied and ruled by a chieftain called Nagasunehiko, who had very long legs. A battle ensued, during which Itsuse no Mikoto was killed, and the brothers lost. Too late, Jimmu realized that the reason for their defeat had been that they had been facing the sun while fighting, which blinded them and rendered them clumsy.

Jimmu now took over as a chieftain. He commanded his forces to move to the Kii Peninsula and, later, to the Kumano Region, from where his army was more strategically positioned as the sun shone on their backs rather than their faces. The second battle was victorious and Nagasunehiko was killed.

Now, Jimmu's forces moved to the Yamato Province. A divine guide was sent by Takamimusubi, the god of agriculture, to aid them on their way: It was a mythical three-legged crow called Yatagarasu, who was also the incarnation of the sun.

In Yamato, Jimmu's forces defeated an ethnic group known as the Emishi. The chieftain of Yamato, Nigihayahi, though he used to be an ally of Nagasunehiko, accepted Jimmu's rule. Jimmu ascended the throne and became the first emperor of the whole of Japan.

But Japan didn't have a name. One day, as Jimmu was climbing the Nara mountain, from which top he planned to chart the country and the Seto Inland Sea, he noticed a curious phenomenon: Dragonflies were mating on the top of the mountain, creating heart shapes from their bodies. As Jimmu was observing this, a mosquito suddenly flew close to him and landed on his arm, intent on biting him and stealing some of his royal blood. But immediately, one of the dragonflies flew to Jimmu's defense and killed the mosquito. Grateful for this deed, Jimmu named the Japanese islands the Dragonfly Islands, which in ancient Japanese read *Akitsushima*.

According to the legend, Jimmu's reign was a long and peaceful one. He was supposed to have died when 126 years old. He is the protoplast of the Imperial House of Japan, also known as the House of Yamato, which nominally rules Japan to this day.

CHAPTER 3

Gods

Given the nature of Shinto, the list of deities that can be found in the Japanese tradition is nearly endless. In this chapter, I will present to you a long, but not nearly complete compendium of the most interesting and important Japanese gods; in the next chapter, we will learn about the goddesses. This overview will include deities from ancient times, as well as those who are still present in Japanese folklore and urban myths to this day. It will also include Shinto gods as well as Buddhist deities.

Aizen Myō-ō

The first god on our list is a Buddhist deity. Also known as Rāgarāja, he is worshiped in the esoteric Buddhist tradition, especially that coming from China. He is one of the Wisdom Kings—the third level of the Buddhist hierarchy of deities and spiritual beings.

Rāgarāja's task is to transform an individual's earthly desires, especially love, and lust, into spiritual awakening. He is most commonly depicted as a red-skinned man sitting cross-legged in a lotus position, with three pairs of hands. The expression on his face is fierce, and he often possesses a third eye and hair made of flames. They represent the burning feeling of rage and lust. Despite Rāgarāja's propensity of liberating and transforming earthly desires, Buddhist followers would often pray to him asking for good luck in love and marriage. In Japan, he is also known to protect the shores from any invaders from the sea. As such, he was especially popular during the Heian Period, when he was especially revered by the lower classes (Goepper, 1993).

Ajisukitakahikone

Ajisukitakahikone is a Shinto god (kami) of agriculture and thunder. His thunderous tendencies were uncovered when his close friend and brother-in-law, Ame-no-Wakahiko, died. When Ajiksukitakahikone came to his funeral, he was mistakenly taken for his deceased friend brought back to life, as they had looked very much alike. Enraged that he had just been connected to a dead man (and therefore made impure), Ajiksukitakahikone drew his sword and destroyed the hut where the funeral was being held, and then kicked it, transforming it into the Moyama mountain in Mino province. Then, Ajiksukitakahikone flew away, and so great was his anger that it lit up the sky.

Amatsu-Mikaboshi

Amatsu-Mikaboshi was one of the gods that emerged from the mutilated body of Kagutsuchi. Not much is known about him except for the fact that he was malicious in nature and always rebelled against the authority of the other gods. During the Asuka and Nara Periods, when Chinese Buddhist influences on Japan were the strongest, Amatsu-Mikaboshi became a personification of Venus. This, later, would lead to a new description of his nature: He was now the god of all stars, less malicious, subdued by his brother, Takemikazuchi, the god of thunder.

Amatsumara

Amatsumara is the god of blacksmiths. He resides in the realm of the gods, Takamagahara, where he is the blacksmith of the gods.

We have only one myth pertaining to Amatsumara: One day, the sun goddess Amaterasu, angered by her brother Susanoo, hid in a cave, depriving the Earth of her light. A plan had to be devised in order to lure her out: So, the god of wisdom, Omoikane, devised a plan.

He ordered Amatsumara to make a beautiful mirror. Then, they hung it in the tree, which they also decorated heavily. Preparations were made for a holy celebration, and the goddess of joy, Ame-no-Uzume-no-Mikoto was brought to a state of holy frenzy. This caused her to bare her breasts and genitals which, in turn, made the gods laugh.

When Amaterasu heard the rumble of laughter, she was intrigued and mildly annoyed. Why were the gods so happy when she wasn't among them? So she called out from her cave, asking what all the fuss was about.

One of the gods responded that the deities were happy because they had just discovered a goddess who was even better than Amaterasu. At this, the sun goddess couldn't contain herself anymore; she pushed away the boulder that was barring the entrance to the cave and peeked out.

The gods acted instantly; they immediately placed Amatsumara's mirror in front of Amaterasu. Dazzled at her own reflection and clearly thinking that this was the new, greater goddess, Amaterasu became distracted. The gods caught her hands and pulled her out of the cave, which was then immediately blocked, preventing her from going back in. And thus, with the help of Amatsumara's mirror, the Earth regained its sun.

Ame-no-Koyane

Ame-no-Koyane was regarded as the ancestor of two very powerful Japanese clans, the Nakatomi clan, and the Fujiwara clan. He served as the priest to the gods, tasked with the performance of Ukei, a special divination ritual. He also had a second job: To be a spiritual advisor of the Imperial Palace of Japan. It was Ame-no-Koyane who performed the ritual that caused the goddess Ame-no-Uzume-no-Mikoto to bare herself and, as a result, to cause Amaterasu to leave her cave.

Ame-no-Wakahiko

Ame-no-Wakahiko is the god of grain, to whom several interesting stories are tied. In one of them, it was said that he was sent by the gods to become the ruler of the Earth. He was supposed to report back to them as soon as he established his rule; however, when he descended on the Earth, he found a beautiful maiden there, fell in love, and forgot about everything.

Eight years passed, and the gods didn't hear back from Ame-no-Wakahiko. So, they sent a supernatural bird to look for him. When Ame-no-Wakahiko saw the bird, he shot it with his arrow; however, he didn't manage to kill it, and it still managed to fly back to the heavens, breast pierced. There, one of the gods saw the wounded bird, and pulled the arrow out of its breast; then, in anger, threw the arrow back to the Earth. By sheer bad luck, the arrow pierced Ame-no-Wakahiko in his sleep. He died on the spot.

We know the rest of the story: During Ame-no-Wakahiko's funeral, his best friend Ajisukitakahikone was confused with him, and as a result, destroyed Ame-no-Wakahiko's funerary hut. Ame-no-Wakahiko's body was transformed into Moyama mountain.

We also have another story tied to Ame-no-Wakahiko. It was written during the Muromachi Period and it's likely that its author was Emperor Go-Hanazono (1418–1471) (Satō, 2017). In this tale, the god resembles more a human man, albeit of noble standing.

The story goes as follows: Prince Ame-no-Wakahiko was a shapeshifter who had the power of transforming into a serpent. When he wished to get married, he sent a letter to a wealthy man, demanding that his three daughters were married to the serpent. This was a peculiar request, and the women had no idea that the serpent was the prince in disguise. Both the eldest and the middle daughter refused to marry him, but the youngest daughter consented.

A new house was built for the couple. It stood on a bank of a large pond where the serpent purportedly lived. When the youngest daughter went there after her marriage ceremony, the serpent emerged from the lake. The woman was scared, probably regretting her decision already; but the snake spoke to her, calming her down, and instructed her to cut off his head with a fingernail clipper.

She did as she was instructed, and suddenly, the snake shed its skin and a handsome young man emerged. He hid the snakeskin in a chest and then revealed to his bride that he was a powerful prince—and for a time, they lived happily together.

But an important errand demanded that Ame-no-Wakahiko leave his wife for a little while. He instructed her to wait for him and to never open the chest with the snakeskin; if she did, she would never see him again.

Nonetheless, the woman asked Ame-no-Wakahiko what she was supposed to do if he didn't come back for a long time. He told her to go search for him in Kyoto and buy a gourd from a woman who would know where he was.

The couple parted, and the woman waited. Her sisters visited her in the meantime, having learned that the repulsive snake which they had rejected was, in fact, a beautiful man. Now, they were envious and nagged their sister to open the box with the snakeskin. Even though she initially resisted, the woman finally caved in and opened the box.

Only smoke emerged from it; the skin wasn't inside. But the woman now knew that her husband was lost to her; so in a last desperate attempt, she decided to search for him, and set out for Kyoto.

In Kyoto, she bought the gourd as instructed; its vines allowed her to climb up to the realm of the heavens. There, she met several personified stars: The Evening Star, a comet, and the Pleiades. All of them tried to help her but didn't know who her husband was. Finally, she met a mysterious man sitting on a palanquin; he told her to seek a palace built of azure stone.

The woman found the palace. Inside, she found Ame-no-Wakahiko. But she wasn't safe there: Ame-no-Wakahiko's father was a demon (called an oni) and set out to kill the woman, so her husband had to magically turn her into various everyday objects in order to hide her.

But the demon was smart, and in the end, he found the woman out. He then set out four impossible tasks on her: To herd cattle numbering a thousand during one day and one night; to move a million grains of rice from one place to another; to spend a night in a house full of centipedes, and then, full of snakes.

The woman, however, was determined to get her husband back. With his help and his magic, she accomplished all of the tasks, outsmarting the demon. He was forced to allow the couple to see each other, but only once a year, during the Tanabata, the Japanese Star Festival (Satō, 2017). Thus, ended the story of the two tragic lovers.

Amenohoakari

Amenohoakari is the God of the sun and agriculture; he is also the deification of Nigihayahi, the chieftain who, according to the legend of Jimmu, accepted Jimmu's authority over Japan. There are no other stories about him preserved in the myths.

Amida Nyorai

Amida Nyorai, also known as Amitābha, is another Buddhist deity; a Buddha of longevity and pure perception. According to one story, during his life on earth, he used to be a monk named Dharmākara, who made a number of vows, aiming to create a pure world that would be governed by the rules of Buddhist enlightenment. In one of these vows, he promised to anyone who would call upon his name at the hour of their death, that they would be reborn in that perfect land.

So, from then on, Buddhist followers would aspire to travel to that westernmost land of bliss created by Amitābha. It was a land of many names, and full of bliss.

Amitābha is often depicted sitting in the lotus position, with hands directed outward and downward—a symbol indicating that his compassion and help could reach even the lowest of beings and save them from suffering.

Azumi-no-isora

Azumi-no-isora is a Shinto god of the seashore. He is, however, a lesser god, and would often be hired as a navigator on sea voyages—more of a supernatural helper than a deity in his own right.

Bishamonten

Bishamonten is the Japanese version of the Indian-Buddhist Vaiśravaṇa, one of the Four Heavenly Kings—gods who oversee the four cardinal directions. Bishamonten himself is the guardian of the North.

However, the Japanese version of the god acquired his own specific set of characteristics. He is worshiped as the god of war, clad in armor and with a spear in his hand. In his other hand, he would hold his symbolic treasury in the form of a small pagoda house.

Bishamonten is also believed to be one of the Seven Lucky Gods: A group of deities, (most of them originally Buddhist, but some of them had also been Chinese Taoists), who grew to be worshiped as the bringers of good luck. Initially, they were revered mostly by merchants who prayed to them to be successful in their trade transactions; however, today, everyone who feels such need could pray to them. Today, they are mostly worshiped as a group.

As one of the Seven Lucky Gods, Bishamonten is said to protect those who follow the rules, especially as pertaining to military honor. Apart from being a protector of warriors, he also defends holy places from all evil.

Daikokuten

Daikokuten, originally Mahākāla, is another god of Buddhist provenience, and one of the Seven Lucky Gods. He is the deity of good fortune and wealth. Originally a benevolent, but also a fearsome and powerful figure, his nature in Japanese tradition changed into that of an always-smiling, harmless god. Most Japanese depictions of Daikokuten show him smiling broadly. However, he is also considered a deity of ignorance and the simplicity of life that comes with it.

Daikokuten is especially tied to one of the Buddhist schools, erected by a monk by the name of Saichō (767–822). According to the legend, when he was building a monastery on the slopes of Mount Hiei (close to Kyoto), the god appeared to him in the form of an old man and offered him protection.

Over time, Daikokuten became conflated with a native Japanese god called Ōkuninushi (of whom we'll speak later). Both gods were depicted carrying a sack on their shoulders, most likely full of riches, and both were also, to some extent, considered gods of fertility. But sometimes, especially in folk religion, Daikokuten would be identified with the handicapped god Hiruko/Ebisu.

Unsurprisingly, Daikokuten reached his biggest popularity among the merchants, who would pray to him for good fortune in their endeavors.

Daruma

Daruma, or Bodhidharma, is the deified founder of Zen Buddhism. He is also credited with bringing a version of Buddhism into China, from where it transferred to Japan—no wonder his importance is really great. He lived in the 5th or 6th century C.E. In China, numerous legends are tied to his biography.

In Japan, Daruma became an inspiration for the so-called Daruma dolls: Round dolls made of papier-mâché, painted in bright colors (although the most popular one is red), with blank eyes which their owner is later encouraged to fill in one by one when they complete a task they set out for themselves (Punsmann, 1962). They are often gifted as a symbol of good luck, but, as might be expected, they also serve as motivation on a very human level which has nothing to do with divine intervention: Every time the doll's owner looks at the halfway-filled eyes, they are reminded of their goal.

The explanation behind the ties of a legless doll to Daruma is that, according to the legend, the monk had once sat in meditation for nine years straight, which caused his arms and legs to atrophy and fall off. Despite that extraordinary lack of awareness of bodily needs, Daruma still, however, kept falling asleep as he meditated; so after nine years, he cut off his eyelids to prevent himself from doing so—hence the doll's blank eyes.

Ebisu

We have already mentioned Ebisu/Hiruko—the handicapped first son of Izanagi and Izanami. Although he is of native Japanese origin, as a result of later Buddhist influence, he was numbered amongst the Seven Lucky Gods—the only Shinto deity to undergo such transformation.

According to the legend, when Izanagi and Izanami found out that their son was boneless and sent him adrift to the sea, he was washed ashore near Ezo (modern-day Hokkaidō), where he was cared for by the Ainu: The indigenous people from that region.

When Ebisu was three, a miracle happened: He grew his bones (or, according to different versions of the legend, his arms, and legs). He was still slightly deaf, but his life on the seashore, among the Ainu, seemed to be full of joy: He became known as "the Laughing God" and a patron of fishermen. Perhaps because of his initial handicap, Ebisu is associated with jellyfish.

Even today, among the fishing communities in Japan, a prayer to Ebisu before a day's work is commonplace. It is believed that he sometimes transforms into a shark and keeps the ocean calm and clean by washing ashore any debris. If someone pollutes the sea, Ebisu becomes enraged.

But Ebisu also has other tasks. Along with Daikokuten, he is worshiped as a patron of shopkeepers. As such, he is even sometimes depicted as Daikokuten's twin or son and apprentice.

Fudō Myōō

Fudō Myōō is a wrathful Buddhist god, one of the Wisdom Kings. Initially known in the Indian Sanskrit tradition as Acala, he became one of the most prominent deities for numerous Japanese Buddhist sects. He is depicted as a blue- or black-skinned man sitting in the lotus position, holding a lasso and a sword, with a fierce, angry expression on his face. His eyes are mismatched and he has two fangs, one directed upwards and one downwards. It's a symbol of the duality of the universe and human existence: The fang facing upwards signifies a soul's path towards enlightenment, while the one facing downwards is a path of the deities who descend on the earth to teach the people the way of true wisdom.

From his very introduction to Japan at the beginning of the 9th century, Fudō Myōō became an important deity who would be invoked as a protector of the state. His popularity grew rapidly and soon, he became the most important of all the Wisdom Kings in Japan.

Despite his fearsome appearance, it is believed that Fudō Myōō can rescue individuals, as well as the whole state, from all evil. Many miraculous stories about him delivering his worshipers from danger have been told since his introduction to Japan.

Fūjin

Fūjin, the demon-god of the wind, is one of the eldest Shinto gods (Roberts, 2010). He and his brother Raijin, the god of lightning, are believed to have emerged from Izanami's body after she died. She took the pair of them to Yomi, the Underworld, where they clung to her decaying body; but when Izanagi went to Yomi in an attempt to become reunited with his wife, and subsequently fled from there, horrified by her sight, Fūjin and Raijin escaped into the world.

Fūjin is depicted most often as a green-skinned demon with a terrifying expression and an outstretched windbag over his head.

Fukurokuju

Fukurokuju is one of the Seven Lucky Gods. However, he wasn't originally borrowed from the Sanskrit tradition, but from the Chinese Taoist star god Shou, who was believed to have been a human before his incarnation into a god: A hermit who could live without eating.

Fukurokuju is both the god of the stars—especially of the southern polar star—and of wisdom and longevity. He is depicted as an old bald man with long whiskers and an extremely elongated forehead, with his additional attributes being a crane and a turtle—both symbols of longevity.

Hachiman

Hachiman, or Yahata, is a result of the mixing of Shinto and Buddhist traditions: Although initially he was believed to be an incarnation of the legendary Emperor Ōjin (270–310), his cult was incorporated into Buddhist temples after the arrival of Buddhism in Japan.

The history surrounding Emperor Ōjin's life is a part of Japan's legendary history described in Kojiki and Nihon Shoki. He was supposed to have been birthed by Empress Jingū after she had invaded the Korean Peninsula, during which time he remained in her womb for three years. Those years might symbolize three harvests, as later, as Hachiman, Ōjin became the god of fertility (Aston, 2013).

As the deification of Emperor Ōjin, Hachiman also became the divine ancestor and patron of the Imperial Family. After the arrival of Buddhism in Japan, he joined the Buddhist pantheon as the protector of the state.

Traditionally, Emperor Ōjin was also regarded as the ancestor of a warrior clan of the Minamoto. They took him as their patron, and thus, Hachiman became revered by the samurai class. Over time, however, his cult spread to the peasantry and to other social classes—and as a result, today, Hachiman's shrines are numerous and his cult is very popular.

Haniyasu no kami

Haniyasu no kami is a term referring to two gods, Haniyasu-hiko and Haniyasu-hime, who are both deities of pottery and clay. There are conflicting accounts pertaining to their birth: One tradition says that they were born out of clay that was left after Izanagi and Izanami created the Japanese archipelago; another, that they were both out of Izanami's feces after her death (Ashkenazi, 2008).

Idaten

Idaten, also known as Skanda, is another Buddhist god, the guardian of Buddhist monks and their monasteries. He originated from the Chinese Buddhist pantheon, where he was believed to have been a virtuous king who always followed the Buddha's teachings, and was tasked to protect the temples in his stead when Buddha attained nirvana.

Inari Ōkami

Inari Ōkami is perhaps one of the most popular Shinto gods. He is a patron of numerous concepts: Fertility and agriculture on one hand and industry on the other; he also presides over rice, tea, and sake, the traditional Japanese alcoholic drink. But most importantly, he is the patron of foxes, who are important animals in Japanese tradition, often representations of spirits and divine beings, as we will see in the following chapters.

Although Inari Ōkami is often referred to as a male god, he can also be depicted in a female form, or in an androgynous one—perhaps a result of the conflation of three separate deities. The preferred gender under which Inari Ōkami is depicted varies depending on a region, or on a person's individual beliefs. All in all, Inari is a very universal deity that caters to all demographics and social groups.

Inari Ōkami's attested worship started around the 8th century, though it could have been earlier by as many as 300 years (Smyers, 1996). Since the 9th century, his worship began to spread and was closely tied to the kitsune—foxes with paranormal abilities, whom we will talk about in Chapter 6.

During the Edo Period, Inari Ōkami's worship as a god bringing luck was popular in Shinto as well as in Buddhism; however, as the attempts to separate and 'purify' both religions became stronger, there were some attempts to remove his shrines from Buddhist temples.

Today, the shrines of Inari are one of the most popular ones in Japan. The entrance to an Inari shrine would most often be marked by red torii, a traditional T-shaped gate. The offerings most often left at the shrines would include rice, sake, and sushi rolls with fried tofu.

One of the most important Inari shrines is located in Kyoto, on a mountain that got its name from the god. The Fushimi Inari Shrine sees numerous pilgrims every year. The pilgrimage usually starts at the foot of the mountain and is preceded by ritual purification with water.

Izanagi

Having mentioned the creator god at length already, let us focus on the part of the story yet untold: How Izanagi fled from Yomi and what happened later. Izanami, embarrassed by having been shamed by Izanagi, sent a number of thunder gods to chase after him as he was running away, but Izanagi managed to distract them: He disentangled a comb and a vine that were keeping his hair together and threw them at the gods. The objects turned into grapes and bamboo shoots. The gods stopped and ate them.

But the pursuit wasn't over. The gods caught up with Izanagi yet again at a mountain pass. This time, Izanagi threw peaches at them, and finally managed to repel them. This led to the god declaring the peach to be a sacred fruit and ordering it to be grown among humans, so that it may help them in their hour of need.

In the end, Izanagi blocked the entrance to Yomi with a huge rock. Izanami, furious at this, declared her intention of killing a thousand people every day to avenge her shame. Izanagi replied that he could create a thousand and more each day, to undo her destruction.

Now came the time for Izanagi to purify himself, having had so much contact with death. He washed himself in the river and that was when, according to one tradition, his previous children with Izanami finally came to this world: When he washed his left eye, the sun goddess Amaterasu came out of it; when he washed the right eye, the moon god Tsukuyomi-no-Mikoto emerged; and finally, when he washed his nose, he produced the storm god Susanoo-no-Mikoto.

Then, Izanagi decided to divide the world among his three children. The Takamagahara, the first Heaven that arose out of the chaos, was given to Amaterasu; Tsukuyomi received the night; and Susanoo was given the seas. But Susanoo wasn't happy with his gift and he kept raging and crying out, causing storms and drying up rivers, and demanding from Izanagi to be dispatched to his mother. Izanagi, furious, finally expelled him from the world.

Here, the narrative of Izanagi ends.

Jizō

Jizō, who comes from the Sanskrit tradition, was originally a Bodhisattva named Kṣitigarbha. In Japanese tradition, he is the protector of all the vulnerable, including children and expectant mothers, as well as travelers. For this reason, his statues can be found by the roadsides and close to graveyards.

Jizō also protects the souls of deceased children, including aborted and miscarried fetuses. The souls of the children are said to be delegated to endlessly construct small towers out of stones, which are repeatedly toppled by demons; Jizō is said to protect the children from the demons and to comfort them, hiding them under his cloak.

Around 1600, a tale called *The Tale of the Fuji Cave* was composed (Kimbrough, 2006); in it, the deceased children were building a stone tower, but the demons sent violent winds and flames in order to thwart them. The flames reduced the children's bodies to ash and charred bones, which were then received by Jizō, who built them back to be whole and that is how they received their eternal happiness.

Because of these legends, the statues of Jizō and his shrines are often surrounded by small piles of stones, sometimes dressed in tiny children's clothes. Those are the offerings of the bereaved parents who lost their children, hoping that Jizō would receive them and comfort them after their death.

Jurōjin

Jurōjin is another one of the Seven Lucky Gods, and another who was originally a Chinese Taoist; similarly to Fukurokuju, he might have been influenced by the Chinese god of the southern polar star. He is the God of longevity since before he became a god, he was supposed to have been a man who lived on earth for 1,500 years.

Jurōjin is often portrayed as a small, smiling old man with a staff and a fan, and is accompanied by a deer, a symbol of longevity. Paintings and statues of Jurōjin are believed to bring their owner good luck.

Kagutsuchi

Kagutsuchi is the feral child that caused the tragedy between Izanagi and Izanami: The god of fire whose birth brought Izanami's demise. His subsequent murder by Izanagi and the creation of various gods and volcanoes out of the mutilated parts of his body marked the beginning of death in the world.

Kangiten

Kangiten, or Shōten, is another Buddhist god (known as a deva), who originated in the Indian Sanskrit tradition, where he is known as Ganesha. Kangiten is a very dualistic god: On one hand, he creates obstacles for those who try to attain enlightenment; despite being a god, he is still governed by earthly desires and very quick to be angry at those who offended him. On the other hand, he can be very helpful to people who have a special connection to him and can grant even wishes which seem impossible. Overall, Kangiten's perception as he was adopted from India through China and to Japan, changed from that of an almost-demon to a god who can battle demons.

Interestingly, Kangiten's depictions aren't kept public. His image is considered to be too sacred to be seen even by his monks, with only a select few being allowed to see them after training and having performed special rituals. We know, however, the way Kangiten is portrayed: As a dual male-female person, both of them with an elephant's head, embracing, but in a non-sexual way. It is a curious image, not found anywhere outside of East Asia; it might represent the god embracing his shakti, that is, his primordial essence (Agrawala, 1978).

Because of the mysteriousness of Kangiten's image, in the Heian Period, his cult was reserved only for the imperial court and banned from private worship. As a destroyer of demons, Kangiten was invoked in rituals of subjugation; according to a legend, when a vengeful spirit of a scholar, poet, and statesman Sugawara no Michizane (845–903), who would later become the god Tenjin, was bringing storms to the land, a monk prayed to Kangiten who managed to pacify the angry ghost.

During the Edo Period, Kangiten's worship gradually spread, even though it still remained somewhat esoteric. Some attempts were made over the years to slow down this process, with some priests emphasizing Kangiten's more destructive, demonic side in order to prevent common people from treating him like a god who could grant each and every wish. But, nonetheless, the cult spread.

In one Japanese legend, Kangiten used to be an angry demon who lived under a legendary Mount Vinayaka, known as the "Elephant-headed Mountain" or the "Mountain of Obstacles" (Faure, 2015). From there, he commanded an army of demons, destroying the humans. There was only one way to tame him: The bodhisattva of compassion, Kannon, assumed a very enticing female form and came before Kangiten. The demon immediately fell in love. But she had one condition: He had to convert to Buddhism if they were to be married. He agreed, leaving behind his evilness, and she embraced him and led him toward bliss.

Konjin

Konjin is the Shinto god of metals, associated with the directions on the compass. He is closely tied to Onmyōdō, a system of Japanese science and divination based on the principles of Chinese philosophy: The working of the five elements in accordance with the belief in yin and yang, the opposing, but also interconnecting, forces.

Because encountering Konjin was believed to be a sign of bad luck—the god could be very violent and fond of hurling curses at people—a system of geomancy was developed in order to establish Konjin's position, which depended on a year, a lunar month, and season. Geomancy is a special form of divination that uses the energies of the earth in order to harmonize a person with their environment. In Chinese philosophy and religion, it is known as feng shui; in Japan, a katatagae. A special calendar was developed based on these practices, which allowed people to avoid Konjin on any given day of the year. This calendar was especially popular during the Heian Period and would be consulted when moving a house, traveling, and undertaking public works.

Kōjin

Kōjin is the god of fire and the hearth, and sometimes even, specifically, of the stove and the kitchen. He is of ambivalent nature: On one hand, a deity of destructive fire, on the other, a symbol of the subjugation of the said destruction in the family hearth. Because of that, a tablet with his depiction would be kept near the hearth—or, in a more modern household, in the kitchen.

Kōjin is said to burn away all impurity. He also watches over households and reports any evildoers to his superior, a god of a particular village, town, or city. The Shinto gods being very diligent governors of the land—a better version of a human government—would then convene in Izumo Province, during the tenth month of the Japanese lunar calendar, when they would discuss all the human misdeeds and decide upon punishments.

Kuebiko

Kuebiko is a very folk saint: A patron of agriculture, knowledge, and folk wisdom whose form is that of a scarecrow. Kuebiko can't walk, but can talk and impart wisdom to those who ask him for advice. In the *Kojiki*, only Kuebiko knew the true name of another god, a dwarf who would later become a helper of Ōkuninushi, an important kami of whom we will speak in a bit.

Today, Kuebiko is worshiped not only as a patron of folk wisdom but also of scholarship in general.

Kukunochi

Kukunochi is the god of trees. He might have initially been a spirit of trees who lived inside them. In some versions of the myths, he was a child of Izanagi and Izanami. Today, he is evoked in a ceremony of blessing new houses.

Kuraokami

As already mentioned, Kuraokami is the dragon-god of ice who was born out of the parts of Kagutsuchi's body mixed with Izanagi's tears. He lives in the mountains and brings rain and snow to the world. Alternatively, he might be a water snake who lives in deep waters.

Kuraokami has his own shrines where he is worshiped during the dry times of the year.

Nesaku

Nesaku is a star god who, according to some versions of the myth, was created from the blood of Kagutsuchi when his father Izanagi murdered him.

Ninigi-no-Mikoto

Ninigi-no-Mikoto is very important to the foundation myth of Japan; as a grandson of Amaterasu, he was also the great-grandfather of Emperor Jimmu. He is said to have descended from Heaven to the earth, bringing treasures with him: Later, they would become the regalia of the Japanese Imperial Family. The treasures were: The legendary sword Kusanagi no Tsurugi; a mirror called Yata no Kagami; and a jewel Yasakani no Magatama. The sword was the symbol of valor, the mirror—of wisdom, and the jewel—of benevolence. The same mirror is said to have been later used to lure Amaterasu out of her cave when she hid.

The regalia are said to have been kept by the Imperial Family of Japan until 1185 when the sword was lost during a civil war, during a battle fought at sea (Turnbull, 2006). A replica was supposed to be then forged (Selinger, 2013). To this day, the presentation of the regalia is a crucial element of the ceremony of the enthronement of the new emperor. The items are kept in sealed containers and are only seen by the emperor and chosen priests during a ceremony, which is not public (Holland & Kobayashi, n.d.). Even the location of the items outside of the ceremony is not certain, and any attempts to examine their archaeological value are rejected (Holland & Kobayashi, n.d.).

But let us come back to Ninigi-no-Mikoto. After he'd been sent to bring order to the earth, he built his palace on the top of Mount Takachiho on the island of Kyushu. He also started looking for a wife. The god of the mountain where he settled presented his two daughters to him as prospective brides: Konohanasakuya-hime and Iwanaga-hime. Ninigi chose Konohanasakuya and rejected Iwanaga, for which she cursed him, taking away his immortality. And thus, the line of the gods would gradually become the line of humans, living shorter and shorter lives.

Ninigi and Konohanasakuya had three sons, the youngest of whom, Hoori, would become Jimmu's grandfather.

Ōkuninushi

Ōkuninushi is one of the most important gods in the chronicles of *Kojiki* and *Nihon Shoki*. He, along with his numerous brothers, is the son of the god of storms Susanoo, and through him, the grandson of Izanagi and Izanami. He was the original ruler of the earth before Ninigi-no-Mikoto was sent by Amaterasu to replace him.

As the ruler of the earth, Ōkuninushi resided in the Izumo Province, and his eventual subjugation might have been a symbol of the subjugation of the said province in 250 C.E. (Palmer, 2016).

There are numerous myths tied to Ōkuninushi. First of them is a famous folk story known as *The Hare of Inaba* (Antoni, 2015). It was written down in the *Kojiki* and tells a tale of a feud between the clan of hares and the clan of sharks. The conflict led to a brutal war; at last, there was only one shark and one hare left, and the hare hopped over the shark, trying to trick him. But the shark snapped at the hare and flayed him from his fur.

Enter Ōkuninushi, who was passing by the area with his brothers—they were all going to woo the princess of the region of Inaba. The hare, being in enormous pain, asked the god and his brothers for help. But the brothers were cruel and advised the hare to wash himself in the salty seawater, and later, to lay on the shore in order to dry up. Unsurprisingly, this caused the poor hare even more pain.

But when Ōkuninushi saw the hare's suffering, he gave him good advice: To wash in fresh spring water and to later roll in the pollen of cattails, which resemble fur. Thus, the hare's fur was restored. Ōkuninushi now revealed his true nature as a god to the hare and the hare blessed him in return, promising him that he would be the one to win his princess' hand.

But that is not where the story ends. Ōkuninushi won the princess, but his brothers were furious about this. They devised a plot to kill him: First, they took him to the Hoki Province and forced him, on the pain of death, to catch a wild red boar. There was only one problem: The supposed prey wasn't a boar at all, but a large rock heated up to hotness so much so that it was red, and hurled down the hill by the brothers.

Ōkuninushi burnt himself so much that he died, but his mother petitioned the gods so that they would bring him a new life. The gods relented and brought Ōkuninushi back to life, making him even stronger and more handsome.

So, the brothers devised a second plan: They tricked him into a trap. He walked onto a tree log that had been split open, but the moment he jumped into the opening, they snapped it shut, killing him a second time.

Yet again, Ōkuninushi's mother managed to restore his life, but this time, she advised him to escape to the Kii Province, on the southern shores of the Japanese archipelago. Only there he would be safe from his brothers. There, he would also be able to find his father, Susanoo, and receive counsel from him.

Ōkuninushi did as he was instructed. But before he found Susanoo, he happened upon his daughter and his half-sister, Suseribime. When he saw her, he immediately fell in love with her—something that was not to his father's liking. So, Susanoo laid four challenges on his son.

First, he invited Ōkuninushi to his palace, where he ordered him to sleep in a room full of snakes. Fortunately, Suseribime had a magical scarf that she gave to Ōkuninushi; when he wrapped himself in it, he was safe from the snake's venom.

Then, Susanoo put Ōkuninushi in a room full of centipedes and bees; but the scarf protected him from them as well.

Seeing that his challenges were no match for Ōkuninushi, Susanoo devised a different plan: He shot an arrow over a field and ordered Ōkuninushi to fetch it. But unbeknownst to him, he set the whole field on fire.

Seeing the flames rising all around him, Ōkuninushi was near despair; but suddenly, he saw a little field mouse. The animal led him quickly to a hole where he could hide and escape the fire. Later, when the flames died down, the mouse also fetched the arrow for him.

Susanoo, now seriously wanting to humiliate his son, summoned him to his palace again. There, he ordered him to comb through his hair and pick out the lice and centipedes that lived there. Ōkuninushi obediently did so, but as he was going, he also covered his father's head with a special paste prepared by Suseribime. It tangled the hair and caused Susanoo to fall asleep. When he did, Ōkuninushi tied his hair to the rafters that were keeping his palace together. Then, he stole his father's bow and arrows, as well as his koto (a stringed musical instrument), took Suseribime with him, and fled the palace.

As they were running away, Ōkuninushi accidentally brushed Susanoo's koto over tree bark. The instrument made a noise that woke his father up; as he lifted his head, the rafters to which his hair had been tied gave way and the whole palace fell down on his head. Injured and furious, but not dead, Susanoo then pursued the couple to the very borders of Yomi, the Underworld.

But as he saw that his son was constantly outrunning him, Susanoo finally had to reluctantly give him the blessing to marry Suseribime. Then, he declared him the lord of the land of the living, whom he remained up until Ninigi-no-Mikoto replaced him.

There is a number of other tales tied to Ōkuninushi. He is said to have wooed many goddesses and to have won them through his gift of poetry, but this made Suseribime very jealous. Ōkuninushi was close to leaving her, but she also persuaded him to stay with her with a song, and so, the couple was reunited.

When he was staying with Suseribime in Izumo, Ōkuninushi one day saw a tiny god sailing on the sea in a bean pod. Ōkuninushi asked the stranger his name, but he received no reply. He then tried to ask around for the man's identity, but without success—until a toad told him to ask Kuebiko, the scarecrow god of wisdom. Kuebiko told Ōkuninushi that this was Sukunabikona-no-Kami, a god of healing. Knowing his name, Ōkuninushi was able to form an alliance with the other god, who soon became his companion and close friend. From then on, they would rule the earth together.

At last, the time has come for Ōkuninushi to give up his rule. The sun goddess Amaterasu sent a number of messengers to Ōkuninushi, but all of them either didn't report back or became distracted with other matters. One of them was Ame-no-Wakahiko, the God of grain whose subsequent death and funeral we have already talked about. At last, the god of thunder, Takemikazuchi-no-Kami, was sent to Ōkuninushi and, after winning strength contests with his sons, managed to persuade Ōkuninushi to cease his control over the earth.

Omoikane

Omoikane is the god of wisdom and intelligence. The gods would often ask him for counsel—for example, when the sun goddess Amaterasu hid in a cave, it was Omoikane who came up with a solution.

Oshirasama

Oshirasama is the protective god of the home. Sometimes, he would enter a person's house, and it is believed that when it happens, men in the house cannot eat meat and only women are allowed to touch it.

Oshirasama is a half-person, half-horse.

Ōyamatsumi

Ōyamatsumi is one of the gods who were born from Kagutsuchi's mutilated body. He is the deity of mountains, sea, and war. He was also the father of Konohanasakuya-hime and Iwanaga-hime, the two young women who were offered to Ninigi-no-Mikoto in marriage. It was through Ōyamatsumi's divine power that Iwanaga-hime cursed Ninigi-no-Mikoto with a shortened lifespan after he rejected her as his bride.

Raijin

Raijin is the violent god of lightning who emerged from Izanami's body after her death. His very characteristic depiction features him as a muscular, half-naked man with a terrifying expression on his face and hair flowing in the air. His attributes are taiko drums, traditional Japanese percussion instruments—it is believed that he plays them in order to create thunder. In depictions and in worship, Raijin is often paired with his brother Fūjin.

In the most famous myth featuring Raijin, he emerged from Izanami's rotting body when she was already in Yomi. Different aspects of Raijin arose from different parts of Izanami's body, and when Izanagi saw this, he was terrified. As the god was fleeing from the Underworld, Raijin, and other demon-gods pursued him. From that point onward, Raijin would rage and cause mischief in the world.

Another story tells how Raijin was captured. He caused a massive storm, so big in fact that the emperor sent his messenger to capture him. The messenger first tried to persuade Raijin to come willingly; but when this failed and Raijin laughed in the messenger's face, he prayed to the bodhisattva of compassion, Kannon, who finally managed to capture Raijin. The god of thunder was then delivered to the emperor in a sack. The emperor promised that he would let him go, but only if from now on, he only brought rain and fertility to Japan, and not violent storms. Raijin promised and was let go; and in the future, indeed, he was less destructive, unless it was against Japan's enemies. It is said that when the Mongols invaded Japan in the 13th century, Raijin repelled them with his storms.

Ryūjin

Ryūjin is another one of the Japanese dragon-gods. He is the tutelary deity of the sea, representing the devouring nature of the ocean through his large mouth. However, over the timespan of Japanese history, the sea has been a source of life and food more often than it was a destructive force—hence, Ryūjin is considered a positive god and a patron of Japan. His storm was supposed to have drowned the Mongol fleet in the 13th century.

But Ryūjin also has the power to change into a human and, apparently, also possesses the knowledge of medicine.

There are several stories tied to Ryūjin; one of them is an origin story of how the jellyfish lost their bones. It is told that one day, Ryūjin had a very particular craving for a monkey's liver. So, he sent his servant, a jellyfish, to get him a monkey.

But the monkey was more clever than the jellyfish: When the jellyfish caught up with it, it said that it kept its liver in a special jar in the forest and had first to go and fetch it. The gullible jellyfish agreed, and thus, the monkey got away. When Ryūjin heard about this, he was so angry that he beat the jellyfish repeatedly, crushing all its bones.

Another story tells how Ryūjin was able to control the high and low tides with special jewels, called kanju and manju. The legend says that the god helped Empress Jingū in her attack on Korea, manipulating the tides with those jewels. Jingū first threw the kanju into the sea when she saw the Korean navy; it allowed the sea to recede, stranding the Korean fleet in the sand. The crew had no choice but to leave the ships; but then, the empress threw the manju, and the sea came back with double force, drowning the Koreans.

Seidai Myōjin

Seidai Myōjin is the god of sports. He is vastly popular to this day, worshiped especially in the Shiramine Shrine in Kyoto as the patron of football and kemari, the traditional Japanese version of football.

Shōtoku Taishi

Shōtoku Taishi, also known as Prince Shōtoku, was initially a semi-historical, semi-legendary figure. He was supposed to have lived between 574 and 622 C.E. and was a regent under Empress Suiko of the Asuka Period. During his time, he was a famed reformer of the administration and one of the first promoters of Buddhism. He ordered the construction of one of the first Buddhist temples, the Shitennō-ji in modern-day Osaka. He was also, famously, one of the first people to call the Japanese archipelago "the land of the rising sun," which he did in his letter to the Chinese emperor (Varley, 1977).

Over the years, a number of legends arose around Prince Shōtoku, and he eventually came to be worshiped as a god. According to one of the legends, when the sage-god Daruma came to Japan, he met Prince Shōtoku. Daruma was dressed as a beggar and refused to give his name to the prince, but Shōtoku gave him food and drink anyway. He also gifted Daruma with a purple cloak and sang as he was sleeping.

The next day, the beggar died. Shōtoku was sad and ordered his burial; but after some time, it was discovered that the man's coffin was empty and only the folded purple cloak lay inside. The prince retrieved the garment; he now knew that he had met a great sage.

Shōtoku is a very popular figure in Japan to this day, and a number of institutions have been named after him. He also appeared on coins and banknotes.

Suijin

Suijin is the god of water of a benevolent kind: He lives in rivers, streams, lakes, wells, and waterfalls. He is the guardian of the fishermen. On the other hand, through his ties to water, he is also the god of fertility, and by association, of motherhood and childbirth. He was often worshiped by people who wanted to provide fresh water and the right sanitary conditions for expectant mothers.

Suijin is worshiped in a number of shrines and during a variety of religious festivals. Most of these festivals are tied to agriculture, as it is a custom to pray to Sujin to ensure enough water for the crops, or to bring bounty to the fishermen. Expectant mothers also pray to Suijin for a safe delivery—and everyone prays to him for deliverance from drowning.

Sukunabikona

Sukunabikona is the god of hot springs, sake brewing, healing, magic, agriculture, and knowledge. He is the tiny partner and friend of Ōkuninushi who helped him build and govern the land of Japan. It is said that he invented cures for the most common illnesses, as well as protection spells, in order to help Ōkuninushi with his governing. He was especially efficient with his help against insect and snake bites.

But Sukunabikona himself wasn't impervious to illnesses. One day, he fell sick. To cure him, Ōkuninushi took him to a hot spring in Dōgo Onsen (today's city of Matsuyama). He put Sukunabikona into the spring and then fell asleep. When he awoke, his friend was completely cured and he was dancing on the stones near the spring—an act that left imprints in the stone, which are visible to this day.

Ōkuninushi and Sukunabikona's partnership ended when one day, Sukunabikona climbed the millet crop; it dipped under his weight and then rebounded, flinging him all the way to the Underworld. Ōkuninushi was very sad after the disappearance of his friend.

Sumiyoshi sanjin

The Sumiyoshi sanjin are a pair of two gods, Sokotsutsu no O no Mikoto, and Nakatsutsu no O no Mikoto—gods of the sea and sailing. They might also be a personification of the Orion stars. According to an alternative version of the legend, both gods were born when Izanagi purified himself after his visit to Yomi.

Susanoo-no-Mikoto

Finally, we come to the famous god of storms, the brother of Amaterasu and Tsukuyomi, the son of Izanagi and Izanami, and the wrathful father of Ōkuninushi. Susanoo-no-Mikoto is both a turbulent, angry god of storms and a hero who is credited with battling many monsters. There are numerous stories tied to him in Japanese chronicles and legends, and some of them we have already told, but let us complete this picture.

One version of the legend about the birth of Tsukuyomi, Amaterasu, and Susanoo said that Susanoo was immediately expelled from the earth by Izanagi due to his violent nature. Of course, he was not content with that state of affairs and tried to come back. Upon the pretext of saying one last goodbye to Amaterasu, he ascended the Takamagahara, making the heavens shake and cry out.

Amaterasu, though she was suspicious of Susanoo's intentions, agreed to meet him. Susanoo then proposed that they both participate in a ritual that would prove his good intentions: Ukehi, a trial by pledge. Each participant was supposed to chew and spit out an object brought by the other person entering the pledge.

Susanoo gave Amaterasu his sword; she broke it into three parts, chewed them, and spat them out. Three goddesses were formed from those parts. Then, she gave Susanoo her necklace which he broke into five parts, chewed, and spat out—and thus, five gods were born. Then, Amaterasu declared that the gods, since they were born out of her necklace, belonged to her, and the goddesses belonged to Susanoo.

Susanoo's good intentions were proven, and he roared in victory. Now, he could declare his true intentions: He started ravaging Amaterasu's rice fields and defiled her palace. Furious, Amaterasu fled from the heavens and hid in a cave—a start to the story we already know. For his transgressions, Susanoo was thrown from the heavens forever.

There are many stories about Susanoo and his exploits during his banishment. He killed a goddess who produced food from the orifices in her body and replenished the earth's food supply; but more importantly, he encountered Yamata no Orochi, a monstrous serpent. In Izumo province, that giant snake had devoured all seven daughters of an elderly couple whom Susanoo met on his way—and the time was coming when the eighth daughter, Kushinadahime, would also be killed and eaten.

Susanoo promised the distressed parents that he would kill the snake. To do this, he transformed himself into a comb which Kushinadahime then put in her hair. When the serpent approached, the daughter, as instructed, offered him a drink of a particularly strong sake, pretending that it was a gift. The snake guzzled it all down and fell asleep, drunk. Then Susanoo turned back into his mighty form and killed the monster.

He then proceeded to hack the serpent's body into pieces. But when he struck the tail, his sword broke. He hacked some more with a broken sword until he heard a metallic sound: A weapon was hidden in the serpent's tail. Susanoo took it out; it was a magnificent sword which Susanoo named Kusanagi no Tsurugi; later, he would use it as a reconciliatory gift when he met his sister Amaterasu again; and Amaterasu would gift the sword to Ninigi-no-Mikoto—and thus, it would become a part of the Imperial Regalia of Japan.

Having killed the serpent, Susanoo wanted to erect his palace in Izumo. He appointed Kushinadahime's father as his steward and married Kushinadahime. Later, he would also marry other women and have many children with them—one of them Ōkuninushi, though some accounts say that he was only his descendant and not his direct son. The incident with Ōkuninushi which we have already described also took place around the palace that Susanoo had erected in Izumo.

As we can see, there is much contradiction in Susanoo's image: A disruptor of peace and a troublemaker on one hand, and a noble slayer of a serpent on the other. There is some evidence to suggest that he was originally a Korean god, imported to Japan; and perhaps that is one of the reasons why his image is so ambiguous (Gadaleva, 2000).

Tajimamori

Tajimamori is a legendary hero from the Kofun Period, who lived during the reign of Emperor Suinin (ca. 29 B.C.E.–70 C.E.); but today, he is worshiped as the god of sweets.

According to the legend, Emperor Suinin ordered Tajimamori to get him a magical fruit—most likely a tachibana orange. In order to do this, the hero set out on a ten-year-long journey, but when he returned with the fruit, the emperor was already dead. Tajimamori gave half of the fruit to his widow; the other half he put on the emperor's grave. Then, he sat by the grave and cried in sadness; soon, he died there out of grief.

After his death, Tajimamori became associated with the fruit he carried and, by association, also with sweets. Today, he is worshiped by the confectioners and producers of sweets.

Takemikazuchi

Takemikazuchi is the god of thunder, one of the gods who emerged from Kagutsuchi's body. He would often be sent by the gods from heaven to the earth in order to subdue the earthly gods, among them Ōkuninushi. Takemikazuchi battled and subdued his sons, which forced Ōkuninushi to relinquish his control. His combat with Takeminakata, in which he crushed his hand, became the first ever known instance of sumo wrestling.

Years later, when Emperor Jimmu was conquering Japan, an old man came to him with a mighty sword. When Jimmu asked him what the weapon was, he said that he had had a dream in which the gods wanted to send Takemikazuchi to subdue the earth yet again. But the god of thunder said that this time, only his sword in Jimmu's hand would be sufficient to conquer Japan. And indeed, the sword instantly cut all of Jimmu's enemies.

Takeminakata

Takeminakata, the god who fought with Takemikazuchi, is the deity of wind, water, hunting, warfare, and agriculture. Historically, he was especially worshiped by the samurai.

He was believed to have been an ancestor of the Suwa clan and is now worshiped in the Suwa Grand Shrine next to Lake Suwa in Nagano Prefecture.

Takeminakata's defeat by Takemikazuchi is depicted as rather shameful in *Kojiki* (Philippi, 1968). There, Takeminakata begged for his life after Takemikazuchi crushed his arm. But in other versions of the myth, it was portrayed as more of a noble defeat; in those versions, Takeminakata was thrown to the ground, as it befitted a first-ever sumo wrestling (von Krenner, 2013).

After his defeat by Takemikazuchi, Takeminakata traveled the land, where he had a number of adventures, most of which involved fighting with divine opponents in a similar style as he did with the messenger from heaven. Most notably, he defeated Moriya, a local god from the Suwa Prefecture. For that, he was besieged by Moriya's compatriots, but some of the people from Suwa swore allegiance to him. Thus, he became the first king of the Suwa and the ancestor of the Suwa clan.

Later, as the king of Suwa, Takeminakata was often portrayed as a god who had the ability to turn into a water serpent.

Tamanoya

Tamanoya is the god of jewelry, most specifically, of the Magatama beads from the Kofun Period. These were tear- or comma-shaped beads made of jade, very characteristic of the era. In the myth about Amaterasu and Susanoo exchanging gifts as a part of their pledge, Amaterasu's necklace was made of Magatama beads.

Ta-no-Kami

Ta-no-Kami is primarily the god of the farmers, as he is believed to preside over the rice harvest. He is worshiped mainly in spring and autumn when the rice is subsequently planted and harvested. Although there are different ceremonies depending on the region, most of them feature dances and eating rice cakes.

Similarly to Kuebiko, a scarecrow is often believed to be Ta-no-Kami's representation. In this form, he repeals the spirits of violent animals and birds from the fields.

Tenjin

Tenjin, the god of scholars and learning, is another example of a historical figure who became deified. Contrary to most of them, however, the earthly form of Tenjin—the politician, scholar, and poet Sugawara no Michizane (845–903)—wasn't only a legendary figure, but definitely a historical one.

As a politician, Sugawara was a governor of the Sanuki Province who came into conflict with the powerful Fujiwara clan, which ultimately led to his banishment and death in exile. As a poet, he was renowned for his works both in Chinese and Japanese.

However, Tenjin's first emergence as a god wasn't tied to his poetry and scholarship. In 930, 17 years after Sugawara's death in exile, Kyoto was struck by a series of lightning and heavy rain, as well as a plague. During these events, many members of the Fujiwara clan died and their houses were destroyed; soon, this was interpreted as a sign that Sugawara's angry spirit was enacting revenge from behind the grave. To pacify him, Sugawara's titles and offices were posthumously destroyed and the edict of his banishment was burned; furthermore, a cult of Tenjin, "the Sky Deity," was established (Pawasarat, 2020).

Over the years, however, Tenjin was less remembered for his anger and more for the poetry he composed during his lifetime. During the Edo Period, his works were widely commented on and renowned, and slowly, his cult morphed from that of a deity of the elements, and more into a deity of learning.

Tenjin is still very popular today: Many Japanese students pray to him before their exams and thank him later if the result is favorable. His role as an angry god has been completely eclipsed by his intelligence.

Tsukuyomi-no-Mikoto

As we have mentioned many times, Tsukuyomi-no-Mikoto was one of the original triads of gods birthed by Izanagi and Izanami. Tsukuyomi is the god of the Moon, and unlike his siblings Amaterasu and Susanoo, he mostly didn't engage in conflicts over the domination of the world. However, there was one instance in which he angered his sister.

One day, Amaterasu sent Tsukuyomi to represent her at a feast thrown by Ukemochi, the goddess of food. But when Tsukuyomi saw the way in which she produced food, he was disgusted. She created fish by spitting into the ocean; game, by spitting into the forest; and a rice paddy, by coughing into a rice bowl. In his disgust, Tsukuyomi killed her.

Soon, Amaterasu found out what happened. She was so angry at her brother that she moved into an entirely different part of the sky, refusing to ever see him again. And thus, their subsequent roles as heavenly bodies were established: Amaterasu as the Sun, and Tsukuyomi as the Moon.

Yakushi Nyorai

The final god on our list is, yet again, a Buddhist deity. Yakushi Nyorai is the Buddha of medicine who has the power of eliminating afflictions by entering the state of the so-called samadhi, or, meditative consciousness. In Japan, he was one of the important Wisdom Buddhas and, even though over the centuries, some of his importance was transferred onto Jizō, he is still invoked in funerary rites.

Yakushi Nyorai is often portrayed surrounded by the so-called Twelve Heavenly Generals, who are his protective minor deities.

CHAPTER 4

Goddesses

The list of Japanese goddesses, even though shorter than that of the gods, is still an extensive one. Let us now talk about them and their fascinating world.

Amanozako

Amanozako, in a way, is Susanoo's daughter—he spit her out when his angry spirit built up inside him. As a result, Amanozako is monstrous: She has long ears and a long nose, as well as fangs that can chew even metal; she can also fly.

There is really no single area of expertise that Amanozako occupies herself with. In a way, she is a trickster goddess—she always acts against social norms and displays unquenchable anger.

Amaterasu-Ōmikami

Amaterasu, the sun goddess whom we have already met many times, is probably the most important goddess in the Japanese pantheon. She is the ruler of the whole of Takamagahara and the primary ancestress of the Imperial House of Japan.

We have already told the most important myths about Amaterasu: About her birth; her conflict with Susanoo and her subsequent hideout in a cave; and how she was lured out of it. We also know about her conflict with her other brother, Tsukuyomi, and how she was sending messengers to the earth to put it under the jurisdiction of her descendant, Ninigi. She then gave Ninigi three of the treasures that would later become the sacred treasures of the Imperial House of Japan: The sword that Susanoo gave her after he slew the serpent; and the mirror and the jewel that were used to lure her out of her cave.

There are a number of stories involving Amaterasu that originate from various times during the reign of different emperors. Many of them tell origin stories behind various shrines dedicated to the goddess, the most famous of them being the one in Ise in Mie Prefecture. One myth tells a story of how the legendary Empress Jingū was possessed by various gods, including Amaterasu, who told her about a rich land over the sea, which, in the end, prompted her invasion of Korea.

Over the years, the cult of Amaterasu became very important, sometimes even to the point of neglect of other kami—a veritable cult of the sun (Wheeler, 2013).

Ame-no-Uzume

Ame-no-Uzume is the goddess of the dawn, but also of joy, art, meditation, and revelry. This combination might seem incongruous, but let us not forget that it was Ame-no-Uzume's trance-induced dance and taking off her clothes that prompted the gods to laugh and, in turn, intrigued Amaterasu so much that she peeked out of the cave in which she had been hiding.

Later, when Ninigi was sent to the earth by Amaterasu, Ame-no-Uzume was ordered to accompany him. However, as they were dismounting from the sky, a lesser deity, Sarutahiko Ōkami who, at the time, was the leader of the earthly gods, blocked their path. Ame-no-Uzume, who was very clever, decided to use her female charms to flirt with Sarutahiko, who, as he became distracted, let Ninigi pass.

It is said that later, Ame-no-Uzume fell genuinely in love with Sarutahiko. They married and were the ancestors of one of the prominent Japanese clans, the Sarume clan.

Benzaiten

Benzaiten was originally a Hindu goddess who was adopted by the Japanese through Chinese culture around the 6th century. She is the goddess of learning, arts, and speech. She is one of the Seven Lucky Gods and is believed to give money to those who pray to her.

Benzaiten is often depicted with eight arms that hold different objects: A sword and a Japanese lute, and sometimes a special jewel that grants wishes.

Izanami

We already know so much about Izanami, her act of creation of the Japanese archipelago and of the primary Shinto gods, as well as her death and the events that transpired in the Underworld. But do we know what happened to Izanami later?

She was trapped in Yomi as Izanagi ran away from there and blocked the entrance with a large boulder. It seems that from now on, the previously loving couple of creator gods would be in perpetual conflict: Izanami vowed that she would kill a thousand of the inhabitants of the earth every day, to which Izanagi replied that he would bring to life 1,500 people every day to make up for that. From then on, that duality between life and death would define Izanami and Izanagi.

Kannon

Kanoon was originally Guanyin, the Chinese-Buddhist bodhisattva of compassion. In China, she was initially depicted as a man, but in Japan, she is predominantly female. We have already met her on a couple of occasions: When she enticed Kangiten with her beauty and captured Raijin. But apart from her association with compassion and taming that which is violent, she is also regarded in Japan as a protector of travelers—and in the modern world, she is believed to prevent cars from accidents. Because of her gentle nature, she is also associated with vegetarianism.

There are many local versions of Kannon. She is worshiped as a protector of the elderly and mothers going through childbirth and raising young children. When the first Christian missionaries arrived in Japan and tried to convert the Japanese people, they often compared Kannon to the Virgin Mary.

Kaya-no-hime

Kaya-no-hime is the goddess of grass and fields and, more broadly speaking, vegetation. She is the wife of Ōyamatsumi, the god of sea and mountains, and according to some, one of the many children of Izanagi and Izanami whom they had before the most important triad. Kaya-no-hime is also the mother of Konohanasakuya-hime, the goddess of Mount Fuji, whom we will talk about in a bit.

People often pray to Kaya-no-hime before cutting down trees as a building material, so that they could create a sturdy home. She is also regarded as the inventor of herbs, and so, their beneficiary properties are regarded as her work.

Kisshōten

Kisshōten, also known as Kichijōten, was originally a Hindu Buddhist goddess. She would sometimes be worshiped as one of the Seven Lucky Gods; however, there are variants of this group of deities where she is not listed. Her specialty is beauty and happiness, as well as fertility.

Konohanasakuya-hime

Konohanasakuya-hime is a special goddess: The deity of Mount Fuji, as well as all volcanoes, who is said to be surrounded by cherry blossoms. Because of this combination of the most iconic elements of Japan, she is often considered a literal embodiment of Japanese life. It is worth noting that, unlike many male gods associated with fire, storms, or volcanoes, Konohanasakuya-hime is gentle and prevents the volcanoes from erupting, rather than causing them to.

There are a couple of legends tied to Konohanasakuya-hime. She was the chosen bride of Ninigi-no-Mikoto, for which her sister, Iwanaga, cursed him with taking away his immortality.

But that wasn't the end of the problems. After only one night with Ninigi, Konohanasakuya-hime became pregnant—something that made Ninigi suspicious. The goddess was so angered by her husband's accusation that she shut herself in a hut without doors or windows. Then, she set the hut on fire—after all, she was the volcano goddess, and if her child was truly to be hers and Ninigi's, it wouldn't be harmed.

And that is what happened: Inside the hut, Konohanasakuya-hime gave birth to three sons: Hoderi, Hosuseri, and Hoori. Hoori, the youngest, would later become the grandfather of Emperor Jimmu.

There is another legend about Konohanasakuya-hime, which was written in the 11th century (*Ancient tales*, n.d.). In this tale, a boy named Yosoji lived in a village that had been struck by a smallpox plague; and one day, Yosoji's mother fell ill, too. So, the boy went to a fortune-teller, who told him to gather water near Mount Fuji and give it to his mother.

The next day, Yosoji went on a trek. But when he was nearing the mountain, he came to a crossroads. There were three possible paths, and he didn't know which one of them to take.

Suddenly, a young girl clad in a white robe appeared before him. She said that she knew the area, and guided him to a stream. Yosoji gathered some water for his mother; but he wanted to cure his neighbors and the whole village, too.

The girl told him that she would meet him at the crossroads in three days' time. It would take five more trips for the water to cure the village, she said. With this promise, she left Yosoji, and he came back to his mother and gave her water to drink.

And the girl's word was true: Five trips later, the whole village, including Yosoji's mother, was cured. The villagers thanked the boy profusely, but he refused to accept gratitude; it was all thanks to the girl. So, he went to hike up Mount Fuji one more time, in hopes of finding the girl and thanking her.

But when he came to the now well-known spot where the stream had been flowing, he found the place completely dried up. The girl was nowhere to be seen, either.

Yosoji started praying. He wished for the girl to reveal her name to him so that he would know whom to thank. And then, the woman appeared before him one last time; she said that her name wasn't important. But she had camellia flowers in her hair, and when she turned away, a cloud descended from the top of Mount Fuji and picked her up. Then, Yosoji finally realized: The girl was Konohanasakuya-hime herself.

Kushinadahime

Kushinadahime was the woman whom Susanoo-no-Mikoto rescued from the terrible serpent and later married. Today, she is mostly worshiped alongside her husband in multiple shrines throughout Japan.

Tamayori-hime

Tamayori-hime is the mother of Emperor Jimmu. She is the daughter of Watatsumi, the water dragon who emerged from Kagutsuchi's severed body. She met Ugayafukiaezu—Jimmu's future father—when he was still a little child and she was sent to care for him by her sister, Toyotama-hime, who was the child's mother but had abandoned the child. As Ugayafukiaezu grew up, he started to love his aunt and eventually, they were married. Not much more is known about Tamayori-hime from that point.

Toyotama-hime

Toyotama-hime, the grandmother of Emperor Jimmu and sister of Tamayori-hime, was much more tied to the sea—the domain of her father, Watatsumi—than her sister. After she gave birth to Ugayafukiezu, she immediately returned to the sea, leaving the child on the seashore and in the care of her sister.

But how did it happen that she gave birth in the first place? Toyotama-hime had lived with her father in his palace made of fish scales, at the bottom of the sea.

But one day, a young prince—Hoori—came to the seashore in search of a fishing hook he had lost. The hook had been borrowed from his older brother, Umisachi, and Hoori was scared that he would be very angry if he learned about the loss.

At the same time, Toyotama-hime came to the shore; she needed fresh water from a nearby well. Hoori came up to her and asked for a drink. Captivated by his beauty, Toyotama-hime offered it to him; she later related the whole affair to her father.

Watatsumi recognized that Hoori was a prince from a renowned house; so he invited him to dine at his underwater palace, where he and Toyotama-hime were soon married. They lived happily together for three years.

But then, Hoori revealed that he still had unfinished business to attend to the matter of Umisachi's hook. As it happened, the hook had caught in the throat of one of the fish at the palace. Hoori retrieved it and was sent to the surface with some advice from his wife and father-in-law. This allowed him not only to return the hook to his brother but also to overpower him.

Then, Toyotama, who returned to the surface with her husband, announced that she was pregnant. Hoori built her a special house for safe delivery which was made of cormorant feathers.

Toyotama then went into labor. She had only one condition for the safe delivery: Hoori couldn't watch her as she gave birth. He complied and waited outside of the house.

But unfortunately, as it's often the case with these things, Hoori couldn't rein in his curiosity, and he peeked inside. But to his horror, he didn't see his wife in the hut: Instead, a giant crocodile was nursing the baby. Hoori cried out in anguish, and the crocodile looked up: It was, of course, still Toyotama-hime—a true daughter of her dragon father—who had shapeshifted to give birth.

Ashamed of having been seen in her monstrous form, Toyotama-hime immediately returned to the sea, leaving the child in the hut. Soon after, she sent her sister, Tamayori-hime, to care for it. We know the rest of the story.

Toyouke-Ōmikami

Toyouke-Ōmikami is the goddess of agriculture on one hand, and of industry on the other. The legend says that originally, she had been worshiped in the Tanba Province. But one day, during the reign of one of the legendary Japanese emperors, Yūryaku (418–479), the emperor had an unsettling dream. Amaterasu herself came to him and said that she couldn't supply enough food for the people in Japan; but there was a goddess who could, for she was responsible for the meals of the gods. It was Toyouke-Ōmikami, and the emperor had to bring her over from Tanba.

So the emperor built a place of worship for Toyouke-Ōmikami in Amaterasu's Ise Grand Shrine; the famine was averted, and from then on, Toyouke-Ōmikami became Amaterasu's food supplier.

There is another legend tied to the goddess, from before she was called from Tanba. It is said that one day, Toyouke-Ōmikami was bathing in a spring and left her cloak on the shore. An elderly couple saw it and took it, rendering the goddess unable to return to the heavens. The couple then used the robe to bind the goddess to themselves and force her to enchant their homemade sake so that it cured every illness.

But after ten years of this, the couple threw the goddess away from their home, and she was forced to wander aimlessly through the earth—until she was called upon her new mission.

Ugajin

Ugajin is the deity of the harvest who can take both male and female forms. In the feminine version, she is depicted with the body of a coiled snake and the head of a woman. Sometimes, she would be fused with the Buddhist goddess of learning, Benzaiten—a snake representing the aquatic aspect of the goddess. Thus, Ugajin would sometimes be treated as Benzaiten's essence.

Ukemochi

We have already mentioned Ukemochi—the goddess of food whose way of producing nourishment by spitting it out offended Tsukuyomi-no-Mikoto so much. But another version of this story is that Ukemochi's encounter was not with Tsukuyomi, but with Susanoo, who asked her for food, which she produced out of her mouth, nose, and rectum. Disgusted—and also suspecting that Ukemochi had poisoned the food—Susanoo killed her. From her body, silkworms crawled out, and various crops grew out of various parts of her body: Rice, millet, wheat, and soybeans. Thus, the most popular crops grown in Japan were born.

Wakahiru-me

Wakahiru-me is the goddess of the rising sun. She is the daughter of Amaterasu, and can be sometimes interpreted as an aspect of her, specifically, of the sun rising in the morning.

Wakahiru-me is also the divine weaver: She makes garments for the gods. There is one fragmentary legend that says that the perpetual troublemaker, Susanoo, once threw a flaming pony at the heavens and killed Wakahiru-me who was sitting at her loom and spinning (Turner & Coulter, 2001).

Wakahiru-me closes our overview of goddesses in the Japanese tradition. In the next chapter, we will talk about heroes: Some of them human, some semi-divine, and most of them interacting with the gods.

CHAPTER 5

Heroes

We are now slowly descending from the immortal plane in order to meet some human heroes from Japanese myth and folklore. But we will not leave the gods and goddesses entirely behind: Our protagonists, whether brave princesses, unassuming heroes, or extraordinary children, will interact with gods, spirits, and other creatures more often than not. Let us now learn their stories.

Hachikazuki

Our first heroine is a princess. The tale of Hachikazuki was first recorded between the 14th and 16th centuries and tells a story of a young girl who finds her love (Seiki, 1966).

An elderly couple had a beautiful daughter, whom they loved dearly, but also guarded against any possible wrongdoers.

One day, the elderly mother of the girl fell ill. Soon, she was on her deathbed; her time had come. As her last wish, she made Hachikazuki swear that she would wear a wooden bowl on her head at all times, in order to cover her otherworldly beautiful face. The girl swore to do so.

After the mother's death, the father remarried. The stepmother didn't care much about Hachikazuki; in fact, she was so cruel that the girl had to escape the house and travel to a different city, where she hired herself as a servant in a noble household.

She served there for a while until the son of her master spotted her one day as she was bathing. In order to wash her face, Hachikazuki took the bowl briefly off her face. The young nobleman perceived the beauty of the girl and immediately fell in love with her. When there came a time for him to choose a wife, he insisted that Hachikazuki would be listed among the candidates.

And, in the end, everything ended happily: The young nobleman chose Hachikazuki and immediately, the bowl cracked into pieces and fell off her head. It not only revealed her beauty to the world but, as it also turned out, it contained a plethora of gems that the girl now possessed as her dowry. Her noble origin was also revealed. The couple married and, presumably, lived happily ever after.

The story of Hachikazuki is a Japanese example of a Cinderella-type story—a type of tale that could be found all around the world. But when it comes to Japan's immediate surroundings, this type of tale, albeit in a slightly different variant, was recorded in China in the 9th century (Beauchamp, 2010).

Issun-Bōshi

Issun-Bōshi literally means "One-Sun Boy," but is often translated as "The Inch-High Samurai," since *sun* in this context refers to the Japanese measurement unit, around 3 centimeters. It's a story about the most unassuming of heroes, but probably, given his size, the bravest one. It was written between the 14th and 16th centuries.

Yet again, this story starts with an elderly couple. They couldn't have children, so they prayed to the three Sumiyoshi sanjin gods. The deities heard their prayer, but the child who was born never grew taller than one *sun*.

Nevertheless, the couple loved the boy dearly. They named him Issun-Bōshi on account of his height and gave him everything he needed.

But the boy had one dream: He wanted to become a samurai. From the moment he was born, he'd heard stories about brave warriors who lived by the samurai code. And Issun-Bōshi was brave; after all, he had to be brave, living in a world that, from his perspective, had been made for giants.

So one day, Issun-Bōshi decided to go to the capital. He prepared his journey well; he fashioned a boat out of a rice bowl and a paddle out of a chopstick. He even prepared his weapon: A needle became his sword, and a straw his scabbard. Thus equipped, he set out on his journey.

In the capital, he found employment in a nobleman's household. However, he still felt like the family dismissed him, treating him only like a small child. But soon, he would find a way to prove himself.

The family whom Issun-Bōshi was serving had a young daughter. One day, as the girl was walking to a palace, she got kidnapped by an oni—an ogre-like demon. Issun-Bōshi, who was accompanying her on her journey as an escort, tried to fight the oni back, but he got swallowed by him in the process.

Fortunately, Issun-Bōshi didn't lose his needle-sword. Inside He started stabbing the oni from the inside—making life unbearable for the demon because of the constant pricking. At last, the oni had to spit Issun-Bōshi out. He was, in fact, so fed up with Issun-Bōshi that he fled to the mountains, leaving the girl behind.

He also left a magic hammer. It had the power of granting its owner wishes if they tapped it on the ground. Now, Issun-Bōshi, who had been in love with the girl whom he was serving, but was unable to pursue his feelings because of his height, wished to grow to an average human height. When his wish was granted, the brave samurai married the girl, with the blessing of her family who were amazed at his bravery. And thus, they lived happily ever after.

Kintarō

The story of Kintarō is the most traditional tale of a brave hero with supernatural strength who battled monsters. His road to glory wasn't easy, however.

Kintarō was born to a princess named Yaegiri. Unfortunately, during that time, her husband, a samurai by the name of Sakata, was engaged in a feud with his uncle, a very powerful and dangerous man. Afraid for her child's life, the princess had to flee and leave the child in the wilderness surrounding Mount Ashigara.

There, the child was picked up by a yama-uba, a type of spirit that could probably best be translated as a mountain witch. The witch decided to raise the little boy who, from the very start, showed signs of restlessness and great strength.

As Kintarō grew up, he was getting stronger and stronger. Soon, he would be able to uproot trees with his bare hands and crush rocks in his fists. He was plump and of a ruddy complexion, and he never grew cold, only wearing a short bib with a Japanese character for 'gold' embroidered on it; that is how he became known as Kintarō, "the Golden Boy."

From a very early age, Kintarō befriended animals—there were no children to grow up with on the mountain slopes—and even learned their language. Soon, the wild beasts of the forest became his companions and mounts. He wrestled bears like a real sumo and, with the help of his animal friends, defeated monsters and demons. He would also be helpful to humans, assisting them with cutting trees.

When Kintarō grew up, he was spotted in the forest by the leader of the powerful Fujiwara clan by the name of Minamoto no Yorimitsu (948–1021). The samurai and lord were so impressed by Kintarō's strength that he immediately beckoned him to come to Kyoto with him and to become his retainer. In Kyoto, after some strenuous training, Kintarō became a member of Minamoto's special guard, also known as Shitennō—a group of four retainers of special qualities.

In Kyoto, Kintarō lived a long and prosperous life, having found his birth mother and brought her to live with him. Here, the old story ends; but Kintarō lives on even today, as he is an exceptionally popular folk hero, with numerous books, manga, anime, and even action figures dedicated to him. Dolls representing Kintarō are often gifted to mothers who have given birth to baby boys; the tradition is that the possession of such a doll will help the boy become as courageous and strong as Kintarō himself. There are also shrines dedicated to his worship.

Kiyohime

The story of Kiyohime is a tale of a woman whose love was scorned, and about the disastrous consequences. The earliest versions of the story come from the 11th and 12th centuries, subsequently (Szostak, 2013).

Our tale starts with a young Buddhist monk who was traveling south on a pilgrimage from his homeland in the area of modern-day Fukushima. On his way there, he took up an offer from a steward of a vast manor house and decided to lodge there for a night.

The steward had a daughter, the beautiful Kiyohime. When she saw the monk, she immediately fell in love with him. Knowing that he will soon be gone, she decided to act quickly and confessed her feelings. But the monk, who did not return them, also lacked integrity and honesty to speak truthfully about his lack of affection; instead, he promised Kiyohime that he would return to her after his pilgrimage—only to get rid of her advances.

But Kiyohime wasn't stupid. She realized that the monk was, in reality, rejecting her, and as soon as he set off, she pursued him, filled with rage. The monk hurried along the way until he came to a river. He bought off the ferryman, instructing him to transport him across the river, but to refuse such transport to a girl who was closing on him.

The ferryman did as instructed. Now, angered even more, Kiyohime jumped into the river and swam to the other shore; but while she was in the water, her rage transformed her into a vicious serpent.

When the monk saw his pursuer in her new monstrous form, he ran as quickly as he could to the nearest temple and asked the monks who resided there to hide him. They complied, telling him to hide under a bonshō bell—a conical bell—the kind which are very common in Buddhist temples.

But Kiyohime, in her serpent form, now had heightened senses. When she slithered into the temple, she smelt the monk hiding under the bell and coiled around it. She banged the bell several times with her tail, causing it to vibrate, and then roared fire from her mouth. The bell started melting, and the monk died in agony inside.

The story of Kiyohime is not only that of a dangerous woman scorned; but also of the danger of giving false promises.

Momotarō

The story of Momotarō is yet another one of those stories about boy heroes. Momotarō's name means "the Peach Boy," as he was born from a peach; his story was written down in the Edo Period, though it probably existed in the oral form earlier than that (Kahara, 2004).

As usual in these stories, it starts with an old childless woman. One day, she was washing her clothes by the river, when she saw a giant peach floating on the water. She caught the peach immediately—she was poor and needed to find sustenance where she could—and brought it back home to her husband.

But when the couple opened the peach in order to eat it, they discovered a little boy inside. The boy was a small child, but he was already articulate: He said that it was the gods who decided for him to become their son. The couple rejoiced and named the boy Momotarō.

Very quickly, it turned out that the boy had supernatural strength. When he was only five, he was capable of cutting trees down with his knife; and when he became a teenager, he heard of a band of demons—oni—who terrorized the area. So, of course, Momotarō decided to seek them out and defeat them.

Momotarō's journey was long. On his way, he met several supernatural creatures: A talking dog, a monkey, and a pheasant. They all agreed to help him on his quest if he fed them along the way.

Finally, Momotarō found the place where the oni dwelled: The island of demons, Onigashima. The boy's animal friends helped him infiltrate the fortress made by the demons, and he barged inside, beating the oni until they submitted to him. In the end, he captured the chief of the demons, named Ozaki, and returned home with loads of treasure and his new animal friends in tow.

This is where the story of Momotarō ends—but by no means the end of his popularity as a character. Over the years, especially at the beginning of the 20th century, the figure of Momotarō was incorporated into Japanese school curriculum, aimed at teaching children bravery, how to care for their parents, and how to battle threats. The tale of the boy was used for patriotic purposes, with Momotarō being often made into a military commander who punished the oni for their wrongdoings (Kahara, 2004). However, that usage of the tale was also criticized, as the metaphorical reading of the story suggested strongly that all foreigners should be treated like the demons were treated in the tale (Kahara, 2004). Momotarō was also used as an icon for war propaganda during World War II (Antoni, 1991). After the war, however, the perception shifted and the highly simplified version of the tale was no longer taught in schools.

Urashima Tarō

Urashima Tarō was a simple fisherman who was rewarded for his kindness. His story was recorded relatively early—around the 8th century (Holmes, 2014).

One day, Urashima Tarō was walking by the seashore, coming back from a day of hard work. Suddenly, he spotted a group of children; they were all gathered around a small turtle, torturing and taunting it. Urashima Tarō, since he was a kind man, decided to interfere; he scolded the children for their cruel behavior and released the turtle back into the sea.

The next day, as he was making his usual walk back home, Urashima Tarō met a turtle again, but this time, a far bigger one. The turtle said that the smaller kinsman whom the fisherman had saved the day before was no other than Otohime, the daughter of Ryūjin, the dragon-god of the sea. Now, she wanted to thank him for his kindness; and so, he was invited into the palace below the sea. The giant turtle gave Urashima Tarō magical gills so that he could breathe underwater—and off they went.

And so, Urashima Tarō saw the wondrous palace of Ryūgū-jō, the Palace of the Dragon God, where he met Ryūjin himself, as well as his daughter, who was now a beautiful princess in a human form. Urashima Tarō was given a tour of the palace and admired its wonders: On each side, it overlooked a different season of the year, and it was enormous. Urashima Tarō agreed to stay in the palace for three days; but later, he wanted to come back to the surface, as he had an aging mother whom he needed to take care of.

Otohime was unhappy about the fisherman's departure, but she said that she understood, and she gave him a parting gift: A magical box, called tamatebako, which was supposed to protect him from all harm, but which he was supposed never to open. Thus equipped, Urashima Tarō was brought back to the surface.

But he was so astonished when he walked onto the shore and didn't recognize his surroundings! A larger city now stood on the seashore, his old home was nowhere to be seen, and none of the people he met were his neighbors. He tried asking around for his mother, but nobody had heard about her; at last, he asked if anyone knew a man by the name of Urashima Tarō.

That is when he learned the terrible truth: 300 years had passed since he had been taken to the underwater palace. Urashima Tarō was now a name of a legend—a man who one day vanished from the seashore, never to be seen again.

Crushed by the weight of his discovery, Urashima Tarō wept on the seashore. He took out the box he had received from the princess: It was supposed to protect him from harm, but what did he care about harm now? All of his friends and family were gone; his life had been uprooted.

He opened the box.

A cloud of white smoke emerged from the inside; in a flash, Urashima felt himself aging rapidly, all the years he spent underwater catching up with him. He wrinkled and sagged, and a long white beard grew from his chin. A cry came from the sea; it was the cry of the divine princess. Very soon, Urashima died of old age.

The story of Urashima Tarō is perhaps the most heartbreaking tale of the ones we have told so far: A story of a man who was supposed to have been rewarded for his kindness, but whose mortal idea of a reward clashed with that of immortal gods. In the end, what is the difference between a reward and a punishment for those whose lives last forever?

Uriko-hime

The tale of Uriko-hime is slightly similar to that of Momotarō, in that it tells a story of a girl born out of a melon fruit. The tale has circulated in an oral version for centuries, and there are more than 100 versions of it all over the Japanese archipelago (Immos & Ikeda, 1973).

But this is what most of the versions agree on: The melon from which Uriko-hime was born was found in a river by an elderly couple, much as it was in the case of Momotarō. And in this case, the couple was overjoyed by the discovery and decided to raise the little girl, who soon became a beautiful young woman.

One day, Uriko-hime's parents had to leave the house after some errands. They left the girl cooking dinner for them but warned her not to open the door for any strangers. Uriko-hime complied and came back to her cooking.

Unfortunately, a yokai—a type of demon—saw the parents leave and the girl being left alone. The yokai's name was Amanojaku and it was known as a particularly vicious demon who could devour souls and prompt people to do wicked deeds.

When Amanojaku saw that the girl was alone, it appeared behind the front door and started calling to her. It beckoned her to open the door only a crack, and no harm would come to her. Unfortunately, Uriko-hime was slightly naive, so she agreed to the demon's plea. She opened the door, but couldn't close it again; Amanojaku forced itself inside the house. Then, it devoured the poor girl and flayed the skin from her body. The demon put the skin on and when the elderly couple came back home, it impersonated Uriko-hime to perfection.

This went on for several days. The couple didn't recognize the change, except that the girl seemed slightly moodier than before; the yokai also wrought mischief in the house whenever given the chance.

But fortunately, one day, a bird sat on the roof and started singing beautifully. This was the real Uriko-hime, reincarnated. As she sang, her parents realized that they could understand the bird's song. With horror, they discovered the truth. The story is vague on what happened later, but presumably, Amanojaku was expelled from the house.

The story of Uriko-hime closes our overview of heroes from Japanese myth, but this is by no means the end of folklore stories from this tradition. In the next chapter, we will learn some more about supernatural creatures such as the already mentioned oni and yokai; and in the last chapter, some more folktales will await your attention.

CHAPTER 6

Supernatural Creatures

Japanese mythology and folklore abound not only in numerous gods and goddesses but also in supernatural creatures. Broadly speaking, there are several categories under which those creatures—spirits, demons, shapeshifters—can fall; but as we will see, not all of them are very easily classifiable. But all of them live very close to us and can interact with us almost at every turn in our lives. Below is the selection of the most important or interesting creatures.

The Obake

Most broadly speaking, the obake are shapeshifters: Special types of spirits that can change their form. In their natural form, they would often be animals, such as foxes or raccoons, or even everyday objects; but they can either transform into spirits or gain supernatural qualities in their primary forms. Let us see what types of creatures are considered obake in Japan.

Bakeneko

The bakeneko are supernatural cats. They look like ordinary cats, except for a couple of small differences: Their pupils change shape and color depending on the time of the day, and when petted, their fur produces sparks. The bakeneko are very stealthy and quiet, and they have a rather ferocious nature, even if to the naked eye they seem very docile and gentle.

At first glance, that description seems to at least partly apply to most ordinary cats; but the bakeneko are almost always old—over seven years, or, in some regional versions, over twelve or thirteen. Sometimes, they are spirits of cats who had been brutally killed by humans, and reincarnated into a new cat, only to enact revenge. For these means, they can even shapeshift into a human or possess a human.

The bakeneko have peculiar tastes: They could lick blood or lamp oil. The latter especially was often treated as a sign of a strange event to come. One possible explanation behind that odd behavior is that during the Edo Period, lamp oil was often made with various fish oils, which could attract cats.

There are many legends concerning the bakeneko from various regions (and time periods) in Japan. The oldest ones center around temples, as cats were often kept by the monks in order to protect the sacred texts from being eaten by rats. It was a belief that those cats could transform into spirits.

One more elaborate story concerning the bakeneko is of a man named Takasu Genbei, who had a pet cat that one day went missing. Very soon after this happened, Takasu's mother started behaving very oddly: She refused to socialize with people and would shut herself in her room.

One day, Takasu and other members of his family decided to check in on his mother; so they peeked inside her bedroom. But instead of a well-known middle-aged woman, they saw a giant cat wearing her clothes and munching on dead rodents.

Takasu burst into the room. Quickly, he killed the giant cat, and in a moment, its carcass turned back into an ordinary small cat—Takasu's pet that had gone missing. And when the family tore up the floorboards in the house, they found the skeleton of the unfortunate mother: It had been cleared clean of all flesh. The poor woman must have been possessed and devoured by the bakeneko.

The second legend took place in the Hizen Province, in the westernmost corner of Japan, in the household of the daimyō Nabeshima Mitsushige (1632–1700). The daimyō had just executed his retainer, Ryūzōji Matashichirō, because he displeased him during a board game. Ryūzōji's mother, unable to console herself after her son's death, committed suicide, having confided her sorrows in her pet cat. As she was dying, the cat licked the woman's blood and became the bakeneko.

The cat sneaked into Nabeshima Mitsushige's castle. There, he started tormenting the daimyō, so that he couldn't sleep for nights on end. Finally, Mitsushige's new retainer killed the cat, ridding his lord of the trouble.

This story became very popular in Japan, to the point where in the mid-19th century, numerous dramatizations of the story were written, which was then followed by films in the 20th century.

Kitsune

The kitsune are supernatural foxes that grow wiser the older they get—and they can grow quite old, often more than 50 or even 100 years. They can shapeshift into humans and, though some are mischievous, most are friendly to people, and could even become their guardians, friends, or lovers. The special status of foxes in Japanese culture most likely comes from the fact that they repel rats and can guard rice reserves by burrowing themselves in them.

All kitsune are said to serve Inari Ōkami.

One of the oldest tales involving a kitsune comes from the 9th century. It tells a story of a man who got married and had a child with a beautiful woman who had an odd animosity toward dogs. She was, of course, a kitsune; and her child and their descendants, too, soon turned out to possess similar powers. Unfortunately, they often used them to do evil deeds.

This old story marks the beginning of a trend visible in many kitsune stories that came after: In those, the kitsune would often turn into beautiful women. Those women would often stroll alone at dusk and have 'fox-like' faces: High cheekbones, thin eyebrows, narrow eyes, and face. Sometimes, a woman like that would cast a shadow in the shape of a fox.

But foxes could sometimes, instead of turning into women, possess them. They would often enter the bodies of young girls through the tips of their fingers (crawling under their fingernails) or through their breasts. Although sometimes the possession would be a peaceful one, causing the victim only to slightly change their facial expression and, sometimes, even to gain wisdom, most of the occurrences are said to be violent in nature. The victims would show signs of madness, such as frothing at the mouth, running around naked, or speaking and writing in an unknown language (Hearn, 1988). The only way to rid the victim of the fox spirit would be to perform an exorcism at the shrine of Inari Ōkami; if it failed, the victim could even be beaten to death in order to drive the spirit away, and if even that failed, the whole family of the victim could be ostracized by society (Hearn, 1988). Even today, a psychiatric condition known as kitsunetsuki, in which a patient believes to have been possessed by a fox, is being diagnosed in Japan—it is endemic to Japanese culture, which shows how a system of beliefs can affect not only a person's worldview but also their mental health (Haviland, 1999).

Kodama

The kodama are the spirits of the trees, or, perhaps more accurately, shapeshifting trees. They can travel around mountain slopes however much they wish, but their tree always provides a safe haven for them.

Outwardly, the kodama trees look like ordinary trees, but they become cursed when a person attempts to cut them down. Sometimes, blood could even pour out of them if they are hurt by an ax. Usually, a knowledge of which trees in a given area are kodama trees would be passed from generation to generation.

When traveling, the kodama can take on an appearance of eerie lights or animals, but they can also sometimes turn into humans.

Mujina

The mujina are shapeshifting badgers. They are closely related to the tanuki—the raccoon dogs—of whom we'll talk about in a bit. In their natural form, the Mujina are mostly harmless, if a bit mischievous: They would often produce music drumming on their inflated bellies, and create fairy lights.

But the trouble starts when they shapeshift. The belief is that they can turn into almost anything, and there are some forms in which they are definitely more dangerous than others. If they turn into a woman, they can seduce men. One of the earliest accounts mentioning a mujina, the *Nihon Shoki*, mentions that they can turn into women and sing seductive songs (Aston, 2013).

The mujina's favorite form, however, is purportedly that of a Buddhist monk clad in black robes, with an inverted lotus leaf on his head. In this form, they would live underneath a temple, causing mischief.

Sometimes, the mujina can even turn into objects or buildings. In one folk story, a mujina turned into a house in which an unsuspecting traveler stayed during the night and then scared him out of his wits (Harada, 1976). The main reason for those numerous and often fantastical transformations is supposedly that the mujina like to test the extent of their shapeshifting powers and see how perfectly they can imitate objects or people's mannerisms. However, it is said that only a man of real integrity would be capable of telling an ordinary person or an object from a mujina.

Even though they are tricksters, the mujina know the meaning of gratitude. In one story, a man who had been feeding a family of badgers for some time, was later saved by two of them when burglars broke into his house and threatened his life (Casal, 1959). The badgers transformed into giant sumo wrestlers and scared the burglars away.

The mujina are slow to anger, but if they get furious, they are a force to be reckoned with. If their den gets destroyed or their family member killed, the mujina can use their shapeshifting powers to confuse the perpetrator and cause their death, luring them to a fatal accident through a series of transformations.

Tanuki

Tanuki, also known as bake-danuki, are supernatural raccoon dogs. They are closely related to the mujina and share some of their traits, such as turning into women and singing songs or deceiving men. It is believed that before the arrival of Buddhism in Japan, the tanuki were considered divine, but they lost such status after the implementation of new religious beliefs onto the archipelago.

The tanuki are predominantly pranksters. In many folktales—we will learn some of them in the next chapter—they are presented as foolish and comical. Although they have better skills at shapeshifting than, say, the kitsune, they mostly only use those skills for fun. Their comical image is further established by the way they are often depicted: With large scrotums, using their testicles as drums or flung over their backs like traveler's packs.

There are several famous tanuki in Japanese folktales. The most well-known form is a triad of "three famous tanuki of Japan:"

Danzaburou-danuki

The tale of Danzaburou-danuki comes from Sado Island in the eastern part of the Japanese archipelago. It is hard to track the origin of the tale, as it was passed down through generations orally.

Danzaburou-danuki was the chief commander of all the tanuki on Sado Island. He liked playing tricks: Transforming into a wall and blocking people's passage, producing fake golden leaves and then selling them as real ones—and many others.

Despite all this, he wasn't malicious. He was just as likely to lend money to people in need as he was to trick the greedy ones. But he didn't like to share his power; Sado Island doesn't have any foxes on it anymore, and there are several stories relating how Danzaburou-danuki drove away all the kitsune from there.

One day, a kitsune wanted to cross the sea to Sado Island, and so he asked Danzaburou-danuki for a safe passage. The tanuki, having no wish to let the kitsune live on Sado, decided to go for a trick. He told the fox to shapeshift into zōri (thonged Japanese sandals), which he then put on his feet. It was a perfect disguise, he explained: Nobody would suspect a thing.

But, as they were already crossing the sea, Danzaburou-danuki tossed the sandals into the sea, and the kitsune, who didn't manage to shapeshift back to his real form in time, drowned. From that point on, no kitsune tried to settle on Sato.

Shibaemon-tanuki

The legend of Shibaemon-tanuki comes from Awaji Island. In behavior, Shibaemon-tanuki was very similar to Danzaburou-danuki. He liked drumming his belly and selling fake golden leaves, disguised as a human. To balance out the chaos, he would also guide lost travelers through the pathways around Mount Mikuma, where he lived with his wife.

One day, Shibaemon-tanuki decided to go to Osaka and watch a famous play. So, he disguised himself as a man, and his wife as a woman, and they set off on their journey.

They were like a pair of overexcited tourists: They had never been to Osaka before, and they were dazzled by the bustling city. In the middle of sightseeing, they decided to hold a contest of disguises.

First, Shibaemon's wife turned herself into an attendant in a procession led by a daimyō. Shibaemon's task was to recognize her in the crowd, which he did, although it was difficult since her disguise was near-perfect.

When it came to Shibaemon's turn, he spotted a procession of feudal lords. When his wife saw the procession, she approached one of the lords immediately. "Oh, you're good," she said, "but I recognized you."

This proved to be a mistake: The man was not, in fact, Shibaemon, but a real lord. For her impudence, the poor woman was struck down and killed where she stood.

Shibaemon was struck with grief. However, he still had a play to see, and he decided he didn't want to waste his ticket. So, he went into the theater; but unfortunately, somebody in the audience had brought a massive dog. Shibaemon was immediately scared of it but managed to suppress his fear.

That is until the dog started barking at him. Startled, Shibaemon turned uncontrollably into his tanuki form, in which the dog killed him. News traveled far and wide from Osaka of a tanuki killed by a dog; and when the inhabitants of a small village by the slopes of Mount Mikuma heard this, and then they didn't hear Shibaemon drumming his belly anymore, they immediately knew that he was dead.

Yashima no Hage-tanuki

Yashima came from a town of the same name, which is now a district of Takamatsu City in Japan. The story of his life is tied to that of the patriarch of the Taira clan, Taira no Shigemori (1138–1179), who was said to have saved the tanuki's ancestor from an arrow wound. As a show of gratitude, the tanuki and his descendants protected the Taira clan, and when it went into oblivion, they became the protectors of one of the temples which the clan had founded.

And that is when Yashima no Hage-tanuki's life started. He was the protector of the temple and, thanks to his mastery of disguises, he became the chief of all tanuki in the area. He would create mirages in the air and show them to people, and, of course, his power of shapeshifting was without contest.

One day, Yashima was challenged by no other than Shibaemon-tanuki. He boasted that he was the best shapeshifter in Japan, and so, the two tanuki met and decided to challenge themselves to a contest of disguises.

On the morning of the contest, Shibaemon awoke and, to his horror, saw a massive fleet sailing on the sea on the horizon. He cried out in alarm, thinking that a war was coming; but as soon as he did, the fleet disappeared and Yashima appeared before him: The fleet had been his disguise. Yashima, glad that he had won, started boasting about his victory far and wide.

But Shibaemon was far from being done. Remembering the misfortune with his wife (and, in this version of the tale, not being dead yet), he now did the same thing to Yashima. He seemingly disguised himself as a member of an entourage of a daimyō, and when Yashima cried out and approached one of the soldiers, he was instantly struck with a spear for his insolence. The soldier, of course, had been a real one.

Shibaemon, as an act of courtesy, threw Yashima a funeral. After his death, Yashima's spirit started possessing people. However, he wasn't malicious; instead, he mediated between people and helped them out.

Tsukumogami

The tsukumogami are a special kind of shapeshifters: Everyday objects, especially tools, that acquired supernatural abilities. A popular belief is that any object which is older than 100 years would acquire self-awareness and become alive—although that number by itself might not always be literal but a symbol of a thing being very old.

What happens when an object becomes a tsukumogami? Like other types of shapeshifters, it could turn into a human of any age or gender; into a spirit; or into an animal. It seems that those shapeshifters would later become mostly deceiving and mischievous in nature so people would mostly try to get rid of old things.

As Buddhism came to Japan, the traditional Shinto belief in the Tsukumogami became merged with the Buddhist belief in reincarnation, and so the sentient objects started to be seen as reincarnated souls of those who did not manage to attain enlightenment. Today, this symbolic meaning of the tsukumogami is mostly lost, and they permeated Japanese popular culture, appearing in anime, manga, books, and films.

There are different types of tsukumogami. Some examples include: Abumi-guchi (a furry monster emerging from a stirrup of a dead soldier); Bakezōri (a possessed sandal that makes noise around the house); Biwa-bokuboku (a sentient biwa, that is a Japanese lute); Boroboroton (an animated futon which attempts to strangle its owner at night); Chōchin-obake (a possessed lantern); and Ungaikyō (possessed mirror which shows a monstrous reflection of those who look into it).

The Yōkai

The yōkai is perhaps the broadest category of supernatural beings in Japanese folklore. In some ways, the obake could also be classified as a type of yōkai. Most broadly speaking, the yōkai are spirits: All supernatural creatures that aren't gods. They aren't demons; instead, they can be both benevolent or malevolent, or simply mischievous.

There is an almost innumerable amount of various yōkai in different regional tales from Japan. Below is the selection of those most famous, interesting, or sometimes even astonishing.

Abura-akago

Abura-akago is a child-like spirit. It lives inside andon lamps—traditional Japanese cubical hanging lamps which could be found both at homes and in temples. When in a lamp, this spirit licks and eats the oil inside; but it can also travel between lamps in the form of a ball of fire. In that latter form, they can haunt the crossroads, confusing the travelers who walk in the dark.

Aka Manto

Aka Manto is perhaps the most peculiar yōkai. The belief in it is widespread in modern Japan and it is more often described as an urban legend than a folklore figure; however, urban legends are mostly just folklore transposed into modern times.

So, who is Aka Manto? It is a spirit living in public bathrooms. It wears a red cloak and a mask and is always equipped with a blue and a red roll of toilet paper. It appears in bathrooms whenever someone occupies a stall; some say that it most often happens in female bathrooms, as the spirit is male; and mostly to those who chose the last stall in a row.

Aka Manto would then ask the victim a question: Would they prefer a blue or a red roll of paper? This has to be ignored, as either choice would mean the victim's death: The red roll means laceration and getting drowned in one's own blood, and the blue one means strangulation and all the blood being sucked out of one's body. So, unsurprisingly, getting out of the bathroom stall as soon as possible and running away is the best option.

It is said that some people tried to outsmart the Aka Manto. They would say that they preferred a roll in a different color. But that doesn't end well either; the spirit could then drag the victim's body to the spirit world. Specifically, if a victim said they preferred yellow paper, their head could be forced into the toilet and they could drown.

The belief in Aka Manto most likely started in the 1930s, specifically among children and teenagers in public schools (Meyer, 2016). It isn't difficult to imagine a school prankster standing behind the belief. But however it started, the odd but dangerous spirit of the public bathrooms now entered the world of the Japanese supernatural.

Akaname

Continuing with the scatological theme—Akaname is a filthy, green monster the size of a child's stature that licks filth from bathtubs and bathrooms. It is literally born out of filth in bathrooms that have been neglected.

Although Akaname is ugly and unpleasant to see, it doesn't harm people; it contents itself with licking filth. The unpleasantness of the creature, however, is enough to spur people into keeping their bathrooms clean.

Akugyo

Akugyo is an aquatic yōkai—a sea monster if you will. It's a giant fish that mostly lives in the southern seas by the shores of the Japanese archipelago. It doesn't seem to be actively malicious towards people; however, its size means that boats can often get stuck between their fins and destroyed.

Amabie

Amabie, broadly speaking, is the Japanese equivalent of a mermaid or a merman. It is slightly different in appearance from the merpeople from European traditions: It has three fin-like legs and a beak-like mouth. It also has the power of prophecy, it can emerge from the sea and predict either a good harvest or an epidemic. Amabie's presence was reported at various points in Japanese history, usually before natural disasters occurred.

There are also different variants of the Amabie. Some can cry out like apes, others glow in the dark; yet others can put on a monk's garb and would pass as monks, if not for their three legs.

Recently, Amabie had a bit of a resurgence because of the COVID-19 pandemic. The image of the creature warning against the disease became quite popular in Japanese social media (Alt, 2020).

Hone-onna

Hone-onna's name literally means "bone woman." Her existence is attested in one folk story in which an animated female skeleton visited a man whom she used to be in love with when alive. She would visit him every night and stay away until the morning; the man didn't realize that the creature was a skeleton, and not a woman herself, since she had put on a disguise. He only realized what was going on when a neighbor peeked into his bedroom and spotted him embracing a skeleton.

Kappa

Kappa, one of the best-known yōkai in Japan, is a reptile-like creature with humanoid features which lives in rivers and ponds. It is the size of a small child, and yet, it possesses considerable strength as it likes engaging in sumo wrestling. Its skin is scaly and slimy save for its back, where it wears a turtle shell. Its hands and legs are webbed, and on the top of its head, it has a small indent, in which the water in which it lives is accumulated.

Although Kappa is a yōkai, it demands people to worship it like a god and can get considerably angry when they don't comply. It would typically attack its victims in water, and remove their organs through their anus. It can also devour whole men and rape women who come to bathe in rivers. More mundanely, a Kappa would also cause drowning—for which reason it has often been used as a cautionary tale for children to prevent them from swimming in deep and treacherous waters (Ashkenazi, 2008).

In order to placate a Kappa, an offering of a cucumber—its favorite food—should be made. In more dire and desperate circumstances, there are a few ways to survive an encounter with a Kappa. Firstly, since it likes when people are polite, one should bow to it, and it would return the bow; then, the water which is accumulated in the indent on the top of its head would spill, and it wouldn't be able to straighten until the water is refilled. During this time, the victim might make their escape—or they can refill the indent, after which the Kappa would be forced to serve the person until the end of their days.

A different method is slightly more dangerous: To engage in sumo wrestling with the Kappa and use this opportunity to spill the water from its indent.

Once a Kappa is forced to serve a human, it would irrigate their fields and bring them fresh fish; they could also cure various diseases, as their affinity for removing organs from their victims also means they are quite skilled in medicine.

Nure-onna

Nure-onna is a hybrid: A creature with the body of a snake and the head of a woman. Nure-onna's hair is always wet, and it lives in rivers and seas, where it often lures sailors to their death. There are different ways in which it can do that. It can appear to be a young woman washing her hair in the water or drowning, which then turns out to be a deadly snake when the sailors come closer; or, alternatively, it can hand over a sleeping baby to a man, begging him to hold it for her—but when the baby is already in the man's arms, it turns into a heavy stone which he can't drop, and he drowns, or a Nure-onna eats him. There is only one way to prevent oneself from that fate, and that is, to wear slippery gloves.

Shuten Dōji

Shuten Dōji is a special case on our list: Rather than being a category of being, he was an individual, a powerful leader of spirits or demons (*oni* in Japanese, which is a special, usually malicious, subcategory of yōkai), who got defeated by Minamoto no Yorimitsu, the same leader who employed Kintarō. The story about their showdown was described in a 14th-century text and goes as follows (Reider, 2010):

Shuten Dōji lived near Kyoto, during the times of Emperor Ichijō (986–1011). He would lure and kidnap young maidens. When this fact was noticed in Kyoto, an investigation started, until at last the emperor's advisors established that it was Shuten Dōji, the king of the spirits, who was responsible. So, the emperor commanded Minamoto no Yorimitsu to take a crew and go on an expedition to get rid of the monster.

Minamoto left Kyoto in 995. On his way, he and his party met various gods disguised as human helpers; they advised them to disguise themselves as yamabushi—ascetic monks. Thus, they could approach Mount Ōe where Shuten Dōji lived unobserved.

As they approached, the party met an old washerwoman who was doing laundry by the river. They asked her for the whereabouts of the demons, and she said that they were near. She also explained that she had been kidnapped by Dōji when she was young, and forced into servitude. Most girls were met with the same fate; however, some of them had been ripped apart and devoured by Dōji's pack of demons.

The party moved forward until they finally found Dōji's lair. Pretending to be priests, they asked for lodgings. The demon, even though he was wicked, couldn't really refuse the holy men. He invited them inside and gave them a drink of sake, then told them his version of the story: How he and his band of demons had been driven away from nearby Hira

Mountains, and how they did everything they could to survive. It was quite a sorry tale, but it didn't negate the fact that the demons had been kidnapping young women.

Then, Minamoto shared his own sake with Dōji. It was a drink given to him by one of the disguised gods—much stronger than regular sake. As Dōji and his demons fell asleep, Minamoto and his party dressed back in their armor and attacked the defenseless hosts. The disguised gods came to their aid and held down Dōji as Minamoto hacked his head off.

But this wasn't the end of Dōji; his head was still alive and biting after being cut off. It jumped at Minamoto's head, but thankfully, he had been wearing a double helmet, so the demon's sharp teeth didn't manage to cut through it. Soon, the head stopped biting and the demons were defeated. The warriors then set free the maidens who were being held hostage.

Tengu

The Tengu is a spirit rather hard to define. He can take on many forms, from a large bird to a monkey, but he usually has a humanoid face with a long nose or a beak. What he likes most, however, is putting on the garb of a priest, especially of the ascetic yamabushi, and impersonating him. In this form, Tengu was most likely borrowed from Chinese folklore (de Visser, 1908).

What is Tengu's specialty? As a monk impersonator, he most often has malicious intent; he is the enemy of Buddhism, and often robs temples, leads priests astray, or kidnaps them (although they usually don't vanish without a trace, just end up miles away from the places they've been in before). Sometimes, he would even possess women and, in that form, try to seduce holy men. The belief is that Tengu himself is a spirit of a monk who was unholy during his life.

One interesting story featuring a Tengu was written down in the 12th century, in the war chronicle *Hōgen Monogatari* (de Visser, 1908). It tells the story of Emperor Sutoku (1119–1164), who was supposed to become a Tengu after his death. After being deposed from the throne and having raised a rebellion, he died in torment and swore to come back as an angry demon.

However, not all Tengu are bad. Over time, the image of the spirit shifted from that of a destroyer of temples to their protector. In the 18th and 19th centuries, the Tengu appeared in many folktales as protectors of forests (de Visser, 1908).

They also changed their appearance from fearsome to slightly comedic spirits. For example, in one folktale a Tengu lost one of his attributes—a fan that could enlarge people's noises—to a little mischievous boy (Seki, 1966). The boy then used the fan to extend the nose of a nobleman's daughter and promised to change it back to a normal shape in exchange for her hand in marriage. But his pranks finally caught up with him: As he was falling asleep one day, he accidentally used the fan on himself and his nose got so long that it reached the heavens.

Yamauba

Yamauba is a female spirit. She lives in forests and would take on the appearance of a young beautiful woman washing or combing her long black hair. Sometimes, if a hunter accidentally shoots in her direction, she would catch his bullet in her hands. But the youthful appearance is only a deception: In reality, Yamauba is an old crone and a dangerous one at that. She delights in eating little children. However, some of the children are special and Yamauba would rather raise them—the mountain witch who raised Kintarō is said to have been a Yamauba.

In general, there are two conflicting portrayals of a Yamauba: As a dangerous witch-eating traveler, and as a supernatural helper who would help out those who are unfortunate. Embodying this second portrayal is a short tale of two stepsisters who were gathering fruit in a forest. The older sister was kind, even though she suffered torment from her stepmother; the younger sister was cruel and selfish. A Yamauba then appeared and gave the older sister a sack full of treasure, while cursing the younger sister to an unhappy fate.

The Yūrei

The yūrei can also be classified as a type of yōkai—however, a very specific type. They are the closest to what we would call ghosts, the spirits of dead people. Even though the Shinto religion doesn't hold very specific views on the afterlife—except that a spirit of a good person would eventually join their ancestors—there is a belief that ghosts of those who died a violent death (such as murder or suicide) would then haunt the living, sometimes to enact revenge for their sudden death. There are some common characteristics of a yūrei: White clothing and long, black, disheveled hair; the lack of feet (they instead float in the air), and lifelessly dangling hands.

Funayūrei

The Funayūrei are vengeful spirits of those who died at sea. Since they drowned in shipwrecks, they want the living sailors to join them, so they would often use ladles to fill boats with water and sink them. Some of them would even form crews and sail through the sea in ghost ships. They usually use bad weather—rains, storms, fog—to lure sailors to their deaths. Sometimes, they tamper with the ship's compasses.

There are several ways to defeat the Funayūrei. Some accounts state that one has to stop one's ship immediately and stare at the ghost; others, that one has to stir the water and startle it. Some objects thrown into the sea are also said to distract and repel the Funayūrei: Flowers, incense sticks, or rice.

Depending on the region, there are different types of Funayūrei that have been spotted over the centuries. For example, around the region of Kyushu, a Funayūrei called Ugume would pretend to be a ship or an island, and it would steer sailors off their course. It could be repelled by throwing ash into the water or by smoking tobacco.

Goryō

The Goryō are the vengeful spirits of aristocrats. Most of them are said to have died as a result of a famine, disease, or murder... And they are also believed to be capable of bringing about the misfortunes that ended their life. For this reason, the Goryō are often worshiped in shrines as a preemptive measure. Some can even become gods—as was the case with Tenjin, whom we've already met.

Ikiryō

The Ikiryō are a bit of a special case: They are disembodied spirits who left people who are still alive. It is a belief that a person who experiences very violent emotions, especially holding a grudge against someone, can unleash an Ikiryō who can later haunt their victim, even over a large distance. They also have the power to curse or possess the other person.

But sometimes, not only vengeance brings about the Ikiryō. Extreme feelings of love, infatuation, and obsession can also be the cause. In one tale, a teenage boy by the name of Matsunosuke was possessed by the spirits of two women who were in love with him, and he would talk to them even though they were not there physically; they would also cause him to fly up in the air. Only an exorcism from a priest delivered the boy from his condition.

During the Edo Period, the separation of the soul from the body by creating an Ikiryō was considered an illness (Hearn, 2020). It was believed that an out-of-body experience was a part of that condition, as well as seeing one's identical double.

Kuchisake-onna

Kuchisake-onna is a singular spirit. It is said that during her life, she was a beautiful woman who got disfigured horribly.

Her husband was a samurai, and spent most of his time away from home; Kuchisake grew lonely and started an affair. When her husband learned about this, he enacted a truly cruel punishment: He cut her mouth from ear to ear.

It is no wonder that after her death, Kuchisake became a vengeful spirit. She would roam the streets with her face covered by a mask, with a knife in her hand. She would accost her victims and ask them, "Am I beautiful?" If a person responds negatively, she would kill them; if affirmative, she would take off her mask and show her mutilated face, asking, "Even now?" If the victim screams in fear or says "No, now you are not beautiful," she would cut them with her knife in half. If, however, they say "Yes," Kuchisake-onna would take out a pair of scissors and cut the victim's mouth so that it resembles hers.

There are a few ways to survive an encounter with Kuchisake-onna unscathed. One can distract her by throwing money or candies at her; or one can cleverly respond to her questions, saying that she is neither beautiful nor ugly, but average; when Kuchisake ponders on that answer, her victim might be able to run away.

Oiwa

The story of Oiwa might be the most popular Japanese ghost story ever created. It is a story about betrayal that carries even beyond the grave, which is said to have historical basis in the 17th century (*Oiwa*, n.d.).

Oiwa was a young girl married to a samurai by the name of Iemon, who was unhappy in that marriage. Iemon did not act according to the samurai code and was instead a thief and a wasteful man. So one day, Oiwa said to herself that enough was enough, and she decided to separate with him and return to her family home.

But Iemon was not also a man without honor, but also quick to anger. He ran after Oiwa, presumably intent on dragging her back to his home by force. However, on the road, he was stopped by Oiwa's father, Yotsuya Samon. Samon knew all about Iemon's misconduct with his daughter and demanded that Samon divorce Oiwa and let her come back to her family.

Iemon wouldn't have this. He murdered Samon where he stood and then pursued Oiwa. He now put on a weeping act: He reported that Samon had been murdered on the road by a ruffian; then, he swore revenge on that imagined man and begged Oiwa to reconcile with him and help him find the murderer. Oiwa, stricken by grief, agreed.

They lived together for some time until Oiwa became pregnant. It was a hard time since, due to Iemon's poor management, they were destitute. Oiwa's pregnancy was difficult, and there was hardly any money for doctors; she managed to give birth to a healthy child but became sickly herself. As might be suspected of a bad husband, Iemon wasn't at all concerned for Oiwa; instead, he came to resent her, because she lost her beauty.

But soon, another factor came into play: Next to Iemon and Oiwa's house lived a rich doctor who had a beautiful daughter, Oume. Oume fell in love with Iemon and dearly wished to marry him, which she confided in her father. The doctor was clever and decided to help his daughter in a most immoral way.

He pretended to prescribe a special ointment for Oiwa—but in reality, it was poison that was supposed to leave her with a disfigured face. Poor Oiwa had no idea what she was taking—and even after applying the ointment, she didn't look in the mirror, so she had no idea what happened.

As suspected, Iemon now not only was distant towards his wife; he actively hated her. At the same time, the doctor came to him and persuaded him to divorce Oiwa and marry his daughter instead; he also promised him all his family fortune if he did so. Iemon agreed; and soon, he started selling all his family possessions, including Oiwa's and their child's clothes, to be able to afford the pompous marriage to Oume.

But Iemon decided to behave even more cruelly. He still didn't have a legal reason to divorce Oiwa: Her lack of beauty was definitely not enough. So, he hired a friend, Takuetsu, who agreed to rape her, and wanted to later accuse her of infidelity.

The next night, Takuetsu broke into Oiwa's bedroom. As he approached her, she screamed and accidentally uncovered her face; upon seeing it, Takuetsu was terrified and immediately abandoned his plan. He talked to Oiwa and explained everything; after which, he showed her her own reflection in a mirror.

Oiwa's horror was hard to behold. Frantically, she tried to cover the scarred part of her face with her hair, but as she started brushing it, it fell out in clumps. Then, she started screaming; in a flash, she understood all the ways in which she had been wronged by Iemon.

In a bout of madness, she reached into a cupboard and pulled out a sword. Then, she thrust it into her own throat.

Oiwa fell to the floor; Takuetsu, terrified, fled the scene. As Oiwa was bleeding to death, she cursed Iemon's name till her last breath.

But when a serving girl discovered Oiwa's body and related the news to Iemon, the cruel samurai couldn't quite conceal his contentment. The servant soon became suspicious, so quickly, Iemon killed her, and disposed of her body along with Oiwa's. In his maliciousness and stupidity, he was thinking that now, he was finally free to marry Oume and that all his troubles were behind him.

But Oiwa's curse was already in place. On his wedding night, Iemon couldn't sleep; as he tossed and turned in his bed, he suddenly saw Oiwa's disfigured face. Terrified, he reached for his sword and slashed at the apparition, only for it to disappear and reveal that he had in reality killed his new wife, Oume.

He didn't know what to do. He jumped from his bed and decided to get help from his new father-in-law; maybe the doctor could still help Oume. But as he ran, he suddenly saw the ghost of the murdered serving girl before him; again, he slashed at it with his sword, only to discover that he had killed his father-in-law.

Iemon ran and ran, but everywhere, Oiwa's ghost pursued him. It hid behind every corner, looked at him from paper lanterns, and stood in his way when he walked down the streets. In the end, he escaped to a hermitage high up in the mountains—but even there, Oiwa's ghost haunted him. He could no longer tell what was real and what was not; in the end, he went mad, and soon after, died.

The tragic story of Oiwa remained in oral tradition until 1825, when it was dramatized by Tsuruya Nanboku (1755–1829) in a form of a kabuki play (a traditional Japanese dance-drama), under the name *Tōkaidō Yotsuya Kaidan* (*Ghost story of Yotsuya in Tokaido*) (*Yotsuya Kaidan*, n.d.). It had multiple film adaptations in the 20th century.

Okiku

Okiku is another girl whose tragic fate became a popular and dramatized ghost story. It was initially a folk story which was later adapted into a bunraku (puppet) play in 1741 (Monnet, 1993).

Okiku was a serving girl. As, sadly, is often the case in situations like these, her master, a samurai by the name of Aoyama Tessan, got infatuated with her and was making rather forceful advances on her, claiming that he wanted to marry her. However, Okiku refused.

Scorned, Aoyama decided to take his revenge. He hid one of the very precious Delft plates (earthenware imported from the Netherlands) and made Okiku believe that she had lost it. A crime for losing such a precious possession would be death.

Okiku frantically counted and recounted the plates, but the one missing was nowhere to be found. She had no other choice than to confess her perceived crime, so she went to Aoyama and told him everything.

Now, the samurai decided to enact his plan. He pretended to be magnanimous and offered to overlook the whole matter if Okiku decided to become his lover.

But Okiku still refused. Enraged, Aoyama pushed her down a well, where she fell to her death.

But this was by no means the end of the story. Okiku came back as a ghost and tormented Aoyama. She would count to nine—recounting the Delft plates—and then emit a great shriek instead of the number ten, which represented the tenth plate she had supposedly lost. Aoyama couldn't get rid of the ghost until he found a priest who exorcized the ghost through a special ritual and by shouting "Ten!" loudly at the apparition.

Over the years, the story acquired many adaptations. Some of them had Aoyama peacefully contemplating his mistake; others, him committing suicide out of madness. A belief was formed that Okiku's ghost hadn't been exorcized, but instead haunted the wells.

Ubume

With the Ubume, we are coming back to categories of spirits rather than individual apparitions. They are ghosts of women who died pregnant or during childbirth. They would roam the streets, carrying bundles in their hands which, at first glance, resemble a swaddled child. However, when an Ubume would try to give away the bundle to a passer-by, they would quickly discover that it is only a rock wrapped in cloth. The rock would become heavier and heavier until it's impossible to hold, causing damage.

There was a way of preventing a woman from becoming an Ubume. If she died during childbirth and the child died as well, one had to bury her with the child in her arms—or, if the child was still in her womb, one had to cut it out and put it into her arms. If this was impossible, putting a doll in a woman's arms was an option.

Zashiki-warashi

The folk stories about Zashiki-warashi come mostly from the Iwate Prefecture. Those spirits are said to live in storage rooms, and they are mostly harmless, if not auspicious. They are said to bring good fortune to the families in whose houses they live.

Zashiki-warashi can be both male and female. They have red faces and short-cropped hair, and they live from three to fifteen years. They would often perform mild pranks in the household they live in, such as making rustling sounds or leaving footprints in ash or bleach powder.

Other Supernatural Creatures

There are some creatures in Japanese folklore that aren't easily classifiable: Hybrids; not-quite-gods but not spirits either… Let us now learn their stories.

Kirin

Kirin was originally a Chinese creature, known as Qilin; from there, it traveled to Japan, Korea, and Vietnam. It's a hybrid: It has horse-like hooves and the body of a Chinese dragon, as well as antlers on its head. However, in Japan, it is depicted as more deer-like than dragon-like.

In China, Kirin is considered a portent of someone very wise being born, be it a sage or a ruler. It retained its position as a good sign in Japan.

Komainu

The Komainu are another type of hybrid creatures: Half-lions, half-dogs. Their statues guard Shinto temples. There are two types of Komainu: Those that guard the entrances and those that are kept inside, in spaces not available to the public. They are supposed to repel the evil spirits from holy places.

Kyonshii

Kyonshii is yet another creature borrowed from Chinese culture—it is a special type of vampire known in China as Jiangshi. It's an animated corpse: Very stiff and dressed in a shroud, it moves around by hopping with its arms outstretched. It doesn't drink blood, however; instead, it sucks out people's life force.

There are many ways one can use to repel the kyonshii. Some of them include: Swatting it with a broom; holding one's breath; or dropping a bag of coins and thus distracting it, so it starts counting the coins instead of pursuing its victim.

Mizuchi

Mizuchi is a Japanese dragon. It is strongly connected to the aquatic dragon deities, such as Okami. Over time, it became conflated with creatures such as the Kappa.

Mizuchi is first mentioned in the chronicle *Nihon Shoki* as dwelling in the Takahashi River and poisoning the water (Aston, 2013).

Over time, several cases of seeing a Mizuchi have been reported, and most possibly, not all of them were referencing a singular creature, but rather, a category of creatures. In another story from the *Nihon Shoki*, a man named Agatamori was supposed to have defeated a Mizuchi (Aston, 2013). He came near a pool and threw three white-flowered gourds (or long melons—very light and bottle-shaped fruits) into the water, challenging the Mizuchi to drown them. Because the fruits were so light, the dragon couldn't sink them with his mighty claws; so he resorted to transformation and changed himself into a deer. That was the moment Agatamori was waiting for: He shot the deer with his arrow, killing it.

Namazu

Namazu is a peculiar monster: It is a giant catfish that lives deep in the water in the center of the earth. Its movements often cause earthquakes. It belongs to the god of thunder Takemikazuchi, who frequently tries to tame it; but when he lets his guard down, the fish thrashes and causes trouble.

It is believed that the connection between a giant fish and an earthquake came from an observation of catfish getting unusually active and restless before earthquakes, a fact that was later scientifically proven (*Sensitivity*, 1933).

CHAPTER 7

Folktales

Throughout this book, I have told you many myths and folktales connected to gods, heroes, and supernatural creatures. But in this last chapter, we will learn stories that we haven't heard before—and which form the corpus of some of the most celebrated tales from Japanese traditional imagination. Many of them will be stories of ordinary people meeting unusual ends—and either emerging successful, or losing everything. They were written down in a traditional Japanese art form known as the monogatari—a prose narrative similar to a novel.

The Tale of the Bamboo Cutter

Our first tale is one of the earliest known written monogatari—it was composed either in the 9th or 10th century (Keene, 1993). It tells a tale of how an ordinary man found a supernatural princess.

There once was a bamboo cutter by the name of Taketori no Okina. He was an old man who toiled away day by day, earning his meager income. But one day was special for him; as he was cutting the bamboo, he came across an unusual shiny stick. When he cut it, he saw a little girl sleeping inside; she was no bigger than the size of a thumb.

The cutter and his wife didn't have their own children, so, as is often the case in these types of stories, they decided to take the girl home and raise her as their own child. They named her Nayotake no Kaguya-hime (which literally meant "Shining Princess of the Young Bamboo").

From that point on, every time Taketori cut a new bamboo stalk in the forest, he would find a gold piece in it. This improved his family situation considerably; soon, he was rich.

Nayotake also grew very quickly. In only three months, she transformed from a child into a beautiful young woman. Soon, news traveled far and wide about a beautiful maiden and an heiress to a fortune; although Taketori and his wife initially tried to shelter Nayotake from suitors, it soon proved futile.

Among others, five nobles arrived at Taketori's house, all intent on marrying Nayotake: Prince Ishitskuri, Prince Kuramochi, Minister Abe no Mimuraji, Grand Counselor Ōtomo no Miyuki, and the Middle Counselor Isonokami no Marotari. Taketori, after some persuading, agreed for Nayotake to choose between them.

But Nayotake wasn't interested in any of them. Not wanting to offend them by rejecting them outright, she devised five tasks which were, nonetheless, impossible to complete. They were all about bringing five objects which no mortal should touch or even see: The begging bowl of the Buddha; a branch made of jewels that only grew on a mythical island of Hōrai; a robe made of skins of Chinese mythical fire rats; a jewel from a dragon's neck; and finally, an impossible object: A cowry shell born of a swallow.

Initially, all the nobles dispersed in pursuit of their tasks. But very soon, they realized how impossible the tasks were, and decided to cheat. Prince Ishitskuri gave Nayotake a fake stone bowl; Prince Kuramochi gave her a branch laid out with Japan's finest jewels, which nonetheless were by no means mythical; the Minister bought a robe from a Chinese merchant, but didn't test it for being fireproof; the Grand Counselor honestly tried to pursue a dragon, but was deterred by a storm; and the Middle Counselor fell down a cliff when trying to reach to a swallow's nest, and died.

When three out of five suitors came back to Nayotake, she saw through their deceit immediately. The bowl didn't reflect the holy light of the Buddha; finding a merchant who had sold Kuramochi the jewels wasn't a difficult task; and the Minister's robe burned immediately in the fire. Disgusted, Nayotake sent the suitors away.

And then, an extraordinary thing happened: The Emperor of Japan himself came to Nayotake's house and proposed. When she saw him, she was immediately taken to him and didn't burden him with an impossible task. However, she still told him she couldn't marry him, because she wasn't a native of his country; she had come from a different place.

The Emperor drove away, but he kept in contact with Nayotake through letters for three long years. In the meantime, the girl grew more and more restless; every full moon, she would cry, and wouldn't respond to the bamboo cutter's questions. At last, when she became more and more upset, she revealed the truth: She had come from the Moon, where she was a princess. She had to return to her people, even if they didn't want her; she said that she had committed a crime (whose nature she nonetheless didn't want to reveal), and that is why she had been sent to the Earth as banishment.

Now, Nayotake started preparing for her journey back; she knew that soon, messengers from the Moon would come and get her. Meanwhile, the Emperor sent his escort to protect her from the wrath of the Moon people.

But the protection was clearly not enough; when an embassy from the Moon finally came to get Nayotake, everyone was blinded by an unearthly light and fell to the ground. Nayotake left her robe behind, wanting her foster parents to have something to remember her by; she then put a drop of the Moon elixir of immortality and attached it to a letter to the Emperor. With great pomp, she ascended into the sky.

The bamboo cutter and his wife wept dearly for their daughter whom they grew to love. They became so sad that they got ill. Meanwhile, a messenger came with Nayotake's last letter to the Emperor, relating the news. The Emperor went sick with sadness, and immediately asked his messenger which mountain was the tallest one in Japan, and therefore the closest to the sky.

The messenger told him that the highest peak of the Suruga Province in the south was reportedly the tallest mountain. He had probably expected the Emperor to climb it in order to be closer to his lost love; but instead, the wise monarch ordered the letter and the elixir of immortality to be brought to the mountain peak and burned. He wanted to make his will known to the Moon princess: He was trying to forget about her, and he was rejecting immortality, for it made no sense to never die, and yet be unable to see his love ever again.

And thus ended the melancholy tale of the bamboo cutter and his adopted daughter, the Moon princess.

Bunbuku Chagama

Bunbuku Chagama is a humorous and heartwarming tale about a tanuki and its exploits. The oral fairy tale version of the story was written down in the 19th century (Mitford, 1871).

There was once a chief priest in a temple. Every day in the evening, he liked to drink some tea, and he owned a magnificent tea kettle. But one day, the moment he put the kettle on the hearth, it suddenly started moving, and then sprung out a raccoon-like tail, transforming into a tanuki.

The monk didn't like this turn of events. He employed his novices to subdue the tanuki and kept it in confinement; then, he sold it at a market—thus, having no idea what he lost.

When a peddler bought a seemingly completely ordinary kettle, it transformed into a Tanuki in his hands. The peddler, startled, almost dropped it; but the tanuki said that it would perform acrobatic tricks if the peddler promised to treat it well. The bargain struck, and the peddler went around, showing the tanuki on the roadsides and during circus-like shows. He shared all his food with the creature, and as an exchange, it walked on ropes and spun around to the delight of the spectators.

Soon, the peddler amassed a great fortune—thus proving that whoever meets a tanuki, should do well if they treat it with dignity.

The Crab and the Monkey

The Crab and the Monkey is a story of violence and retribution. It can be read a bit like a parable, or a metaphorical animal fable. It was first published in the 19th century, ending a time of oral transmission (Ozaki, n.d.).

A female crab was once out on a walk. While strolling, she found a rice ball, a true treasure. She presented her findings to her friend, a monkey. But the clever and manipulative creature persuaded her to trade the rice ball for a persimmon seed. The crab wasn't happy about the exchange, but she couldn't find it in herself to refuse.

However, her discontent soon turned to joy when the seed planted in the ground slowly grew into a tree. The crab was now in possession of a fortune that didn't run out immediately.

There was one problem, however: The crab couldn't climb the tree. She had to ask the monkey to do it for her—something that her sly acquaintance decided to exploit. He quickly climbed up, but instead of throwing some of the fruits down for the crab, he started eating all the ripe persimmons. When the crab realized what was happening and started protesting, the monkey threw unripe, hard fruits at her, injuring her. Shocked, the crab, who had been pregnant, gave birth before her time—and then shortly died.

But when the crab's offspring grew up, they decided to take revenge on the greedy and malicious monkey. They amassed unusual allies for their confrontation: A chestnut, a cow dung, a bee, and a heavy mortar. They decided to storm the monkey's house, where they hid, the chestnut in the hearth, the bee in the water container, the cow dung on the floor in an invisible spot, and the mortar on the roof.

The monkey entered his home. Immediately, he went to the hearth and tried to warm himself; but from there, the chestnut jumped, causing him to burn his face. Outraged and in pain, the monkey ran to the container full of water to cool off the burn; but there, the bee was waiting for him and stung him immediately. The monkey was now mad with pain; he ran out of his house, clutching at his burning face; but he didn't see the cow dung on the floor and slipped on it. Then, it was left to the mortar to finish the job. It fell from the roof, crushing the monkey's skull and killing him.

The point of the story is relatively simple: Harsh, retributive justice will come sooner or later for evildoers. The flourish is, however, the unusual use of the animal characters and objects who took part in how justice was served.

The Crane Wife

The Crane Wife, or, *Tsuru Nyōbō*, is a very unusual, and yet heartbreaking, love story. For ages, it circulated in oral tradition and has now many variants, being one of the best-known Japanese folktales (Adams & Seki, 1976).

The story starts simply enough: A man married a beautiful woman, whom he loved dearly. But he had no idea that the woman was a shapeshifting crane. She loved him and decided to make the sacrifice of changing into a human in order to be with him.

The man was a silk merchant. Every night, his wife would weave silk brocade for him, which he would later sell. In order for the brocade to be of extraordinary quality, she used her own crane feathers which she plucked every night. But this made her increasingly weaker.

Soon, she became very sick. Her husband, of course, noticed this and demanded to know what the matter was. Very reluctantly, she told him. She was afraid that his love for her would disappear when he discovered her true nature.

In tears, he said that his love for her didn't diminish. But she had to stop what she'd been doing; he didn't need that kind of sacrifice from her.

But she had been doing this all for them and their love, she responded. For her as a crane, life didn't exist without sacrifices.

The man disagreed. He said that love should be pleasurable, and one didn't have to sacrifice one's own core for it.

The wife frowned. This disagreed with everything she believed in. But instead of arguing further, or trying to understand her husband's point, she turned back into a crane and then flew away. Her husband didn't deserve to be with her if he didn't believe that love requires sacrifices.

The Crane Wife is a tragic story: Supernatural or not, it is about two people with different worldviews and values who cannot find a middle ground and overcome their difficulties, even though they love each other.

Hagoromo

Hagoromo is one of those folk stories which have been turned into a play—the traditional Japanese dance-drama. Although the stories the play is based on were first recorded around the 8th century, the earliest known performance of the play dates to the 16th century (Tyler, 2004).

Hagoromo uses a motif of a swan maiden, slightly similar to that of a crane wife. It's a story about a tennin—a celestial female spirit—who left her feather cloak on a shore. It was later found by a fisherman who refused to give it back to the shapeshifting swan if she didn't perform a special dance for him.

In the play, the swan maiden's dance is the most important part of the whole performance. According to the story, it was a beautiful thing to behold, and it represented the phases of the moon; at the end of it, the maiden disappeared into mist.

There isn't much more to the story; it's more of a scene than a plot, showing a mortal's encounter with the otherworldly and the miraculous.

Hanasaka Jiisan

Hanasaka Jiisan is another one of those stories about a single miracle. It, unsurprisingly, tells the tale of an old childless couple to whom something extraordinary happened.

The couple didn't have children, but they had a dog whom they loved dearly. One day, the dog dug in their garden and found a bag full of gold coins. When the news about this spread, a neighbor came to the couple, saying that it must be proof of the dog having the ability to find hidden treasure. He begged the couple to lend him the animal for only one day, so it could sniff around and dig in his own garden. Reluctantly, the couple agreed.

But when the dog went on the reconnaissance round, it only found some old bones. Enraged, the neighbor kicked the poor animal so hard that he killed it. But he wasn't going to tell the truth to the couple. Instead, he claimed that the dog had just dropped dead; it must have been sick.

The couple wept profusely for their friend and companion, and buried it in their garden, in the exact spot where it had found the gold. That night, the dog's master had a dream: The dog came to him alive and spoke, saying that he should chop down the fig tree growing in his garden and make a mortar out of it.

The man awoke and related his dream to his wife. They decided to do what the dog asked of them. They chopped down the tree, made a mortar, and then tried to grind rice in it; but the moment they did, the rice turned into gold.

Yet again, their neighbor learned of this and demanded to borrow the mortar. But when he put his rice inside, it turned into rotting berries. Again, furious, the man threw the mortar to the ground and then burned it for good measure.

But then, the dog's master had another dream. The dog told him to sprinkle its ashes on the cherry trees in his garden. When he did so, the next day, the cherries blossomed instantly, even though it wasn't their time of the year.

As it happened, a local daimyō was passing by the house. When he saw the beautiful cherry blossoms in the garden, he marveled and gave the old couple lavish gifts for such a beautiful display.

Yet again, the neighbor tried to replicate the same deed that the couple had done, but when he tried to sprinkle his cherry trees with the dog's ashes, a wind picked up and blew the ashes straight into the daimyō's face; for that, he was thrown into prison. When he finally got out, he no longer had a house, and the inhabitants, having discovered his past transgressions, threw him out of their village. Thus, justice was served.

Kachi-kachi Yama

Kachi-kachi Yama is another folktale with a tanuki as a main character; but instead of being the usual harmless trickster, he is the villain of the story. The title can be translated as "Fire-Crackle Mountain," since it is the landmark near which the story takes place, and provides an important plot point to the tale.

One day, there was a farmer whose fields were being repeatedly plundered by a tanuki. Having endured months of this, the man finally came to a breaking point and managed to catch the tanuki and tie it to a tree. He wanted to kill it and cook it for dinner.

But later that day, the farmer's wife passed by the tree. The tanuki started crying and screaming, begging the woman to set him free, and in exchange, he would help her make mochi, a rice dish which she was supposed to prepare. The woman agreed to free the tanuki, only for the malicious creature to immediately kill her.

But this wasn't the end of the creature's maliciousness. He shapeshifted into the form of the now-dead farmer's wife, went to the farmer's home, and cooked some soup. But it wasn't just any soup; he used the flesh of the dead woman to make it.

And thus, the tanuki completed his terrible revenge. When the farmer ate the soup, he turned back to his natural form and revealed the full extent of his scheme. Then, he ran away, leaving the man in utter shock, grief, and mortification.

But the story was by no means over. Now, as the news spread of the tanuki's terrible deed, a rabbit, who had been a neighbor and a friend to the farmer and his wife, came over and promised the man that he would avenge his wife's death.

The rabbit was clever: He didn't just plan out the damage he would cause the tanuki; first, he pretended to befriend him. Only when the tanuki trusted him and let him into his confidence, did he start playing cruel tricks on him. For example, he once sneakily threw a full bee's nest on the tanuki's head. The bees stung him painfully, and when he asked his 'friend' for help, the rabbit rubbed in ointment made of spicy peppers, thus making the wounds even worse.

But then, the rabbit played an especially cruel trick on the tanuki. One day, the tanuki was carrying some sticks for the fireplace in his home. Unbeknownst to him, the rabbit had set fire to the kindling, but the tanuki didn't notice, since it was strapped to his back.

However, after some time of walking, he heard a crackling sound. He asked the rabbit if he could hear it, too. The rabbit feigned innocence, telling the tanuki that they were passing close to Kachi-Kachi Yama, the fire-breathing mountain that made a crackling noise. No wonder the tanuki was hearing it.

When the flames reached the tanuki's fur, it was already too late to put them out. The creature was burned badly—however, he was still alive, and writhing in agony.

Now, the tanuki knew that the rabbit was no real friend. Having licked his wounds, he challenged the rabbit to a contest; the one who lost would also lose his life.

For the challenge, both creatures built boats that would allow them to traverse a lake. The tanuki, even though manipulative and clever, lacked wisdom, and made his boat out of mud, while the cleverer rabbit made his boat out of a tree trunk.

Even so, the competitors were evenly matched in the beginning; but soon, the tanuki's boat started dissolving in the water. The rabbit stopped paddling in his canoe and turned, satisfaction written in his features: He had achieved his revenge. He then proclaimed that the whole point of the rivalry had been to avenge the farmer—and paddled away, leaving the tanuki to sink. The story ends with the rabbit coming to the farmer's house and announcing that he had achieved his goal. The farmer thanked him profusely, and they remained fast friends till the end of his days.

Kasa Jizō

Kasa Jizō is probably the most Buddhist of tales told in this chapter, aimed at teaching its followers the value of kindness. It starts with a well-known premise: A poor old couple who shows generosity to a supernatural being.

The couple lived in the snowy part of the country, and because of their poverty, would often not even be able to afford some basic kindling. As the day of the New Year was approaching, they realized that they couldn't even afford to make the traditional rice meal, mochi.

The old man decided to try everything. He took some homemade bamboo hats, called kasa, and walked down to the nearest village to sell them. But the road to the village was long, and a blizzard was coming. Soon, the man couldn't even move an inch, and he decided to come back home—only, he didn't even know which direction his home was anymore.

So he walked blindly until suddenly, he almost bumped into holy statues. After a moment, he recognized them as the statues of Jizō, the protector of the vulnerable. He took out his bamboo hats and decided to offer them to the Bodhisattva. However, he didn't have enough hats to cover the heads of all statues; so he took out his hand towel and thus protected them from the snow. Then, he continued on his journey. He finally managed to make it back home safe and sound, and his wife understood why he couldn't bring her the New Year's mochi.

The couple went to sleep. But in the middle of the night, they were suddenly awoken by a thumping on the door. When the old man managed to get out of bed and open the door, there was no one outside—but there was a pile of treasures and food laying on the doorstep. There was mochi, but also vegetables and gold coins.

The old man looked into the distance, where the blizzard was still raging. Faintly, he saw the Jizō statues on the horizon, walking away. They had repaid him for his kindness.

Kobutori Jiisan

Kobutori Jiisan is a tale about an unholy miracle, which was first recorded in the 13th century (Hearn, 1918). It tells the story of a man who had a tumor lump on the right side of his face, and how it magically disappeared.

The man with a lump was a woodcutter. One day, he went into the forest to do his day's work but was surprised by a heavy downpour. He hid in a hollowed-out tree, where he was easily overlooked by anyone who was passing by.

And soon, a very peculiar group gathered outside of his hiding spot. It was a gathering of the on. Some of them had only one eye, and some were mouthless. They soon sat down in a circle and, despite the continuing rain, managed to build a magnificent bonfire. Then, they drank sake and made merry, singing and dancing.

There was something alluring in that gathering, and the woodcutter found himself wanting to join, instead of hiding in a dark and wet tree hollow. After a while, he overcame his fear and let his presence be known.

It was a risky venture, but the demons seemed more entertained by his presence than angered by the fact that he oversaw them. He was a curiosity to them, and they beckoned him to sing and dance with them. After the meeting was finished, the oni told the man to come back the next day. The man agreed, but the demons still wanted a guarantee that he would come back.

So they decided to keep one of his possessions as an assurance. The problem was, the man was poor, and had almost nothing on him—so the demons decided to take away his lump. They removed it smoothly and without any pain, and there wasn't even a scar left. The man was overjoyed.

When he came back to his village, the people immediately noticed the lack of his disfigurement. A neighbor, who had a similar problem—only the lump was on the left side of his face—wished to know everything about the woodcutter's adventure. He then managed to persuade him to take his place the next day, so that he might get his own lump removed.

The man agreed, and the neighbor hid in the same tree hollow he had found the previous day. Like the man before him, he let his presence be known when the oni gathered around the bonfire. But unlike his friend, his dancing skills were not the greatest, and the demons were more irritated than entertained. As a punishment, they not only didn't remove the man's lump but 'gifted' him with his friend's lump instead. Now, he had two lumps on both sides of his face.

This story can be read as a cautionary tale against the envy of our neighbors—but also, as a warning against the oni, whose behavior might be volatile and the contact with whom might not end well for mortals.

Shippeitaro

Shippeitaro might be one of the most famous animal characters in Japanese folklore. The fairy tale about this helper dog has many versions; below, I will present the most well-known one.

There was once a brave warrior who went on a quest for adventure. He entered an enchanted forest and, because he couldn't find the way back before dusk, he slept at a magical shrine in the middle of the woods. During the night, he heard many voices outside the shrine: Cats meowing and wailing, chanting some hymn whose words sounded like "do not tell Shippeitaro!"

The next day, the warrior went to the nearby village. He soon learned that the famed Shippeitaro was a dog owned by an overseer of the local prince and that he was a vicious protector against demonic cats who lived in the forest. However, there was one danger that the villagers believed Shippeitaro couldn't protect them against the spirit of the nearby mountain, to whom they had to sacrifice a girl every year. As it happened, the time for another sacrifice had come. The terrified girl asked the warrior for help.

He agreed to aid her, and he decided to use Shippeitaro after all. The girl was supposed to be locked in a cage and put in the temple where the warrior had spent the night, but the warrior knew that Shippeitaro guarded the shrine. So, he borrowed him from the overseer and put him in the cage instead of the girl.

As suspected, the so-called mountain demon took the form of a giant cat. When he arrived at the temple, it was dark; he didn't see who was sitting in the cage. So, he opened it, and immediately, Shippeitaro jumped out, killing the cat. Once this was done, the warrior joined him, and together they rid the forest of all demonic cats. Afterward, Shippeitaro was celebrated in the village as a hero.

Shita-kiri Suzume

Shita-kiri Suzume is a story about friendship, jealousy, and greed. It starts where most Japanese fables do: With an old couple. The old man was a woodcutter who earned his living honestly and never complained about his lot in life. His wife, however, was greedy and of a malicious disposition.

One day, as the man was cutting wood, he noticed an injured sparrow lying on the ground. He took pity on the poor animal and took it home, where he fed it some rice in hopes that it could help the bird to recover.

But when the man's wife saw this, she was angry. The man was wasting precious food on some insignificant creature, she said. They had an argument, but the man didn't stop caring for the bird.

But the next day, the man had to go back to work. He left the bird in his wife's care, but she had no intention of feeding it. Instead, she went out fishing. As she was gone, the bird, who was slowly recovering, hopped around the house and found a sash full of starch, which it ate. When the woman came back home and noticed this, she got so angry that she cut out the bird's tongue and kicked it out of the house.

When the man came back home, his wife told him what happened. Angered and upset, the man went out in search of the bird. He asked some other sparrows for its whereabouts, and they led him to its nest. There, he was greeted with honors as the bird's friend and savior.

At the end of the gathering, the sparrows wanted to send the man home with a gift. They presented him with a small and a large basket and asked him to choose. The man was old and frail, so he chose the smaller gift, as he knew he wouldn't be able to carry the large basket home.

When he came back and opened his gift, he discovered that the basket was full of gold. He told the whole story to his wife, including the part where he chose the smaller gift. Unsurprisingly, the greedy wife was immediately angered by the fact that her husband didn't go for the larger basket, and decided to seek out the sparrows on her own and come back with large treasure.

She found the sparrows; they, despite having been treated poorly by her, gave her the basket anyway. However, there was one catch, she couldn't open it before she got home.

But the woman couldn't contain her curiosity. She decided to only have a sneak peek when on the road—unfortunately, the moment she opened the basket, deadly snakes, insects, and other creatures immediately crawled out of it, scaring her to her death. Thus, the punishment for her greed was served.

Tawara Tōda Monogatari

The last tale in our collection is an epic one. It is a legendary tale of Fujiwara no Hidesato, a noble warrior who lived in the 10th century. Several prose narratives dating from around the 14th century have been preserved about him (Kimbrough & Shirane, 2018). In English, his story was first translated under the title *My Lord Bag of Rice* (Kimbrough & Shirane, 2018).

The tale goes as follows: In the Ōmi Province in central Japan, a giant snake was attacking travelers. Fujiwara no Hidesato decided to confront it; but as he was crossing near the snake's dwelling, it didn't attack him.

That night, a beautiful woman came to him. She told the warrior that she was the one transforming into a snake; she had been driven out of her home by Lake Biwa (the largest lake in Japan), where a giant centipede was devouring her kin. Fujiwara agreed to go there and get rid of the monster.

The centipede was truly enormous, and its legs were blazing with fire so that when it descended from the mountains, it looked as if an army carrying a thousand torches was marching down. Fujiwara, not deterred, shot two arrows at the centipede but missed. He then prayed to Hachiman, the god of war, to help him kill the creature. This time, the arrow stuck to its body and killed it.

Fujiwara was rewarded profusely for his deed. The serpent woman gave him, among other gifts, a bag of rice that never ran empty. It was on account of this gift that he got his nickname: Tawara Tōda, meaning "The Bag of Rice."

The story of the brave hero closes our journey of Japanese folklore.

Conclusion

You have now reached the end of the book; I hope this was an entertaining and illuminating journey. As you probably already realized, this overview of figures and stories from Japanese myth and folklore was by no means an exhaustive one—after all, we are speaking of a culture that believes in thousands of gods and creatures. There is always more to discover, and I hope that this book will prove an inciting incident for your own fascinating journey through the Land of the Rising Sun.

From the creator gods in ancient chronicles to monsters from modern urban myths, the Japanese tradition is full of love, betrayal, fear, strange creatures, and extraordinary endings—just at the tip of your finger. I hope that this book will serve you as a guide on your way to discovering even more wonders.

References

Adams, R. J., & Seki, K. (1976). *Folktales of Japan*. University Of Chicago Press.

Addiss, S., Yamamoto, A. Y., Jordan, B. G., Secor, J. L., Welch, M., Wolfgram, J., Fister, P., Lillywhite, J., Yamamoto, F. Y., Foresman, H., Deguchi, M., & Carpenter, J. L. (2005). *Japanese ghosts and demons: Art of the supernatural*. G. Braziller In Association With The Spencer Museum Of Art, University Of Kansas.

Agrawala, P. K. (1978). On a four-legged icon of Ganapati from Ghosai. *Artibus Asiae*, *40*(4), 307–310. https://doi.org/10.2307/3249822

Alt, M., Yoda, H., & Komatsu, K. (2018). *An introduction to yōkai culture: Monsters, ghosts, and outsiders in Japanese history*. Japan Publishing Industry Foundation For Culture.

Alt, M. (2020). *From Japan, a mascot for the pandemic*. The New Yorker. https://www.newyorker.com/culture/cultural-comment/from-japan-a-mascot-for-the-pandemic

Ancient tales and folklore of Japan: XXXI. Yosoji's camellia tree. (n.d.). Www.sacred-Texts.com. https://www.sacred-texts.com/shi/atfj/atfj33.htm

Antoni, K. (1991). Momotaro and the spirit of Japan. *Asian Folklore Studies, 50*.

Antoni, K. (2015). On the religious meaning of a Japanese myth: The white hare of Inaba. *Comparative Mythology*, *1*(1), 61–72.

Ashkenazi, M. (2008). *Handbook of Japanese mythology*. Oxford University Press.

Aston, W. G. (2013). *The Nihongi: Chronicles of Japan from the earliest times to A.D. 697*. The Japan Society of the UK.

Beauchamp, F. (2010). Asian origins of Cinderella: The Zhuang storyteller of Guangxi. *Oral Tradition, 25*(2), 447–496. https://doi.org/10.1353/ort.2010.0023

Bocking, B. (2016). *Popular dictionary of Shinto.* Curzon.

Cali, J., Dougill, J., & Ciotti, G. (2013). *Shinto shrines: A guide to the sacred sites of Japan's ancient religion.* University Of Hawai'i Press.

Casal, U. A. (1959). The goblin fox and badger and other witch animals of Japan. *Folklore Studies, 18*, 49–58. https://doi.org/10.2307/1177429

Chamberlain, B. H. (2008). *A translation of the "Ko-ji-ki" or records of ancient matters.* Forgotten Books.

Davisson, Z. (2018). *Yūrei: The Japanese ghost.* Chin Music Press.

Deal, W. E., & Ruppert, B. D. (2015). *A cultural history of Japanese Buddhism.* Wiley, Blackwell.

Dejima Nagasaki: Japan experience. (2013). Www.japan-Experience.com. https://www.japan-experience.com/all-about-japan/nagasaki/attractions-excursions/dejima-nagasaki

Encyclopedia of Shinto. (n.d.). 國學院大學デジタルミュージアム. https://d-museum.kokugakuin.ac.jp/eos/

Ernst, D. (2019, September 26). *Essential guide to Japanese monsters.* Bokksu. https://www.bokksu.com/blogs/news/essential-guide-to-japanese-monsters

Farris, W. W. (2009). *Japan to 1600.* University of Hawaii Press.

Faure, B. (2015). *Protectors and predators: Gods of medieval Japan.* University of Hawaii Press.

Gadaleva, E. (2000). Susanoo: One of the central gods in Japanese mythology. *Nichibunken Japan Review: Bulletin of the International Research Center for Japanese Studies, 12*(12), 168.

Goepper, R. (1993). Aizen-Myoo: The esoteric king of lust: An iconological study. *Artibus Asiae. Supplementum, 39*, 3-172. https://doi.org/10.2307/1522701

Tyler, R. (2004). *Japanese nō dramas.* Penguin Books.

Harada, V. H. (1976). The badger in Japanese folklore. *Asian Folklore Studies, 35*(1), 1–6. https://doi.org/10.2307/1177646

Haviland, W. A. (1999). *Cultural anthropology.* Harcourt Brace College Publishers.

Hearn, L. (1988). *Glimpses of unfamiliar Japan: In two volumes.* Rinsen Book.

Hearn, L. (1918). *Japanese fairy tales.* Boni and Liveright.

Hearn, L. (2020). *The romance of the Milky Way.* BoD – Books on Demand.

Henshall, K. G. (2012). *A history of Japan: From Stone Age to superpower.* Palgrave Macmillan.

Henshall, K. G. (2014). *Historical dictionary of Japan to 1945.* The Scarecrow Press.

Holland, O., & Kobayashi, C. (n.d.). *Japan's ancient and mysterious royal regalia.* CNN. https://www.cnn.com/style/article/japan-enthronement-royal-regalia/index.html

Holmes, Y. (2014). *Chronological evolution of the Urashima Tarō story and its interpretation.*

Immoos, T., & Ikeda, H. (1973). A type and motif index of Japanese folk-literature. *Monumenta Nipponica, 28*(2), 255. https://doi.org/10.2307/2383873

Jun'ichi, I., & Thal, S. E. (2000). Reappropriating the Japanese myths: Motoori Norinaga and the creation myths of the Kojiki and Nihon Shoki. *Japanese Journal of Religious Studies, 27*(1/2).

Kahara, N. (2004). From folktale hero to local symbol: The transformation of Momotaro (the Peach Boy) in the creation of a local culture. *Waseda Journal of Asian Studies, 25,* 35–61.

Keene, D. (1993). *Seeds in the heart: Japanese literature from earliest times to the late sixteenth century.* Henry Holt & Co.

Kimbrough, R. K. (2006). Translation: The tale of the Fuji Cave. *Japanese Journal of Religious Studies, 33*(2), 337–377. https://doi.org/10.18874/jjrs.33.2.2006.1-22

Kimbrough, K., & Shirane, H. (2018). *Monsters, animals, and other worlds: A collection of short medieval Japanese tales.* Columbia University Press.

von Krenner, W. G. (2013). *Aikido ground fighting: Grappling and submission techniques.* Blue Snake Books.

Littleton, C. S. (2002). *Shinto: Origins, rituals, festivals, spirits, sacred places.* Oxford University Press.

Lovelace, A. (2008). Ghostly and monstrous manifestations of women: Edo to contemporary. *The Irish Journal of Gothic and Horror Studies, 5.*

Meyer, M. (2016). *Aka manto.* Yokai.com. https://yokai.com/akamanto/

Mitford, J. (1871). *Tales of old Japan.* Macmillan And Co.

Monnet, L. (1993). Connaissance délicieuse or the science of jealousy: Tsushima Yūko's story "Kikumushi" (The Chrysanthemum Beetle). *Japan Review, 4,* 199–239.

Nelson, J. K. (2006). *A year in the life of a Shinto shrine.* Seattle Univ. Of Washington Press.

Nukariya, K. (2016). *The religion of the samurai.* Routledge.

Oiwa. (n.d.). Yokai.com. https://yokai.com/oiwa/

Ozaki, Y. T. (n.d.). *The quarrel of the monkey and the crab*. Etc.usf.edu. https://etc.usf.edu/lit2go/72/japanese-fairy-tales/4848/the-quarrel-of-the-monkey-and-the-crab/

Palmer, E. (2016). *Harima Fudoki : A record of ancient Japan reinterpreted*. Brill.

Pawasarat, C. (2020). *The Gion festival*. Catherine Pawasarat.

Perez, L. G. (1998). *The history of Japan*. Greenwood Press.

Philippi, D. L. (1968). *Kojiki*. University Of Tokyo Press.

Picken, S. D. B. (1994). *Essentials of Shinto: An analytical guide to principal teachings*. Greenwood Press.

Picken, S. D. B. (2011). *Historical dictionary of Shinto*. Scarecrow Press.

Punsmann, H. (1962). Daruma, a symbol of luck. *Folklore Studies, 21*, 241–244. https://doi.org/10.2307/1177354

Reider, N. T. (2010). Shuten Dōji (Drunken Demon): A medieval story of the carnivalesque and the rise of warriors and fall of oni. In *Japanese Demon Lore: Oni from Ancient Times to the Present* (pp. 30–52). University Press of Colorado.

Roberts, J. (2010). *Japanese mythology A to Z*. Chelsea House Publishers.

Sansom, G. B. (1982). *A history of Japan*. Stanford U.P.

Sato, H. (2012). *Legends of the samurai*. Duckworth.

Satō, M. (2017). Transforming an ancient myth into a popular medieval tale. In *Japan on the Silk Road* (pp. 339–363). Brill.

Seki, K. (1966). Types of Japanese folktales. *Asian Folklore Studies, 25*(1), 1–220. https://doi.org/10.2307/1177478

Selinger, V. R. (2013). *Authorizing the shogunate: Ritual and material symbolism in the literary construction of warrior order*. Brill.

Sensitivity of fish to earthquakes. (1933). Nature, 132(3343), 817–817. https://doi.org/10.1038/132817b0

Smyers, K. A. (1996). "My own Inari": Personalization of the deity in Inari worship. *Japanese Journal of Religious Studies, 23*(1-2), 427–452. https://doi.org/10.18874/jjrs.23.1-2.1996.85-116

Szostak, J. D. (2013). *Painting circles: Tsuchida Bakusen and Nihonga collectives in early twentieth century Japan.* Brill.

Theodore, W., Gluck, C., Tiedemann, A. E., & Dykstra, Y. K. (2001). *Sources of Japanese tradition.* Columbia University Press.

Totman, C. D. (2014). *A history of Japan.* John Wiley & Sons.

Totman, C. D. (2008). *Japan before Perry: A short history.* University Of California Press.

Turnbull, S. R. (2006). *Samurai: The world of the warrior.* Osprey.

Turner, P., & Coulter, C. R. (2001). *Encyclopedia of ancient deities.* Oxford University Press.

Wheeler, P. (2013). *The sacred scriptures of the Japanese.* Henry Schuman.

Varley, H. P. (1977). *Japanese culture: A short history.* Holt, Rinehart And Winston.

de Visser, M. W. (1908). The Tengu. *Transactions of the Asiatic Society of Japan., 36*(3), 107–116.

Yotsuya Kaidan. (n.d.). Www.kabuki21.com. http://www.kabuki21.com/yotsuya_kaidan.php

Made in the USA
Columbia, SC
17 October 2024

44571270R00362